COMPLETE BOOK OF

Drills for

Winning

Football

COMPLETE BOOK OF
Drills for
Winning
Football

MICHAEL D. KOEHLER

PARKER PUBLISHING COMPANY
West Nyack, New York 10994

Library of Congress Cataloging-in-Publication Data

Koehler, Mike.
    Complete book of drills for winning football. / Michael D. Koehler.
        p. cm.
    ISBN 0-13-087046-3
    1. Football—Training.   2. Football—Coaching.   I. Title.
    GV953.5.K64 2000
    796.332'2—dc21   00-041646
                                                                CIP

Acquisitions Editor: *Connie Kallback*
Production Editor: *Jacqueline Roulette*
Interior Design/Formatting: *Robyn Beckerman*

Printed in the United States of America

10 9 8 7 6 5 4 3 2 1

ISBN 0-13-087046-3

PARKER PUBLISHING COMPANY
West Nyack, New York 10994

www.phdirect.com

ACKNOWLEDGMENTS

The author wishes to thank the following coaches for sharing some of their favorite drills for this book:

Frank Lenti, Mt. Carmel High School, Chicago

Don Drakulich, Aviano High School, Italy

Jeff Johnson, Marquette High School, Ottawa, IL

Paul Adams, Deerfield High School, IL

George Kelly, the University of Notre Dame

Greg Royer, Deerfield High School, IL

ABOUT THE AUTHOR

Mike Koehler played fullback and linebacker for Marquette University and the University of Nebraska. He coached football for 31 years, contributing to an overall record of 245-70. He was a school and district-level administrator, and has been an adjunct professor of educational administration and supervision since 1974. Currently, he is devoting all his time to writing, teaching at the university level, speaking at conventions, and consulting with schools on coaching, the eligibility and recruitment of student athletes, and sports in schools. Mike is the author of scores of articles for professional journals, a nationally syndicated radio show, a newspaper column, and the videotape, *The ABCs of Eligibility for the College-Bound Student Athlete,* which is being marketed by the College Board. It currently is in its second edition.

Mike has written 14 books, the most recent being *The Administrator's Staff Development Activities Kit, Counseling Secondary Students with Learning Disabilities, The Athletic Director's Survival Guide, Advising Student Athletes Through the College Recruitment Process, Building the Total Athlete, The Department Head's Survival Guide,* and *The Football Coach's Survival Guide*, all with Prentice Hall. He also has written *Leadership Through Collaboration,* released by Eye on Education. He currently is in the planning stages for two more books, one a biography of his grandfather, Jim Thorpe, and is involved in a variety of speaking engagements across the country.

Mike has been married to wife Pat since 1962, has three delightful daughters: Kathleen, Carrie, and Peggy, three fine sons-in-law: Bruce, Dwight, and Dave, and enjoys time spent with his two grandchildren, Eric Michael and Cassie Jean.

For additional information or to contact Mike for consultation or in-service presentations, write or call:

Mike Koehler
Ideation, Inc.
8246 Voss Road
Minocqua, WI 54548
715-358-8802

or

15380 N. 100th St.
Unit 1116
Scottsdale, AZ 85260
480-661-4818

ABOUT THIS RESOURCE

I coached football for more than 30 years and I'm convinced the best piece of advice I ever gave an athlete was: "Trust your body." Football players who are unable to trust their bodies think too much; invariably, they compromise nature's built-in instrumentation and inhibit any physical intuition that defines their uniqueness as athletes. As a result, their performance suffers.

Yogi Berra, the venerable Mr. Malaprop of the sports world, said, "You can't think and hit at the same time." The uninformed giggled and were thankful for another "Yogi-ism." Coaches and experienced athletes, however, nod in solemn agreement, recognizing that the effective performance of any athletic skill depends on the *body's* memory and its ability to perform skills spontaneously and instinctively.

Football coaches at all levels, particularly in community and youth leagues, are constantly searching for drills that promote such spontaneous performance in their athletes. They also want to develop game skills and introduce variety and fun to daily practice schedules. Even veteran coaches may discover they have fallen into predictable and boring practice sessions and need exciting new drills to stimulate the interest and the performance of their players.

Good drill books are vital to coaches. Young coaches need them to develop programs with tried-and-true strategies and techniques to assure good player fundamentals. Veteran coaches need them to add spark to their repertoire of effective, but perhaps outdated, practice activities and drills. All coaches need them, not only to introduce variety, excitement, and change into practice sessions, but also to remind themselves of the skills their players must master.

The latter point is important for head coaches. A resource of this type not only provides a variety of drills for every position on the team, it also identifies the skills players require to perform effectively in each position. This book, then, is important for any coach who may need periodic reminders about the skills that have to be emphasized during practice sessions. Head coaches may want each assistant to have a copy or, at least, to have access to one.

Inexperienced coaches will benefit from the pointers found with each drill. The pointers provide examples of exactly what coaches should say to players or look for during the execution of the drill. Coaches from youth league to high school programs will benefit from this aspect of the book, perhaps the most important part of the book for them.

While many veteran coaches have experiences and knowledge that extend beyond the scope of these coaching pointers, the book is still useful to them. The range of drills contained in each section can help even veteran coaches teach solid fundamentals, maintain player motivation, emphasize important safety procedures, and introduce the variety athletes require to stay tuned in during practice.

Changing rules and improved performance techniques also require new drills. The relatively new rule permitting hand checking, for example, introduced a variety of drills and strength-training techniques for backs and linemen. The availability of such drills and conditioning techniques is important for all coaches.

This book also contains suggestions for organizing practices and for promoting safety for players. Player safety is one of the most important responsibilities of any football coach. Young athletes are inclined to do some crazy things in the heat of the moment. A good coach has to be alert to this possibility and protect such players from themselves. One thoughtless moment in a scrimmage or a game can result in life-long disability for a player. For the coach, thoughtlessness can cause player mismatches that result in unnecessary injury.

That's why many of the drills emphasize safety tips. The drills and diagrams in the book are also provided in an easily reproducible format. Coaches who want to use one or more drills or safety tips during an upcoming practice can simply duplicate the page(s) and take them along, referring to them periodically. This aspect of the book will guarantee its use by all the coaches in the program.

Exciting new drills are the coaching equivalent of new jokes for stand-up comics who will "borrow" material to improve their routines. Some will even claim to have created it, but that's OK. Good drills belong to all of us because they do such good things for young athletes. On that basis alone, a new drill book is a temptation to even the most experienced coach, especially if it contains a variety of novel and updated ideas.

This book will not gather dust on a shelf in the coaches' office. It will be reviewed often by all coaches, whether first-year or veteran. Because it offers drills for every player on the football team, including special teams, and identifies necessary skills for each player, it is the most comprehensive resource currently available. As such, it will introduce variety into practice sessions and, most important, will remind all coaches of the needed fundamental skills players require to perform safely and effectively.

Mike Koehler

CONTENTS

4   RUNNING-BACK DRILLS 65

5   RECEIVER DRILLS 111

6 OFFENSIVE-LINEMAN DRILLS **161**

7 TACKLING DRILLS 203

8 DEFENSIVE-LINEMAN DRILLS 219

9 LINEBACKER DRILLS 263

10 DEFENSIVE-BACK DRILLS. 305

11 DRILLS FOR THE ENTIRE TEAM 337

12 SPECIAL-TEAM DRILLS 361

SECTION 1

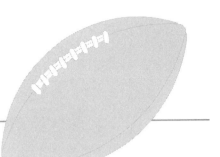

PRACTICE REALLY CAN MAKE PERFECT

First, a Quick Story:

I coached for several years with a first-generation Greek American who readily attributed most of his personal and professional success to his parents' old-country values. I enjoyed working with Paul because hard work, integrity, and common sense characterized much of his behavior. I discovered first-hand the impact of his parents, particularly his father, during the first few years of our relationship.

Paul and I were helping his parents move some furniture early one Sunday morning, after football practice had just started. In a thick Greek accent, his dad asked, "How good is team?"

Paul answered, "Pretty good, Pop, but we don't have a quarterback."

His dad asked, "What? You have no boys want to be quarterback?"

I responded: "Oh, sure, we have five kids who are trying mighty hard, but not one of 'em looks any good."

Paul's dad persisted: "Five boys try to be quarterback?"

"Yeah," said Paul.

"Then why you say you have no quarterback?"

Paul smiled. "They're just not very good, Pop."

His dad smiled, shrugged his shoulders slightly, and responded, "Coach 'em!"

Maintaining a Focus on "Coach 'em"

It was a lesson I never forgot. It synthesized every principle of coaching I have learned since. It may have been history's shortest butt chewing. In a brief but memorable moment, Paul's dad told us to stop whining and do our jobs. For years afterward, "Coach 'em" was the way to fill key positions. Whenever we questioned player performance, we asked ourselves, "What's the problem? They can't learn—or we can't teach?" Practice became a continuing challenge for us to become better teachers.

That's what practice is: the opportunity for coaches to help players refine their skills and learn the strategies and assignments that promote a team effort. It's our best chance to give players something to believe in—us, the program, and, most importantly, themselves.

One More Quick Story:

Several years ago, we were preparing to meet an especially tough opponent in the semifinals of the state playoffs. They ran the triple option better than any team we had ever played, plus they were big and fast. On paper, they were the better team. Years of experience enabled us to make such an admission. You see, experience also taught us that acknowledging an opponent's superiority is the first step to beating him. Impending defeat was, for us, a chance to overcome his superiority by finding a way to use it against him.

For example, we discovered that no one that season had attacked the mesh to force a hurried pitch from the quarterback. Our defensive coordinator decided to rush our outside backer right at the mesh as soon as he saw the quarterback open to his side. Normally, our outside backer maintained an outside-in responsibility on the pitchback. The playside safety, who normally had an inside-out responsibility on the quarterback, was told to cover the pitchback. We called the adjustment a "safety/backer switch" and convinced the team the strategy, if executed properly, would win the game.

It did, although I'm not sure it was the defensive adjustment or the team's belief in it that won the game. Who cares? Our defense reacted so hard and so fast to the mesh that the opposing quarterback barely had enough time to put the ball in the fullback's gut before our backer was in his face. Two of his pitches ended up on the grass, both recovered by us, one for a touchdown.

The kids worked hard in practice to perfect the strategy. They believed that this one defensive adjustment was just what they needed to beat one of the best teams in the state. They believed so strongly in the adjustment they **made it happen.** Teams that believe in themselves are like that. When they believe in their coaches and in themselves, they realize success by the sheer force of their collective will. They master not only adjustments but routine assignments. They may not be the better team on paper, but they win—because they believe they will. Practice helps create such belief.

TAKING A CLOSER LOOK AT PRACTICE

Football has more than its share of good teams that, like some pool players, hit and hope. They hit as hard as they can and hope that something drops. Don't get me wrong. Hitting is good, especially if it's hard hitting. Hoping is good, too, as long as it's accompanied by hard work. But if you're hoping, get hopping. Dreaming about victory may help establish a goal, but it doesn't make things happen. Old adages are usually true: the smaller the head, the bigger the dream.

The derivation of the word practice denotes action. Practice is doing and doing requires purpose. Purposeless action is wasted movement and too many football teams "practice" wasted movement. By way of example, I recently offered a couple hours of my time to a local junior high team and got my ideas about wasted movement reinforced by something they were doing early in practice.

On the field for no more than 15 minutes, the coaches had the entire team running "ladders," sprints to the ten and back to the goal line, to the twenty and back, to the thirty and back, and so on. They followed this exercise with 100-yard sprints, to the point where a few of the kids had to walk the last fifty yards. Winded and exhausted, the kids were then told to break into their groups for fundamentals. A half hour later, the coaches were complaining about a lack of enthusiasm and the apparent unwillingness of most of the kids to pay attention and learn.

Who wants to practice form tackling when he can barely stand up? I'm the first to admit that conditioning is essential for every football program, but emphasize it at the end of practice, even for an entire practice. But when you're emphasizing conditioning, don't expect your players to listen and learn, too. When a youngster is thinking only about his next breath or a longing to get lost next to the water fountain, don't expect him to concentrate on the intricacies of the swim technique or the timing of the counter dive option.

The key word is purpose. Good teams and good coaches have hope. Great teams and great coaches have purpose. They establish a clear sense of direction and then move purposefully in that direction. Every practice must reflect this sense of direction.

MORE ABOUT PURPOSES

Purposes are goals. They represent targets for action, desirable outcomes, planned accomplishments. As such, they motivate. If compelling, goals push us in certain directions; they sustain a sense of mission, a reason for action. To realize such goals, coaches and players need to break them down into smaller, realizable steps. That's what practice is—a series of well-coordinated steps leading to the realization of one or more goals.

Determining Needs

In a sense, then, purposes for practice are solutions to problems, the kind that interfere with the realization of goals. Coaches, for example, are constantly seeking answers to the following questions:

- What fundamental skills do players need?
- How are these needs influenced by rules changes: no blocking below the waist, the use of hands in blocking, etc.? More immediately, how are these needs affected by player performance in practice or in recent games?
- What elements of our offense or defense require better execution?
- What adjustments must we make in our offense and/or defense to improve our chances against upcoming opponents?
- What skills or changes in execution do some or all players need to guarantee the success of these adjustments?
- What conditioning needs do we have?
- What motivational needs must be satisfied?
- What changes in team or individual discipline must be emphasized?
- What personnel changes must be made because of recent injuries?
- What changes in offense or defense must be made and mastered to accommodate these new players?
- What skills or knowledge do these replacement players need to perform effectively?

Obviously, the relevance and importance of each of these questions is influenced by coaches' observations, players' opinions, and game tapes. Each of these sources of information is important to identify team needs and for solutions to be introduced in practice sessions. The good coach, then, is constantly aware of his team's needs, identifies solutions to resolve these needs, and coordinates each practice session to enable his team to master the solutions.

Communicating the Needs

Having identified the team's needs and possible solutions, the coach must communicate them. Such communication gets everyone on the same page and, if shared effectively, promotes a common sense of purpose.

- **Conditioning need**—We ran out of gas in the fourth quarter! What do we have to do about it?
- **Execution need**—We didn't use the right blocking scheme even once on the defensive tackle when we ran the inside belly counter at five.
- **Fundamental need**—Look at the film! Every time we run a dropback pass no fewer than two defensive linemen are chasing the quarterback! How can he find receivers? He's too busy trying to survive!
- **Motivational need**—Watch this. How badly did we want to make that goal line stand? What does it take to make a goal line stand, boys?

- **Discipline need**—Hey, I'm getting pushed out on the field more than the ball boy! The first thing we do today is practice sideline behavior!

Practice sideline behavior? You bet! Smart coaches pay attention to specifics such as taking the field, breaking down into groups for pregame activities, lining up for the national anthem, and assuring *disciplined* sideline behavior. Practice is important for all kinds of player activities, not the least of which is disciplined behavior on and off the field.

Trust Your Body

No single reason for practice, however, is more important than memory training. It's important not just for players to execute offensive and defensive assignments but to perform fundamental and advanced skills routinely. Body memory is *at least* as important as mind memory. The best advice a coach can give any athlete is: Trust your body. All athletes must allow their athletic ability to express itself spontaneously, to let the body's built-in instrumentation throw a football or run to daylight.

Some youngsters are born with a kinesthetic sense that slows down time. They are able to see everything around them during performance, whether they execute triple somersaults, back walkovers, or quick openers. Few athletes have this ability. It is a gift—and only marginally coachable. The tailback with eyes in the back of his head was born that way. No amount of coaching or drill time can compensate for nature's shortcomings.

Practice sessions are not the place for talent implants. Even the best coaching won't create athletic talent where there is none, but it will refine the team's existing talents. It will also develop the athletic skills that players need to execute their assignments. Well-planned practice sessions drill fundamental and advanced skills into the body memory of every athlete so that the skills are taken for granted and performed spontaneously. Once this happens, players are able to progress to more sophisticated skills and to concentrate on their offensive and defensive assignments.

Yogi Berra's comment "You can't think and hit at the same time," is well-received by knowledgeable coaches. Conscious thought slows down athletic performance. The gymnast who thinks through a back walkover falls off the balance beam. The halfback who thinks about the right cut makes no cut. The well-coached athlete's body remembers skills and trusts itself to perform them the instant they're needed.

Maintaining a Focus on the Needs

On that basis, coaches want two things to happen when a play is called: They want players to know their assignments (mind memory) and they want them to execute those assignments to the best of their ability (body memory). Practice assures each of these; it's a time to master both the assignments and the skills needed to win football games. Such mastery is impossible without a sustained focus on the needs the team is trying to resolve.

If one of those needs is conditioning, the entire team must work harder, both aerobically and anaerobically. At such times, the coach may want to focus generously, if not exclusively, on activities that promote cardiovascular efficiency. Good conditioning wins close games in the waning minutes. Conditioning can never be overrated.

But be careful not to work your players at cross purposes. When the team is gasping for air, don't introduce two new plays to beat a stunting Gap Stack 44. As the late Hall of Fame Coach Vince Lombardi once said, "Fatigue can make cowards of us all." My experience has been it also can make us pretty stupid. If the two new plays are the focus, then, organize practice around them and give the team enough time to master them:

- Explain the reasons for them; in essence, how they will counteract a particular defense.
- Describe how they fit into the existing offense.
- Explain what new skills, if any, will be needed to execute these plays.
- Explain and demonstrate the actual execution of the plays and the skills.
- Provide enough time for the players to walk through the plays and, later, to run through them at half speed. Walking through offensive or defensive assignments is the essential first step to learning them. It's also the critical first step in learning new skills. Like mind memory, body memory requires structure and meaning. Both are provided with deliberate, sequential steps that enable players to catch on and to practice the relationships among different movements.
- Have them execute the plays at full speed, explaining adjustments in speed, footwork, backfield paths, and coordination with line blocking.
- Finally, incorporate the plays into timing sessions and scrimmages.

All this takes time, especially if the team has similar adjustments to make on defense. During this time, coaches must avoid mixing and matching. In other words, introduce two counter plays that involve different but similar movements at two different times. Or promote mastery of a new blocking scheme before introducing another one, especially if they are to be used against similar defenses.

Also, keep reminding the team of the need for better conditioning, for new or improved skills, and/or for the reasons behind the adjustments in offense or defense. Avoid nagging; kids stop listening to nagging. But they do respond positively to reminders that capitalize on their motivational needs. What are those needs? Consider some or all of the following.

Motivating Athletes During Practice

- *All kids have goals*—When all is said and done, most athletes want to win. Certainly, it isn't their exclusive goal, nor is it the only goal of many coaches. But let's admit it; win-at-all-costs is the concentrated focus of many coaches—and, by extension, many kids. It is a preoccupation that has defiled sports, schools, and the coaches and players themselves. It sounds almost contradictory but winning does help satisfy the motivational needs of athletes.

Achievement, belonging, recognition, responsibility, deference, dominance, and many other ego and social needs relate directly to winning. When these ends justify the means and when winning becomes an end in itself, however, young athletes hear mixed messages and athletic competition teaches lessons that run counter to the expectations of most coaches, athletes, and parents. Balance is the key and it must be evident during practice sessions.

Use practices and meetings, then, as opportunities to mention the individual commitment and the teamwork required to make a winning effort. Mention specific tasks that relate to the players' goals. The team that wants to win must master its assignments, continually refine its fundamental skills, adapt to new strategies, put forth more effort in practice, help teammates, listen to coaches, engage in positive self-talk, and behave in ways that reflect character and self-discipline.

Because young athletes want to win, they are motivated to do these things, especially when coaches remind them of the relationship between their responsibilities and their personal and athletic goals. It's safe to say that one of the coach's most important responsibilities during practice is to convince players to make the effort to realize their individual and team goals. Following are some suggestions:

- *Athletes need a knowledge of results*—The knowledge of how they're doing is motivating to athletes. It promotes improvement. One of my early experiences on the golf course found me slicing shots into every water hazard. For a while I appreciated the considerate but strained silence of my partners, but finally shouted, "Will someone tell me what I'm doing wrong?"

Once they gave me a few pointers, I couldn't wait to practice their advice. When a piece of advice worked, I immediately sought more. I discovered through such experiences the best time to offer advice is when someone *asks for it*. I was most inclined to use suggestions when *I* felt I needed them. Believe it or not, this concept works for football players, too. Establish a trusting relationship with your players and encourage them to ask for help whenever it's needed.

This is possible only when coaches offer suggestions and criticisms in a way that provides *light and not heat*. You'll discover that most of your players are as upset and as embarrassed as you are when they miss a block, get beat deep, run the wrong hole, or blow an assignment. A specific correction, especially if the coach is creative enough to get players to ask for it, is just as motivating to football players as that golf advice was to me. Save the heat for the few players who spend as much time beating the system as contributing to it.

I've also been around long enough to know that some kids need a size 12 where it will do them and the team the most good! I'll do that, too; some players need an occasional jolt out of their dream worlds. But I won't allow a misguided understanding of motivation or a misinterpretation of Lombardi's philosophy to transform me into a fire-breathing dragon. Such coaches may achieve some warped sense of power—but they lose. They fail to understand that it's hard to lead when you're standing behind everyone kicking them in the seat of the pants.

- *Periodic tests help promote a knowledge of results*—Periodic tests promote self-evaluation as well as requests for help. Documented proof is often the harsh dose of reality kids need to refocus on their goals. Bring out the video camera. Take a few moments to show your right tackle that he's not moving his feet on his pass block. Prove to your quarterback that he's throwing consistently off his back leg. Put the stopwatch on all the running backs to retime their 40s or on the quarterbacks to time their seven-step drops.

The key is to resurrect their goals, then document their progress toward realizing them. Their knowledge of such progress—or lack of it—will be motivating. It worked for my golf swing; it will work for them. And it will cause them to compete with themselves: A competition they all can win.

- *Athletes need standards to shoot for*—Excuse the dust on this suggestion, but there's a right way and a wrong way to do everything. The right way has passed the test of time. It works. Make it the standard that guides the performance of every player on your team. Explain such standards at the right time and to the right kids. Some players pick up basic skills fast. These are the players who *make things happen*. Teach them as much as they can absorb—which is a lot.

Other players wander around the practice field wondering *"What happened?"* They may be out of touch, but many of them are big, strong, and/or fast. They may be slow on the uptake, but they can make a contribution. We have to find a spot for them somewhere on the team. But we can't expect them to master fundamentals as quickly as their more gifted teammates. They have to work harder and longer to master even the most fundamental skills.

Look at it this way. Few junior high school math students are ready for pre-calculus in seventh grade. But for those few who **are** ready, someone better be prepared to teach them. The occasional blue chipper picks up football skills faster than a knife and fork—well, almost as fast. Give him/them as much as they can handle. Such coaching can even be handled on the run, between plays in a scrimmage. Gifted athletes are like sponges. They absorb everything.

Conversely, some eighth graders still struggle with fractions. If given enough time and support, these students will master them. Most teachers have learned, therefore, that a lock-stepped approach to teaching math is inappropriate. The best time to teach a particular skill or concept is when the student is ready to learn it. Such readiness involves a mastery of the fundamentals.

Similarly, a lock-stepped approach to teaching football skills scares some kids and helps others. The coach's job is to continually assess the mastery levels of athletes, to teach advanced skills when players are ready for them, and to review fundamental skills as needed.

• *Athletes are motivated by watching each other*—The athlete who watches a fellow teammate master a fundamental or advanced skill is motivated to master it himself. "If he can do it, so can I" underscores the competitive impulses of most football players and urges them toward improved performance. Keep in mind, however, that the team's blue chipper(s) may not be the best example(s) of mastery of advanced or fundamental skills.

Having your highly recruited right tackle demonstrate a reach block may be daunting to most of the linemen. It might even become yet another reason for many of the players to envy him and to regard his skills as peculiarities beyond the grasp of us common folk. On the other hand, the less talented hard worker who masters the reach block becomes a reasonable standard for everyone else on the line, even the blue chippers, who sometimes find themselves relying more on nature's generosity than on their own hard work.

• *Athletes are also motivated when they're watched by others*—That less talented player who demonstrates his mastery of the reach block is motivated to master another difficult technique each time his coach asks him to show his stuff. Nothing motivates us more than praise, especially when we're performing for our peers. The more often my teammates watch me, the harder I want to work and the better I want to do. Kids are pushed to do their best when they know that their peers as well as their coaches are watching them.

• *Athletes are watched most closely when they compete with each other*—All the guards can pull and race to the sidelines. All the quarterbacks can drop seven steps, set up, and throw the football. All the backs can race 10 yards or run an obstacle course. All the defensive backs can back-peddle 15 yards. All the linebackers can shuffle sideways for 15 yards. During such competitions, be sure that the players don't get sloppy in their haste to win. Proper execution is still the primary goal.

A Final Look at Motivation

Football players can be motivated in a variety of ways. Pep talks and other attempts at inspiration, even the occasional browbeating, work at times, but rarely motivate consistently. The coach who focuses on the individual and collective needs of his team and devises strategies to realize them motivates players far more than the yeller and the browbeater. Varying misinterpretations of tradition have sanctioned the browbeater as a motivational force, but even a brief glimpse at his win–loss record usually reveals something else. Winners understand and capitalize on the subtleties of motivation.

All of us have to take an occasional look at ourselves to reassess *our* motivations. We are all motivated to win, or we wouldn't be in this game. But when our motivations to win football games obscure the needs of our teams and jeopardize the emotional and physical well-being of our players, we run into problems, particularly during practice when the groundwork is laid for player commitment and interpersonal relationships that establish winning attitudes and programs.

Assessing the Achievement of Needs

The next step is to monitor team progress toward the resolution of needs. In essence, are the changes we have introduced and the skills we are trying to develop in our players doing what we originally intended? Do we have to adjust the adjustments? If we decided to put the noseguard in the A gap, for example, does he have the quickness and the strength to rip past the center as needed? If he can't, maybe we're better off repositioning him and adjusting the positions of other players to accomplish the defensive adjustment the team needs.

These determinations have to be made relatively early in the week. If the offensive tackle or tight end can't log or reach block the man on his outside shoulder, that sweep play we wanted to run may not work. In fact, it might work against us. Similarly, if the new plays we thought would beat a particular defensive set don't seem to be working, we have to look carefully not only at player execution but at the effectiveness of our planning. Those new plays may be ill-conceived. If so, we'd better change them right away.

Throughout this process, it's also important to remember one thing: **BE FLEXIBLE.** Don't be afraid to introduce new plays or defensive adjustments at any time during the season. The coach who says that we're going to run only five or six plays but we're going to run them so well that no one will stop them—is kidding himself. He's playing right into the hands of opposing scouts. Most teams in Pop Warner leagues or in junior high schools or senior high schools are unable to recruit the players with the skills to run only five or six plays.

Early in each season and periodically throughout the season, therefore, coaches must reevaluate what they are doing and adjust to use their personnel effectively. To do this, they must believe in their players' ability to learn and to execute new plays and skills. Kids are amazingly adaptable and intellectually more capable than many coaches realize. The coach who denies such player adaptability is, more often than not, admitting his own inflexibility. And my experience has led me to believe that inflexibility in a coach inevitably leads to failure.

So believe in your kids. Believe in their ability to adjust. Believe that they will master new skills and plays early in the week in order to give your team the unpredictability and the strategic effectiveness needed to stifle what your opponents do best. If you believe, they'll believe. Self-fulfilling prophecies run two ways. To revisit for the moment one of my early lessons in coaching: "Is it that they can't learn—or that I can't teach?" **COACH 'EM!**

A FEW FINAL WORDS

Practice is the time for improvement, for refinement, for mastery of our fundamental skills and our offensive and defensive execution. It is not a time for carelessness, horseplay, or needless injury. Coaches are well-advised, therefore, to guard against freak injuries to their players. Consider the following suggestions; certainly not startling revelations, just reminders to keep everyone healthy:

• Be sure that one or more coaches are on the field before and after practice. You or one of your staff should be the first one on the field and the last one off. To illustrate, we had a franchise player one year who jogged onto the field and decided to take a quick run through the blaster—the wrong way! The piece of equipment was relatively new, and he was feeling his oats, so he decided to take a freebie.

When it became evident what he was doing, I shouted, "John, stop! You're going the wrong way!" What could have been a serious spinal injury became a good laugh for all of us, and John went on to start 33 games for Notre Dame and to serve as a tri-captain for the Irish in his senior year. I hesitate to think of what might have happened if I hadn't been on the field to stop him.

- Schedule optimal levels of contact. Most football players like contact, at least they're not afraid of it. Some contact during practice is essential if players are to learn proper execution and improve their offensive and defensive timing. But contact is no longer necessary when execution and timing have been mastered. Contact for contact's sake is nonsense. With some teams, the principle of less is more should guide the use of contact during practice.

We had a team one year that had many talented players but not much collective desire to run into their fellow man. It wasn't a question of fear; they just didn't particularly like contact. When a rash of injuries before a big game that season forced us to back off contact, we decided to use the problem to our advantage. We told the kids we were taking contact *away from them* because they were one of the toughest teams we had ever coached and we wanted them to be hungry for the upcoming game.

We repeated our reasons often during practice. We even started hearing comments like: "Come on, coach, just a couple pops today." We responded, "Nope, you guys hit too hard; we don't want you hurting each other. Save it for Saturday." It worked. During the game, they topped out on the hit meter with any of our toughest teams—and no one got hurt. When it comes to hitting, *givers* rarely get hurt. The *recipients* usually get the aches and pains.

- Because most youngsters seem to have unlimited energy, we often forget that their muscles tire easily, in spite of their conditioning levels. Drills should be long enough to teach but short enough to avoid injury. If, for some reason, the players fail to profit from a certain drill one day, use it again the next day or find another drill that teaches the same skill(s).

When I was at Nebraska, Coach Bob Devaney allocated a specific amount of time for each drill. When the time ended, the drill ended, regardless of how well we did. If we didn't do well, we knew we would see it again the next day; it might even be a little tougher. We learned to work as hard as we could. Your players will do the same thing and they won't be victimized by fatigue.

- Provide as much water as your players need during practice. It's a well-known fact that water increases the suppleness of muscles by increasing the flow of oxygen throughout the body. It also promotes perspiration, which is the body's primary cooling mechanism. Youngsters can never drink enough water, particularly on hot days or early in the season, when conditioning sessions are unusually tiring.

On 90-degree days during preseason practice, we even had our kids take off their jerseys and pads and walk under the hose. No matter how hard we pushed them on those days, even in spite of a few verbal blasts to get their attention, we made a lot of friends! The water promoted not only good health for them but great relationships between the players and the coaches.

- Avoid player mismatches. When using these drills, especially if they involve contact, be sure that the players hitting each other are roughly comparable in size and strength. The underdeveloped youngster taking on the blue chipper may provoke a few inspirational moments, but he's risking a weekend, maybe a lifetime of pain. Protect him—sometimes even from himself. We may admire his guts, but let's also teach him forethought. Play smart today and be around to play tomorrow.

- Know your players. The youngster who walks on the practice field each day somewhat afraid of contact may do something impulsively to prove to himself and to others that he's tough. Throwing yourself recklessly in front of a runner or dropping your head and running into three tacklers is not tough. It's dumb. We have to impress on such youngsters, as on everyone else, that tough and smart are complementary terms. Tough is coming out for football in the first place, having the guts to work toward success. Smart is learning the skills, the assignments, and the self-control that promote such success.

- If your kids aren't ready developmentally for some of these drills, don't use them! That's why I included over 350 drills in the book. There's something here for everyone, but some of the drills may demand too much from young football players. Be judicious in your use of the drills and in your expectations of your players. Injured players can't help us on game day.

Most importantly, however, we have a responsibility to our players. Their parents entrusted them to us and the players themselves look up to us. We must constantly earn such trust and respect by caring about our athletes and doing everything we can to promote their emotional and physical safety.

Let's Wrap It Up

Relationships. That's what football is all about. Relaxed and trusting relationships among players and coaches promote good communication and a common sense of purpose. Nothing is more important during practice, when players must learn their assignments and the skills necessary to execute them. Let's face it; drills can get pretty boring. The essential repetition that forces proper execution into the body's memory challenges the attention span of even the most dedicated athlete.

Although the drills in this book have been designed to be fun as well as instructive, even they can become tedious. That's why coaches are encouraged to use them within the proper time frame, long enough to teach, short enough to be fun. That's also why the book provides a variety of drills that teach similar fundamental skills. Vary the drills to teach the same skills. Your players will appreciate it, especially as the season wears on and that favorite drill of yours becomes a pain in the neck to them.

Finally, let your players know that these drills are important not just to help them win but to enable them to *refuse to lose.* We all want to win, sometimes for the wrong reasons. Young athletes like attention; coaches like respect from their peers. Players want to walk tall in school or strut their stuff in front of the girls. Some want trophies or even attention from college scouts. With kids as well as with coaches, winning can become an end in itself, so desirable that it obscures all the other values of athletic participation.

Give me the athlete who refuses to lose, the committed, gut-level tough kid who stands toe-to-toe with the biggest opponent and keeps coming back for more. Certainly, athletes like this want to win, but, more important, they refuse to lose. They develop the character that sees them through the football season and life. We want these kinds of players on our team. These drills can help develop them.

To get your season moving in the right direction, share the following poem with your players. Perhaps post it in the locker room and refer to the concept periodically during practice to get your athletes into the right mindset during drill time. The athlete who refuses to lose wants to master the necessary skills to make himself the complete football player. These drills will help. Good luck with them.

REFUSE TO LOSE

In the stillness of the locker room, before the game begins,
When the slogans and the posters shout a silent need to win,
Refuse to lose.
When your teammates dream of glory and your coaches make demands,
When there's quiet in the locker room and thunder in the stands,
When your teammates pray for victory by joining hearts and hands,
Refuse to lose.
There is no joy in victory save the satisfaction found
When we dig a little deeper, when we get up off the ground,
When we push beyond our limits and disregard the pain,
When the season's toughest challenge provokes the same refrain:
Refuse to lose.
Some players value winning for the glory that it brings:
For the public's adulation, for the trophies and the rings.
They seek the recognition, the honors, and the fame—
Self-indulgent reasons for playing any game.
Refuse to lose.
Athletes who refuse to lose soon earn the greatest prize.
They learn to take on anything, regardless of their size.
They learn that there's no quitting when the game is getting tough,
When pain and perseverance no longer seem enough.
Refuse to lose.
Character is nothing more than what we think and choose;
It's the strength we find within ourselves by vowing not to lose.
It's the act of daring greatly in the face of daunting odds;
It's a promise to our teammates and a partnership with God.
It's the courage to prevail, whatever fortune brings,
When common athletes find the strength to do uncommon things.
Refuse to lose.
The fairest praise good athletes hear, when all is said and done,
Are not the cheers or shouts of joy when games are finally won.
They hear instead an inner voice, frank and unrestrained,
That criticizes how they played or spurs their *self*-acclaim.
So take the trophies and the plaques and put them on your shelves,
And when you look for character—look within yourselves.
Refuse to lose.

KEY TO SYMBOLS

[A/F]	= Air Flate (Shield)		(K)	= Kicker or Kicking Team
(BC)	= Ball Carrier		(KR)	= Kick Receiver
(B)	= Blocker		(L)	= Lineman
(CT)	= Center		(LB)	= Linebacker
(C)	= Coach		(MLB)	= Middle Linebacker
△	= Cone		(NG)	= Nose Guard
(CB)	= Cornerback		(OL)	= Offensive Lineman
V or (D)	= Defender		(OT)	= Offensive Tackle
(DB)	= Defensive Back		(OLB)	= Outside Linebacker
(DE)	= Defensive End		○ or (P)	= Player or Punter
(DL)	= Defensive Lineman		(PR)	= Punt Returner
(DT)	= Defensive Tackle		(QB)	= Quarterback
(E)	= End		(TE)	= Tight End
🏈	= Football		(R)	= Receiver
(FB)	= Fullback		(RB)	= Running Back
(G)	= Guard		(S)	= Safety
(HB)	= Halfback		(S/U)	= Stand-up Dummy (Bell)
(H)	= Holder		(T)	= Tackler
(ILB)	= Inside Linebacker		(T)	= Tackle

SECTION 2

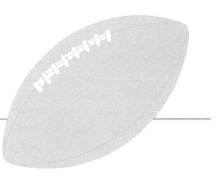

AGILITY DRILLS

This section provides a series of agility drills to be used for pre-practice warming up and flexibility exercises.

1. HIGH KNEE

Purpose: To improve flexibility, to emphasize high knees when running, and to promote a good warm up before practice.

Description: Align the entire team on the goal line in four or five waves, depending on the size of your team. Instruct each wave to run 20 yards, pumping their knees as high as they can and exaggerating their arm movements. This is not a race. Each player must execute to the best of his ability. His knees should be at least waist high, and his exaggerated arm movement should swing his hands from behind his back to over his head.

2. QUICK FEET

Purpose: To develop quick feet, to promote anaerobic strength, and to provide a warm-up prior to practice.

Description: Align the entire team on the goal line in four or five waves. Instruct each wave to run 20 yards, chugging their feet as fast as they can. This drill is not a race. Each player should chug his feet almost as if running in place but moving gradually downfield. Each player's knees should not be high, and his arm movement should be restricted to only a short but quick arc on each side of his body.

3. SEAT ROLL

Purpose: To promote body quickness, flexibility, arm strength, and pre-practice warm up.

Description: Place the entire team on the goal line in four or five waves. Instruct each wave, in turn and on your command, to drop to all fours. Their necks should be bulled and their feet should be making quick, choppy movements. As soon as you point, they should execute a seat roll in that direction. Make sure you point unpredictably: right, right, left, right, left, left. On the command, "Break," they should drop to their stomachs and get up as fast as possible. Keep them moving briskly. This is a good warm-up activity. It also promotes team discipline. Have each wave return to its original alignment for more repetitions.

4. CRAB

Purpose: To develop arm strength and to simulate defensive movement, especially for linemen.

Description: Align the entire team on the goal line in four or five waves. Instruct each group, in turn and on your command, to drop to all fours. Their necks should be bulled, their knees bent, and their arms straight. Command them to move alternately right and left. Each player should crab in that direction. On your command, "Break," each wave should execute a seat roll, get up as quickly as possible, and sprint 10 yards downfield. Each wave should jog to the outside of the activity, return to their original alignment, and follow the coach's commands.

5. HEEL TO BUTT

Purpose: To strengthen the hamstrings and stretch the quadriceps.

Description: Have waves or the entire team run 40 yards, pumping their arms, their backs straight with a good forward lean. Tell them to stride out but to kick themselves in the butt with their heel each time they complete a stride. Run this agility drill in combination with other running drills to promote a good warm up before practice or a game.

6. HANG TIME

Purpose: To strengthen the calf muscles and to emphasize good leg drive when running.

Description: Have waves or the entire team run 40 yards, pumping their arms and driving their knees as high as possible. Tell them to push off the ground with their toes, to push so hard they get good hang time. The better the hang time, the better they are executing. With good hang time, they may cover a yard and a half with each stride.

7. CARIOCA

Purpose: To emphasize hip flexibility and general agility.

Description: Have waves or the entire team run 40 yards. They should be facing upfield, their shoulders at a 90-degree angle to the sideline. When running to the right, they should put the left foot in front of the right foot, then stride with the right, then put the left foot behind the right, and so on down the field. With each sideways movement of the feet, they should rotate their hips. Their shoulders should remain square to the sideline so that the motion is completely sideways.

8. QUARTER EAGLE

Purpose: To work on hip flexibility, warm up the legs and ankles, and promote anaerobic conditioning.

Description: Align the players in waves of four or five. On the command, "Get 'em moving!" the players should start running in place. On your hand signal, they should quickly turn their hips a quarter turn, then return to the front. They should keep their upper bodies facing you and continue running in place throughout the drill. Have them turn their hips three or four times in each direction, each time shouting the direction of the turn.

9. DRIVE 'EM

Purpose: To warm up the legs and upper body and practice an effective running motion.

Description: Align the players in waves of four or five. On the command, "Get'em moving," the players should run in place, driving their knees at least waist-high and pumping their arms vigorously. Tell them to get a good forward lean and to pump their legs as many times as possible before you wave them past you. This is an excellent warm-up drill and should be the first drill you use during agilities.

10. DOUBLE CARIOCA

Purpose: To increase hip flexibility and to promote quick feet.

Description: Align the players in waves of four or five. On the command, "Get 'em moving," they should run in place. By pointing, have them carioca 10 to 15 yards in one direction, then 10 to 15 yards back. Have them carioca twice in each direction before waving each group past you.

11. RUN IN THE DIRECTION

Purpose: To improve lateral mobility and to warm up the knees and the upper body.

Description: Align the players in waves of four or five. On the command, "Get 'em moving," have them run in place, emphasizing high knees. Hand signal the direction you want them to run. Alternate the direction every two to three seconds. Each time you point, they should turn completely and run in that direction, then, on the next signal, pivot 180 degrees and run in that direction. They are to run as fast as they can for four or five repetitions and to shout the direction of the cut each time you point.

12. SHUFFLE IN THE DIRECTION

Purpose: To improve lateral mobility and quick feet.

Description: Align the players in waves of four or five. On the command, "Get 'em moving," they should run in place. Hand signal the direction you want them to shuffle. Alternate the direction every two to three seconds. Each time you point, they remain facing you but shuffle in the direction you indicate. Be sure they don't crossover step but maintain a good, quick shuffle. Each time you point, they should shout the direction.

13. COMPASS RUN

Purpose: To warm up the ankles, knees, hips, and upper body and to promote anaerobic conditioning.

Description: Align the players in waves of four or five. On the command, "Get 'em moving," they should run in place. Hand signal the direction you want them to run. This drill directs them to run back and forth as well as right and left. They should run at full speed and shout the direction each time they change directions: right, left, back, forward. They should back peddle when moving backward, their knees bent and their weight forward. Emphasize high knees and good arm movement throughout the drill.

14. BACK AND FORTH

Purpose: To emphasize back peddling as well as explosive movement forward.

Description: Align the players in waves of four or five. On the command, "Get 'em moving," they should run in place. Point in the direction you want them to run—back or forth. Each time you point, they should shout the direction, then move as quickly as they can. Emphasize bent knees and a good forward lean when they run in either direction. Be sure each wave gets at least three repetitions.

15. STEP AND HOP

Purpose: To promote quick feet, pyelometric exercise, and anaerobic conditioning.

Description: Align all the players in front of the first row in the stadium. On your command, all the players should step up with the right foot, then alternate left, right, left, right on the same row until they hear the whistle. They should not run up the stadium but should step up, down, up, down on the same row.

Vary the drill by having the players hop up and down with both feet until they hear the whistle. This is a good pyelometric exercise and promotes leg explosiveness.

16. HIP HOP

Purpose: To emphasize pyelometric conditioning and to warm up the knees and ankles.

Description: Align all the players on one side of a sideline. On your command, have them hop back and forth over the line, pushing off both feet and moving as quickly as possible. Have them hop the length of the field, then stop for the next drill.

17. RUN THE SQUARE

Purpose: To provide a total body warm up and to promote some competitive aerobic conditioning.

Description: Place four cones in a square exactly 10 yards apart. Align the players in lines on opposite corners of the square as illustrated, the first player in each line five yards from his corner of the square. On your command, have the first player in each line bear crawl (run on all fours) to the first cone, get up and sprint to the second, carioca left to the third cone, backpedal to the fourth, and carioca right to his original starting position. This is a good drill for combining different agility drills when time is short and for promoting some lively competition for everyone.

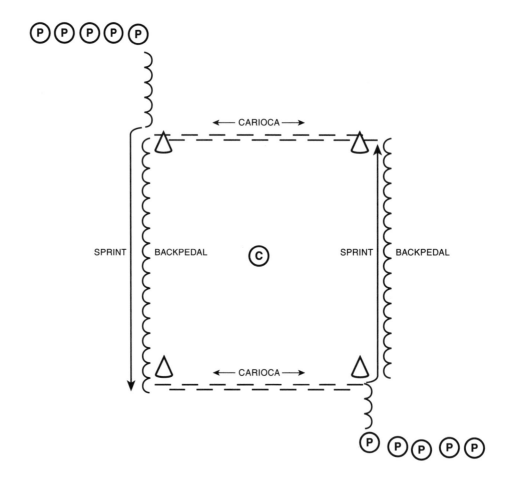

18. GET UP AND GO

Purpose: To emphasize getting off the ground quickly after being blocked and moving quickly to a target. The drill also promotes total body conditioning.

Description: Position four stand-up dummies 10 yards upfield. Position the players in waves of four, each in front of a dummy as illustrated. Instruct the players to lie on their sides, their heads on the yard stripe, and—on your command—to get up as fast as they can and race to the stand-up dummies and knock them over. The first player in each wave to knock over a dummy is the winner.

Vary the drill by having the winners from each wave race each other. Move the dummies farther downfield to intensify the conditioning.

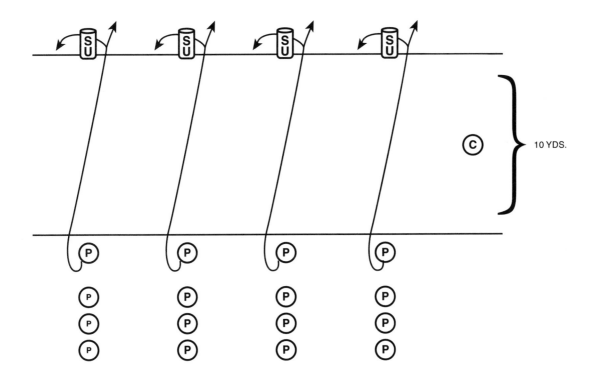

19. SLALOM

Purpose: To warm up the legs, hips and upper bodies, and to promote anaerobic conditioning.

Description: Place five or six stand-up dummies on their sides, approximately two yards apart. Place another stand-up dummy upright nine or 10 yards from the last dummy as illustrated. Position the players two or three yards from the first dummy and instruct them to sprint around and between the dummies as fast as possible. Tell them to emphasize good body lean and to push hard off their outside foot on each turn. After running between the last two dummies, they should sprint to the upright dummy and knock it over. Have them follow each other quickly, so that you have just enough time to put the dummy upright again after each player hits it.

When the last player has sprinted through the dummies, tell the first player to *shuffle* between them. Make sure the players don't crossover step. They are to shuffle between each pair of dummies. When they clear the final dummy, they should once again sprint to the upright dummy and knock it over.

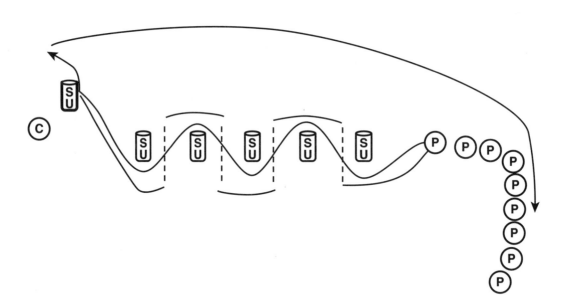

20. ROPE DRILLS

Purpose: To work on foot speed and balance and to promote pyelometric exercise and anaerobic conditioning.

Every Hole

Each player should step with his left foot in each hole on the left side, his right foot in each hole on the right.

Every Other Hole

Each player should step in every other hole on both sides of the ladder, alternating steps.

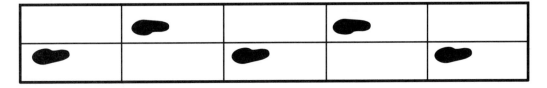

Crossover

Each player should step in every other square, crossing right foot to left and left foot to right.

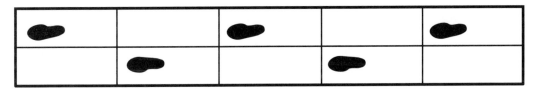

Jump Every Hole

Each player should jump with both feet in every hole.

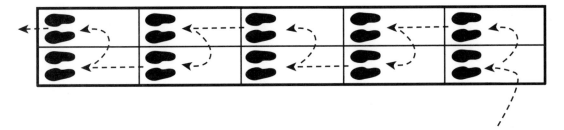

Jump Every Other Hole

Each player should jump off both feet into every other hole, left to right and back to left.

Outside the Lines

Each player should start to the left of the ropes, step with his right foot into the first square, his left into the second square on the right, and his right again outside the ropes. He should repeat the process in the other direction, then back again. See illustration.

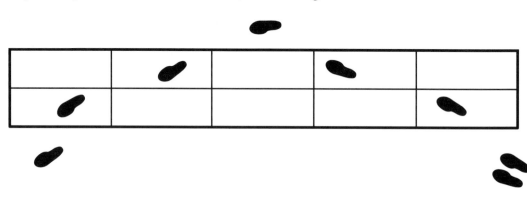

SECTION 3

QUARTERBACK DRILLS

This section focuses on the following skills:

- Stance and starts
- Exchange from center
- Hand-offs
- Faking
- The passing motion
- Footwork during the motion
- Staying in the pocket/sensing and reacting to pressure
- Drop-back passing—3-, 5-, and 7-step
- Sprint-out passing
- Roll-out passing
- Play action passing technique
- Screen passing technique
- Option techniques: the triple option, the buck option, the veer, and the sprint option

21. TARGET SNAP

Purpose:

- To guarantee a consistent exchange between center and quarterback.

Coaching Pointers:

To the quarterback:

- Extend your arm and wrist so that only your hand rests under the center.
- Your arm and wrist should be almost straight, with only a slight bend in the elbow.
- Move your arms forward to maintain contact with the center as he fires out to make his block.
- For purposes of this drill, place only your top hand under the center and allow the ball to drop to the ground after the snap.

To the center:

- Snap the ball firmly into the quarterback's hand as you initiate your block. Hold it for a split second to give the QB time to gain control.
- Be moving forward as you snap the ball. Don't allow the snap to interfere with your blocking responsibility unless the field is unusually wet.

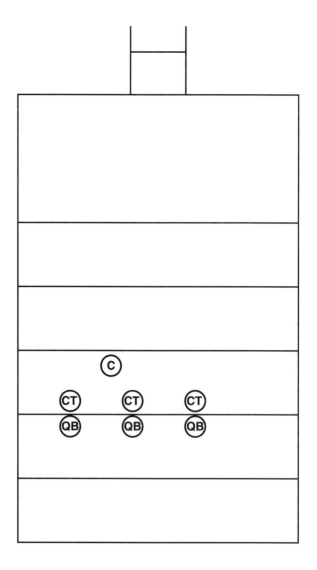

Set-up and Instructions:

- Place tandems of centers and quarterbacks along the goal line or any designated line of scrimmage, approximately five yards apart.
- Have the quarterbacks get in their stances, placing only their top hands under the center. Have the quarterbacks alternate the cadence.
- At the snap, the center moves forward to simulate blocking.
- The quarterbacks let the ball drop to the ground. If it falls straight down, the location of the snap is good. If the ball bounces backward, the snap is too far back on the quarterback's hand; if it bounces forward, the snap is too short.

22. SWITCH SNAP

Purpose:

- To emphasize the fundamentals of a good center/quarterback exchange.
- To switch the roles of the quarterback and the center so that each recognizes the key points in executing a good snap.

Coaching Pointers:

To the quarterback:

- Apply the same pressure on the center every time you take a snap.

To the center:

- After you snap the ball, hold it up there for a split second so the quarterback can gain control of it.

To both:

- Now switch roles. See how difficult the other guy's job is! Notice how important hand pressure and an accurate snap are.

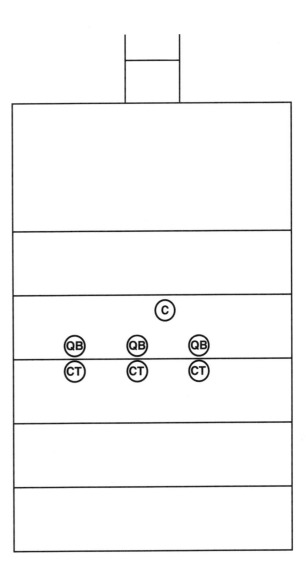

Set-up and Instructions:

Align tandems of quarterbacks and centers along a designated line of scrimmage. Position them approximately five yards apart and tell them to switch places. Instruct the quarterbacks to snap the ball and the centers to receive it. Emphasize consistent hand pressure, quarterback follow-through, and accuracy of snap. Use this drill early in the season and as needed as the season progresses. Be sure to tell the centers to keep their hands sufficiently separated to avoid getting their fingers jammed if the ball is snapped prematurely. This will serve as a reminder as well to the quarterbacks.

23. GET 'N GO

Purpose:

- To emphasize the proper quarterback stance.
- To develop quarterback quickness after the snap.
- To emphasize the importance of getting the ball before executing the play.

Coaching Pointers:

- **Always** follow through with the center to get the ball before executing the play!
- Quarterbacks, keep your feet approximately shoulder-width, a slight bend in your knees, be on the balls of your feet, and maintain a balanced stance.
- Once you get the ball, bring it into your chest and lean in the direction of the play. Fire out of your stance to do your job. GET THE BALL AND GO!

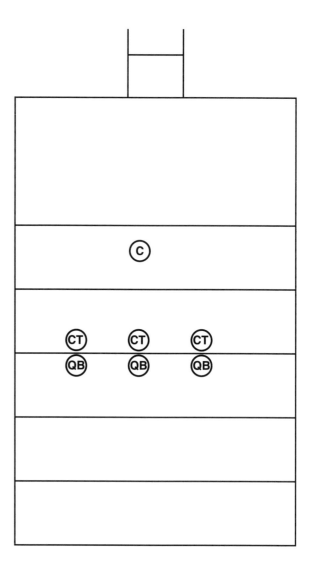

Set-up and Instructions:

Align tandems of quarterbacks and centers along a designated line of scrimmage. Have the quarterbacks face you. You stand 10 to 15 yards downfield. Give them a play and have the quarterbacks alternate the cadence. At the snap, make sure each has good control of the ball before executing the play. The plays should involve quick openers so that the quarterbacks have to work into the line of scrimmage, quarterback sneaks, simulated handoffs to the fullback, sprint-out action, and drop-back passes.

Tell them to emphasize good control of the ball first, foot speed second. Alternate three, five, and seven steps for the drop-back passes. Use this drill primarily early in the season. Once the quarterbacks have mastered the fundamentals, have them compete with each other to see who sprints out and drops back fastest. Remind them not to surrender proper execution for speed. Thoughtless execution results in fumbles. You might even require extra sprints for each fumble, fewer sprints for consistently good execution.

24. FIRE OUT SNAP

Purpose:

- To train the quarterback to keep his hands under the center throughout the entire snap.
- To impress on quarterbacks the snap may change depending on the center's blocking responsibility.

Coaching Pointers:

- Get in a good stance. Be mobile; you're going to have to move with the center to get the snap, then in a different direction to make the play.
- Maintain upward pressure on the center until you have secured the ball.
- As soon as you secure the snap, bring the ball into your stomach to initiate the play.

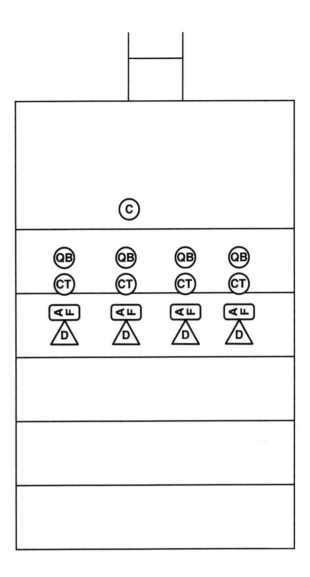

Set-up and Instructions:

Position tandems of quarterbacks and centers on a designated line of scrimmage. Position a defender over each center. Give each defender an air flate and, from a position behind the centers and quarterbacks, tell them what defensive technique to use. For example, they might bull rush the center or slant into either A gap. Have the quarterbacks alternate the cadence, making it loud enough for everyone to hear. Early in the season, you might also have all the quarterbacks give the cadence simultaneously to assure uniformity.

Check to make sure the centers are executing their blocks correctly and the quarterbacks are getting the snap securely.

25. SAME SNAP

Purpose:

- To practice and standardize the exchange from center to quarterback.

Coaching Pointers:

- Place your hands in the same spot on each center.
- Pressure the center! Make sure he knows where your hands are.
- Follow through on the snap. Go with the center as he fires out.
- Centers, if you don't feel pressure, tell the quarterback!
- Quarterbacks! Get a good bend in your legs and have only a slight bend in your elbows so you can follow through with the snap.

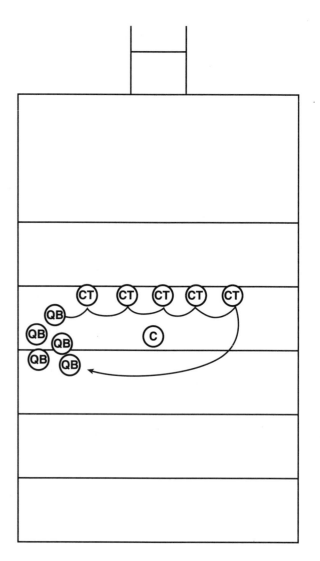

Set-up and Instructions:

Position all the centers on a designated line of scrimmage approximately two yards apart. Gather the quarterbacks to the left of the line as illustrated. Give each quarterback a football and have him work his way down the line of centers, taking a snap from each one. Have him hand his football to the first center, take a snap, then move to the next center giving him the ball. Instruct the centers to take a step forward while snapping the ball to simulate a block. Make sure the quarterbacks follow through with each snap. Give each quarterback at least three repetitions moving down the line.

This is an excellent drill during the preseason for introducing and practicing the snap. It's also good for making sure each quarterback can take a snap from each center. Injury sometimes makes for interesting combinations of players! It's a short drill, too, so use it often during the season—as a quick preliminary for other activities during practice.

26. HANDOFFS

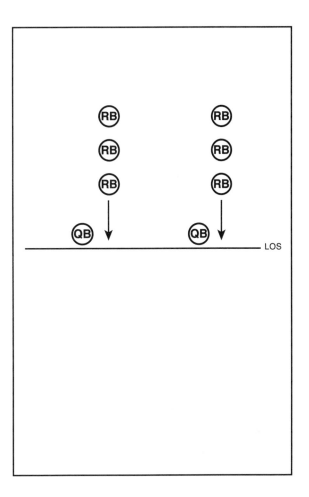

Purpose:

- To master the fundamentals of an effective handoff.

Coaching Pointers:

- Look the ball into the ball carrier's pocket.
- Bend the wrist slightly to snap the ball into the ball carrier's stomach.
- Always aim at the ball carrier's stomach. If the handoff is too low, his knee will jar the ball from your hand. If too high, the ball will hit the breastplate of his shoulder pads, and he won't feel it.
- **His job is to run the football; your job is to get it to him! He has the tougher job; make it easier for him!**

Set-up and Instructions:

Align all the quarterbacks along a designated line of scrimmage. Position a line of running backs to their left. After three or four repetitions, move the line to the right of the quarterbacks so they head off in both directions. Have all the quarterbacks shout the cadence simultaneously the first two or three times you use this drill to develop uniformity in the way the cadence is called. Assure such uniformity early.

A couple days later, have the quarterbacks alternate the cadence, each loud enough so that all the backs can hear them.

This drill consists of three phases:

- **Phase one:** Instruct the running backs to line up in the "home" halfback position, to run a quick opener, and to try to beat the quarterback to the point of exchange. When they reach the point of exchange, tell them NOT to make a pocket but to keep both arms straight alongside their bodies. Tell the quarterbacks to put the ball firmly but gently into the running back's stomach but to hold on to it after the point of exchange. Observe and correct as needed. Make sure the ball makes contact with the ball carrier's stomach. Run this phase several times.

- **Phase two:** Tell the running backs to take the ball only with the arm and hand farther from the quarterback and to keep the near arm straight alongside the body. Check to make sure the ball isn't being pushed through the pocket. The ball carrier's far elbow should be tight enough to the body to prevent that.

- **Phase three:** Take the handoff with both arms but beat the quarterback to the point of exchange! Teach him to get the ball to you as quickly as possible!

31

27. LOOK IT IN

Purpose:

- To emphasize to quarterbacks the importance of looking the ball in when making a handoff.

Coaching Pointers:

- Look the ball into the ball carrier's pocket every time you make a handoff.
- Be sure to wrist the ball gently into his stomach and avoid hitting the breast-plate on his shoulder pads. He has to **feel** the ball!
- Don't look back at the ball carrier after making the handoff. Continue with the execution of the rest of the play.
- Tell me whether you see an open hand or a fist each time you make the handoff.

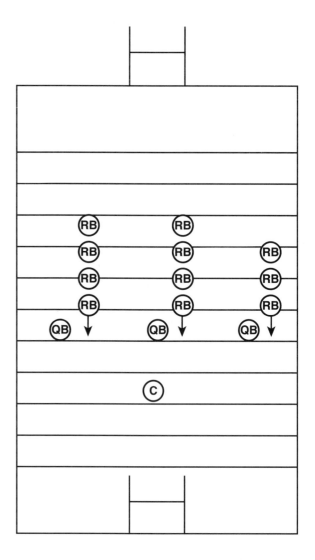

Set-up and Instructions:

Align the quarterbacks along a designated line of scrimmage, approximately 10 yards apart. Place a line of halfbacks to the left of each quarterback. Instruct the quarterbacks to look away, then signal the ball carriers to open their bottom hand or make a fist with it while receiving the handoff. Then instruct the quarterbacks to hand off the ball, looking it in to determine whether the ball carrier has a fist or an open hand. After each repetition, have all the quarterbacks shout "Fist" or "Open hand."

Continue the drill until the quarterbacks look the ball in routinely. This technique can also be used during timing or scrimmage sessions if you suspect that the quarterbacks are not looking the ball in. Without the quarterback's knowledge, whisper to the ball carrier to make a fist or an open hand during the next play. After the play, ask the quarterback to tell you what he saw. Such periodic reminders are easy and very effective.

28. FAKE YOUR WAY

Purpose:

- To emphasize the importance of good fakes.
- To master the basics of good faking.
- To learn to take pride in making a good fake.

Coaching Pointers:

To the quarterbacks:

- Stay low at all times throughout the execution of the play.
- Make every fake and every handoff look exactly the same.
- Don't watch the ball carrier; continue with the play, making every fake as if it's a handoff.

To the ball carriers:

- Maintain a wide pocket when faking; don't knock the ball from the quarterback's hands.
- As soon as he removes the ball, clamp down hard.
- Don't execute a fake; don't make it look like a fake. Make it look like you're running the ball! Run hard, keep your head up, and make appropriate noises!
- One good fake is sometimes better than two or three good blocks!

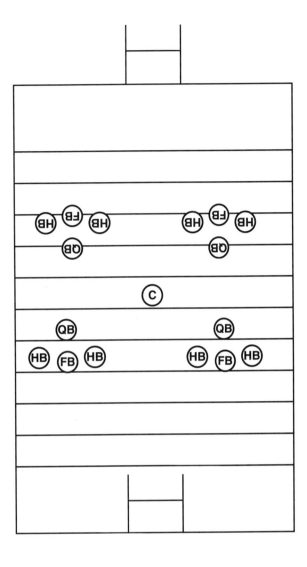

Set-up and Instructions:

Depending on the number of backfields you have, align half of them along a designated line of scrimmage, approximately five yards apart. Align the other backfields opposite and facing them five yards downfield. In essence, all the backfields will be facing each other five yards apart at five-yard intervals along the line of scrimmage. Have one backfield at a time execute a play involving a fake. Have the backfield opposite them shout out who has the ball as soon as they see it.

After making corrections, have the remainder of the backfields alternate executing their plays. Every backfield should execute at least three plays. Award points to the backfield that confuses the observing backfield. Also, have the observing backfield tell the executing backfield why it was so easy for them to identify the fake. Competition and peer pressure sometimes work!

29. WHERE'S THE BALL?

Purpose:

- To emphasize the importance of good faking.

Coaching Pointers:

- Quarterback, keep your weight down. Operate with a good bend in your knees so you can maneuver easily and quickly.
- Running back, run as if you have the ball. Don't act as if it's a fake; act as if it's a run!
- A good fake is better than two good blocks!
- Grunt, groan, bounce off tacklers, cross both arms over an imaginary ball, drive your legs, do whatever you have to do to make the play believable.

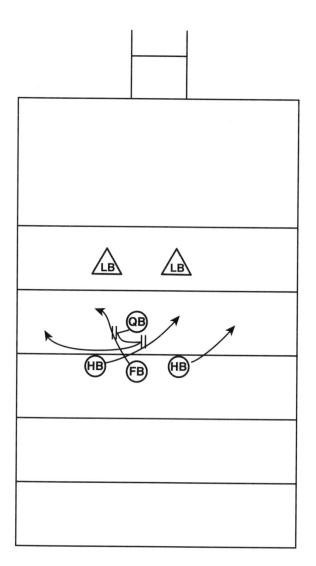

Set-up and Instructions:

Align two inside linebackers as if in a 5-2 set. Face them up to alternating backfields. Have each backfield execute a play from your offense that involves a fake. The plays may involve counters, inside reverses, counteraction fakes, belly plays, fake draws, bootlegs, crossfire action, or any of the misdirection plays you are using. Tell the linebackers to react immediately once they know who has the ball. Praise the backfield that immobilizes the linebackers momentarily or causes them to react to the fake. Correct the backfield that allows the linebackers to react immediately to the ball carrier.

This is an especially good drill for the misdirection offense. Vary the drill by giving two points to the backfield that causes the linebackers to react to the fake, one point if it immobilizes the linebackers. Deduct a point every time the linebackers react immediately to the ball. Give fewer sprints to the winners after practice or buy them a soda the next day.

30. MAKING A PASS

Purpose:

- To develop proper passing technique.
- To drill passing fundamentals into the body memory of every quarterback.

Coaching Pointers:

- Both hands on the ball; keep it in front of you prior to the pass.
- Feet shoulder-width, stay on the balls of your feet, in a balanced stance.
- Step in the direction of your pass.
- Never pass off your back leg.
- Always pass to a spot; always have a target.
- Never raise the ball and hesitate. Passing involves one continuous motion.
- Rotate your upper body forcefully during the passing motion. The strength and quickness of the pass comes more from your upper body, less from your arm.
- Your throwing elbow should be roughly parallel to your shoulder at the start of the passing motion.
- Whip your non-throwing arm hard during the passing motion to help rotate your torso.
- Follow through; roll your weight onto your front leg.
- Your index finger should touch the ball last and your arm should be extended toward your target.

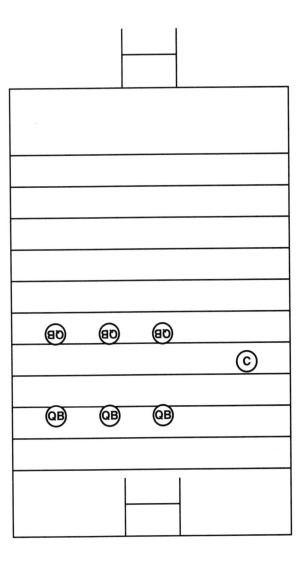

Set-up and Instructions:

Align half the quarterbacks along a designated line of scrimmage, the other half facing them approximately 15 to 20 yards downfield. Have tandems of quarterbacks pass the ball to each other, emphasizing the proper passing motion. Check for proper fundamentals and make corrections as appropriate.

31. TAKE A KNEE

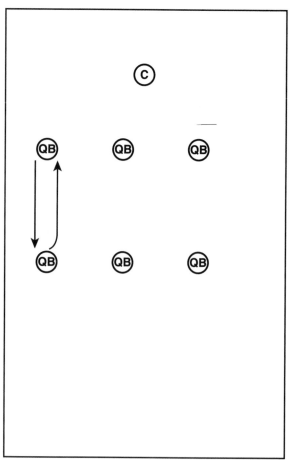

Purpose:

- To emphasize upper body rotation during the passing motion.

Coaching Pointers:

- Always aim for a target when passing the football. Try to hit your partner in the nose or the ear.
- Rotate your shoulders forcefully in the initial stages of the movement so that your torso pivots to either the right or the left.
- Keep the ball high on your chest as you start your rotation.
- When you release the ball with your non-throwing hand, you should be "palming" the ball with your throwing hand, and your throwing arm should be roughly parallel to the ground.
- As you rotate your shoulders and torso to throw the ball, the elbow of your throwing arm should come forward first in order to "whip" the ball to your receiver.
- At the point of release, the ball should touch your index finger last and the palm of your throwing hand should be parallel to the ground.
- Exaggerate the arm extension toward the receiver in order to assure the proper follow-through.

Set-up and Instructions:

Position tandems of quarterbacks facing each other approximately 10 yards apart. Instruct each quarterback to kneel on the knee that is on the same side of his body as his throwing arm. Tell the quarterbacks to play catch, emphasizing upper body rotation throughout the passing motion. Share the previous passing fundamentals with them and check for proper execution throughout the drill. Make corrections as needed. Use this drill as often as needed to condition each player's body memory.

32. ROTATION

Purpose:

- To emphasize upper body rotation during the passing motion.

Coaching Pointers:

- Refer to the pointers outlined in *(31) Take a Knee.*
- Emphasize as well that the quarterback's non-throwing shoulder should be lower than the throwing shoulder. If the non-throwing shoulder is higher, the ball will sail high.
- In addition, if the non-throwing shoulder is higher, the quarterback is not rotating his shoulders and torso forcefully enough to pass with good velocity.

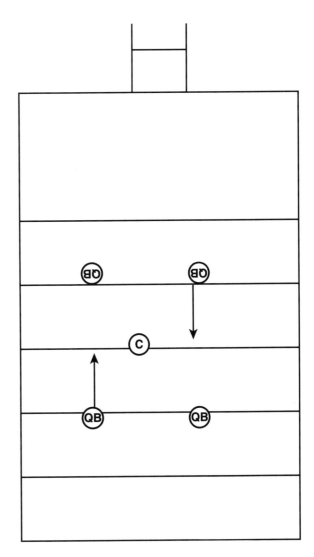

Set-up and Instructions:

Align half the quarterbacks on a yard line, approximately five yards apart. Position the remainder of the quarterbacks 15 to 20 yards downfield, facing the first half. Instruct all the quarterbacks to position the toes of both feet on a designated yard line. Their feet should be shoulder-width, their bodies erect, the ball held with both hands chest high. Instruct them to play catch—without moving their feet.

The drill emphasizes the importance of upper body rotation during the passing motion. After each quarterback passes the ball five or six times, tell them to exaggerate their upper body rotation by having half the quarterbacks move 20 or more yards downfield so that each tandem is throwing the ball 40 to 50 yards without moving their feet. Some of them may not throw the ball that far, but each will realize the importance of upper body rotation.

Variation: Indicate as well that a quick release of the football results not from the arm alone but from the quickness and forcefulness of the rotation of the upper body. To prove this point, have them rotate their upper bodies as quickly as possible. They'll notice how naturally and quickly the arm will follow and how tight the passing motion must be to maintain control of the ball.

33. LEAD STEP

Purpose:

- To emphasize the quarterback's step in the direction of the receiver and the importance of a good follow-through.

Coaching Pointers:

- While you rotate your upper body, take a step in the direction of your receiver.
- Use your non-throwing arm to help whip your upper body around.
- As you release the ball, feel your weight transfer from your back leg to your front leg. You should roll over your front leg as you exaggerate the extension of your throwing arm in the direction of the receiver.
- Reach out to touch the receiver!

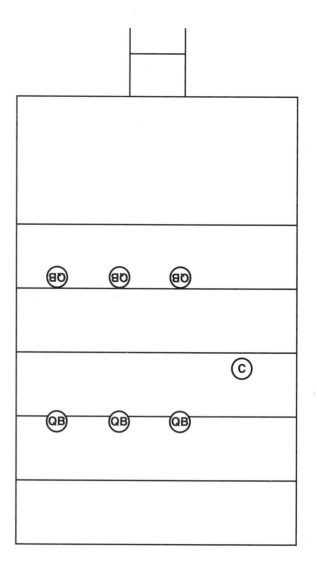

Set-up and Instructions:

Have tandems of quarterbacks play catch. Have them throw the ball 15 to 20 yards. Separate each tandem by five yards so you can watch all the quarterbacks and make corrections as needed. Make sure each quarterback is emphasizing good upper body rotation while he steps in the direction of the pass to his partner. Check to see if the weight of each quarterback is rolling over his front leg as he releases the ball. Also check to see if the follow-through of his throwing arm is well extended toward his receiver. Follow-through is the critical element that enables a quarterback to "feel" the ball to the receiver. The ball should roll off his index finger and the palm of his throwing hand should be parallel to the ground, his fingers pointed at the receiver after the throw.

Devote at least 15 minutes to this drill, making corrections as needed. Use it as often as needed to assure good upper body rotation and follow-through.

34. STEP LIVELY

Purpose:

- To condition quarterbacks to use the correct footwork for three-, five-, and seven-step drop-back passes.

Coaching Pointers:

- Reach on your first step! It should be a deep step but you should retain vision of the secondary.
- On the first step, sit back while you pivot and lean in the direction of the drop.
- On the third step of a five- or seven-step drop, bring the ball into its ready position and drive hard for depth.
- On the next to last step of a five- or seven-step drop, take a small step to begin to regain your balance.
- On the final step, lean away from the direction of the drop so you are erect, balanced, and ready to throw the football.

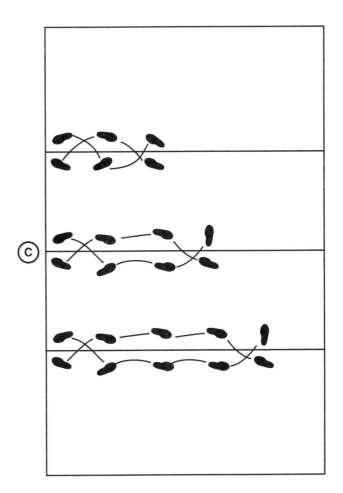

Set-up and Instructions:

Position all the quarterbacks on the sideline facing you. Have as many as possible straddling a yard stripe. Introduce the drill by explaining the above coaching pointers and, knees permitting, demonstrating the steps. Take the quarterbacks through each of the three drops, one step at a time if necessary. Get them in their stances and, without a cadence, shout "One!" Each quarterback should take the lead step away from the center—with depth and as quickly as possible. Check for depth.

Get them back in their stances. Shout "One, two, three," slowly at first, then more quickly. Ultimately, shout out the steps as quickly as you want the quarterbacks to take them. On the five- and seven-step drops, stop them after the third or fourth steps to reemphasize depth. The drill should conclude with you shouting "One, two, three" or "One, two, three, four, five," or "One, two, three, four, five, six, seven" as quickly as you want them to take the steps.

This is an excellent first drill to introduce drop-back passing techniques to the quarterbacks, especially the young ones.

35. FOOTWORK

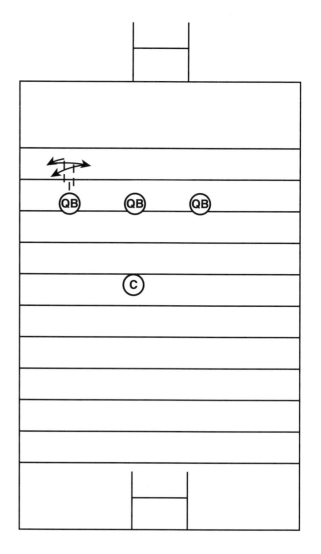

Purpose:

- To emphasize the proper footwork when passing.
- To emphasize stepping in the direction of the receiver.
- To practice follow-through over the front leg.
- To avoid throwing off the back leg.

Coaching Pointers:

- Move your feet!
- Never throw across your body!
- Step in the direction of your receiver!
- Follow through! Roll over your front leg.
- Never throw off your back leg! The ball will sail over your receiver.
- Get a deep enough drop so that you're not forced into throwing off your back leg!
- Don't stride in the direction of your pass until you actually throw the ball.
- Maintain a balanced stance until you find an open receiver.

Set-up and Instructions:

Position one or more quarterbacks 10 to 15 yards in front of you. Have them face you, five yards apart, their toes on one of the yard lines. On the snap signal, have them execute a three-, five-, or seven-step drop. A split second before they complete the drop, point to the right or the left, thereafter alternating right, left, right, left, etc., instructing the quarterbacks to move their feet in the direction you indicate. Each time they change directions, expect them to set up in the appropriate passing position: feet approximately shoulder-width, balanced stance, body erect, the ball held with both hands in front of them. After three, four, or five repetitions, drop your arm in the direction you want the quarterback(s) to throw the ball.

Position receivers 15 to 20 yards downfield on either side of each quarterback, or use stand-up dummies in place of live receivers. To establish competition among the quarterbacks, award points each time a quarterback hits a stand-up dummy. Have the quarterback with the least points put all the equipment away after drill.

36. DEEP DROPS

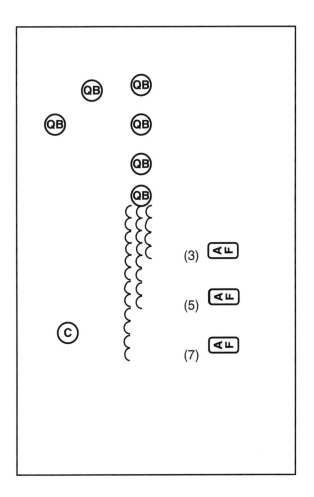

Purpose:

- To train the quarterbacks to get depth on drop-back passes.

Coaching Pointers:

- Take a long first step on all three-, five-, and seven-step drops.
- Drop back quickly. The faster you are, the longer you'll have to throw the ball.
- Use the last step to plant and to set up in your passing position. As soon as you complete the drop, you should be ready to throw the football.
- I want to see quickness in this drill!

Set-up and Instructions:

Position one quarterback on a designated line of scrimmage. Use air flates, scrimmage vests, cones, or other equipment to mark the desired depth of a three-, five-, or seven-step drop. Your knees permitting, demonstrate each drop—half-speed if necessary—to mark the expected depth of the drop. Place the equipment behind the quarterback at each location and instruct him to drop to that depth as fast as possible. Remind him that his first step should be the longest and that each successive step should be made as quickly as possible. The final step should be a plant step that brings his body upright into the passing position.

Alternate the quarterbacks. Each should have at least three repetitions at each of the three depths. Make corrections as needed. Use this drill early in the season to condition all quarterbacks to get the depth they need to see the field and to beat the pass rush. This is a critical drill for all teams that expect to throw the ball successfully. The quarterback, no matter how talented, who develops a lazy drop back compromises not only his own ability but the success of his team's passing attack.

37. QUARTERBACK CHALLENGE

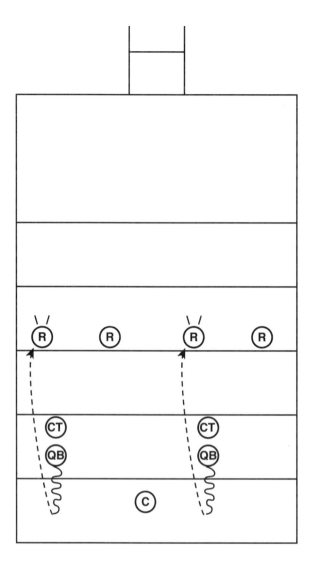

Purpose:

- To emphasize a quick three-, five-, or seven-step drop.
- To set up in a good passing position.
- To step into each pass.

Coaching Pointers:

- Drop three, five, or seven steps as fast as possible, always keeping your shoulders pivoted in order to see downfield.
- When the drop is completed, get into a good passing position: stance balanced and on the balls of the feet, feet relatively close, ball positioned just inside the shoulder under the chin.
- Step **into** each pass with a good follow through.

Set-up and Instructions:

- Two quarterbacks, each with a center, on the 5- or 10-yard line.
- Two receivers for each quarterback 15 to 20 yards downfield.
- Coach stands behind the quarterbacks. Coach calls the cadence.
- Instruct quarterbacks to drop three, five, or seven steps to get into a good passing position, and to throw the ball to the receiver who has his hands up.
- Signal which of the two receivers should raise his hands for each quarterback. Instruct them not to raise them until the quarterback sets up.
- The quarterback who gets the pass off the fastest is the winner, unless he throws off the back leg or to the wrong receiver.
- Give each set of quarterbacks six repetitions, then replace. Mix and match until one of them wins.

38. MOVE AND RESUME

Purpose:

- To train the quarterback to move and resume his passing position whenever he feels defensive pressure.

Coaching Pointers:

- Make your three-, five-, or seven-step drop as quickly as possible and get into your passing position.
- I will simulate a defensive rush. Move away from the pressure, reset, and throw the ball.
- Move quickly and, when you reset, be sure you're in a good passing position.
- When you throw, take your lead step, rotate your upper body, and follow through after releasing the ball.

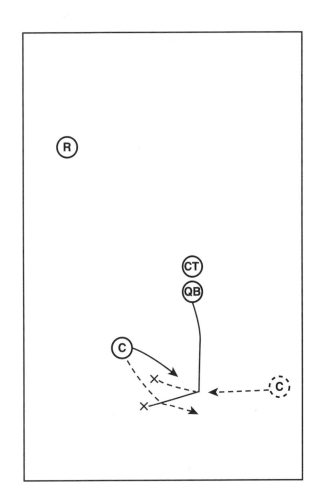

Set-up and Instructions:

Position a quarterback and a center on a designated line of scrimmage. Place a receiver 15 to 20 yards upfield. Instruct the quarterback to take the snap correctly, then execute a three-, five-, or seven-step drop. You stand off to one side and when he completes his drop, put pressure on him by: moving at him from the outside with your hands up; moving at him from the inside with your hands up; moving at him from behind.

Expect him to move, reset in the proper passing position, and throw the ball to the receiver, using the correct passing motion. Make corrections as needed. This is a good drill for quarterbacks, especially young quarterbacks, to teach the basics of avoiding pressure and resetting. Use it early in the season, then follow up with one or more of the drills on pages 44, 45, and 46.

39. PRESSURE

Purpose:

- To get quarterbacks to sense and react to defensive pressure.
- To emphasize using the proper passing motion in spite of defensive pressure.

Coaching Pointers:

- Make your drop as quickly as possible.
- Set up in your passing position: feet shoulder-width, balanced stance, body erect, ball held chest high with both hands. Load the gun!
- As soon as you feel pressure, move away from it and back into the pocket. Don't panic!
- After moving back into the pocket, resume your passing position. Reload the gun!
- Always look downfield; **sense** the pressure.

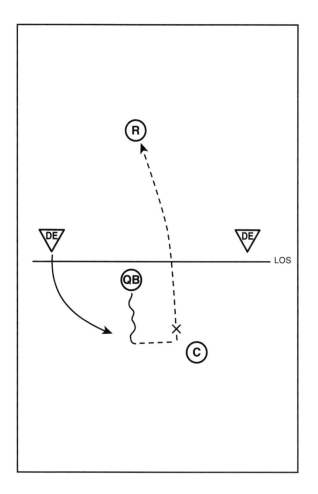

Set-up and Instructions:

Place a quarterback on the designated line of scrimmage and have him execute a three-, five-, or seven-step drop, then set up in his passing position. Have another quarterback be a receiver, positioned 15 yards downfield, facing the passer. Have two more quarterbacks be defensive ends, alternately exerting pressure on the passer.

It's often a good idea for the coach to "roam" during this drill to catch the passer's reactions from several different angles. The coach should instruct one of the two defensive ends to rush the passer from the outside, hesitating momentarily at the line of scrimmage as if defeating a pass block. The quarterback should sense this pressure, move away from it, then back into the pocket, resetting himself before throwing the ball to the receiver. Emphasize quickness of initial drop, proper footwork, and good passing position and motion.

Alternate the quarterbacks so that each gets at least two repetitions. If you have only two or three quarterbacks, vary the drill by having four linemen pass block and pass rush on the outside.

40. SET AND RESET

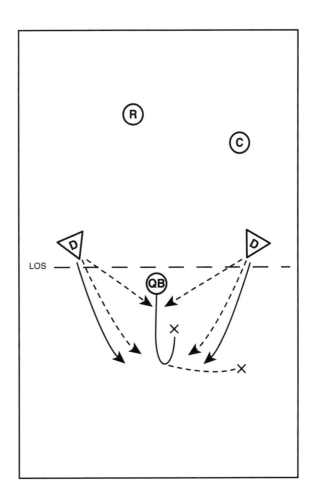

Purpose:

- To train the quarterbacks to sense pressure and to reset before throwing a pass.

Coaching Pointers:

- This drill emphasizes a five-step drop. Take it as quickly as possible!
- Set up immediately in your passing position ready to throw the ball.
- SENSE pressure from the pass rush; don't focus on it. You are focusing on the secondary and your receivers!
- Reset away from the pass rush in the correct passing position. Throw the ball, using good passing fundamentals.

Set-up and Instructions:

Position one quarterback on a designated line of scrimmage. Position two of the remaining quarterbacks as defenders on the line of scrimmage, facing the backfield. Finally, position a receiver, perhaps a fourth quarterback, 10 to 15 yards downfield. Instruct the quarterback on the line of scrimmage to make a five-step drop. Check for proper fundamentals. Signal the pass rush paths you want from the acting defenders. Both can go to the outside or one to the inside, the other outside. Instruct the quarterback to sense the pressure, move away from it, and reset in the correct passing position to make the throw. Tell the quarterback to make the throw only when the receiver raises his hands. Check for proper throwing fundamentals.

Alternate the other quarterbacks so that all of them have at least three repetitions avoiding the pass rush and making the throw. This is a good introductory drill for sensing pass rush and for checking the correct fundamental skills.

41. SENSING PRESSURE

Purpose:

- To teach quarterbacks to react to pressure while focusing on the defensive secondary.

Coaching Pointers:

- Make your drop as quickly as possible.
- While making the drop, keep your head turned so you can watch the secondary coverage.
- Focus on the secondary and find your receivers!
- **Sense** the defensive pressure; don't look for it!
- React to the pressure, reset, and throw the ball—and throw it **correctly,** using the fundamentals!

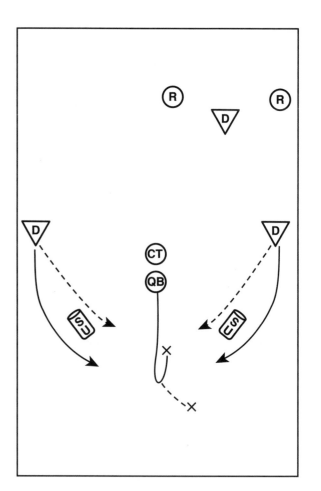

Set-up and Instructions:

Position a quarterback and a center on a designated line of scrimmage. Place one receiver directly in front of the quarterback, approximately 20 yards upfield. Place another receiver closer to the sidelines, also 20 yards upfield. Align one defender halfway between the receivers.

Place two stand-up dummies on their sides as illustrated. Use the alternate quarterbacks or defensive ends as rushers. Standing behind the quarterback, signal the kind of rush you want from each defender. Both can rush from the outside, both from the inside. Or one can rush from the outside, one from the inside. Also instruct the defender in the secondary to move toward one of the two receivers.

Then move to a position where you can watch the eyes of the quarterback. Observe his reaction to pressure. Make sure he is sensing it and maintaining his primary focus on the movement of the defender. Also make sure he is resetting in the proper passing position and executing the correct passing fundamentals.

42. SNAP IT OFF

Purpose:

- To train quarterbacks to read defensive coverage and to develop a quick release.

Coaching Pointers:

- Execute your drop as quickly as possible. Your first step should be deep and fast!
- Set up immediately in your passing position, then read the defender's· reaction.
- Throw the ball immediately to the appropriate receiver as soon as the defender makes his first move. Snap it off—quickly!
- Cover the outside if you throw a flat pass.

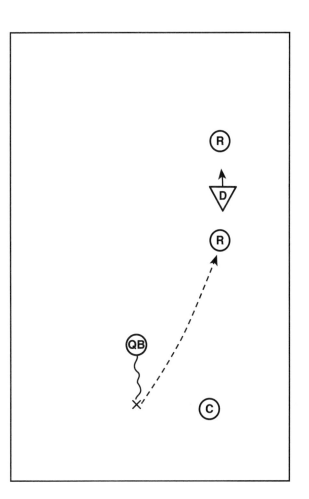

Set-up and Instructions:

Position one quarterback, the passer, on a designated line of scrimmage. Tell him to execute a three-, five-, or seven-step drop. Position one receiver in the flat outside the passer, eight to ten yards downfield. Position a second receiver approximately the same distance outside the passer, 20 yards downfield. Position one defender between the two receivers. Instruct the defender to cover one of the two receivers as soon as the passer sets up. Tell the passer to throw to the open receiver—as soon as the defender makes his first move.

Emphasize the need to read the defense and to snap the ball off as quickly as possible. Vary this drill with more receivers and more defenders, always leaving one receiver uncovered. This is an excellent drill for teaching quarterbacks to read the defense instead of finding their favorite receiver. Have the quarterback throw to both sides of the field and use other players in specific positions as needed.

43. QUICK RELEASE

Purpose:

- To enable the quarterback to release the ball quickly when running a sprint-out pass.

Coaching Pointers:

- When sprinting out, run quickly but under control to the outside in order to stretch the defensive secondary.
- Always hold the ball with both hands, chest-high, ready to throw to the first open receiver.
- Execute the proper passing fundamentals for sprint-out passing: step in the direction of your receiver, rotate your upper body, and exaggerate your follow-through.

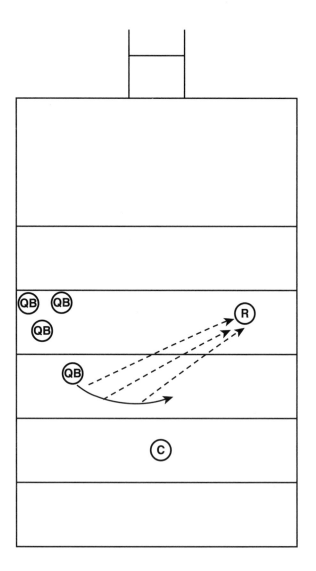

Set-up and Instructions:

Align a quarterback on a designated line of scrimmage. Instruct him to sprint out to his right or left, getting depth and width at the same time. He should run under control, holding the ball chest-high, prepared to throw as soon as the receiver raises his hands.

Position one receiver in the flat, 15 yards deep and 10 to 15 yards outside the quarterback. Instruct him to raise his hands on your signal. Vary your signal, sometimes after the quarterback has taken only two or three steps, sometimes after 20 steps. Alternate quarterbacks after every repetition, varying their release time as much as possible.

This drill is particularly good for emphasizing upper body rotation as the best way to insure a quick release. Use this drill periodically throughout the season to reemphasize good passing fundamentals.

44. BIG CIRCLE

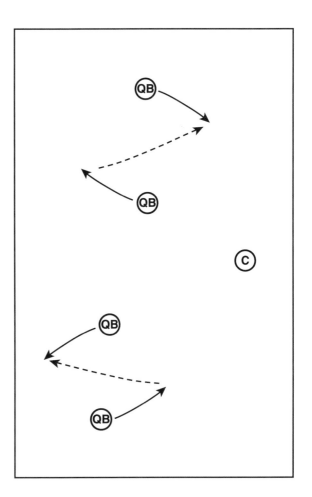

Purpose:

- To train quarterbacks to maintain good passing fundamentals while throwing on the run.

Coaching Pointers:

- Whenever possible, step in the direction of your receiver.

- If the receiver is wide open and you have to throw across your body or, awkwardly, away from your body, don't stride when you throw the ball. Stop your feet and, as much as possible, allow the bottom half of your body to go limp—then throw the ball.

- Always exaggerate your follow-through. Extend your arm and fingers toward your receiver whenever you have to throw the ball awkwardly.

Set-up and Instructions:

Align two quarterbacks 10 yards apart, one of them with a football. Put the remainder of your quarterbacks in a similar alignment. Instruct them to run clockwise in a circle passing the football back and forth. After several repetitions, tell them to run counterclockwise passing the football. Emphasize the above coaching pointers. Remind them to hold the ball with two hands, chest-high, and to exaggerate upper body rotation.

45. PARALLEL PASS

Purpose:

- To maintain proper passing fundamentals when quarterbacks have to throw on the run.

Coaching Pointers:

- Whenever possible, step in the direction of your receiver.
- Whenever hurried—and your receiver is **wide open**—throw the ball without the step in the direction of your receiver but exaggerate your follow-through and try not to be striding when you throw the ball.
- Just before you throw on the run, take smaller steps in order to step in the direction of your receiver.

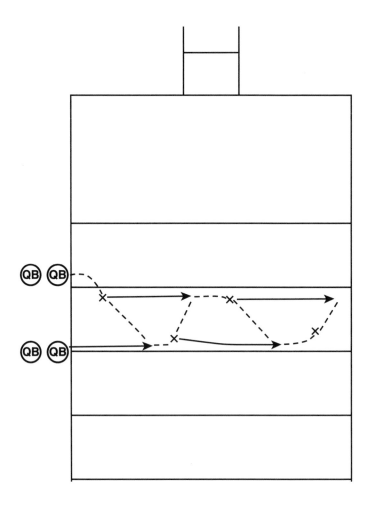

Set-up and Instructions:

Position two quarterbacks on the sideline, 10 to 20 yards apart. Instruct them to run parallel to each other playing catch. The throwing quarterback should run under control, the receiving quarterback should race ahead. Once he catches the ball, he should start to run under control, and the other quarterback should race ahead to receive the pass. Have them alternate until they reach the other sideline.

Remind each quarterback to step in the direction of his receiver, taking smaller steps just before the throw. Also emphasize proper passing fundamentals, including upper body rotation and follow-through. Start a second tandem of quarterbacks after the first tandem has passed the ball twice. Have all the quarterbacks wait on the opposite sideline until you start them again.

This is a good drill to use prior to the introduction of your sprint-out or roll-out passing attack.

46. SPRINT OUT

Purpose:

- To train quarterbacks to get width on sprint-out and roll-out action.
- To emphasize the need to spread the secondary and to put pressure on defenders with outside contain responsibilities.

Coaching Pointers:

- Don't run at full speed but run quickly and under control to a position approximately two to eight yards outside the offensive tight end.
- The actual width will depend on defensive containment, your decision to run or pass the ball, and the location and openness of your receivers.
- Concentrate on taking all the width the defensive containment will give you— or our blocking will take!
- We're sprinting out in order to stretch the secondary and to put pressure on the defense's outside containment.
- Whenever possible, step in the direction of your receiver, especially when you throw the ball.

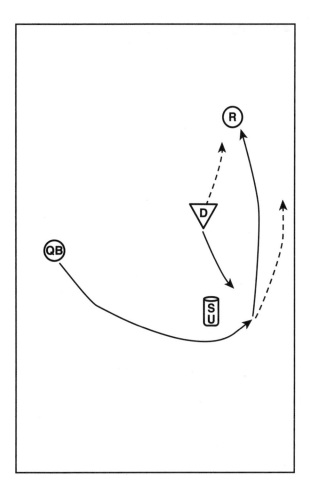

Set-up and Instructions:

Place a stand-up dummy approximately five yards outside the normal location of your tight end and five yards deep in the backfield. Instruct the quarterbacks to roll out or sprint out beyond the dummy and to either run or throw the football based on the reaction of the defender. Instruct the defender to either drop into pass coverage, play a half-and-half containment/coverage responsibility, or put immediate pressure on the quarterback.

Instruct the quarterbacks to force a reaction from the defender who plays half-and-half, to make him commit to either run defense or pass defense. When he reacts to run, have the quarterback throw the ball. Remind the quarterbacks, whenever possible, to step in the direction of the receiver. Every so often, put a stopwatch on the quarterbacks to create some friendly competition.

51

47. STRETCH THE DEFENSE

Purpose:

- To train quarterbacks to get width on sprint-out passes and to read defensive coverage to find the open receiver.

Coaching Pointers:

- Quarterbacks! Get width on your sprint out or your bootleg. Stretch the defense!
- As you approach the center to start the play, get a good pre-snap read of possible secondary coverages. Prior to the snap, have an idea of which of your receivers is likely to be open.
- While you're sprinting out, watch the secondary for seams or openings.
- Don't look for your favorite receiver! Throw to the uncovered man.
- Whenever possible, step in the direction of your receiver. The pass will be more accurate.

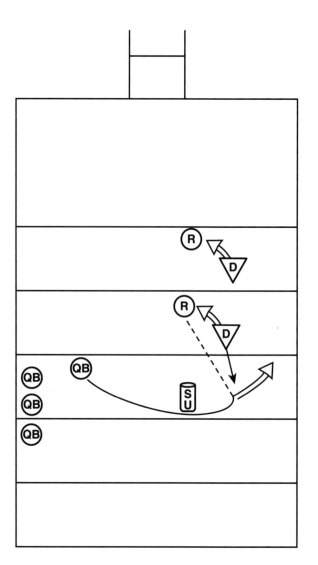

Set-up and Instructions:

Position the first quarterback on a designated line of scrimmage. Place a stand-up dummy eight to 10 yards to his outside. Position two receivers in the secondary, one 10 to 15 yards downfield, the other six to seven yards in front of the first receiver. Position one defender between the two receivers, another in front of the closer receiver—as illustrated.

Hand signal the desired coverage to the defenders before the snap. Have the deep defender cover either of the two receivers. Have the nearer defender cover the nearer receiver or rush the passer. Instruct the quarterback to get his width, read the secondary while sprinting out, throw to the open receiver, or run the ball if both are covered.

Check to be sure the quarterback gets good width, reads the secondary, and, if possible, steps in the direction of his pass. Check for the other passing fundamentals as well. This is a good drill early in the season to emphasize reading the secondary and using good passing fundamentals.

48. HALF LINE

Purpose:

- To enable quarterbacks to read defensive coverages during roll-out or sprint-out passes.

Coaching Pointer:

- Refer to coaching pointers from individual quarterback drills. They all apply here.

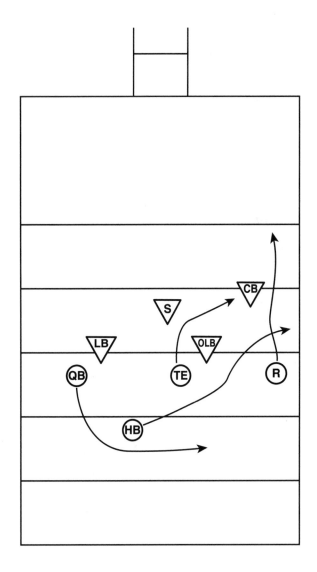

Set-up and Instructions:

Align extra receivers or regular defensive personnel in a half-team secondary as illustrated. The team should consist of at least one safety, one cornerback, one inside linebacker, and one outside backer/defensive end. Signal what coverages you want—man, combo, or zone—and have the outside linebacker/defensive end alternate between rushing the quarterback and dropping to cover the flat.

Call a variety of pass plays/patterns in the huddle and check for proper coverage reads, quarterback mechanics, and receiver techniques. Coach on the run with this drill. Try to get as many repetitions as possible.

49. FIND THE RECEIVER

Purpose:

- To emphasize the importance of reading the secondary to find an open receiver.
- To correct the tendency of some quarterbacks to look for a favorite receiver.

Coaching Pointers:

- Make a pre-snap read. Look at the defense to determine likely coverage. It will give you a hint as to the receiver who is likely to be open.
- Make the drop and set up in the correct passing position.
- AS YOU DROP, read the secondary for gaps in the defense.
- By the time you complete the drop, you should have a good idea of the receiver in the pattern who is likely to be open.
- Throw to the hole in the defense. The throw should be made just before the receiver looks for the ball.

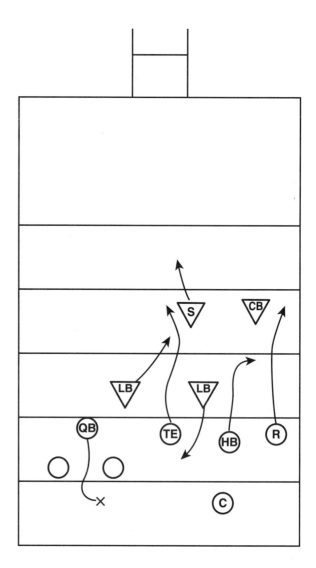

Set-up and Instructions:

Instruct the defense to position themselves for several different alignments, with the specific play alignment to be determined by a hand signal from you. Call a formation and a pass play in the huddle, with the play itself to determine the depth of the quarterback's drop. When the offense gets to the line of scrimmage, signal individual defenders to cover certain areas. Point to deep outside, for example, for the cornerback, deep middle for the safety, pass rush for the outside linebacker, and hook zone for the inside linebacker. For purposes of the illustrated play, this specific coverage will leave the slotback open in the flat.

Continue to call plays and to signal specific areas of coverage for the defenders, always being sure to leave one receiver uncovered. Watch the quarterback's drop, passing position, ability to find the open receiver, and passing fundamentals. Give all the quarterbacks at least six or seven repetitions every time this drill is used. Vary the drill by using the entire field. This is a challenging but essential drill for quarterbacks.

50. FEEL IT IN

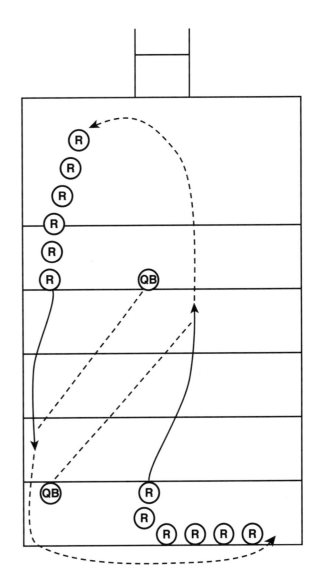

Purpose:

- To teach quarterbacks to throw long passes with touch.

Coaching Pointers:

- The mechanics are the same for all passes, but get some backward body lean before throwing a long pass.
- Exaggerate the follow-through on a long pass, almost as if shooting a basketball.
- **Reach** out to the receiver! **Feel** the ball into his hands!
- Be sure to get some air under a long pass so the receiver can adjust his speed.
- Short passes with low trajectories must be very accurate! Long passes with high trajectories can be less accurate. They let the receiver adjust to the ball.

Set-up and Instructions:

Position half the receivers on the 10-yard line three yards in from the sideline, the other half on the 40-yard line next to the closest hash mark. Tell each line to run a streak or a fly pattern in opposite directions. Tell the quarterbacks, positioned as illustrated, to throw to their respective receivers. Have the receivers catch the ball and give it to the quarterback facing them, get in the other line, and run a pattern in the opposite direction. Give each receiver at least three repetitions and watch the quarterbacks for proper execution. Each should be lofting the ball, letting it roll off his fingers, and "feeling" it into the receiver's hands. The pass should pin the receiver to the sideline and promote a burst of speed from him.

51. BOMBS AWAY

Purpose:

- To coordinate the timing of the quarterback and the wide receiver(s) when throwing deep.

Coaching Pointers:

To the receiver:

- Get down the sideline fast but always have a reserve of speed if the ball is overthrown.
- Catch the ball with your hands at its highest point if the defender has you covered. Go up and get it! At least knock it down so he can't get it!

To the quarterback:

- Keep the pass within your range. Always be able to **feel** the ball to the receiver.
- Get a little air under the ball, so the receiver can adjust his speed as needed.
- Keep the receiver pinned to the sideline. Make the defender's job as difficult as possible.
- If the receiver is wide open, DO NOT overthrow him!

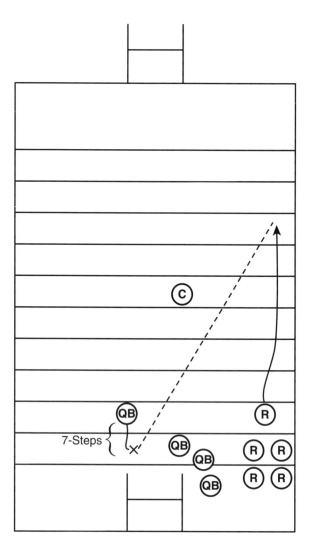

Set-up and Instructions:

Place the quarterbacks on a designated line of scrimmage. Have them drop seven steps and throw the ball as far as they can. Simultaneously, have a wide receiver run down the sideline as fast as he can. In most instances, the receiver will outdistance the passer. If he doesn't, be thankful you have a quarterback with a cannon arm!

But assuming he does outdistance the quarterback, remind the quarterback to drop quickly and to get the ball off as soon as possible. The quarterback must stay within the range of his capability to throw the ball effectively. Continue to time the pass, so that the receiver adjusts his speed and the quarterback drops fast enough and throws the ball soon enough to hit the receiver in stride. Some quarterbacks and receivers may combine for 50-yard passes; others may achieve only 35 yards. Let them know that even a 35-yard bomb can get the job done. You—and they—will want to know their strengths and limitations. This is a very important early-season drill because it will set the tone for the remainder of the season.

52. SELLING THE SCREEN

Purpose:

- To emphasize the importance of and the techniques for selling a screen pass.

Coaching Pointers:

- Take a quick five-step drop and set up in your passing position.
- Look downfield for receivers.
- Sense the oncoming pass rush and drop another five to 10 steps. Make it look as if you're in trouble!
- As you retreat, try to move slightly in the direction of the screen. Don't make it too obvious!
- Movement toward the screen will give you better balance when you throw the ball.
- If you're still backpedaling and you have to throw the ball, hard arm it to the receiver and exaggerate the follow-through; otherwise, you're going to throw short!

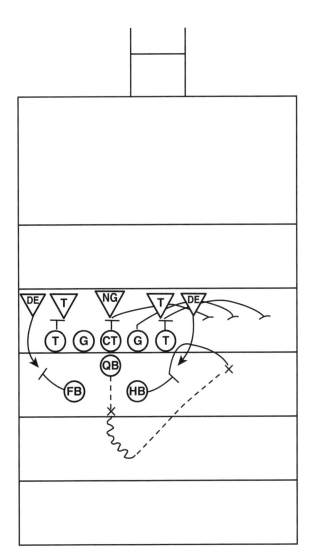

Set-up and Instructions:

Align all the interior offensive linemen and the quarterback on a designated line of scrimmage. Set up a five-man front to rush the passer. Instruct the offensive linemen who are not in the screen to block their men aggressively and to stay with the blocks. Tell the linemen who are in the screen to block their men for three counts—**a full three counts**—then to release them and move to form the screen. Preliminary blocking is critical for a good screen pass. Linemen who simply open the floodgates force the quarterback to run for his life. At that point, the play becomes too obvious and it rarely works.

Instruct the quarterback to take a fast five-step drop, set up in his passing position, and look downfield for receivers. When the linemen release their blocks to move to the screen, have him backpedal or run to either side to avoid the rush. Just moments before getting hit, he should release the ball to the screen man—if the screen man is open. If he's covered, the quarterback should throw the ball out of bounds. On every fourth or fifth repetition, hand signal the defensive end to cover the screen man to test the quarterback's adaptability.

Coordinate this drill with others in this book that emphasize proper execution, especially with the receiver's responsibilities.

53. THUMB UNDER

Purpose:

- To emphasize proper option pitching technique.

Coaching Pointers:

- Look at the pitchback only peripherally. Focus on the defense and what they're giving you. Trust that the back will maintain his pitch relationship with you.

- When you decide to pitch, focus on the pitchback and extend your arm in the back's direction.

- Always execute the thumb-under pitch. It will put the proper rotation on the pitch and make it easy to handle.

- Always put the same velocity on the pitch, neither too hard nor too soft.

- Be sure to pitch the ball in front of the back. If he happens to be looking where to run, he'll still see the ball.

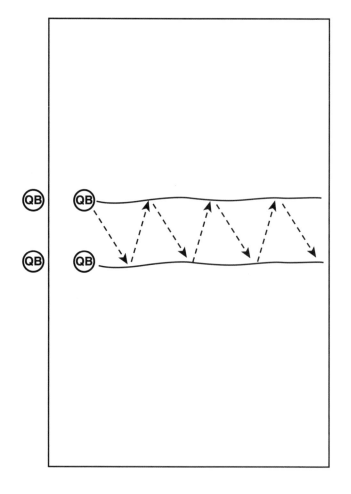

Set-up and Instructions:

Position two quarterbacks on a sideline, two or three yards apart. Have them jog parallel to each other pitching the ball back and forth. Have another tandem of quarterbacks follow them after the first tandem has executed three or four pitches. Be sure each quarterback is executing a thumb-under pitch, that is, holding the ball with both hands, then pitching it so that the thumb on the pitching hand goes under the ball when it is released.

Remind the quarterbacks to pitch the ball at least chest-high to the running back, always keeping it in front of him. Make corrections as needed. This is a good drill prior to the introduction of your option running attack.

54. OPTION DRILL

Purpose:

- To perfect the option ride and handoff to the fullback
- To teach the quarterback to focus on the defensive end throughout the ride and to make a quick decision to pitch or keep the ball.

Coaching Pointers:

- During the drop step to the fullback, two things must happen:
  1. Place the ball in his pocket and execute a good handoff.
  2. Look immediately to the defensive end to determine his strategy.
- In effect, don't look at the fullback at any time during the play. Watch me to toss a ball to you, and focus on the defensive end to determine whether you will pitch or keep the ball.

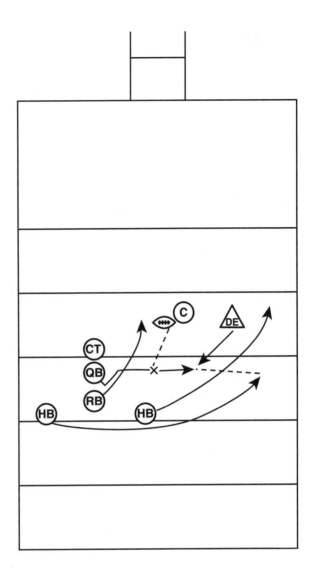

Set-up and Instructions:

Position the backfield in its normal alignment. The illustration suggests a wishbone, but any alignment is appropriate. Be sure that each quarterback receives the ball from the center to assure proper timing. Position yourself two to three yards outside the quarterback and just over the line of scrimmage. As soon as the quarterback completes the ride and the handoff to the fullback, firmly pitch a football to him. He should catch the ball while reading the defensive end, and, based on the end's maneuver, either pitch the ball to the right halfback or keep it himself.

The drill accomplishes two important things. It perfects the quarterback's ride with the fullback and forces the quarterback to focus on the defensive end's strategy. This drill is especially important early in the season when quarterbacks must develop consistent execution. It becomes less important as the season progresses.

55. EITHER/OR

Purpose:

- To train quarterbacks to exploit openings along the line of scrimmage when executing an option play.

Coaching Pointers:

- After making whatever fakes the play requires, look for openings along the line of scrimmage to run the football yourself.
- When you decide to keep and run, lean into the opening and pivot your body. **Lean and pivot!**
- If you keep the ball around the end, you can still pitch the ball downfield. Just be sure it's a safe pitch.
- Always remember first-down yardage. If you can get it yourself, GET IT!
- When you decide to keep and run, you become a ball carrier. Protect yourself and the ball!

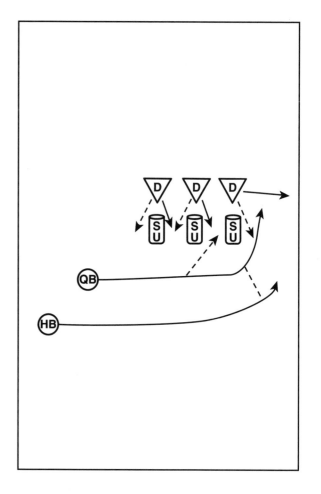

Set-up and Instructions:

Lay three stand-up dummies on their sides on the defensive side of a designated line of scrimmage. Lay them parallel to each other, approximately two yards apart, and place a defender on the defensive end of each dummy. Instruct the quarterback to take the snap, pivot in the direction of the play, and hesitate for a split second, particularly if the option play involves a preliminary fake.

Instruct the halfback to maintain a pitch relationship with the quarterback, usually two to three yards deep and three to five steps in front of the quarterback. This may vary depending on the play and the coach's preference.

Stand behind the defenders and tell them which gaps to fill. Tell the quarterback to read the openings along the line of scrimmage and to take what the defense gives him. He may cut between the first two dummies or the second two, or he may take the play around the end, continuing his option possibility with the ball carrier. Tell the outside defender to take either quarterback or the pitch. Accordingly, instruct the quarterback to either keep or pitch the ball. This is an excellent drill for option teams and promotes the body memory quarterbacks need to make good, quick reads.

56. OPTION READ

Purpose:

- To emphasize a quick read for option quarterbacks.

Coaching Pointers:

- Don't look at the fullback during the ride! Watch the movements of the defensive tackle.

- Your steps and the fullback's path should never vary. Both of you should be able to count on each other to be in the same place all the time.

- If you don't give it to the fullback, look to the defensive end (or whomever you expect to be the contain man) immediately to determine your pitch option.

- Pitch or keep depending on the defender's reactions.

- Remind your running back to maintain a pitch relationship throughout the play, even after you turn upfield.

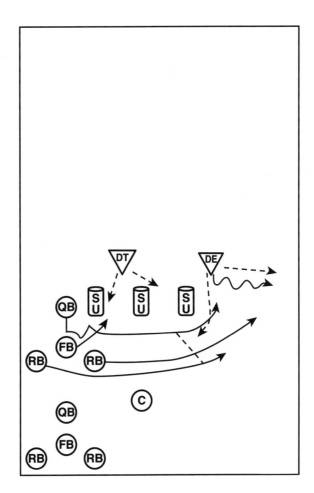

Set-up and Instructions:

Instruct your backfields to get into a wishbone alignment or any desired formation for running your option play. Position three stand-up dummies on their sides to approximate offensive linemen. Put a defensive tackle between the first two dummies, a defensive contain man outside the third dummy. Tell the defensive tackle and the contain man what to do using hand signals. Have the defensive tackle take the fullback sometimes; loop him outside other times. Alternately send the contain man immediately to the quarterback, put him immediately on the pitchback, or have him play soft and slide with the play, forcing the quarterback to commit.

Don't huddle with this drill. Just have each successive backfield run the read option and make corrections on the run. This is a rapid-fire drill and should result in as many repetitions for each backfield as possible.

57. ALL CATCH

Purpose:

- To practice full team pass plays and to throw the ball to every receiver.

Coaching Pointers:

- Quarterbacks, throw the ball on time. Find the seams in the defense and throw the ball just before the receiver looks for it.
- Refer to coaching pointers in other drills. They are all useful here.

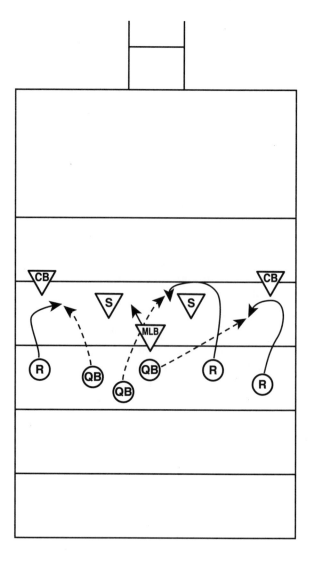

Set-up and Instructions:

Use extra receivers to set up a four-deep defense with one or two inside linebackers. Tell them to execute at least three different coverages. They can call these coverages at random.

Organize a skeleton passing offense but assign a quarterback to each receiver. Call different offensive formations and the pass plays or patterns you want to practice. Instruct each quarterback to read the defense and to throw the ball when his assigned receiver is approaching a hole in the coverage. Alternate the defenders to ensure that every receiver gets at least four or five repetitions.

This drill enables every receiver to catch a football during skeleton practice drills. This not only keeps the receivers engaged but forces them to read the defense and to catch a timely thrown ball. It also forces the quarterbacks to read different coverages before throwing the ball. That's why it's a good idea to alternate the quarterbacks as well. Even when you dummy scrimmage the passing attack on a full-team basis, it's a good idea to assign a quarterback to each of the receivers.

58. SCRIPT SKELETON

Purpose:

- To train quarterbacks to read and throw against as many defensive coverages as possible.

Coaching Pointers:

- Refer to the coaching pointers from the individual quarterback drills. All of them apply here.

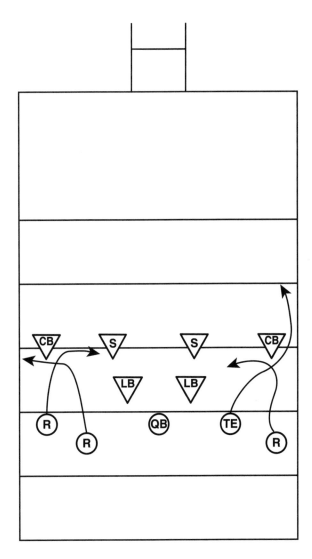

Set-up and Instructions:

Position a skeleton secondary with two 52 linebackers at midfield. Position a skeleton offensive team opposite them. Provide a script to the offense and the defense and run the plays consecutively. Early in the season, the offensive script can list a portion or all of your passing attack. The defensive script can list the probable secondary coverages you expect to see that year. As the season progresses, the offensive script can list the pass plays you expect to use against a particular opponent. The defensive script can list the secondary coverages you expect to see based on scouting reports.

Scripting provides a quick-paced drill and guarantees against unnecessary interferences during important practice sessions. You can even provide drawings for the defense to clarify their assignments. This is a good drill at any time of the season.

59. FIND THE HOLE

Purpose:

- To emphasize the importance of reading the secondary to find open receivers.

Coaching Pointers:

- Make a good pre-snap read to determine the secondary's likely coverage.
- As you drop back, read the secondary to determine the coverage.
- Don't look for your favorite receiver! Find the hole or the seam in the secondary! Throw into the hole!
- You find the hole; your receiver will fill it!

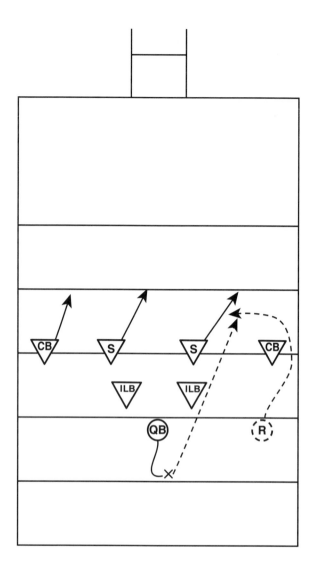

Set-up and Instructions

Set up a skeleton defense consisting of linebackers and a secondary. Give them a specific coverage; vary it from play to play. Put the quarterback in his normal alignment and have him run a three-, five-, or seven-step drop. Tell him the pass play you want him to visualize and to make a pre-snap read to determine the likely secondary coverage. Have him shout what he thinks the coverage is. Then have him drop, read the coverage, find the hole in the coverage, and visualize where his receivers are likely to be. Instruct him to visualize the open receiver and throw into the hole of the coverage.

Check to determine the accuracy of the quarterback's pre-snap read and his ability to find the holes or the seams in the defense. Remember, he is not throwing to a receiver; he is throwing into the hole he finds in the secondary. He must visualize his receivers, specifically the open receiver.

Use this drill in conjunction with the receiver drill (112) Fill the Hole. Run them independently of each other, then combine them to see if the quarterbacks and receivers are doing a good job reading secondary coverages.

SECTION 4

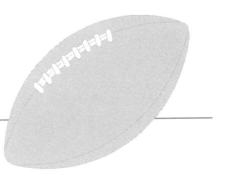

RUNNING-BACK DRILLS

This section focuses on the following skills:

- Stance and starts
- Hand-offs
- Faking
- High knees
- Shoulder drop
- Open-field running
- Ball switching
- Spinning technique
- Leg drive
- Run-blocking technique
- Pass-blocking technique
- Pass receiving from backfield position: routes, hot receiver, etc.

60. STANCES

Purpose:

- To develop a comfortable, appropriately balanced stance for running backs.

Coaching Pointers:

- Keep your head up; always concentrate on what the defense is doing.

- Stay balanced; don't give the defense any clues about the direction of the play.

- Put most of your weight on your arm only when we have very short yardage to pick up and we don't care who knows where we're going.

- Keep your tail up and your knees at shoulder-width to maximize explosiveness out of your stance.

- Relax your non-weightbearing arm. Use it to drive you out of your stance. **Reach** with it!

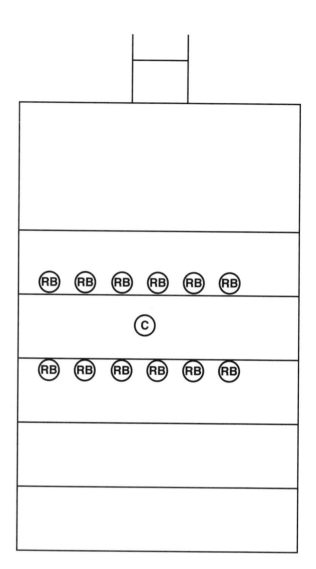

Set-up and Instructions:

Position half the running backs at arm's length on a designated line of scrimmage. Position the other half 10 yards downfield, facing the first half. This is a three-phased drill:

- **Phase one:** When you say "One," have them bend at the waist and put their hands on their knees, checking to make sure that their feet are slightly pigeon-toed and approximately shoulder width. Make corrections as needed.

- **Phase two:** When you say "Two," have them bend farther, placing their elbows on their knees, checking to make sure their knees are shoulder width.

- **Phase three:** When you say "Three," have them roll forward into their stances, making sure their necks are bulled and their backs are approximately parallel to the ground. Have them hold the stances long enough for you to make corrections.

Later, vary their stances as needed—or allow them to vary their own stances—based on individual preference or comfort—as long as the stance **works!**

61. STARTS

Purpose:

- To develop explosive starts for running backs.

Coaching Pointers:

- Explode out of your stance! Use your arms—drive them hard!
- You're a sprinter during your first two or three steps, a running back after you get the ball!
- Stride out! High knees! Make the pocket only after your first two or three steps.
- Make a noise—grunt and groan. It tightens the muscles and increases explosiveness.
- Generate speed and keep high knees. Tacklers don't like high knees!

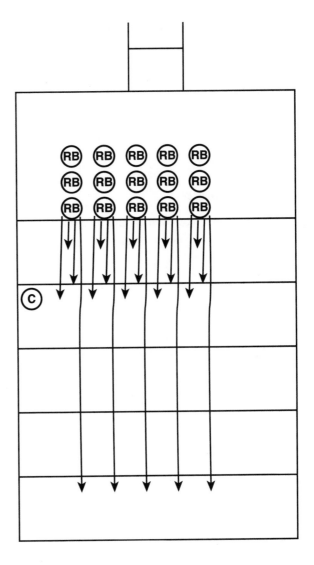

Set-up and Instructions:

Position the running backs in equally numbered waves, the first wave on a designated line of scrimmage. On your cadence, have the first wave explode out of their stances and drive hard for five yards. Have them come to the back of the pack and give the cadence to successive waves. Make corrections as needed. Look at their stances as well.

After two or three repetitions, have each wave run 10 yards, then 15. Finish the drill with one timed 40-yard sprint. Announce the winner and his time. This is a preseason drill and good for creating a little early competition. Beyond the actual competition, every once in a while time everyone, so that all the backs can compete with themselves to improve their speed. Congratulate them every time they do.

62. TRUST AND FEEL

Purpose:

- To train running backs to take a secure handoff.

Coaching Pointers:

- Fire out of your stance and hit your top speed as soon as possible.
- Make a good pocket for the quarterback.
- Fire out, keep your head up, and make the pocket after the first two steps.
- Clamp down hard on the ball as soon as you feel it, covering both points with your hands.
- Tell the quarterback if you don't feel the handoff.

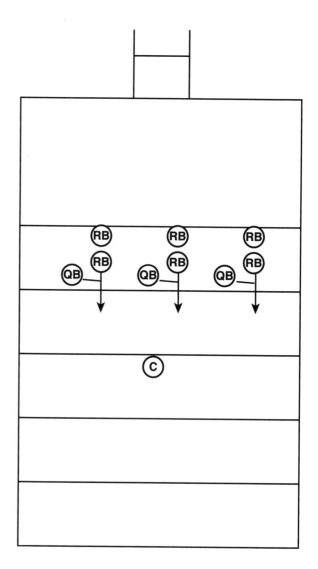

Set-up and Instructions:

Position all the quarterbacks on a designated line of scrimmage, each with a line of halfbacks. Halfway through the drill, switch the halfbacks to the other side of the quarterback so they take the handoff from both sides. Alternate the cadence among the quarterbacks. Instruct the running backs to get into their stances, shut their eyes, and fire out when they hear the snap count. Tell them to keep their eyes closed until they have secured the football. Tell the quarterbacks to look the ball into the pocket, being sure to pressure the ball into the running back's stomach.

Emphasize **feel** throughout this drill—and **trust.** The running backs have to trust that the quarterback will get the ball to them, and they have to trust themselves to feel and take the ball securely. Use this drill in conjunction with one or more of the other handoff drills in this book.

63. OOOO/AHHH

Purpose:

- To practice making and receiving good handoffs.

Coaching Pointers:

- Look the ball in; gently pressure it into his stomach.
- Don't look at the ball when you're receiving it; look straight ahead.
- When you're in the left line, say "oooo" when you feel the pressure of the handoff. When you're in the right line, say "ahhh." If you don't feel any pressure, don't say anything.
- Don't be in a big hurry. Make and receive good handoffs.

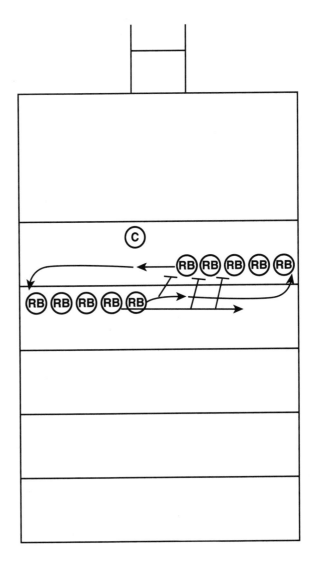

Set-up and Instructions:

Place all the backs on a designated line of scrimmage. Separate them into two halves and have each half face each other. Give a football to the first player in the left line. Instruct him to move down the line and hand the ball to the first player in the other line, who should be moving toward him. Have all the players in both lines do the same thing, each going to the back of the line after the exchange. Continue the drill until each player gives and gets the ball at least three times.

If you don't hear either an "oooo" or an "ahhh" during a particular exchange, remind the player(s) to pressure the ball into the stomach. Tell the players to remind the quarterbacks of the same thing as needed.

64. TAKE AND CUT

Purpose:

- To train running backs to take a secure handoff.

Coaching Pointers:

- Keep the elbow of the arm opposite the quarterback fairly tight to your body so he can't push the ball through the pocket.

- Clamp both arms on the ball, cupping the points with your hands.

- Never look for the ball; the quarterback's job is to get it to you.

- You watch the defense for daylight; your job is to run with the football!

- Hit the hole as fast as you can! Beat the quarterback to the hole, and keep your head up!

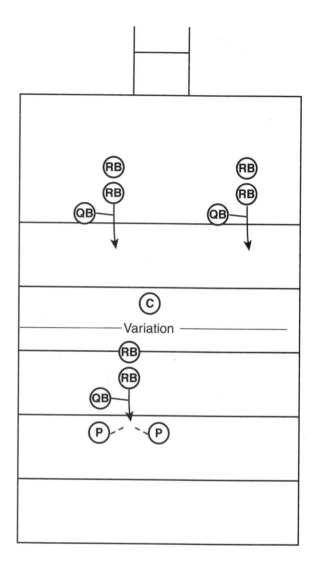

Set-up and Instructions:

Position all the quarterbacks along a designated line of scrimmage, each with a line of halfbacks in their home alignments. Switch the lines of halfbacks halfway through the drill so they take handoffs from both sides. Have the quarterbacks take turns calling the cadence. Tell the running backs to focus on you throughout the exchange and to hit the hole as fast as possible. As they receive the ball, signal them to cut right or left or to keep running straight ahead. Tell them not to anticipate your hand signal by slowing down but to keep running as fast as possible. They have to TRUST THEIR BODIES to make the right cut.

Check the quarterbacks for stance, snap, and execution; the running backs for stance, start, speed, and execution.

Variation: Position players on either side of the running back after he receives the handoff. Instruct them to pull at his arms or to try to grab the football.

65. GET A GRIP

Purpose:

- To emphasize ball security after the handoff.

Coaching Pointers:

- As soon as you receive the handoff, cup both points with your hands.
- Continue to secure both points until you're out of traffic.
- If you encounter two or more tacklers after breaking into the secondary, recup both points to protect the ball during contact.
- Don't be afraid to swing your arms and the ball in traffic, as long as you have a firm grip on both points.
- Maintain a good forward lean. That protects the ball even more.

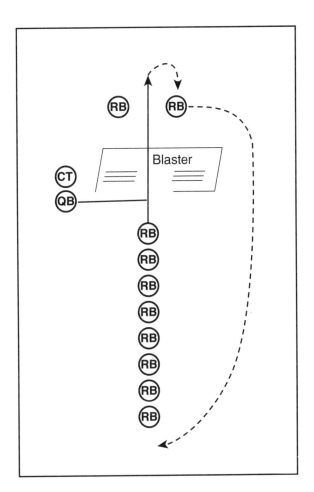

Set-up and Instructions:

Position two players facing each other on the exit side of the blaster. Position a line of running backs on the other side of the blaster, with a quarterback on one side. Be sure to switch the quarterbacks to the other side halfway through the drill to guarantee that all running backs get handoffs from both sides. Tell the quarterbacks to make the exchange immediately in front of the pads on the blaster, so the running backs have contact as soon as they receive the ball. Tell the two players on the exit side of the blaster to use both hands to grab for the ball when the running back comes through. They should try to pull both of the running back's arms to force a fumble. Switch the players as needed and be sure that each running back gets at least two repetitions from both sides of the quarterback.

66. SELL JOB

Purpose:

- To emphasize to running backs the importance of selling a fake.

Coaching Pointers:

- Whether you are running the ball or faking, run hard!
- Sell yourself; attract attention when faking!
- Always run the same way, whether carrying or faking.
- During this drill, you won't know whether you're getting the ball or not. Run hard no matter what!

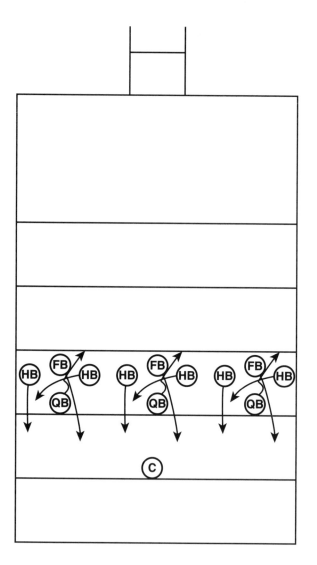

Set-up and Instructions:

Align all the backfields on the same designated line of scrimmage. Have them run one at a time so you can watch each play closely. Give them a variety of misdirection plays to run, ranging from bootlegs to belly or veer plays. Instruct the quarterbacks to decide to whom they want to give the ball. They can decide to keep it, too. In essence, they are the only ones who know who will be running with the ball. Tell the running backs to be prepared for either a handoff or a fake and to run the same way—whether or not they have the ball. Have each backfield run on its own cadence, and watch the play to identify who has the ball. As soon as you see the ball, shout out who has it.

Establish some competition among all the backfields. See who can fake out the coach! Whenever some backfields do an especially good job—even if they didn't fake you out—shout out the wrong player anyway. Every time they can say "Gotcha!" to a coach, kids get motivated!

67. HIGH KNEES

Purpose:

- To practice effective handoffs and high knee action for running backs.

Coaching Pointers:

- Look straight ahead at me; don't look at the handoff.
- Hit the hole as hard as you can! Beat the quarterback to the point of attack. Make him stretch to get to you!
- Don't throw your feet out to the side when you come to the bags. Lift your knees. Get 'em up in the air!
- Maintain a forward lean while you drive your knees. It's hard to tackle a guy who's all knees and shoulder pads!

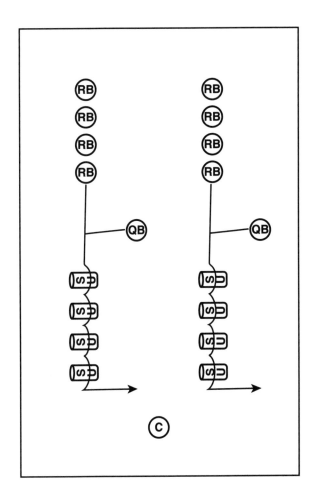

Set-up and Instructions:

Position the quarterbacks on a designated line of scrimmage, each with a line of running backs to his right or left. Alternate the positioning of the running backs so they all get handoffs from both sides of the quarterback. Place three or four stand-up dummies on their sides in front of each row of running backs with just enough room between each dummy for the running back to take one step. On your cadence, have the quarterbacks execute the handoffs and have the running backs step over the dummies.

Check the execution of the handoffs as well as the leg drive and the forward lean of the running backs. Don't let them throw their feet out to either side as they jump the dummies; make them get their knees in the air. When they clear the final dummy, point in the direction you want them to cut. Tell them to cut hard—on a 90-degree angle, if possible. This is a good drill early in the season.

68. BAG GAUNTLET

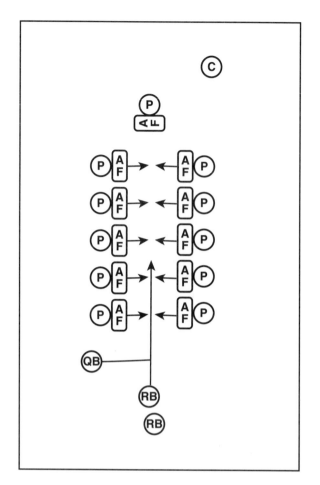

Purpose:

- To emphasize the importance of a good handoff, leg drive, and ball protection.

Coaching Pointers:

- Look straight ahead at the gauntlet; don't look for the handoff.
- Secure the ball after the handoff. Get your hands over both tips and hold tight!
- Run through the gauntlet with high knees; drive your legs hard, and maintain a good forward lean.
- Hold the ball with both arms and swing them from side to side when you run. That prevents tacklers from grabbing your arms or the ball.
- Lower the boom on the bag at the end of the gauntlet or spin off in either direction.

Set-up and Instructions:

Position a quarterback on a designated line of scrimmage. Put two or three running backs in a line prepared to take a handoff. Create a gauntlet of two parallel lines of extra players in front of the running backs. Have each player in the gauntlet hold an air flate, and instruct each to jam the running back to force a fumble or to break the running back's stride. Finally, position one player at the end of the gauntlet holding an air flate.

On your cadence, have the quarterback hand the ball to the first running back, who runs the gauntlet and either lowers his shoulder or spins off the bag at the end. Check for a good exchange, high knees, forward lean, good protection of the ball, and a good pop on the last bag. Have runners take the bag after each repetition, taking turns in the gauntlet until they become ball carriers again. Be sure that each back gets at least three or four repetitions.

69. HIGH KNEE/FUMBLE

Purpose:

- To emphasize high knees and effective leg drive when running with the football.
- To protect the ball at all times.
- To execute an effective spin when coming out of the pack.

Coaching Pointers:

- After the handoff, secure the tip of the ball with your hand. Hold it within the crook of your arm and hug it!
- Drive your knees high and hard when running through the gauntlet. If you "skate," you'll go down.
- Maintain a good body lean as you drive your legs—and protect the ball.
- After running the gauntlet, lower either shoulder into the dummy and spin off that shoulder. Maintain high knees during the spin.

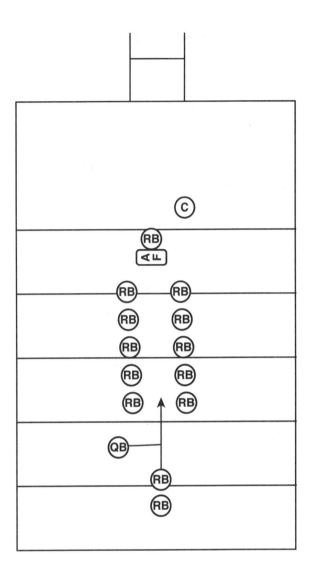

Set-up and Instructions:

Place 10 to 12 running backs into two equally divided, parallel lines, approximately two yards apart. Have the players kneel on their inside knees facing the quarterback and two running backs. Instruct the quarterback to give the cadence and to hand the ball to successive runners in the line. Instruct the running backs to drive their knees, get a good forward lean, and protect the ball while running through the gauntlet. Tell them to spin off the bag after completing the gauntlet.

Instruct the players forming the gauntlet to grab at the ball or the runners' legs as they pass them. They are not to extend their arms or do anything else to trip up or to tackle the runners, just grab at the ball or a foot or a leg. Anything other than that could result in injury.

Each runner should then replace the player holding the bag. The player holding the bag should take a spot in one of the two lines. Simultaneously, one of the players in the front of either line should go to the back of the line of running backs in order to run the gauntlet. Be sure that each player runs the gauntlet at least twice.

70. TRIP 'EM UP

Purpose:

- To emphasize high knees for running backs.
- To develop the ability to break hand or arm tackles.

Coaching Pointers:

- Get some forward lean for momentum and power when you hit the hole.
- But don't lean so much that you can be tripped up easily.
- When in traffic, emphasize an up-and-down action with your legs. That will help you maintain balance, even when someone reaches for your foot.
- Pump your legs up and down like pistons! Generate power.

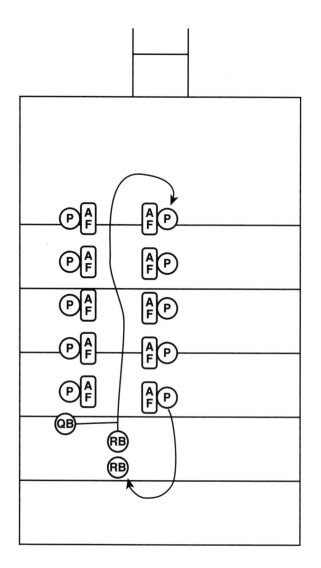

Set-up and Instructions:

Position a quarterback on a designated line of scrimmage and one or two running backs in their home halfback position behind him. Create a gauntlet in front of the running backs, each player in the gauntlet holding an air flate. Tell the players in the gauntlet to kneel and when the running back comes through the gauntlet to swing the bag at his knees to try to trip him up.

Have the quarterback call the cadence and make a good handoff to each running back. After the running back runs the gauntlet, have him go to the back of the gauntlet and work his way to the front to run the ball again. Be sure each back gets at least three repetitions.

Check each handoff and make sure each running back is driving his legs as emphasized in the coaching pointers.

Variation: Prior to the above drill, align all the running backs on a yard line and instruct them to run in place, emphasizing high knee action. Walk among them while they're running and hold your hand in front of them approximately waist high. Tell them to hit your hand with their knees, then go to the above drill. This is a good drill early in the season.

71. PUNISH THE BAG

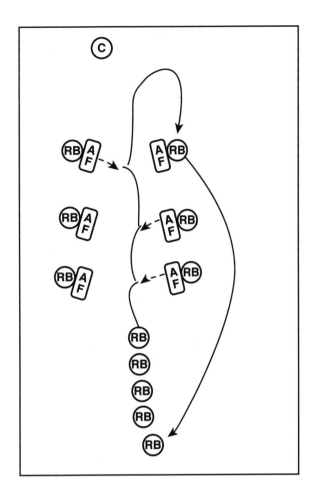

Purpose:

- To emphasize high knees when meeting tacklers.

Coaching Pointers:

- Drop your shoulder and drive your near knee into whichever bag is thrown.
- The bag simulates a tackler. When you can't make a move, always drop your shoulder and drive your knee into tacklers.
- This doesn't mean you hesitate while you're doing it either! Keep driving your legs. Never stop your legs!
- Don't kick the bag high in the air. That's not what I'm looking for. Just get your knee into each bag that's tossed at you.

Set-up and Instructions:

Position the running backs in one or two lines as illustrated. Position a gauntlet of six players in front of the line(s), each on his knees and holding an air flate in front of him. Have each tandem decide who will toss the bag. Only one player in each of the three tandems should toss a bag at the ball carrier's knee.

Instruct each ball carrier to use high knees while running through the gauntlet and to drive a knee into each bag that is tossed at him. Again, the purpose of the drill is not to drive the bag high in the air, just to get a knee into it. Check to be sure that the runner doesn't hesitate while driving the knee. His legs should be chugging throughout the drill.

72. HIGH STEPPIN'

Purpose:

- To emphasize high knees and a shoulder drop whenever tacklers appear unexpectedly.

Coaching Pointers:

- Whenever a tackler suddenly appears and contact is unavoidable, drop your near shoulder and drive your near knee into him.
- Whenever the football is on the same side as your near shoulder, press it tightly to your side as you drop that shoulder.
- Attack the tackler! Destroy the tackle!
- Drop the shoulder and protect the football!
- Keep your legs driving hard throughout the contact.
- Don't expect to be tackled! Expect to keep running!

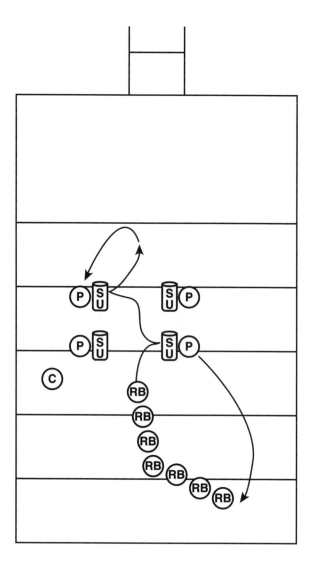

Set-up and Instructions:

Position two tandems of players in a mini-gauntlet, each with a stand-up dummy. The tandems should be facing each other, approximately two to three yards apart, the second tandem approximately five yards downfield from the first.

Align all the running backs in a line in front of the gauntlet and tell them to run through both sets of dummies—prepared to attack the dummy that moves toward them. Before each back runs the gauntlet, hand signal which dummies in each tandem will attack the runner. Check each running back for a good shoulder drop, strong leg drive, a bulled neck, and good ball protection.

Rotate the backs so that each holds a dummy and each has at least three repetitions running the football.

73. DIP AND RECOVER

Purpose:

- To emphasize dropping the shoulder into tacklers, switching the ball, and recovering balance.

Coaching Pointers:

- Drop the shoulder and raise your knee into tacklers, especially when you're pinned in.
- Always switch the ball to the other hand to meet potential tacklers.
- Make a move when you can—always run to daylight! But be prepared to lower the boom when you have to.
- When you lose your balance, recover it by raising your head, sticking out your chest and, driving your knees as high and as hard as you can.
- Always bull your neck when dropping a shoulder. You'll see where you're going and, most important, you'll protect your head!

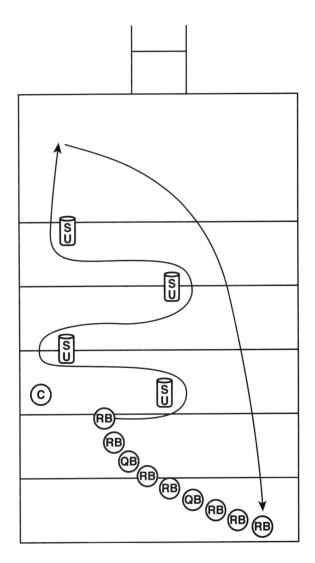

Set-up and Instructions:

Position the running backs and quarterbacks in a straight line as illustrated approximately five yards to the left of a cone or a stand-up dummy. Position four or five cones or stand-up dummies as illustrated, approximately eight to 10 yards apart. Holding a football in his right arm, each back should run half to three-quarter speed to the first cone, dip, and touch the ground with the palm of his left hand. He should then recover his balance, switch the ball to his left hand, and, at the second cone or stand-up dummy, touch the ground with his right hand. He should repeat the same process for the next two or three cones, then sprint five to 10 yards upfield.

This is a good drill for an early-season emphasis on ball switching and dropping the shoulder. Once the backs become proficient, vary the drill by having them run full speed toward the stand-up dummies.

74. MOVE AND PROTECT

Purpose:

- To emphasize trusting your body and protecting the ball.

Coaching Pointers:

- Don't consciously **think** when running to daylight! **React!**
- Let your body do the thinking.
- Let it be second nature to you, making your cuts and protecting the football.
- Concentrate only on how hard and fast you're going to run. Let your body do the rest.

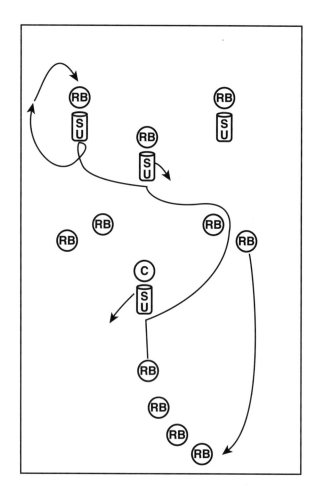

Set-up and Instructions:

Position four stand-up dummies as illustrated, the first five yards in front of the cluster of three. Arrange the cluster of three two yards apart. You hold the first dummy and have a running back holding each of the three dummies behind you. Finally, position two running backs a yard behind you and on each side.

Position some running backs in a straight line in front of you and instruct them to run straight ahead as fast as they can. Tilt your dummy right or left and have the back cut in the opposite direction. Then have the two backs on that side grab for the football. Have the back sprint toward the middle dummy in the cluster and again cut in the direction opposite the tilt. He should then spin off the final dummy.

Be sure to rotate all the running backs so that everyone gets three or four repetitions. Check for quickness, a willingness to trust their bodies, a good spin, and good ball protection.

75. STUTTER CUT

Purpose:

- To emphasize a quick stutter move on an open-field tackler, followed by a cut to daylight.

Coaching Pointers:

- When you come to the tackler in the open field, get on your tiptoes and stutter step quickly.
- Then take a quick **and short** jab step in the direction opposite your intended cut.
- You're doing this to get the first tackler off balance.
- Make your cut based on the movements of the second tackler.
- In other words, make a jab and a quick lean in his direction, then weave in the opposite direction to run to daylight.

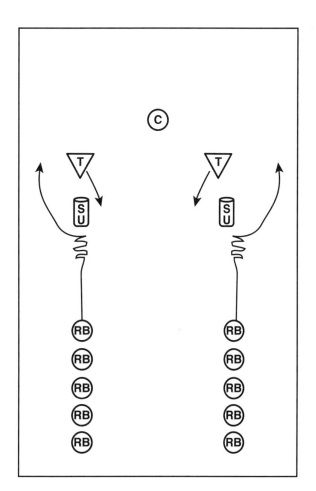

Set-up and Instructions:

Position two lines of running backs facing upfield approximately five to six yards apart. Position a stand-up dummy and a tackler in front of each line as illustrated. Alternate the runners and the tacklers so that each back gets at least three or four repetitions as a ball carrier. Instruct the running backs to stutter step a yard or two before the first tackler (the stand-up dummy), then jab step and cut in the direction opposite the second tackler. The jab step should be just pronounced enough to get the first tackler off balance. Instruct the second tackler to move to the right or the left of the stand-up dummy as soon as he sees the running back start his stutter step.

Check for quick feet, a balanced hit position, and a quick weave before the actual cut to daylight.

76. SWITCH AND LOWER

Purpose:

- To emphasize ball protection and proper body lean when making cuts.

Coaching Pointers:

- Protect the ball by holding one or both tips when in traffic.
- When making a cut or breaking for the sideline, switch the ball away from potential tacklers by reaching **over** the ball with your far arm, grabbing the tip, and switching the ball to that arm.
- After making the switch, be sure to apply pressure to the ball with your hand, the crook of your arm, and your side.
- Once the ball has been secured, drop your body in the direction of tacklers and use your free arm and shoulder to break any tackles.

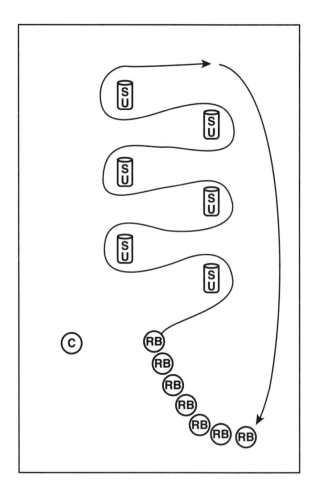

Set-up and Instructions:

Position all the running backs in a straight line and give the first in the line a football. Stagger five or six stand-up dummies as illustrated and instruct each running back to run outside each dummy and cut back to the inside, each time switching the ball to the outside arm. After switching the ball, each back should then lift his inside knee and lower his inside arm and shoulder into the stand-up dummy and knock it over.

Check for effective switching of the ball, ball protection, and running technique. This drill should be run throughout the season to reemphasize ball protection and running technique. It's also a good drill for the team that has had enough contact but needs to review technique.

77. SPIN, DRIVE, AND CUT

Purpose:

- To emphasize a repetition of basic running fundamentals.

Coaching Pointers:

- Get your knees up in the air! Maintain a good forward lean with your upper body.

- Start your spin move the moment you hit the bag or the tackler. Don't give him any time to grab you!

- Whip your off arm hard to help you spin and to get separation from the tackler.

- Drop your shoulder and drive your near knee high and hard into the second tackler. Keep your legs moving at all times.

- Never stop driving your legs!

- High knees and hard-driving legs will help you make the final cut!

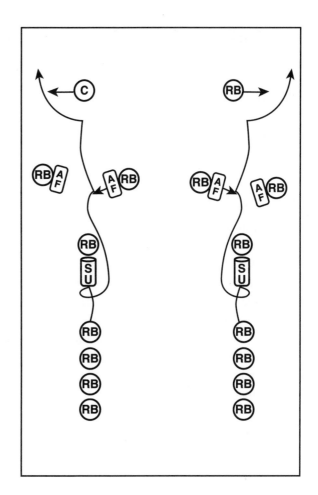

Set-up and Instructions:

Position all the backs in two lines as illustrated. Put one running back holding a stand-up dummy in front of each line. Behind him, position two more running backs to either side, each with an air flate. You stand behind them. Be sure to alternate all the backs so that each gets at least two or three repetitions as a ball carrier.

Instruct each running back to hit the first bag and to spin in either direction, then to drop a shoulder into the player who attacks him with an air flate, finally to cut in the direction of your hand signal.

This is a rapid-fire drill. Try to get as many repetitions as possible for every running back.

78. GET UP AND GO

Purpose:

- To emphasize a variety of running techniques and skills.

Coaching Pointers:

- Get your knees up! Drive them over the dummies. Tacklers don't like to hit runners with high knees!
- Cut low and hard on the cones. Push hard and lean in the direction you want to go.
- Always switch the ball away from potential tacklers. Keep your near arm free to stiff arm or drop a shoulder.
- Attack the last dummy! It represents the last person keeping you out of the end zone!
- Never simply accept a hit from a tackler. Hit him first!

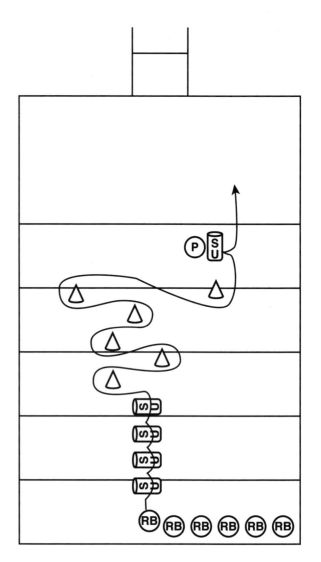

Set-up and Instructions:

Lay four stand-up dummies on their sides parallel to each other in front of a line of running backs. Five yards beyond them, stagger four cones as illustrated. Place another cone 15 to 20 yards to the left, another 40 yards across field from it. Finally, position a stand-up dummy with one player holding it 10 yards upfield of the final cone.

Instruct the running backs to emphasize high knees over the stand-up dummies and to weave low and hard around the cones. After the last cone, have them race to the cone on the left, switch the ball and run across field to the final cone. At the final cone, they should pivot, switch the ball again and run upfield, attacking the final dummy before sprinting into the end zone.

This is an excellent drill any time of the season to reinforce running technique. To make it especially lively, put the stopwatch on each back and enjoy the healthy competition that results.

79. THREE-SQUARE

Purpose:

- To emphasize basic running technique and tackling fundamentals.
- To identify players who like contact— or who, at least, don't mind it!

Coaching Pointers:

To the running back:

- Keep your body low and protect the ball.
- Bull your neck to maintain balance and to protect your head.
- Keep your knees high—drive them hard.
- **BELIEVE** that you can't and won't be tackled!

To the tackler:

- Tackle across the bow. Get your head in front and wrap up the runner.
- Drive your legs and tackle **through** the running back.
- Bull your neck! **DO NOT** align your spine. We don't want injuries, just good fundamentals.

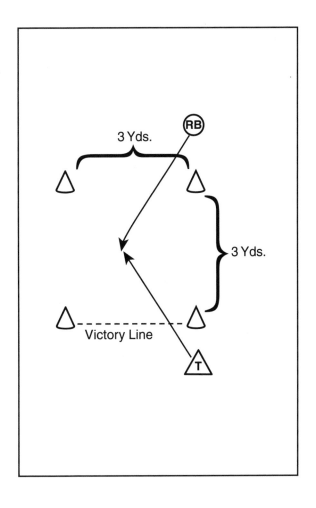

Set-up and Instructions:

Set up cones to form a three-yard square. The tackler starts behind one cone, the running back opposite him. On the whistle, the running back tries to cross the "victory line" with no cut backs or jukes. The tackler tries to stop him.

Use this drill early in the season to find your hitters. It becomes a very competitive drill, so emphasize safety—no head butting or knee or ankle twisting. Blow the whistle immediately when one player has won or if an injury to either player seems possible.

Thanks to Don Drakulich, head coach at Aviano (Italy) High School for this drill.

80. MOVE OUT

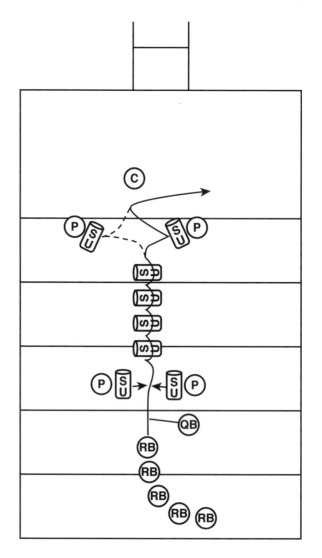

Purpose:

- To emphasize high knees, leg drive, and shoulder drop.

Coaching Pointers:

- Pound through the first two bags. Get your weight down with a good forward lean and drive your legs!
- High knees over the next four bags. Get 'em up in the air!
- Full speed all the way! Drop your shoulder into the bag that attacks you after the high step over the last dummy.
- Attack the last bag; don't just accept the hit. Deliver one of your own!
- Read me for the final cut.

Set-up and Instructions:

Position a quarterback on a designated line of scrimmage. Position a line of running backs to either side of him. Switch the line halfway through the drill to assure that everyone takes the ball from both sides. On the quarterback's cadence, give the ball to the first back in the line and tell him to drive through the first two bags, to use high knees over the next four bags, and to drop the shoulder into the bag that attacks him at the end. Finally, tell him to cut in the direction you point.

Check for good handoffs, leg drive, high knees, shoulder drop, and forward lean. You can also put the stopwatch on everyone to set up some competition. This is a good drill midway through the season to provide a little variety and to review ball-carrying techniques.

81. TWO BAGGER

Purpose:

- To practice leg drive for running backs.
- To introduce good spinning technique.
- To promote positive reaction time.

Coaching Pointers:

- Hit the hole with maximum speed.
- Always spin off the shoulder closer to the tackler.
- Spin hard and fast, throwing the far shoulder hard enough to regain forward momentum after completing the spin.
- Emphasize high knees. Runners won't regain balance fast enough without high knees.
- When tackled from both sides, drive the knees high and hard, almost as if running in place. **Never stop your legs, especially in a crowd!**
- **Bull your neck; protect your head!**
- If you drop your head, you might get hurt. **You definitely won't make a read!**

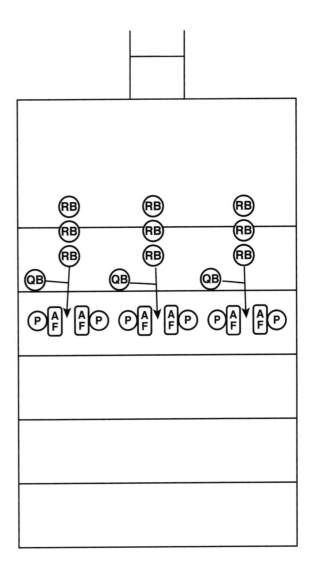

Set-up and Instructions:

Make a line of left halfbacks in their normal three- to four-yard alignment off the line of scrimmage. On the quarterback's cadence, have each run a quick opener. Position two bag holders as illustrated above. Prior to the snap, instruct either or both of the bag holders to attack the runner. Tell each runner to spin if attacked by one bag, to drive the knees high and hard—almost as if running in place—if attacked by both bags, working to split the bags or to spin off one of them.

Vary the drill or complement it by having the running back lead through the hole, blocking the bag that attacks him. Instruct the quarterback to follow the back, making the appropriate cut and spinning off the bag(s) as needed.

82. THREE BAGGER

Purpose:

- To assess and practice reaction time.
- To emphasize the importance of destroying tackles.
- To teach proper cutting technique.
- To emphasize leg drive.

Coaching Pointers:

- Never look at the handoff; the quarterback will get you the ball.
- Hit the hole as fast and as strong as possible.
- Make the appropriate cut, but never anticipate it. Trust your body to make the right read and to react accordingly.
- When you react, react hard. Don't simply absorb a tackle from either side. Attack it and destroy it.
- Bull your neck at all times; never drop your head when attacking a tackler.

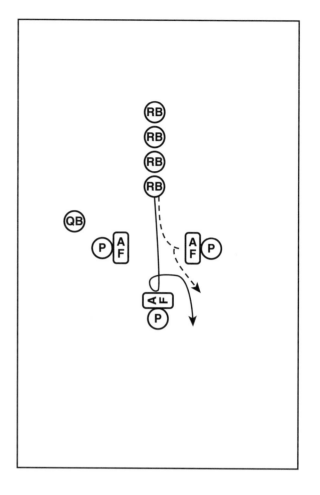

Set-up and Instructions:

Tell the backs to be a line of left halfbacks in their normal alignment to the left of the quarterback. On the quarterback's cadence, have each run a quick opener. Position three bag holders as illustrated above. Prior to the snap, point to the bag holder who is to attack the ball carrier: left, right, or middle. Instruct each ball carrier to attack the bag, driving through or spinning off the middle bag, attacking and driving through either side bag. After the runner gets two turns, have them line up as right halfbacks.

Vary the drill by hand signaling all the bag holders to take a step backward when the ball carrier receives the handoff. Instruct the ball carriers to make a quick cut to either side of the middle bag when this happens. On rare occasions, hand signal all three bags to attack the ball carrier, telling the running back to pick out one bag and destroy the tackle, emphasizing strong leg drive until he breaks into the open.

83. BLAST READ

Purpose:

- To emphasize good ball security, running technique, blocking technique, and use of blockers.

Coaching Pointers:

To the running back:

- Secure the tips of the ball as soon as the quarterback gives it to you.
- Swing your arms and the ball from side to side when you run. Don't let anyone get a hold of your arm or the ball!
- Get a good forward lean and leg drive through the blaster and the gauntlet.
- Read the block at the end of the gauntlet and make the right cut. Cut to the side to which the blocker moves his head.

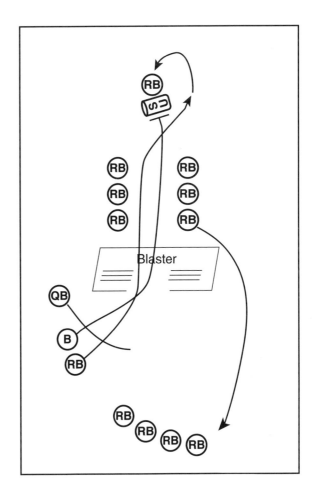

To the blocker:

- Maintain a good base and explode through the block. Keep driving your legs until you hear the whistle.

Set-up and Instructions:

Position a quarterback and a line of running backs on one side of the blaster. On the exit side of the blaster, place a gauntlet of the remaining running backs. Instruct them to grab for the ball as the running back passes them. At the end of the gauntlet, have one of the running backs hold a blocking dummy. Place tandems of running backs in an I formation behind the quarterback. On the quarterback's cadence, have the first back lead through the blaster and block the dummy at the end of the gauntlet. Instruct the other running back to take a handoff, run through the blaster and the gauntlet, and cut off the block at the end of the gauntlet.

Check for a good handoff, good leg drive, good ball protection, an effective block, and a good cut. Have all players rotate through the gauntlet so that each running back has at least three repetitions. This drill should be run throughout the season to emphasize ball-carrying fundamentals.

84. RUN AND BLOCK

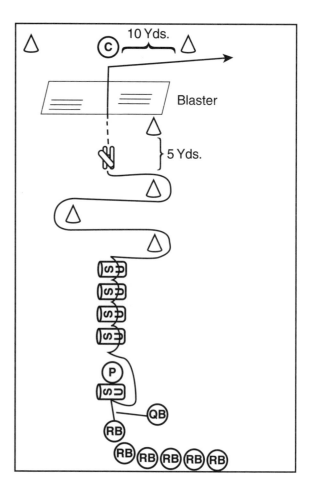

Purpose:

- To emphasize and review blocking and running fundamentals.

Coaching Pointers:

- Hit the hole as hard as possible and spin off the first dummy! Keep your knees high during the spin!
- High knees over the next four dummies! Good forward lean!
- Make good cuts on the cones and switch the ball.
- Hit the popsicle low with a good base and drive it hard for five yards.
- Low and hard through the blaster!
- Cut in the direction I indicate and sprint to the cone.

Set-up and Instructions:

Set up an obstacle course as illustrated. Put the backs in a home halfback alignment and have them go on the quarterback's cadence. They are to run the course full speed. Check for good running and blocking fundamentals. Tell them that if they don't execute properly, they will run the course again. Time each back and record the times. Run the obstacle course again a couple weeks into the season and again mid-season to see who improves his time. This drill creates healthy competition and can become spirited. Players look forward to it. Praise good execution whenever you see it; this drill is also a good teaching tool.

85. SIDELINE

Purpose:

- To neutralize tacklers along the side-lines in order to pick up necessary first-down yardage.
- To emphasize explosion into the end zone.

Coaching Pointers:

- Raise the near knee into the tackler so he doesn't get a clean shot into your body.
- Drop the near shoulder into the tack-ler, driving off the leg closer to the sideline.
- Bull the neck in order to avoid injury to the spinal column.
- Keep the legs driving throughout the motion, almost as if running in place but always driving for the first-down marker.

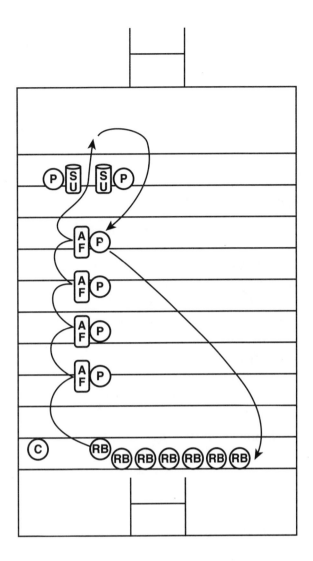

Set-up and Instructions:

Position four players, each holding an air flate, approximately 10 yards apart and no more than four or five yards from the sidelines. Position another two players, each with a stand-up dummy, on a yard line. Instruct each running back, when he receives the ball from you, to posi-tion it in the hand closer to the sideline, then to drive the near knee to lower the shoulder and to deliver a forearm into the players holding air flates as they try to knock him out of bounds. Each should then drive through the stand-up dummies as if on the goal line, low and hard enough to fall into the end zone.

Tell the players holding the air flates to take only two or three steps into the running backs but to hit them solidly with the bag. They are to hit the runners only hard enough to jar them off balance. The same is true of the players on the simulated goal line. Instruct them to leave a one-foot opening between the dummies but to resist each runner.

Rotate the runners and the bag holders. To provide incentive, tell the runners they owe you a lap after practice if they get knocked out of bounds.

86. BASEBALL

Purpose:

- To emphasize effective spinning technique.

Coaching Pointers:

- Drop your shoulder into the tackler but don't sustain contact.
- At the moment of contact, spin hard off the tackler, using your non-contact arm to help rotate your body.
- Drive your legs hard throughout the maneuver, almost as if running in place, to maintain your balance.
- Make a complete spin, regain your balance and forward momentum, and keep running.
- Don't stop your legs throughout the maneuver! **Never** stop your legs when you run with a football!

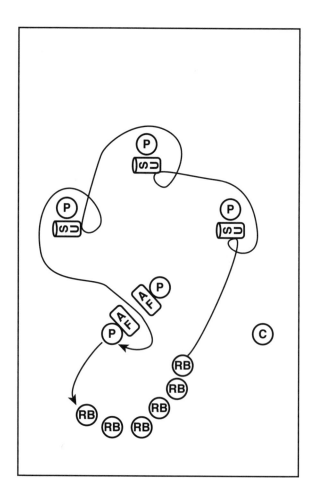

Set-up and Instructions:

Position three players as if on a baseball diamond, one at first base, one at second, another at third. Each should be holding a stand-up dummy. Position two other players on the third base side of home plate, each holding an air flate. Create a line of running backs just behind "home plate." Give the first running back a football and tell him to spin off the bags at first, second and third bases, then to "come home" by blasting through the two players at the plate.

Check for good spinning technique on each of the first three bags and for good leg drive, explosion, and ball protection when blasting through the two final bags. This drill should be run periodically throughout the season, not often but enough to remind the running backs of the need for good spinning technique.

87. KEEP THE BALANCE

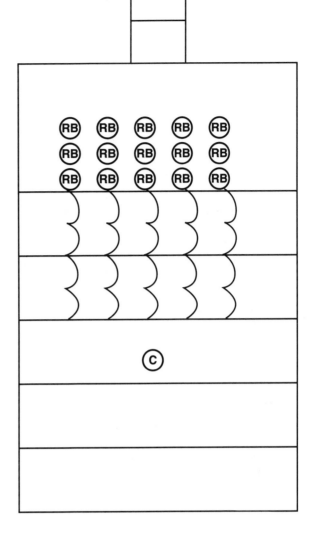

Purpose:

- To practice regaining balance.

Coaching Pointers:

- Whenever you put your hand to the ground to prevent yourself from going down, hold the ball tightly in your other arm.
- Don't swing arm loosely in an attempt to regain your balance. You can regain your balance without taking the chance of fumbling the ball!
- After you catch yourself on your free hand, raise your head and shoulders sharply and push your chest forward.
- Raise your knees and drive them hard to bring yourself upright.

Set-up and Instructions:

Align two or three waves of running backs on the goal line. Instruct the first wave, each holding a football, to start running and after five yards to touch the palm of their free hand to the ground as if stumbling. Check their technique for regaining their balance. After regaining their balance, they should switch the ball to the other arm and, at the 10-yard line, touch the ground with the palm of the other hand. Instruct them to alternate arms every five yards until they reach the 20-yard line. Then run the other waves. Each running back should have at least three repetitions.

This drill can be run independently or it can be integrated with pre-practice agility drills for the running backs.

88. SLED CHALLENGE

Purpose:

- To emphasize a good base and leg drive when executing a shoulder block.

Coaching Pointers:

- Bull your neck and explode up and through the pad!
- Gather your body just before the block, uncoil, and extend **through** the pad.
- When driving your legs, keep your feet approximately shoulder-width to maintain a good blocking base.
- Don't just push the sled; keep driving your legs and working your arms.
- Keep your neck bulled throughout the block. A bulled neck protects your head and maintains your upward and forward momentum.
- Don't be afraid to make some noise when blocking. Grunting tightens your muscles and gives you more power.

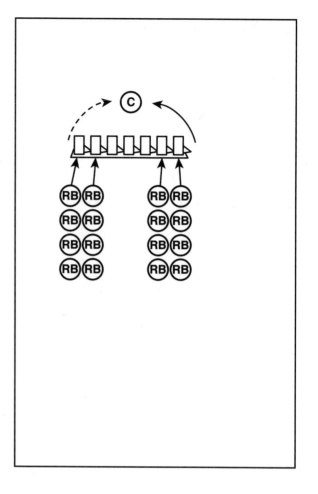

Set-up and Instructions:

Create teams of two running backs. Tell them this is a competition to see which two backs can outdrive the others. Position half the teams on the outside two pads of the seven-man sled, the rest on the opposite side of the sled. Align each tandem approximately three yards from the sled and, on your cadence, have them explode into the two outside pads.

Have them drive their legs until one of the two teams turns the sled. After all the backs have had a turn, pair off the winners of each competition and have them drive the sled until one tandem outdrives the rest. Let the winners rest for the remainder of the drill while everyone else drives the sled for another two or three repetitions. This is an excellent drill for early in the season. It conditions the running backs while it emphasizes fundamentals. It's also a lot of fun.

89. DRIVE OR CRAB

Purpose:

- To practice the fundamentals of the drive (shoulder) block and the crab block.

Coaching Pointers:

For the drive block:

- Bull your neck to protect your head and drive your head and outside shoulder into the defensive end to move him out of the off-tackle hole.
- Maintain a good base with your legs. Keep them wide enough so that you won't fall off or be pushed off the block!
- Always block **through** the man. Don't extend your legs before contact—only after contact.

For the crab block:

- Approach the defensive end as if you plan to shoulder block him.
- At the last second, drop below his waist and attack his outside knee with your far shoulder.
- Drive your far shoulder so that your upper body is on his outside and drop to both hands.
- Move like a crab sideways into his legs, pinning them between your arm and the knee of your leg closer to him.
- Keep moving into his body to stop him from reacting to the outside.

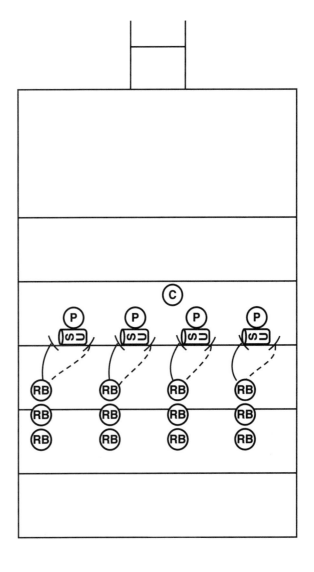

Set-up and Instructions:

Position four stand-up dummies on a yard line, approximately three yards apart. Position lines of running backs two yards to the left of each dummy. Halfway through the drill, reposition them to two yards to the right of each dummy so all the backs get to block with both shoulders. Instruct them first to execute a drive block on the dummy to open up the off-tackle hole for the running back.

After at least three repetitions each, instruct them to execute a crab block to take away the defensive end's outside pursuit path. The drive block will open up the off-tackle hole; the crab block will open up the outside. Check for proper fundamentals, especially a good initial hit, a good base, and a bulled neck for protection.

90. HELP THE BLOCK

Purpose:

- To emphasize blocking fundamentals and to train running backs to help set up blocks.

Coaching Pointers:

To the blocker:

- If the defensive end is closing hard to the inside, take him that way by crabbing him.
- If the defensive end is outside conscious, push him that way by drive blocking him to the outside.

To the running back:

- Help the blocker by making the defensive end think you're going to the outside, then plant and cut into the off-tackle hole.
- **OR** Help the blocker by making the defensive end think you're going to the inside, then bend hard to the outside.
- Always help your blocker by setting up his block. If the play is committed to the outside, sell off-tackle. If the play is committed to the inside, sell outside.
- Always watch your blocker and take what the defense gives you.

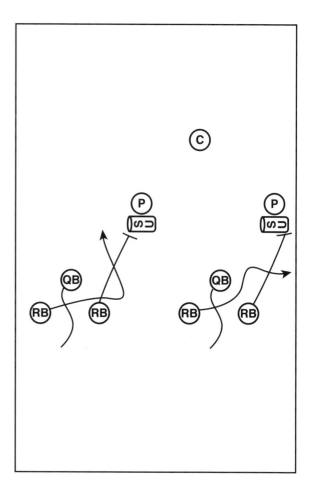

Set-up and Instructions:

Position two stand-up dummies approximately five yards apart. Align a quarterback and two running backs approximately two to three yards inside each dummy. Instruct the players holding the dummies to react to the running back, to be conscious of the off-tackle hole as well as of the outside. Instruct the blocking backs to execute either a drive block or a crab block, depending on the defensive end's reactions. Instruct the running backs to set up the blocks by running hard to the outside and cutting into the off-tackle hole, or by leaning into the off-tackle hole and bending hard to the outside.

This is a good drill for both running backs and blockers, especially early in the season.

91. CRACK BACK I

Purpose:

- To emphasize the fundamentals of a legal crack-back block.

Coaching Pointers:

- Keep your head in front of the man to be blocked.
- Never block him when his back is turned.
- Get as close to him as possible if his back is turned, get into a good hit position and wait for him to turn, always keeping your body between him and the ball carrier.
- Once he turns, hit him!
- Immediately after contact—*if you can*—drop to an inverted crab block, your hands on the line of scrimmage, your legs pointing upfield, and pin the defensive end to the inside.
- Don't expect to pancake him more than once during the game; defensive ends are smarter than that! Most of the time, you may have to shield block him, simply keeping your body between him and the ball carrier!

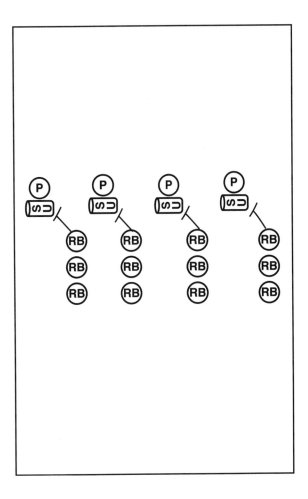

Set-up and Instructions:

Position four stand-up dummies on a yard line. Position lines of slotbacks or wingbacks one to two yards outside the dummies. On your cadence, have them crack-back block the dummies, keeping the above coaching pointers in mind. Hand signal the players holding the dummies to turn their backs to the blockers or to react immediately into them. Check for proper fundamentals, for a shoulder block, a crab block, or a shield block when appropriate. Each requires a different blocking technique and continuing explanation, especially for young players.

Use this drill early in the season and then periodically as the season progresses.

92. PASS BLOCKING

Purpose:

- To emphasize good pass blocking fundamentals for running backs.

Coaching Pointers:

- Get in a good hit position as a pass rusher approaches.
- Depending on the abandon of his rush, decide either to sting him by blocking him high or to chop him by blocking low.
- Don't give him any clues as to which you plan to do. Chop him only at the last second. Always make him think you plan to block him high.
- For purposes of this drill, always block high, using either your hands or your helmet, shoulders and arms, and **keep your legs driving** throughout the block!
- Don't wait for the pass rusher to come to you. Always take two or three steps in his direction before you set up in your hit position.
- That will give the quarterback more room and it will cut down the distance between you and the pass rusher.
- Always invite him to take an outside rush.

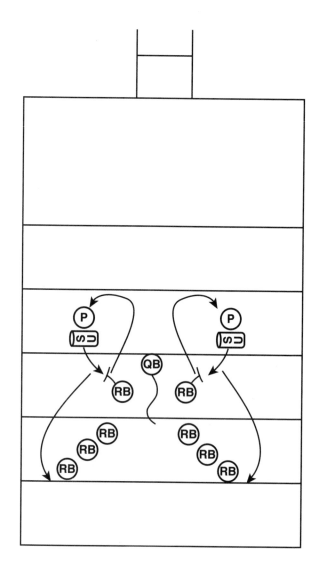

Set-up and Instructions:

Position tandems of running backs behind a quarterback. Align pass rushers in both defensive end positions. Instruct the quarterback to take a five- or seven-step drop. Instruct the running backs to set up in hit positions and block the defensive ends. The defensive ends will be holding stand-up dummies and will either bull rush or try to spin off the blocker to either the inside or the outside of the blocker.

Check for a good hit position and blocking technique. Make sure each back has at least three repetitions. This is an excellent drill for teaching fundamentals and prior to any live blocking.

93. MOVE THE FEET

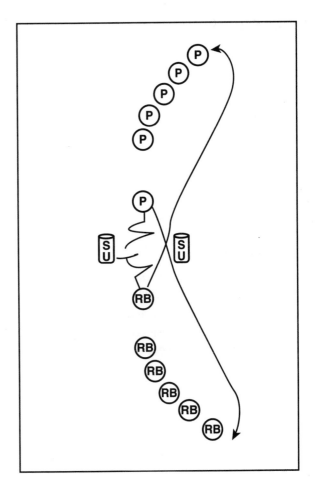

Purpose:

- To emphasize foot speed when pass blocking or shield blocking.

Coaching Pointers:

- Keep your feet moving so that your body is always between the defender and the quarterback or ball carrier.

- Always stay in your hit position—knees bent slightly and on the balls of your feet. It gives you more mobility and more leverage!

- When you jam the defender with your hands, keep your arms within the frame of your body; otherwise, it's a penalty.

- Lock your elbows to keep the rusher away from your body.

- You don't have to punish the defender! Just keep your body between him and the ball.

Set-up and Instructions:

Lay two stand-up dummies on their sides, approximately two yards apart. Position a pass rusher on one end of the dummies, a pass blocker on the other end. Tell the rusher to get past the blocker. Tell the blocker to stop the rusher for at least five seconds. At the end of five seconds, blow your whistle. If you have an unusually large number of backs, run two groups simultaneously. Otherwise, run only one group. You'll want to see all the blockers in order to make corrections. You'll also want the backs to watch each other.

This drill provides an excellent opportunity for players to observe each other. It brings out the best in everyone and provides for some healthy competition. Use it early, then periodically throughout the season.

94. IN THE ARC

Purpose:

- To master effective footwork and explosiveness when pass-protection blocking.

Coaching Pointers:

- Always stay in a solid hit position throughout the drill.
- Chug your feet fast enough to face up to successive pass rushers.
- Sting the pass rusher with your head and shoulders or use your hands, depending on the defender's technique.

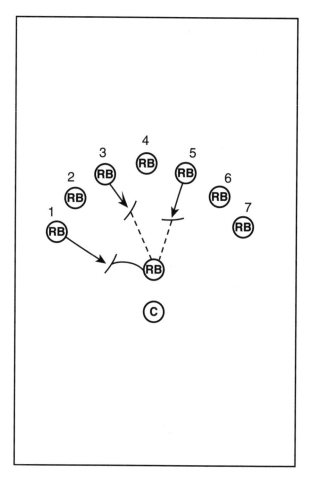

Set-up and Instructions:

Place six or seven (four or five, if you have fewer players) in an arc. Assign each a number. Position a blocker (either a running back or a lineman) in the center of the arc. Instruct the blocker to get into his hit position. Call successive numbers until the blocker has faced up to at least four rushers. Tell the rushers they can use any rushing technique, ranging from bull rush to spinning. Tell the rushers to try to touch you—gently! Vary your position behind each blocker accordingly. Make sure the blocker is staying in a hit position to maximize his explosiveness and facing up to each rusher. Make sure the blocker is attacking—in a controlled fashion—each rusher. Make corrections, then replace the blocker with another player. Also replace one or two of the rushers. Each player should have at least one turn as the blocker.

Variation: Before replacing the blocker, ask the other players to make suggestions for improvement to him.

95. BLITZ BLOCK

Purpose:

- To teach running backs to read blitzing linebackers and to execute the proper block.

Coaching Pointers:

- When you leave the huddle and get into your stance, watch the linebackers for clues that one or more of them might be blitzing.

- If the defensive end is rushing and a linebacker is blitzing, block the one who is closer to the quarterback. That will usually be the linebacker.

- When pass blocking, always block inside out! When the ball is snapped, watch for inside penetration from a linebacker or a missed block. If you see no penetration, look outside for the defensive end, then backside to help out.

- If the linebacker is coming hard, chop him. If his rush is controlled, pass block him.

- Always step **up** to block a linebacker, **out** to block a defensive end!

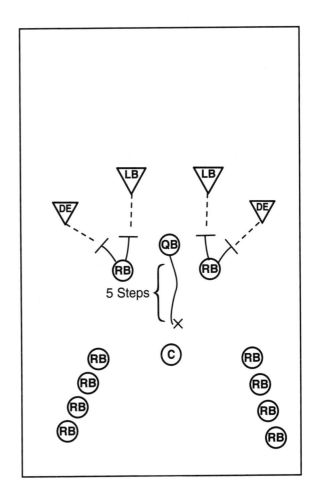

Set-up and Instructions:

Position two running backs in a normal alignment: I, split, pro set, etc. Align two backs as 52 linebackers opposite them and two more as defensive ends. Hand signal one or both linebackers to blitz when the ball is snapped. Do not permit chop blocking for purposes of this drill, but instruct the backs to use the chop block in a game situation, especially if the linebacker is coming hard.

Tell the backs to block the linebacker if he's coming. If he's not coming, have them block the defensive end. The important thing is they read the defense to determine their blocking responsibility. Check for the proper read and for good blocking fundamentals.

96. ISO BLOCK

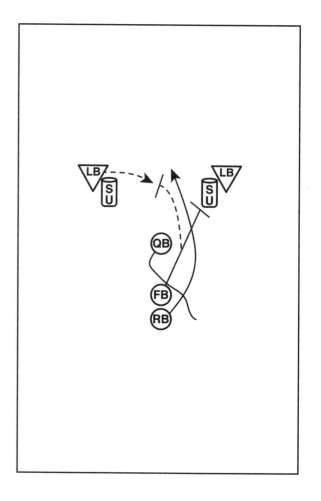

Purpose:

- To emphasize good decision-making when the fullback blocks and the running back runs the isolation play.

Coaching Pointers:

To the fullback:

- Pick up the linebacker's position immediately after the snap of the ball.
- Adjust your path to give you the best blocking angle.
- Gather before contact and explode through him, driving your legs until you hear the whistle.
- Your job is to move him; if you can't, keep your body between him and the running back.

To the running back:

- Read the fullback's block, his head, if possible. Run to the side his head is on.
- Don't hesitate when making this read. Do it while running full speed!
- The most important part of this play is that you hit the hole as fast and as hard as possible.
- **Trust your body** to make the right read and the right cut.

Set-up and Instructions:

Position two backs and a quarterback in an I formation. Position two linebackers, each with a stand-up dummy, in a 52 defensive set. Instruct the linebackers to adjust their reactions, sometimes blitzing straight ahead, sometimes stepping to either side, sometimes taking a step back. Instruct the fullback to read the linebacker's movement and to adjust his path accordingly. Tell the running backs to read the fullback's block and to make the right cut.

Check for speed from both the fullback and the running back into the hole, good blocking technique from the fullback, and the right cut and good leg drive from the running back.

97. GET THE FUMBLE

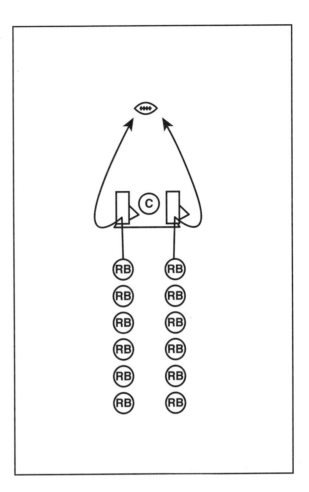

Purpose:

- To emphasize explosion and leg drive while blocking and to teach effective and safe fumble recovery technique.

Coaching Pointers:

- Explode up and through the sled! I want to feel good contact! The front part of the sled should come off the ground!
- Keep a good base throughout the block!
- Drive your arms and keep your neck bulled.
- When you recover a fumble, slide sideways on your body, scooping the ball with the arm closer to the ground.
- **OR** Grab the ball with both hands, then shoulder roll to the ground and get into the fetal position.
- Keep your body coiled and wrap your other arm around the ball.
- This is the only time I want to see one of my football players in the fetal position: roll up in a ball and protect yourself. You're going to attract attention!

Set-up and Instructions:

Position all the running backs in lines in front of the two-man sled. You get on the sled to make it a little tougher for them. Align the first person in each line approximately two yards from the sled. On your cadence, have them explode from their stances and rip up and through the pads on the sled. They should lift you and the sled off the ground. After they take three or four steps, blow the whistle, have them roll to the outside off the pad onto the ground, get up immediately, and recover a ball that you throw behind the sled.

Check for good blocking technique, agility, and aggressiveness to recover the fumble. Be sure they protect themselves while recovering the fumble.

98. HITTING GOLD

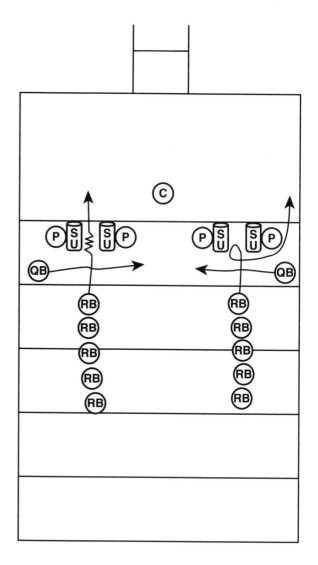

Purpose:

- To master the fundamentals for plunging successfully and safely into the end zone.

Coaching Pointers:

- Unless you have ears like Dumbo, keep your feet on the ground! Go to the air only if you know how to fly!
- Look for an opening, no matter how small, and drive through it.
- Dig your knees as hard and as fast as possible.
- Bull you neck to see where you're going and to protect your head. You can score touchdowns and still avoid injury.
- Get all the forward lean you can. Don't worry about losing your balance and falling on the ground—as long as the ground is in the end zone!
- When you start falling, be sure to do a shoulder roll. Protect yourself.

Set-up and Instructions:

Position two sets of players with stand-up dummies on the one- or two-yard line as illustrated. Position a line of running backs in front of each set of players. Have the first player in each line take a handoff and split the dummies by driving hard into the end zone. Use the above coaching pointers to assure proper execution and safety.

Instruct the players with the dummies to sometimes hold them upright and to meet the ball carrier with good resistance; at other times to push the bottoms of the dummies together so they form a V. Tell the ball carriers that when they meet resistance to drive hard through the dummies or to spin off one of them. Tell them also that when the dummies form a V to drive hard through the opening and to shoulder roll when they hit the ground. Remind them not to dive. Diving is for college or the pros—even then it causes injuries.

99. JUMP CUT

Purpose:

- To master the skill of changing direction by powering off both feet.

Coaching Pointers:

- When you plan to jump cut, land on the balls of both feet and jump diagonally away from the tackler.
- Jump so the tackler can't grab either of your legs.
- After the jump cut, hit the ground running!
- Use this technique downfield when running with the ball or immediately after catching a pass in traffic.
- Get a good bend in your knees and jump hard in either direction. Cover as much ground as you can.

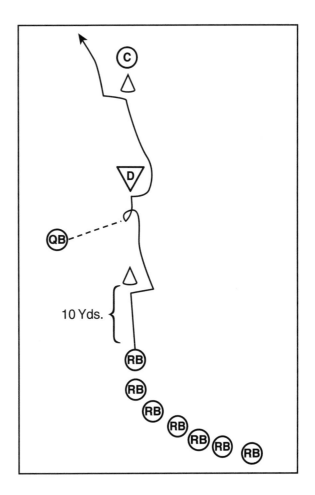

Set-up and Instructions:

Position a line of running backs approximately 10 yards in front of a cone. Give each a football and instruct him to run full speed at the cone and jump cut in either direction. Have him run a five-yard stop pattern, turn and face the quarterback, catch the ball, and jump cut away from an approaching defender. Finally, have him run full speed to the next cone and jump cut in the direction you indicate. Instruct the defender to move toward the running back as soon as he catches the ball and turns.

Give each running back at least three repetitions and check for execution.

100. FOCUS

Purpose:

- To train running backs to focus on the pitch in spite of defensive pressure around them.

Coaching Pointers:

- Maintain your pitch relationship with the quarterback.
- Be prepared for a pitch at any time.
- When the quarterback cuts upfield, maintain your pitch relationship but stay a yard behind him.
- Forget defenders! Focus on the ball! Catch everything he pitches.

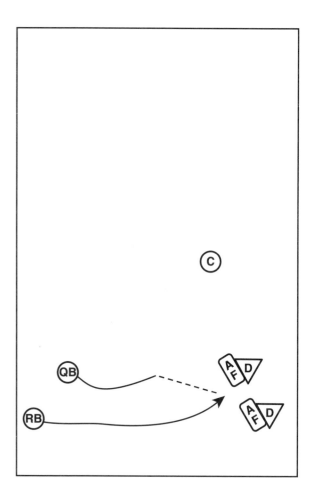

Set-up and Instructions:

Align quarterbacks and running backs in their backfield positions along a designated line of scrimmage. Execute preliminary fakes, depending on the option play, then have the quarterbacks and running backs carry out the pitch. Position two players with air flates outside the play. Instruct them to hit the running back with the bags as soon as he catches the pitch.

Vary the drill by having the bag holders hit the running back a split second before he catches the pitch. They can aim the bags at his hands or make contact with him, not so hard as to knock him down but enough to disrupt his focus.

101. SCREEN PASS

Purpose:

- To develop in running backs the right positioning for catching a screen pass.

Coaching Pointers:

- Attack the defensive end as if to block him.
- Actually make momentary contact, if possible. And don't be in a big hurry! Give the play time to set up.
- If possible, always release downfield of the defensive end. Let him pass you to continue his pass rush, then sneak in behind him.
- Never release in front of the defensive end. He'll see you, sense screen, and stop the play.
- After releasing the defensive end, run an arc of three to five steps, and stop. Create a stationary target for the quarterback.
- Get in a ready position, raise your hands, and catch the ball. Shout GO to the screen and make a touchdown!

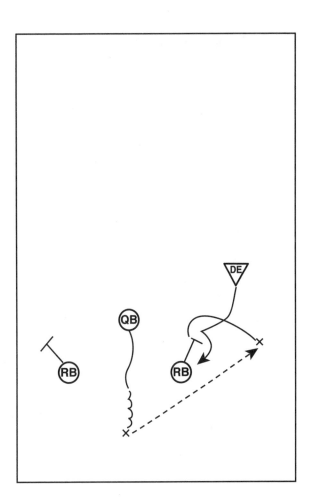

Set-up and Instructions:

Position the backs in their respective backfields. Tell each to run a screen pass. Share the above coaching pointers with the receiver and check for execution. Check specifically for ease of execution, the proper release to the screen area, and the back's ability to become a stationary target.

102. LOOK QUICK

Purpose:

- To emphasize the fundamentals of the swing or dump-off pass.

Coaching Pointers:

To the running backs:

- Look for the ball as soon as you cut. Get your hands up right away. The ball already may be in the air!
- Turn your head and look for the football immediately. Don't wait until the last second.
- Catch the ball with your hands! Don't let it hit your chest!
- Look it in! Don't run with it until you catch it!

To the quarterbacks:

- Firm the ball to the receiver and throw it just before he cuts.
- Don't throw it too early and don't throw it too hard! We don't want him worrying about **you** when he's running a pattern!

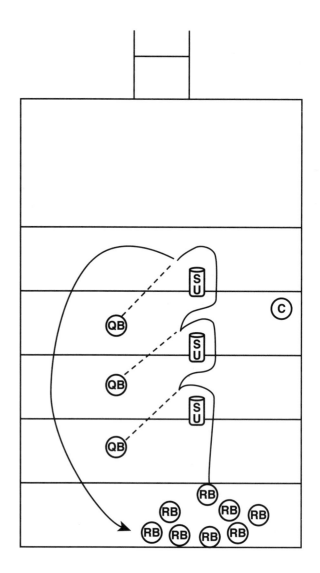

Set-up and Instructions:

Position three stand-up dummies in a line 10 yards apart. Gather the running backs 10 yards downfield from the first dummy. Position a quarterback 10 yards outside each dummy and five yards downfield as illustrated. Instruct each running back to run toward the first dummy looking straight upfield. As soon as he reaches the first dummy, he is to cut inside it and back toward the quarterback, looking for the football and catching it with his hands. He then should throw the football back to the quarterback and head upfield to do the same thing at the next dummy.

Give each running back at least three repetitions. Check for proper fundamentals according to the above coaching pointers.

103. RELEASE ROUTE

Purpose:

- To teach running backs the when and how of releasing on a pass play.

Coaching Pointers:

- Your first responsibility is to block the pass rush inside-out.
- Look for any inside leakage, a missed block, or a blitz overload.
- Help out! Block it! The inside rush is the most immediate problem for the quarterback.
- Then, look to the outside and block outside pressure coming from a defensive end or an outside linebacker.
- As you're stepping to the outside, you can look for inside leakage and adjust your steps. Don't set up on the inside first. Go immediately to the outside but look for inside leakage as you go.
- If no one rushes, release to the area vacated by the outside linebacker. Take what he gives you. If he goes wide, you swing short. If he drops straight back, you go wide.
- Look for the ball immediately. The quarterback may have to dump fast.

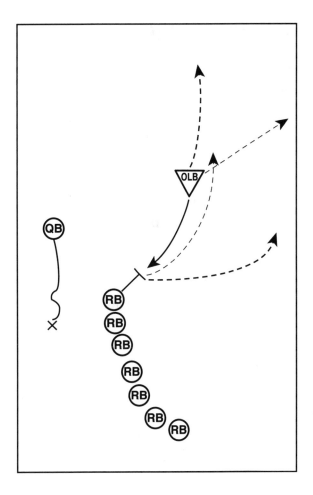

Set-up and Instructions:

Position a quarterback on a designated line of scrimmage. Position a line of halfbacks in their home position and a line of outside linebackers in a rush position. Hand signal the linebackers to either rush the quarterback, drop hard to the outside flat, or drop straight back to the onside hook zone. Instruct the halfbacks to either block the rusher, inviting him to the outside, or to release on a swing short or a swing wide pass route. Check for their blocking fundamentals, their release to the open area, and their pass-receiving technique. Check also for the quarterback's release. His pass should be firm but easily catchable.

104. HIT AND HOLD

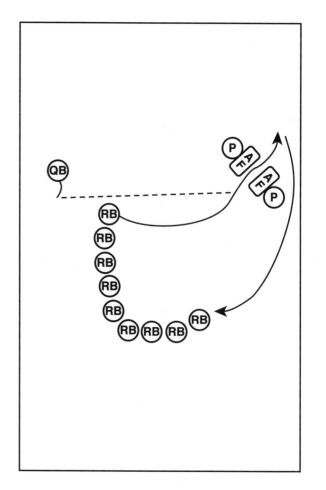

Purpose:

- To emphasize focus on the ball and to disregard potential or actual contact when catching a pass.

Coaching Pointers:

To the running back:

- Watch the ball! Watch it all the way into your hands.
- Nothing else exists **but that ball!**
- Catch the ball with your hands! Look it in, squeeze it, and cradle it into your arms!
- As soon as you cradle it, protect it with the three pressure points: your hand over the tip, the crook of your elbow, and your rib cage.
- Catch the ball **before** you run with it!
- Run a swing route so that you're heading upfield and can pivot your body to make the reception.

To the quarterback:

- Throw the ball firmly; don't knock him over with it.

Set-up and Instructions:

Position a quarterback on a designated line of scrimmage. Position a line of running backs in a right halfback position next to him. Halfway through the drill, position the running backs in a left halfback position so they get practice catching the ball from both sides. Position two players, each with an air flate, 10 yards outside the running backs and a yard from the line of scrimmage.

Instruct the running backs to execute swing routes from their home halfback position and to focus on the football and running with it afterward. Tell the two players with air flates to hit each running back just after he catches the pass: "Don't hit him too hard; you're not trying to knock him over, just give him enough to think about while he's trying to catch the football!" When the running backs become accustomed to the drill, have the players hit them with the air flates **as** they catch the pass. Check for general execution and for focus on the football.

SECTION 5

RECEIVER DRILLS

This section focuses on the following skills:

- Varying speed
- Catching with the hands
- Maintaining focus on the ball
- Confusing defenders
- Pass routes
- Play-action versus traditional dropback techniques
- Being a pass *deceiver*
- Finding the seams and holes in the secondary
- Understanding unspoken communication with the quarterback to adjust routes
- Stalk blocking techniques
- The shoulder block: when and how
- Shield blocking techniques
- Tight ends reading hot-receiver responsibilities

105. FEEL THE BALL

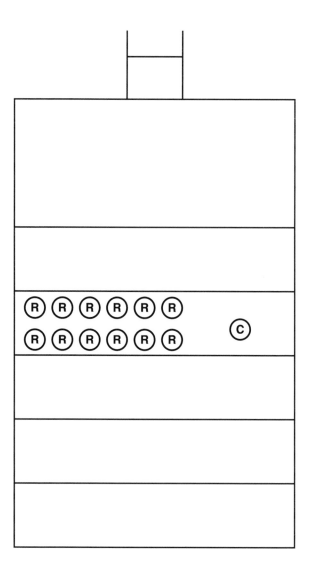

Purpose:

- To emphasize soft hands and reaction time when catching the football.

Coaching Pointers:

- Look the ball in; watch it all the way into your hands. **See** it when it hits your hands.
- Cushion the ball as it hits your hands; give with it to soften the catch.
- As your hands give with the ball, **feel** it! Feel the grain as it touches your hands. Caress it; you **like** that ball!
- Focus on nothing but the ball. See nothing but the ball when it's in flight and when it hits your hands.

Set-up and Instructions:

Pair all the receivers approximately three to five yards apart. Give each pair a football and have them play catch. Each should underhand spiral the ball to the other, varying the location of each toss. Check each pair for focusing on the ball, watching the ball into their hands, and feeling it. Feel is very important. This is a good preseason drill for emphasizing the most essential fundamentals of catching a football.

106. RELAXED ARMS

Purpose:

- To emphasize the need for receivers to relax their arms and hands when catching the football.

Coaching Pointers:

- When running a pass pattern, keep your arms as relaxed as possible when catching the football.
- When your arms and hands are relaxed, you react better to the football and catch it more softly.
- Relaxed hands are soft hands!
- For purposes of this drill, hold your arms and hands at your side—completely relaxed. Then react when you see the ball!
- **Feel** the ball. Pull it in softly as it touches your hands!

Set-up and Instructions:

Position half the receivers on a yard stripe, each with a football. Position the other half two yards behind them so that all the receivers are paired up. Have the second line turn their backs on their partners. Instruct the players with the footballs to arc them over the heads of their partners. Their partners should be looking straight ahead and up to find the balls. Their arms should be completely relaxed at their sides. If their arms are relaxed, their hands will be relaxed. When they see the ball, they should snap their arms and hands up to catch it. Remind all players to keep their arms and hands relaxed and to feel the football when they catch it.

Continue to alternate the lines—one throwing, the other catching—until all the receivers have had at least 10 to 15 repetitions.

107. SQUEEZE IT

Purpose:

- To emphasize to receivers the need to look the ball in, to catch it with the hands, and to squeeze it.

Coaching Pointers:

- Look the ball into your hands!
- Don't catch the ball in your body. Extend your arms toward the football and grab it with both hands.
- Reach for the ball! Go get it!
- If you wait for it, a good defender will get it first!

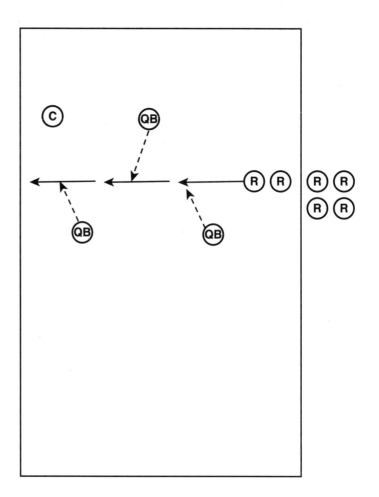

Set-up and Instructions:

Position a line of receivers on one of the sidelines. Position three quarterbacks at 15-yard intervals across the field as illustrated, each 10 yards away from the designated path of the receivers. On your signal, have each receiver run straight across the field, catching a ball from each of the three quarterbacks. After each receiver catches the ball, he should two-handed chest pass it back to the thrower. Accuracy back to the thrower is unimportant. That he catch the ball with his hands so that he can two-handed chest pass it back to the thrower is the important element of the drill.

Check for concentration on the ball, arm extension, and the use of both hands when making the reception.

108. SOFT HANDS

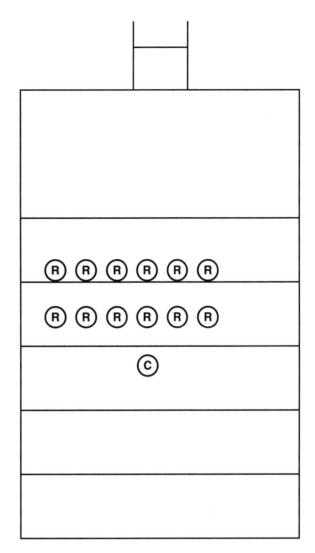

Purpose:

- To train receivers to use soft hands when making a reception.

Coaching Pointers:

- Don't fight the ball! **Ease** it into your hands!
- Don't squeeze it until you're done catching it!
- Soft hands depend on your whole body.
- Catch the ball by allowing it to continue on its original trajectory after you first touch it—right until the moment you nestle it into your arms.
- Keep your eyes on the ball throughout the entire process. Follow it in flight—right into your arms!

Set-up and Instructions:

Pair off all the receivers, give each pair a football and have them play catch. Instruct them to extend their hands toward the ball when it's in flight and, after touching it, allow it to continue its original trajectory until they nestle it in. The movement should be exaggerated in order to emphasize the importance of easing the ball into their arms. Have them alternately face each other and turn their backs to each other to simulate different pass-receiving positions.

Check for extended arms to initiate the reception, a soft follow-through, and eye contact with the ball throughout the motion. This is an excellent preseason drill for emphasizing fundamentals.

109. HARASSMENT

Purpose:

- To teach receivers to handle harassment when they come off the line of scrimmage and when breaking past linebackers.

Coaching Pointers:

- If the defender pushes you or jams you on the line of scrimmage, don't hesitate to use your hands to push off or to use any of the other techniques we've practiced so far.
- Rip through any defender who stands in front of you or tries to impede your forward progress.
- Don't put your hands on him to leverage him if you're already downfield, but don't hesitate to rip through a defender who attempts to block your pattern.
- When you find yourself in that kind of traffic, be sure to extend your arms toward the ball and use your hands to make the reception.

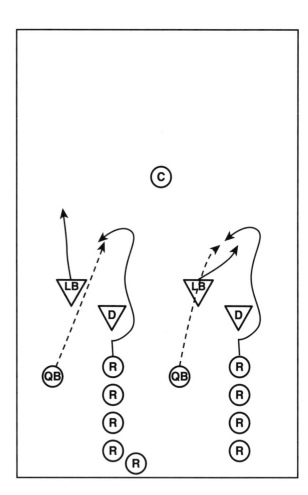

Set-up and Instructions:

Position two lines of receivers facing upfield, each with a quarterback. Position a linebacker just to the inside of each line of receivers as illustrated. Position another defender head up on the first receiver in each line to impede the receiver's move off the line of scrimmage.

Instruct the receivers to rip through the defender on the line of scrimmage or to use any of the techniques they already have practiced. Then have them read the linebacker's drop and move to an open area to catch the football. Check to make sure they find the right seam in the defense, come back to the ball, extend their arms, and catch the ball with their hands.

110. DRIVE OFF

Purpose:

- To teach receivers to release quickly off the line of scrimmage.
- To emphasize the need to take away the defender's cushion and inside or outside advantage.

Coaching Pointers:

- Especially when running a short or intermediate pattern, come off the line of scrimmage hard to force a fast and deep drop from the defender.
- Run directly at him to take away any outside or inside leverage.
- Recognize that an inside alignment suggests man-to-man coverage; an outside alignment suggests zone.
- Run your pattern accordingly, looking for the seams in either of the coverages.

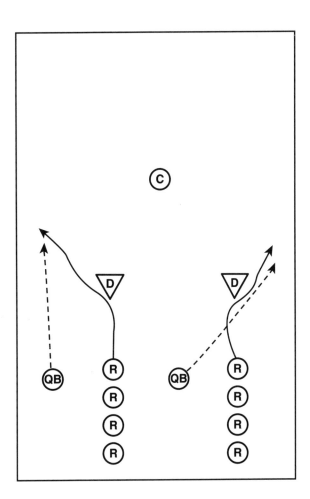

Set-up and Instructions:

Position two or three lines of receivers on a designated line of scrimmage as illustrated, a quarterback to the inside of each. Position a defender five or six yards upfield aligned either slightly to the inside, the outside, or head up on the first receiver in each line. Communicate the alignment you want by hand signaling the defenders.

Tell the receivers what pattern to run. Teach them to run posts against inside alignments, flags against outside alignments. Vary the patterns and the alignments. Have the quarterbacks alternate the cadence. On the snap count, have the receivers attack the defenders according to the coaching pointers listed above. Be sure they release quickly off the line of scrimmage, take away the defender's inside or outside cushion, and execute good patterns. Also be sure the quarterbacks throw the ball at the right time.

Combine this drill with other receiver drills. It complements several of them.

111. RIP OUT

Purpose:

- To train receivers to release off the line of scrimmage past a containing, bump-and-run defender.

Coaching Pointers:

- On the snap count, release off the line by taking a jab step in one direction, then driving off the step in the opposite direction and ripping through the defender.
- Rip the forearm and shoulder that are on the same side as your jab step through the opposite side of the defender.
- Drive the forearm and shoulder hard enough to get your extended arm behind him, then drive your elbow into his back to get the leverage to free yourself.

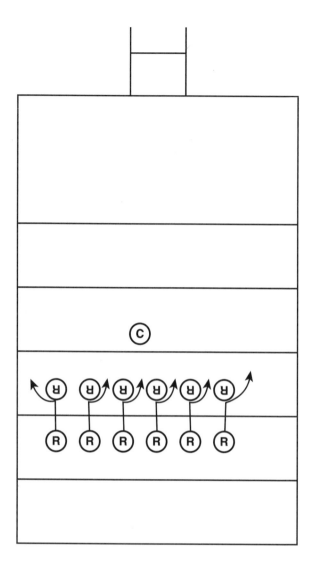

Set-up and Instructions:

Position half the receivers on a designated line of scrimmage, the other half opposite them. Pair off the receivers and instruct them to alternate being a receiver one time, a defender the next. Tell them to defend by preventing the receiver from releasing off the line. Instruct the receivers to use the rip-out technique to free themselves. Give each receiver at least five or six repetitions. Check to make sure the move is aggressive, almost hostile. This is a technique to be used against a strong, tough defender.

Variations: Modify the drill by emphasizing the following techniques:

- Drifting in either direction
- Swimming
- Hand-swatting
- Feinting and spinning

As you get into the season, lengthen the drill by aligning the receivers as indicated above and instructing them to alternate among all the above techniques.

112. FIND THE BALL

Purpose:

- To emphasize the fundamentals of catching the football with the hands.

Coaching Pointers:

- Lift your head up and look back when you hear the word "Ball!"
- Find the ball and catch it with your hands. Nestle it in and cradle it into your arm.
- Once in your arm, protect the ball with the three pressure points: cup the tip with your hand and press the ball into your rib cage with your forearm and elbow.
- **Catch** the ball before you tuck it away and run! If the ball is below your waist, catch it with your thumbs out. If above your waist, catch it with your thumbs in.
- Catch it with your hands! Look it in!

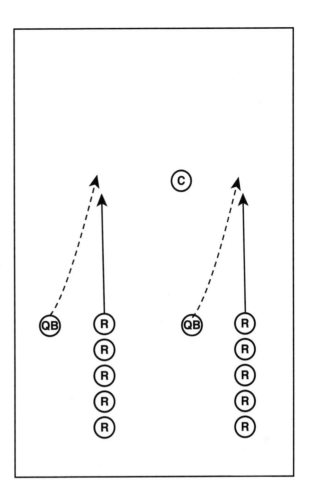

Set-up and Instructions:

Position the receivers in two lines as illustrated, each with a quarterback in his normal alignment. Have the quarterbacks alternate the cadence. On the snap count, have the first receiver in each line run three-quarter speed straight ahead. Instruct them to keep their eyes straight ahead. When they hear you shout "Ball!" they should look back and up to find the ball, catch it with their hands, and tuck it in. Check for proper receiving technique and ball protection.

This is a good preseason or early season drill.

113. SHOULDER LOB

Purpose:

- To train receivers to react to passes thrown over their shoulders.

Coaching Pointers:

- When running hard downfield close to the sideline, pivot your head as much as possible to get a good view of the ball.
- If the ball is thrown over your near shoulder (the shoulder away from the sideline), catch the ball in stride with your hands.
- If the ball is thrown over your far shoulder (the one closer to the sideline), adjust your body lean so that you don't have to turn your head to keep the ball in sight.
- Turn your head and your body back to the ball only if you have to, usually only when the ball is underthrown.

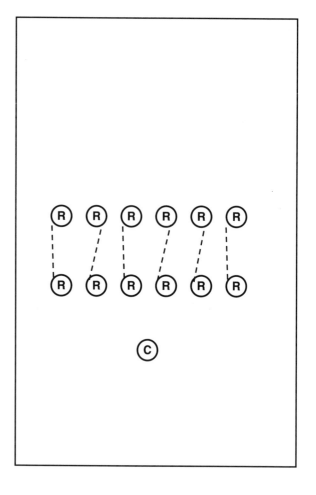

Set-up and Instructions:

Pair off the receivers and have them alternate turning their backs to each other and catching soft passes over their shoulders. Instruct the receiver to follow the flight of the ball over his near shoulder and to make the catch with his hands, thumbs out. Tell him to adjust his body lean if the ball is thrown slightly over his far shoulder.

Instruct the ball tosser to throw underhand spirals over his partner's near shoulder and over his far shoulder. Alternate tosser and receiver so that each gets three or four repetitions looking over each shoulder.

114. FIND IT

Purpose:

- To train receivers to locate the ball in flight and to catch it aggressively with their hands.

Coaching Pointers:

- Find the ball and go to it. Catch it aggressively!
- Make whatever body adjustments are necessary to catch the ball with both hands.
- Always stay alert to the quarterback. There's no telling when he might have to throw the ball!

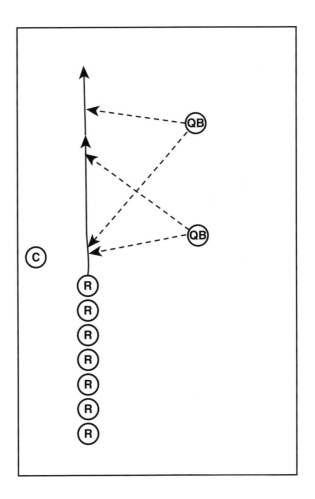

Set-up and Instructions:

Position a line of receivers on a designated line of scrimmage. Position two quarterbacks upfield and 10 yards to the right of them as illustrated, one 10 yards upfield, the other 25. Instruct the receivers to run upfield at half to three-quarter speed and to be prepared to find the ball when they hear the word "Ball!" and catch it aggressively with both hands.

You give the snap count and, as the receiver is running upfield, point to the quarterback you want to throw the ball. You might point to the first quarterback when the receiver is opposite him or after the receiver has passed him. You might point to each quarterback in quick succession to test the receiver's reflexes. You might point to the second quarterback as soon as the receiver comes off the line of scrimmage.

Check for alertness, the ability to find the ball, and an aggressive catch with both hands.

115. OVER THE SHOULDER

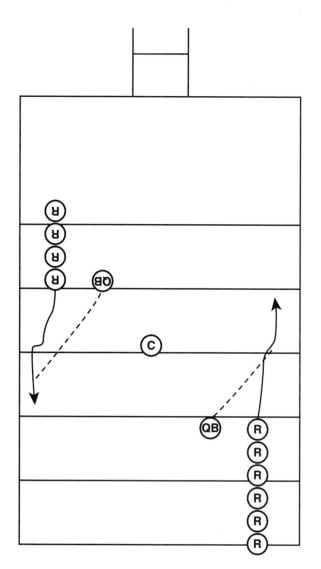

Purpose:

- To train receivers to adjust their bodies to catch deep, slightly off-target passes.

Coaching Pointers:

- When running a deep sideline pattern, if the ball has been thrown slightly over your outside shoulder, adjust your body—**not your head!**
- Turn your head only as a last resort to find the ball!
- Instead, lean your body toward the sideline, maintain your focus on the ball, and try to catch it over your inside shoulder.
- Trying to stay inbounds is secondary to catching the ball!

Set-up and Instructions:

Position a line of receivers three to four yards inside each sideline, a quarterback five yards farther inside each line as illustrated. Instruct the receivers to run sideline patterns at half to three-quarter speed. Tell the quarterbacks to throw the ball over the heads and slightly to the outside of the receivers so the receivers have to adjust their bodies while the ball is in flight.

Check to make sure the receivers adjust their bodies to make the reception over their inside shoulders and turn their bodies only if they have to. Give each receiver four to five repetitions and alternate them so each receiver runs along both sidelines.

116. IN BOUNDS

Purpose:

- To train receivers to stay in bounds after making a reception on the sideline.

Coaching Pointers:

- Be aware of where you are in relation to the sideline.
- Don't look down at it! Learn to sense where it is; that's why we're doing this drill!
- Focus on the ball! Be sure to catch the ball; being in bounds is secondary.
- Try to step in bounds with your lead foot. If you try to drag your rear foot, your lead foot may already be out of bounds.
- Put the lead foot down while catching or immediately after catching the ball.
- **Catch the ball first!**

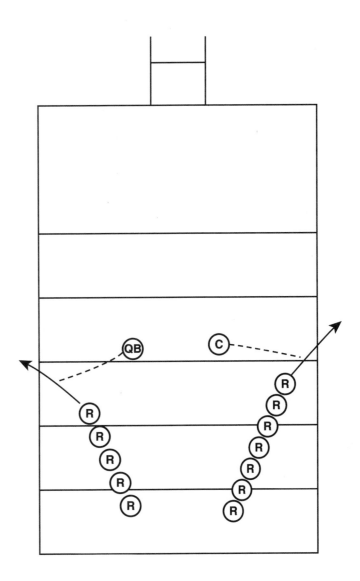

Set-up and Instructions:

Position a line of receivers angled toward the sidelines. Tell each receiver, on your signal, to run toward the sideline, at three-quarter speed, to catch the pass, and to stay in bounds by bringing the lead step down as quickly as possible. Check to be sure each receiver focuses on the ball, is aware of the sideline, and executes the fundamentals as described in the coaching pointers.

This drill should be used often enough to teach the receivers to sense the sideline without looking before catching the ball. The primary focus should always be on the ball.

117. DEFLECTION

Purpose:

- To teach receivers to react to a deflected pass.

Coaching Pointers:

- Focus on the ball; always focus on the ball!
- You can't **think about** reacting to a deflected ball! Let your body make whatever adjustment is needed.
- Relax. Always stay relaxed when catching a football. If you stay relaxed, you'll react quicker. Just let your body do it. **TRUST YOUR BODY!**

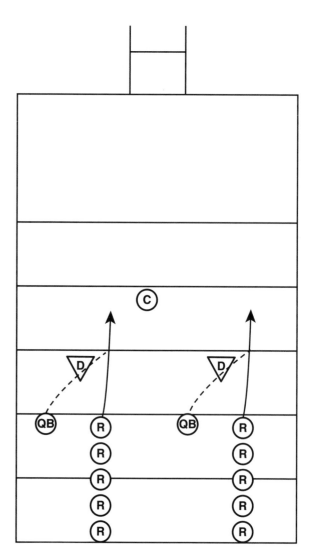

Set-up and Instructions:

Position two lines of receivers as illustrated, with one defender approximately five yards upfield of each line. Have a quarterback for each line. Tell the quarterbacks to throw the football to the first receiver in each line but to keep it within reach of the extended hands of the defender. Instruct the defender to deflect the pass by touching the ball in flight. The defender should not bat the football high in the air but deflect it slightly off its path.

Check for focus on the football and a relaxed and spontaneous reaction to the deflected ball.

118. ATTENTION GETTER

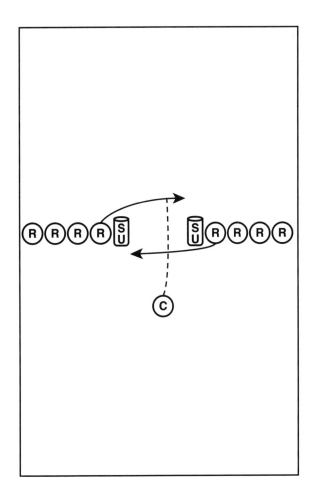

Purpose:

*   To train receivers to maintain focus on the football.

Coaching Pointers:

*   When the football is in the air, it should be the **only** thing you see!
*   Don't allow yourself to be aware of **anything** else.
*   Catch the ball with your hands! Watch it all the way into your hands. Watch it **hit** your hands!
*   After it hits your hands and **only** after it hits your hands, squeeze it!
*   Keep your hands and arms loose and relaxed up to the point the ball hits your hands.

Set-up and Instructions:

Position two lines of receivers facing each other as illustrated. Keep the two lines staggered about one yard apart. Put two stand-up dummies as illustrated to maintain the distance between the two lines. On the snap count, have the first receiver in each line run toward the center of the field. You (or a quarterback) throw a football as the two players approach each other. The receivers in one line should be told to harass the receivers in the other line, by putting their hands in the air, almost touching the ball in flight, or anything to get the receiver's attention off the ball, short of touching the ball or the receiver.

Be sure the receivers focus on the football and catch it with their hands. Have the players get in the back of the line after each turn. Be sure that every player gets at least four or five repetitions as a receiver.

119. FOCUS ON THE BALL

Purpose:

- To emphasize the need for receivers to focus on the ball when it's in the air and to ignore distractions.

Coaching Pointers:

- Focus 100% of your attention on the football! **Nothing** exists but that football!

- Watch it all the way into your hands. Watch it **hit** your hands!

- For purposes of this drill, when you catch the first ball, tuck it into your left (or right) hand. Catch the second ball one-handed.

- Concentrate, concentrate!

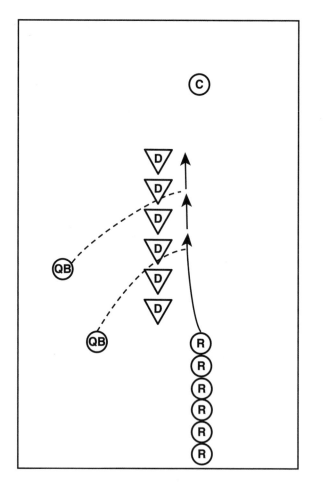

Set-up and Instructions:

Position six or seven receivers in a straight line (gauntlet) at a 90-degree angle to a designated line of scrimmage as illustrated. Align them one to two yards apart. Position the remainder of the receivers as defenders three yards downfield of the line as illustrated. On the quarterback's cadence, have the first receiver in the line run half speed parallel to the gauntlet. Have the quarterback throw the ball just over the gauntlet, immediately or after the receiver runs a few yards. Instruct the players in the gauntlet to distract the receiver. They can do anything they want, but they can't touch the ball or the receiver. They can put their hands in front of his eyes, wave at the ball, or move suddenly toward him.

Check for concentration and pass-receiving techniques.

Variation: Vary the drill by having two quarterbacks throw balls. Have the receivers catch and tuck away the first ball, then catch the second one-handed. Both balls should be thrown so the gauntlet can distract each receiver. This variation is a lot of fun but only after the receivers have developed good technique.

120. BIG HAND

Purpose:

- To train receivers to catch the ball with one hand.

Coaching Pointers:

- Catch the ball with one hand only when you have to, only when there's no other way to make a reception. Otherwise, always use two hands when catching the football.
- When reaching to make a one-handed catch, make the receiving hand as big as possible! Stretch the fingers!
- Cup the point of the ball with your hand and grasp it firmly, then ease it back into your body.

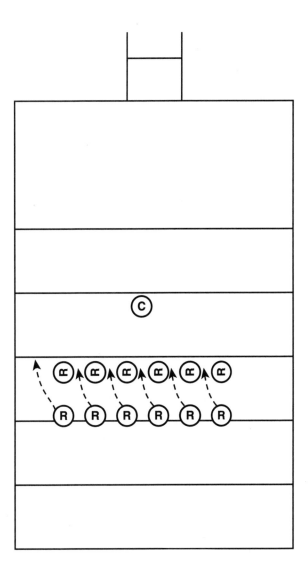

Set-up and Instructions:

Pair off all the receivers. Position them five yards apart, give each pair a football, and have them play catch. The receiver should alternate between standing sideways and turning his back to the thrower. He should take two or three steps parallel to the thrower or away from him while the ball is being thrown. The ball should be thrown either behind him or in front of him. Check how well he cups the ball with his hand. Have the two players alternate until each has had at least five or six repetitions.

121. COME BACK

Purpose:

- To emphasize the need for receivers to always come back toward the quarterback when catching a pass.

Coaching Pointers:

- Unless it's impossible because of where the ball is thrown, always come back to the quarterback when making a reception.
- This doesn't mean that you're taking three or four steps back to him; just plant your upfield foot when the ball is in the air and come back to it.
- This separates you from the defender and makes his job harder.
- **NEVER** just wait for the ball to come to you! Come back to it! Go get it!
- **NEVER** round off a cut so that you drift back into the defender! Every time you do that, you risk an interception or a broken pass.

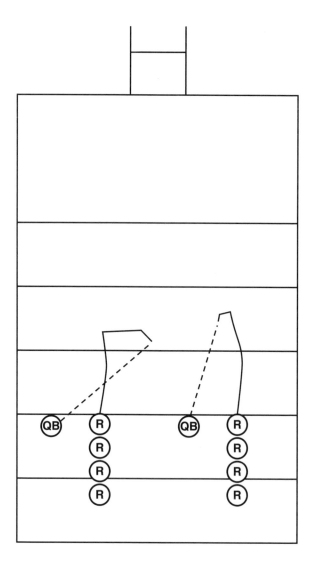

Set-up and Instructions:

Position two lines of receivers on a designated line of scrimmage, as illustrated, each with a quarterback. Have the quarterbacks alternate the cadence and have the first receiver in each line run a pattern. Emphasize the most common patterns: square outs, posts, flags, and curls.

Instruct the quarterbacks to throw the ball on time, just before, or as the receiver makes his cut. Check the receivers for good initial cuts and for a good plant with the upfield foot to come back to the ball to make the reception.

This drill should be run frequently throughout the season to remind receivers of proper fundamentals.

122. TUCK IT IN

Purpose:

- To emphasize the importance of securing the football after a reception.

Coaching Pointers:

- After you catch the ball, secure it as quickly as possible.
- Bring it into your body immediately and, if in traffic, hold it with both hands!
- When you start to run, tuck it in. Remember the three pressure points: cup your hand over the tip of the ball, secure the other tip in the bend of your arm, and press the ball against your rib cage.
- Focus on the ball when you're catching it and focus on it when you're running with it.
- Don't let anyone strip it! When in traffic, hold it close to your body with both hands!
- And get low. Bull your neck and lower your shoulders to protect yourself as well as the ball.

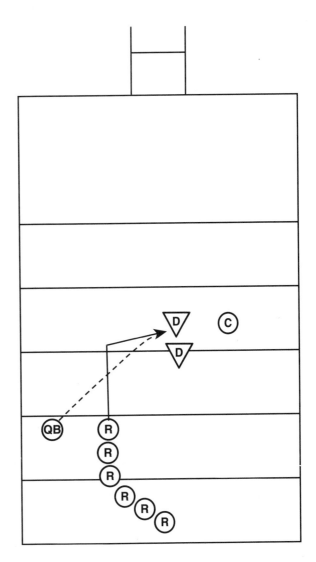

Set-up and Instructions:

Position a line of receivers and a quarterback on a designated line of scrimmage as illustrated. Position two defenders upfield and two to three yards outside of them. One of the defenders should be six to seven yards upfield; the other, four or five. Tell the receivers to run a square-out pattern so that they split the defenders. As soon as the receiver catches the ball, have the defenders grab an arm and try to pull it loose.

Make sure the receiver runs a good square-out pattern, the quarterback throws the ball on time, and the receiver secures the ball. Alternate the receivers and the defenders and give each receiver at least four repetitions. This drill is an essential during early season practices.

123. GAUNTLET

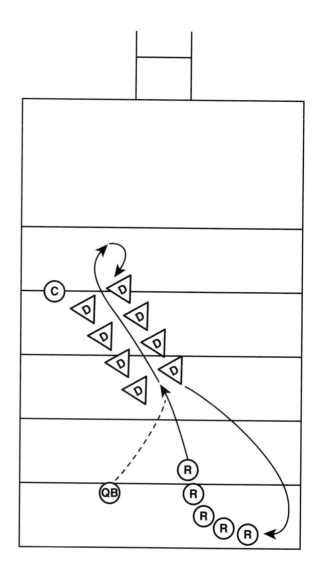

Purpose:

- To emphasize ball protection and good running technique after catching a pass.

Coaching Pointers:

- Catch the ball with your hands whenever possible and tuck it in immediately after the catch. **CATCH, CUP,** and **CLAMP!**
- If you're in traffic, secure it with both arms and make sure there's no air between the ball and your body.
- When in traffic, cup both tips of the ball with your hands and, as you run, lead with your elbows.
- Swing your arms from side to side if you want—as long as you have both tips protected. You'll have more speed and defenders will have a tougher time grabbing the ball.

Set-up and Instructions:

Position a line of receivers on a designated line of scrimmage with a quarterback to their inside. Position a gauntlet of players to the inside of the receivers and, as illustrated, approximately two yards upfield of them. Have the receivers execute a quick in route, then run through the gauntlet. Tell the players in the gauntlet to grab for the ball or for the receiver's arms. Don't just swipe at the ball! Pull it out of his hands!

Check the coaching pointers listed above. Run this drill periodically throughout the season to remind receivers of the need to protect the football.

124. BURST AND SPIN

Purpose:

- To emphasize ball protection and good running technique after catching the ball.

Coaching Pointers:

- After catching the ball with **your hands,** bring it into your body and secure the tips with both cupped hands.
- If in traffic, bend at the waist, lower your shoulders, and bull your neck in anticipation of contact.
- Don't be a receiver of contact; be a **giver!**
- Drive your legs hard through all contact! **Never** stop your legs!
- Pump your knees! Don't skate.
- Whenever you spin off a tackler, swing your non-contact arm hard and pump your legs high to maintain your balance.
- Come off the spin low so you can take on any additional contact.

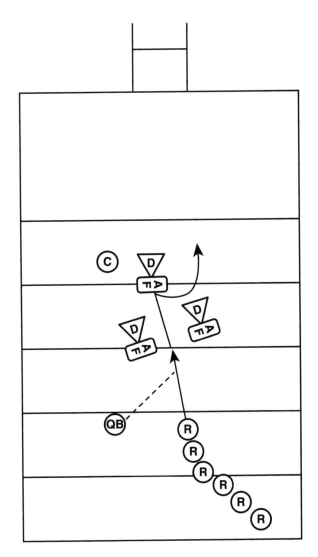

Set-up and Instructions:

Position all the receivers in a straight line pointing upfield, a quarterback to the inside of the line in his normal alignment. Position three defenders with air flates to the inside of the first receiver in the line, as illustrated. Instruct the receivers to run in patterns, catch the ball, and burst through the first two bags. Tell the bag holders to give good resistance but not to hit the receiver before he catches the ball. After he bursts through the first two bags, have the receiver spin off the third bag—in either direction.

Check the coaching pointers listed above. As the season progresses, combine several of these drills. For example, run this drill and add a defender head-up on the receiver to harass him.

125. COME BACK AND HIT

Purpose:

- To review the importance of coming back to the ball and learning to disregard immediate contact during and after the reception.

Coaching Pointers:

- Make a good initial cut, then be sure to come back to the ball to make the reception.
- **FOCUS** only on the ball! **SEE** only the football.
- This is a hard catch. If you're tough, you'll make it!
- Catch the ball and tuck it in. Always protect the football, then lower your shoulder into the defender(s).

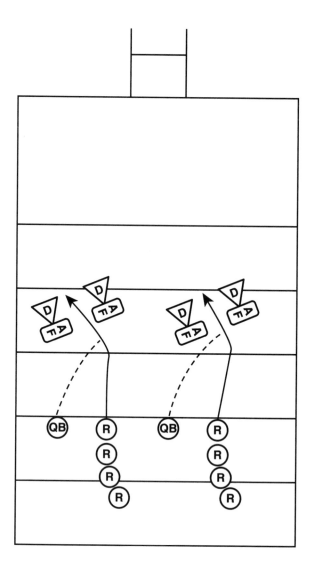

Set-up and Instructions:

Position two lines of receivers on a designated line of scrimmage, each with a quarterback. Position two defenders with air flates approximately 12 to 15 yards upfield of each line, slightly to the inside of each receiver. Have the quarterbacks alternate the cadence and tell the receivers to run post patterns toward the defenders. Have the defenders hit the receivers with the bags at the moment of the reception or immediately afterward.

Check to make sure the receivers make good initial cuts, come back to the ball, disregard the contact, and protect the ball after making the reception and cutting upfield.

This drill is excellent for emphasizing focus on the football. It also teaches receivers that making good cuts and coming back to the football creates a safe buffer between themselves and the defenders.

126. GET IT AND GO

Purpose:

- To teach receivers to run aggressively with the football after a reception.

Coaching Pointers:

- **Catch the football** and tuck it in before you start running.
- Find the first down marker and know what yardage you need for a first down.
- If you're close, put the ball in your outside arm and lower the boom on tacklers. You attack the tacklers! Get the first down!
- If you're not close to first-down yardage, get what you can and get out of bounds before contact.
- Sometimes it's wise to save yourself for another play!

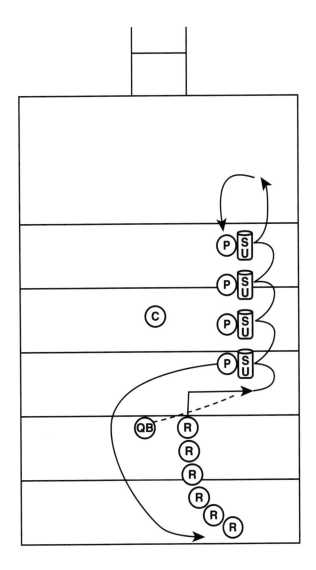

Set-up and Instructions:

Position a line of receivers on a designated line of scrimmage approximately 15 yards from the sideline. Position a quarterback to their inside and align four or five players with stand-up dummies upfield as illustrated, approximately three yards inside the sideline.

Have the receivers run square-out patterns and, after catching the ball, head up the sideline, lowering a shoulder into each stand-up dummy. Instruct the players with the dummies to lift the dummy and punch it into the receiver to try to force him out of bounds.

Check for a good, sharp cut on the square out, a timely pass, and a thumbs-inside reception if the ball is properly thrown. Also make sure the receiver carries the ball in his outside arm, bulls his neck, drops his inside shoulder, and drives his legs through all the contact. Run this drill periodically throughout the season to remind receivers of ball-carrying techniques and the wisdom of getting out of bounds at certain times!

127. REBOUND

Purpose:

- To practice jumping for a high pass, landing in a protected and secure position, completing the circle, and executing a jump step to avoid defenders.

Coaching Pointers:

- Go up and get the ball!
- Catch it with your hands, pull it into your stomach as you land, and secure it with one or both arms.
- Regardless of the direction you hook, complete the circle when you land. For example, if you plant your right foot and hook to your left, when you land, keep turning to your left. Always complete the circle after running a hook pattern!
- When the defender attacks you, jump step in either direction to avoid him. (See *(99) Jump Cut* in the running backs' drills. Use it with the receivers.)

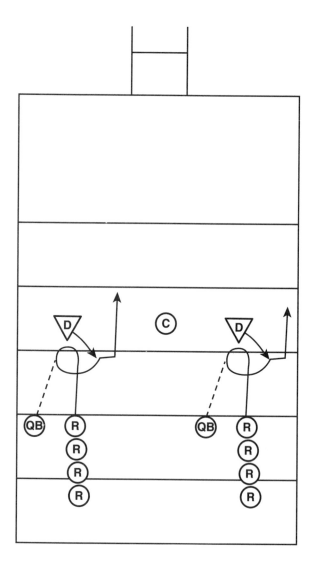

Set-up and Instructions:

Position two lines of receivers as illustrated, each with a quarterback in his normal alignment. Position one defender on each line of receivers, approximately six yards into the secondary. Have the receivers run inside hook patterns simultaneously and tell the quarterbacks to throw the ball high so that the receivers have to jump for them. Instruct the receivers to catch the ball as explained in the coaching pointers and to "complete the circle" when they land. Instruct the defenders to attack the receivers as soon as the receivers turn upfield. Tell the receivers to execute jump steps to avoid the tackles.

This drill should be used only after receivers have learned to catch the ball with their hands, to jump step, and to protect the ball. It integrates several skills and gives receivers a good feel for the big picture.

128. GO GET IT

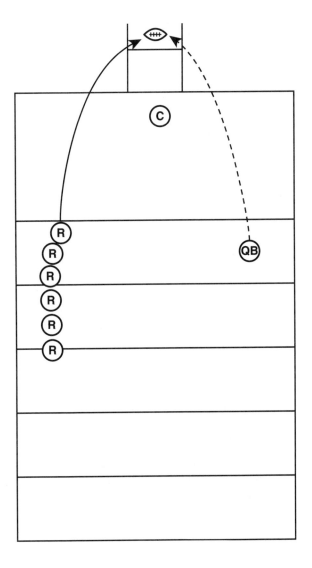

Purpose:

- To train receivers to catch the ball at its highest point.

Coaching Pointers:

- **Never** try to catch a lofted pass in the basket! Don't wait for it to come down to you. **Go get it!**
- Jump for the ball and catch it with your hands at the ball's highest point!
- After catching it, squeeze it and bring it down securely with both hands.
- Then put it in your arm and run if traffic permits.

Set-up and Instructions:

Angle a line of receivers on the goal line facing the goal post as illustrated. Position a quarterback on the 5-yard line and tell him to throw the ball over the crossbar to the receivers, forcing each one to catch the ball at its highest point.

Check to make sure the receivers are getting off the ground and reaching for the ball at its highest point. Each should catch it with his hands and bring it down securely with both hands. This drill should be repeated often throughout the season; most receivers, especially young ones, need frequent reminders to **go up and get** high passes.

129. SCOOP IT

Purpose:

- To train receivers to scoop low-thrown balls off the ground.

Coaching Pointers:

- Run your pattern as instructed and look for the ball immediately.
- If it's thrown low—so low that you have to go to the ground—let your legs go limp and lean forward into the ball.
- Leave your feet only if you have to, **but catch the ball!**
- Position your arms as if you're holding a load of laundry, your arms together, your elbows as close as possible, and your hands spread wide, your thumbs pointing outward.
- Scoop the ball and draw it into your body, then shoulder roll onto the ground.
- Make sure you catch the ball before you shoulder roll!

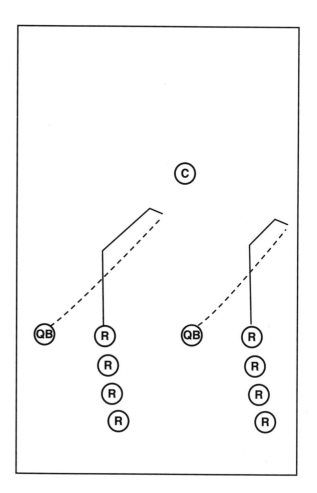

Set-up and Instructions:

Position two lines of receivers as illustrated, each with a quarterback in his normal alignment. Instruct the receivers to run a specific pattern and tell the quarterbacks to throw the ball low. Tell the receivers to catch the ball and run with it if they can. If they have to go to the ground to catch it, check for proper execution as explained in the coaching pointers.

130. DROP AND RECOVER

Purpose:

- To train receivers to come off the ground to catch the football after being knocked down.

Coaching Pointers:

- If knocked down while running your pattern, push off the ground and look for the football. Complete the pass pattern while continuing to look for the ball.
- Doing this successfully requires extra effort and an obvious desire to catch the football!

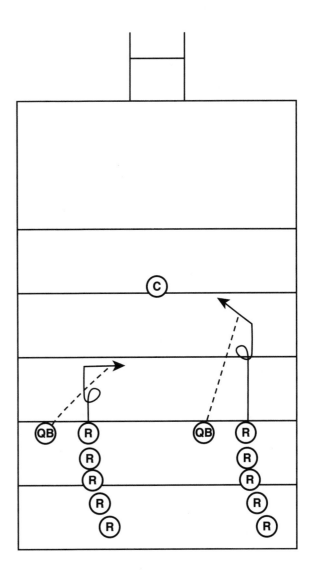

Set-up and Instructions:

Position two lines of receivers on a designated line of scrimmage, each with a quarterback. Have the quarterbacks alternate the cadence. On the snap count have the first receiver in each line run a pass pattern: a square out, post, or flag. Just before the cut, have them execute a shoulder roll or a forward roll and get off the ground as quickly as possible, then complete the pattern. Instruct the quarterbacks to throw the football just as the receivers are getting off the ground. Each receiver should find the ball and react quickly to make the reception.

This is a good drill to introduce a little variety into your practice sessions. It serves a purpose and players have fun with it.

131. STUTTER STEP

Purpose:

- To emphasize the stutter step as a way to immobilize defenders.

Coaching Pointers:

- Run the first part of the pattern at approximately 80% speed.
- Just before making your cut, stutter step two or three times, then jab step and drive hard in the direction of the cut.
- Stutter step by getting on your toes and shuffling two or three times.
- While stutter stepping, read the defender's moves and drive in a direction away from him—to a hole or a seam in the defense.
- As the defender moves toward you, you already should be moving past him into your pattern.

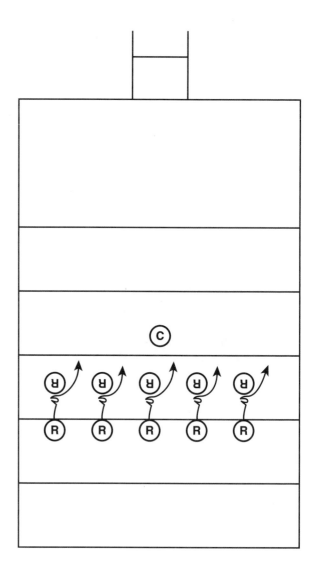

Set-up and Instructions:

Position half the receivers on a yard line, the other half facing them approximately six yards downfield. Pair them off and have them take turns being receiver and defender. Tell the receivers to run either post or flag patterns, the defenders to react to them. They can all run simultaneously. Correct poor execution and reward proper execution by having the receiver model the technique for everyone else. Give each receiver at least five or six repetitions. This is a quick drill; combine it with other drills emphasizing receiver technique.

132. BODY FAKE

Purpose:

- To practice the body fake and jab step when approaching a defender.

Coaching Pointers:

- Just before you cut, jab step and make a one-quarter turn in the opposite direction.
- When the defender crosses over, drive hard in the opposite direction—into your pattern.
- If running an outside pattern, approach the defender at an angle that takes away his outside cushion.
- If running an inside pattern, approach the defender at an angle that takes away his inside cushion.

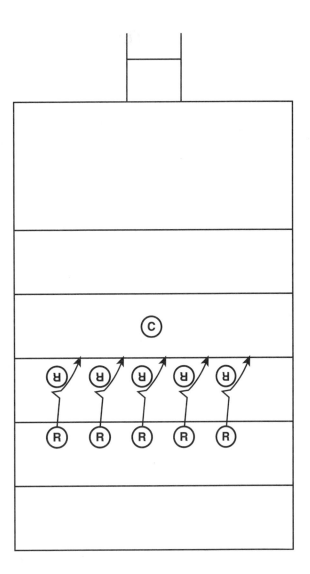

Set-up and Instructions:

Position half the receivers on a yard line, the other half facing them approximately six yards downfield as illustrated. Pair them off and have them alternate being receiver and defender. Instruct the receivers to jab step and one-quarter turn in the opposite direction of their intended cut. Be sure they make it deliberate enough to force the defender to crossover step. At the moment the defender crosses over, the receiver should be driving in the opposite direction to complete his pattern.

This is a good preseason and early season drill to emphasize pass-receiving techniques. As the season progresses, combine this drill with others to give the receivers several options to confuse the defenders. These drills should be used often enough to make sure all the receivers have approached mastery of these techniques by at least the first or second game.

133. QUICK PIVOT

Purpose:

- To emphasize the head and shoulder pivot as soon as the receiver completes a cut.

Coaching Pointers:

- In the middle of your cut, start to pivot your head and shoulders in the direction of the quarterback.
- You won't have time to pivot your complete body, so be sure to turn your head and shoulders so you can find the ball quickly.
- If the quarterback is doing his job right, the ball will already be in the air.
- Find the ball and turn the rest of your body to make a good reception.

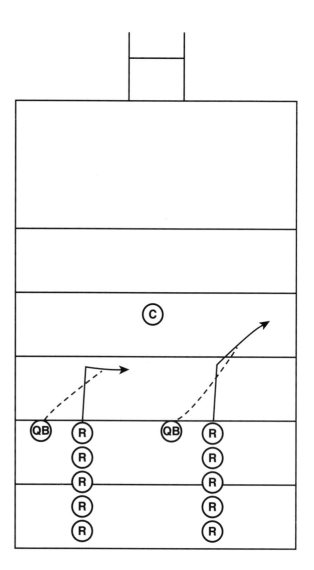

© 2001 by Michael D. Koehler

Set-up and Instructions:

Position the receivers in two separate lines as illustrated, each line with a quarterback. Instruct the receivers to run square-out patterns or flags. Instruct the quarterbacks to throw the ball a split second before the receivers make their cuts. Check to make sure the quarterbacks throw soon enough—but not too soon. The receivers don't need to be shell-shocked, just to learn to find the ball in the air!

Make sure the receivers are pivoting their heads and shoulders soon enough to find the ball right away. Run this drill early in the season and periodically throughout the season.

134. PLANT AND CUT

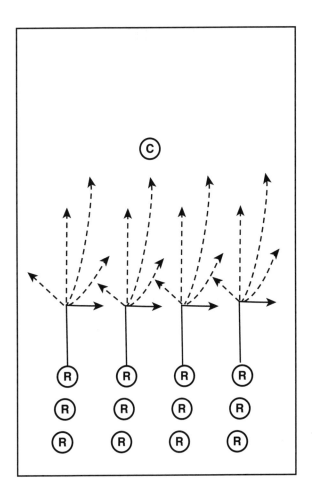

Purpose:

- To emphasize proper cuts on a variety of patterns.

Coaching Pointers:

- Remember to use all the techniques you've been learning: body fake, head feint, stutter step, and variable speed!

- For purposes of this drill, you won't be reacting to a defender, but you can **imagine** one! Visualize him and make sure you plant hard on your cuts to avoid him!

- We'll be running square ins and outs, posts, flags, streaks, and fly patterns. Remember, a fly pattern is straight upfield from where you line up. Use variable speed with it. A streak involves a quick slant-out move first, followed by a move straight upfield. Variable speed is good with this pattern, too.

Set-up and Instructions:

Position all the receivers in three or four waves on the goal line or a designated line of scrimmage. Instruct each wave, when it's their turn, to run a square out. Be sure that each runs a solid 90-degree cut and accelerates hard to the sideline. Then have them run posts, flags, streaks, and fly patterns in succession. Include any comeback, Z, or other patterns you include in your passing attack. Correct as needed, checking for the use of the receiving techniques mentioned in the coaching pointers.

This is a good drill any time of the season. It also provides excellent conditioning for the receivers at the end of practice.

135. THREE CONES

Purpose:

- To emphasize to receivers the importance of making a good cut and finding and catching the ball.

Coaching Pointers:

- Make your cut and turn your head immediately toward the quarterback. Find the quarterback!
- Chances are the ball already will be in the air. Be prepared to catch the ball with your hands.
- Keep your arms and hands relaxed as you make your cuts to improve your reaction time.
- Don't let the ball hit your body! Reach for the ball and catch it with your hands!
- After you catch it, bring it immediately into your body and apply the three pressure points on the ball: hand, elbow, and ribs.

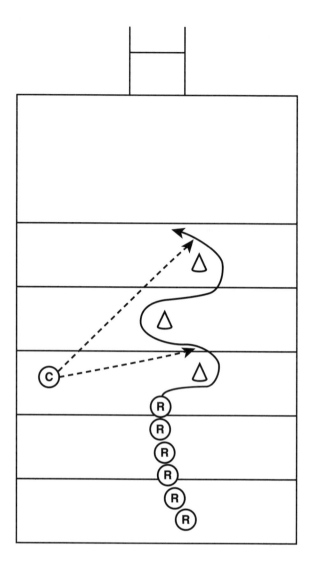

Set-up and Instructions:

Position all the receivers in a line facing three staggered cones or stand-up dummies as illustrated. Position a quarterback or yourself off to the side approximately 10 yards away. Instruct the receivers to make sharp cuts on each of the three cones, looking for the ball after cone one or cone three. Check to make sure each receiver runs a sharp cut, looks to you immediately when coming out of the cut, and catches the ball with extended hands.

Throw the ball two out of three times after cone one so the receivers have a tougher time anticipating the throw. Also be sure to throw the ball before the receiver turns his head toward you—but not so soon that he's afraid for his life! When the ball is thrown too soon, receivers get gun-shy and fail to run their routes correctly.

Thanks to Frank Lenti of Mt. Carmel (Chicago) High School for this drill.

136. SQUARE OUT AND UP

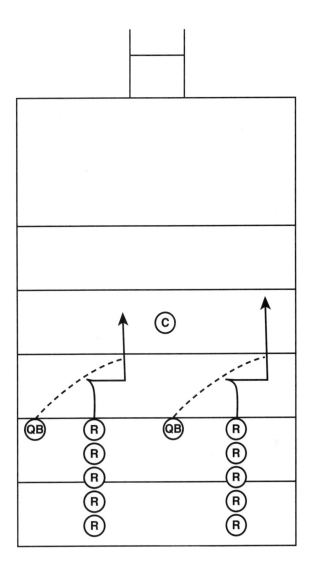

Purpose:

- To teach the fundamentals of executing a square-out-and-up pattern.

Coaching Pointers:

- Stop most of your forward momentum on your next to last step!
- Use your last step as a jab step to make a good 90-degree cut.
- Get in the habit of using a head feint in the opposite direction of your cut.
- Use the feint when the defender has taken away your cushion. You don't need the feint when the defender is favoring the side away from your cut.
- Don't round out the cut! Get away from the defender!
- Sometimes you may even have to come back to the ball!

Set-up and Instructions:

Position two groups of receivers approximately 15 to 20 yards apart, as illustrated, each with a quarterback. Have the first receiver in each group alternate running a square-out-and-up pattern. You'll want to watch both groups carefully. Have each receiver make a head feint on the out move, look back at the quarterback deliberately, then plant hard to make the up move. For purposes of this drill, the receiver should not look back for the ball until after his third step. When he does look back for the ball, it should already be in the air. You may also want to instruct the receiver to turn up field only when the quarterback pump fakes to him. A good pump fake will help influence the defender and it's a good signal to the receiver to make his move.

Check for a good head feint on the first cut, a deliberate look back to the quarterback, and good timing on the actual pass.

137. VARIABLE SPEED

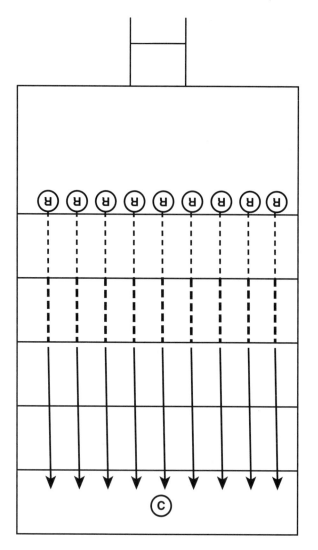

Purpose:

- To teach receivers to appear to be running at full speed but to vary their speed when running a deep pattern.

Coaching Pointers:

- Shorten the length of your stride and drive your arms less vigorously when running at anything less than 100% of your speed.
- Run only at 70% to 80% of your top speed when running a streak, a post, a flag, or any other deep pattern.
- Always save a reserve of speed to outrun the defender or to catch up to the ball on a deep pattern.
- Put the defender to sleep with something less than your top speed. Then, when the ball is in the air, **LEAVE HIM!**

Set-up and Instructions:

Position all the receivers on the goal line. On your snap count, have them run the first ten yards at 80% of their top speed, the next 10 yards at 90% of their top speed, and the final 20 yards at top speed. Check to see that all receivers are running approximately at the same speed for the first 20 yards. The faster players will outdistance the others for the final 20 yards. Be sure that the slower players are still running at less than their top speed throughout the first half of the drill. Many of them will have to go full out to stay with the faster players. This will defeat the purpose of the drill. Break them into separate groups if necessary.

This is a good, competitive drill for all the receivers, especially if they are divided into groups of comparable speed.

138. ANGLE CUT

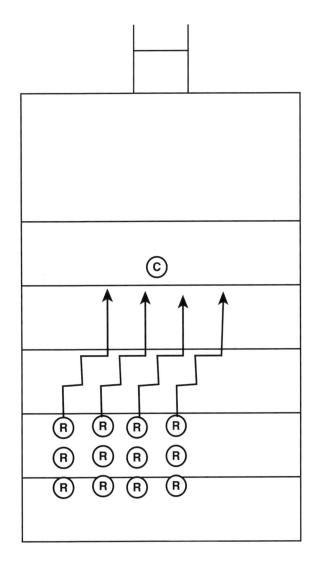

Purpose:

- To emphasize the fundamentals of executing 90-degree cuts and maintaining visual contact with the quarterback.

Coaching Pointers:

- On the snap count accelerate at 80% speed straight upfield. Stop your forward momentum on your second to last step.
- Make your last step a jab step to initiate a 90-degree cut toward the sideline.
- On the cut, look back to the quarterback for the ball.
- Take four more steps; slow your momentum on the second to the last step; jab hard on the last step to make a 90-degree cut upfield.
- Take three steps and look to the quarterback for the ball.
- Slow your momentum on the fourth step, then jab step to make another 90-degree cut to the outside. On the cut, look back to the quarterback for the ball.
- **Never** round out a 90-degree cut! **Never** make the defender's job easier!
- Continue making 90-degree cuts outside and upfield until you hear the whistle.

Set-up and Instructions:

Position four or five waves of receivers on a designated line of scrimmage. Have them execute 90-degree angle cuts as illustrated and as described in the coaching pointers. Check to be sure they look back to the quarterback after each cut and, most importantly, that they execute sharp 90-degree cuts. Correct every player who rounds out the cut. Have each wave run 30 to 40 yards upfield at least five times. This is a very important drill.

139. STAY PUT

Purpose:

- To emphasize conformity when running pass patterns.

Coaching Pointers:

- OK! Let's all stand here a minute and visualize how we run our pass patterns. Visualize yourself coming out of your stance and running a (name a passing play or a combination of patterns for them).
- Now let's run the play. As soon as you or another receiver catch the ball, stop immediately. Stand still where you are.
- The next group of receivers will now run the same play, followed by the third and fourth groups of receivers. All of you stop and stand where you are as soon as the ball is caught.
- When all the groups have run, I want to see the receivers in each position standing in approximately the same place.

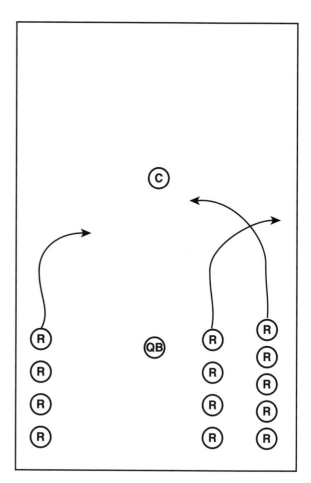

Set-up and Instructions:

Position waves of receivers on a designated line of scrimmage. Have each wave line up in a designated formation. Change the formation as needed. Call a pass play or a combination of patterns and have each successive wave execute it as explained in the coaching pointers above. When all the waves have run each pass play, each position should be standing close to each other.

Once a particular play has been completed, you can also keep the receivers where they are and explain their location in relation to different defensive coverages. Should they be a little deeper, farther inside, farther outside? Where are the seams in a particular coverage? What should they be looking for when executing their pass routes?

The drill provides a lot of learning as well as conformity.

140. CUT ON TURN

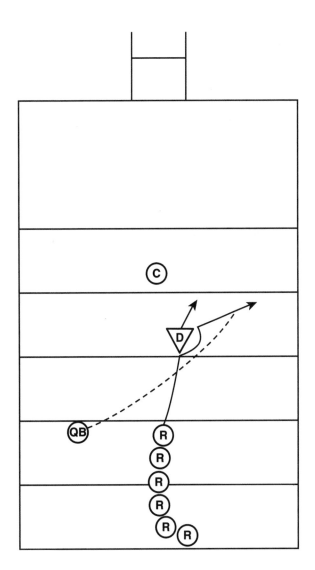

Purpose:

- To teach receivers to cut as soon as the defender turns to "go with him."

Coaching Pointers:

- Approach the defender at only half to three-quarter speed. If you're running a deep post or flag, keep him in his back pedal as long as possible.
- Take away his inside or his outside cushion and approach him so that he turns in the opposite direction of your intended cut.
- Run hard for two or three steps and get him to turn to run with you.
- As soon as he turns, cut hard into your pattern and look for the football.
- The quarterback is looking for the same things. As soon as the defender turns, he'll be throwing the football.
- This technique is good for intermediate passes. We'll use other techniques that are good for longer or shorter patterns.

Set-up and Instructions:

Position a line of receivers on a designated line of scrimmage with a quarterback throwing to them. Position a defender five or six yards upfield. Alternate the receivers and the defenders. Make sure the defender doesn't know the pattern being run. Have the receivers run post or flag patterns according to the coaching pointers listed above.

Check to make sure the receivers make their cuts and the quarterback throws the ball as soon as the defender turns to run with the receiver. The receivers should learn to keep the defender in his back pedal, to move in a direction that forces the defender to pivot, then to cut against the defender's pivot to an open area.

141. HOOK AND BACK

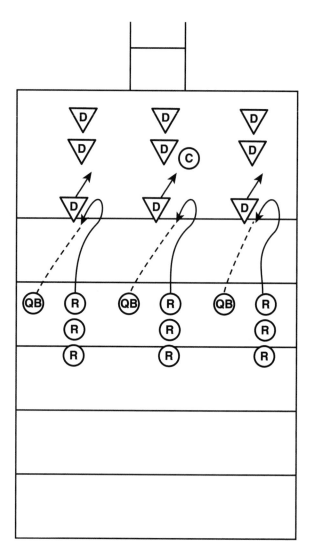

Purpose:

- To emphasize the fundamentals of running a good hook pattern.

Coaching Pointers:

- Know the distance you need for a first down! Look at a point on the field that will give it to you.
- Come out of your stance and run the first few steps of the pattern at about half speed.
- Start running three-quarters to full speed about a yard or two before first-down yardage. You're doing this to drive the defender deep.
- Try to get him to turn and run with you.
- Two to three yards beyond first-down yardage, start a backward lean, plant your outside foot, and **drive hard** away from the defender.
- Always come back to the ball—until approximately one yard beyond first-down yardage!
- The quarterback will be throwing the ball a moment before you make your plant.

Set-up and Instructions:

Position half the receivers on the goal line, the other on the 10-yard line. Tell one line to be receivers; the other, defenders. Have them alternate after each repetition. Instruct the line of receivers to run a hook pattern, emphasizing the coaching pointers listed above. Check to be sure each receiver takes three or four hard steps at the end of the pattern to drive the defender deep, that he has first-down yardage, and that he comes back toward the quarterback to make the reception.

Vary the drill by having quarterbacks throw the ball so that it's in the air when the receivers make their turns. Check to make sure the receivers get their hands up quickly after they make their turns. Run this drill several times during the season to remind receivers of the essentials of executing a good hook pattern.

142. HOOK AWAY

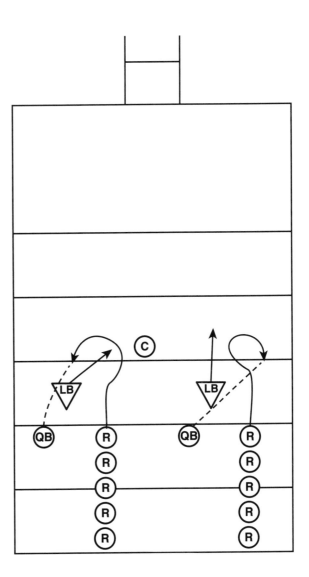

Purpose:

- To teach receivers to read the coverage of linebackers in order to hook into open areas.
- To teach tight ends or slotbacks to read linebacker blitzes in order to be "hot receivers."

Coaching Pointers:

- As you come off the line of scrimmage, read the linebacker's drop.
- Get behind him so he can't see you, then move into an open area.
- If he drops wide, move inside him. If he drops straight back, stay outside him.
- As soon as you turn back to the quarterback, look for the ball!
- Come back to the ball! Don't wait for it to come to you! Go get it!

Set-up and Instructions:

Set up two lines of receivers on a designated line of scrimmage as illustrated, each with a quarterback. Position a linebacker just to the inside of each line, approximately two to three yards upfield. On the snap count, have the linebackers drop to a shallow or a wide hook zone. Hand signal which of the two you want. Tell the receivers to read the linebacker's drop and to hook or curl into the open area. Check for a good read, a smart move into the open area, a timely pass, and a comeback move to the ball.

Be sure each receiver gets at least three or four repetitions. Use this drill as a follow-up to *(141) Hook and Back*.

143. PLAY ACT

Purpose:

- To emphasize the difference between play-action and traditional pass patterns.

Coaching Pointers:

- You're a deceiver as well as a receiver when you run play-action.
- Stalk the defender as if you're going to block him—deceive him—before you release into your pass pattern.
- Take the time needed to do this; don't hurry the pattern. The quarterback needs time to make his fakes.
- If you hurry, he hurries and we don't have the run fake we need to set up the pass.
- If you can, make contact with the defender before releasing into your pass pattern.

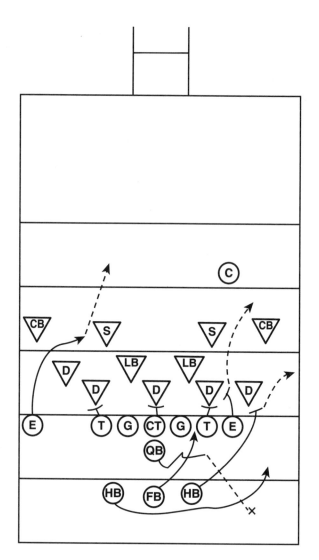

© 2001 by Michael D. Koehler

Set-up and Instructions:

Set up an offensive and a defensive team. Tell the defense to react to the offense as they normally would in a game—without the contact. Call a running play in the huddle. When the ball is snapped, count out loud until the play is completed. You probably will count to three or four. Run the play again, this time without any pass receivers. Have them watch the play standing next to you, counting to themselves as the play is executed.

Put the receivers back in the huddle and call the play-action passing complement to the running play. Count out loud while the play is being executed so the receivers take the necessary time to set up their fakes and to stalk the defenders.

Do this early in the season with each of your play-action passes to impress on the receivers the importance of run fakes and stalking techniques. Later in the season all you'll have to do is count to remind them of the time needed to run each play.

144. PASS DECEIVING

Purpose:

- To distinguish between play-action and conventional pass routes.
- To master stalk and shield blocking techniques.

Coaching Pointers:

- Be a pass **deceiver** when running play-action routes! Make the defender believe that you are approaching to block him.
- Then, when you **do** block him, he'll still be thinking possible pass.
- Don't worry about a devastating downfield block. When shield blocking, just keep your body between the defender and the ball carrier, almost as if pass protecting. Feel free to use your hands.
- Keep moving your feet!

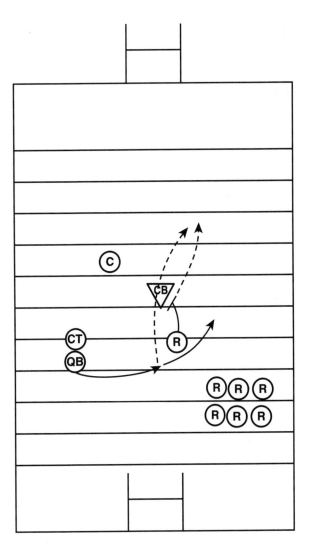

Set-up and Instructions:

Position a quarterback behind a center on one side of the field. Put one pass "deceiver" out to the quarterback's right or left. Place one cornerback or safety six to seven yards off the receiver. Instruct the quarterback to execute a roll out in the direction of the receiver. Use a hand signal to instruct the quarterback to either pass or run. Make sure the receivers are stalking the defender first, then either shield blocking him or releasing on a predetermined pass route. Watch for proper footwork during the stalk and the shield block. Also, be sure that the stalk is as long during a pass play as during a run.

145. READ MY MIND

Purpose:

- To train receivers and quarterbacks to understand when to keep going deep or when to come up short on a deep pattern.

Coaching Pointers:

- Most deep patterns are home runs, but we'll often settle for a first down or a big gain!

- Neither will happen unless you and the quarterback are on the same wave length!

- If the defender has you well-covered on a deep pattern, plant your outside foot and come back hard to the inside after you pick up first-down yardage or at a predetermined distance.

- The quarterback will see that you are well-covered and he will expect you to make the inside move.

- In other words, the defender is always wrong! If you have him beat deep, keep going! If he has you covered, cut inside at a predetermined spot and look for the ball.

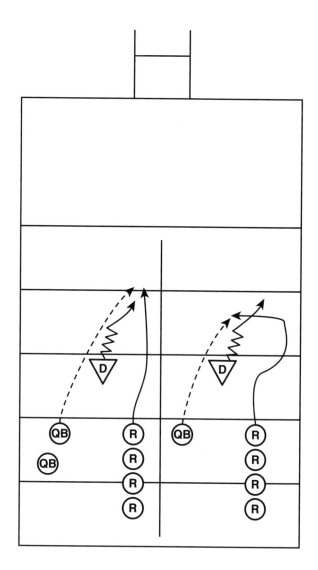

Set-up and Instructions:

Position a line of receivers on a designated line of scrimmage as illustrated, a defender five or six yards upfield of them. Position the quarterbacks to the left. Tell them to throw deep to the receiver if he has beaten the defender, short if the defender has the receiver well-covered. Tell the quarterback and the receiver the predetermined distance at which to make the inside cut if the receiver is well-covered. Hand signal the defender to cover deep or to get beat deep. Tell the quarterback and the receiver to make the right read and adjustment.

Check for the proper reads, good timing, and proper fundamentals. This is an excellent early season drill and can pay big dividends as the season progresses.

146. FILL THE HOLE

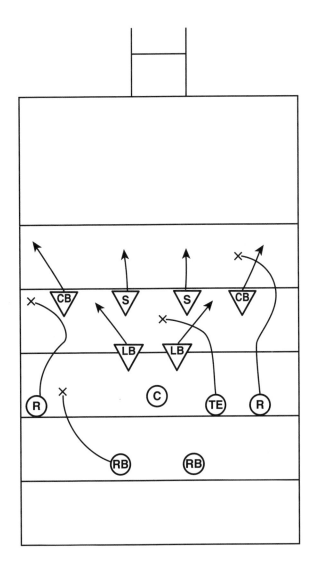

Purpose:

- To emphasize to receivers the importance of finding and getting into the holes in secondary coverages.

Coaching Pointers:

- Don't run your route as if you're following a yellow brick road!
- Watch the defensive coverage! How is your man covering you? Where are the holes and seams in the secondary?
- Run the route assigned to you but try to find a hole in the secondary and get into it.
- The quarterback is looking for the same hole. When he finds it, he's going to throw into it! **You be there!**

Set-up and Instructions:

Position a defensive secondary and linebackers in a variety of alignments and assign them a variety of coverages. Position your receivers on a designated line of scrimmage and give them a pass play to execute. If necessary, instruct the secondary to leave a hole in their coverage. Give the receivers a snap count and have them run their pass play, looking for holes in the secondary. Once they find a hole, tell them to get into it and stop.

Check to make sure the receivers read the coverage and take whatever the defense gives them. Tell them that the quarterback is looking for the same hole and will be throwing into it.

*Run this drill in conjunction with the quarterbacks drill **(59) Find the Hole**. Have the quarterbacks and receivers run them independently at first, then combine them to see if they all are making the right reads.*

147. CRACK BACK II

Purpose:

- To teach the fundamentals of a good crack-back block.

Coaching Pointers:

- Rarely is this a pancake block! When you get the chance, take it! But keep it legal!
- More often, this is a solid shield block. Position yourself so the defender initiates the contact. He should be moving into you.
- You know in what direction he is likely to react once he reads the play. BE THERE!
- The block is always above the waist and your head is always in front of the defender.
- Maintain your balance throughout the block. Keep your body between the defender and the ball carrier.
- Hurry up to your blocking position and wait for the defender to react. WAIT AGGRESSIVELY!

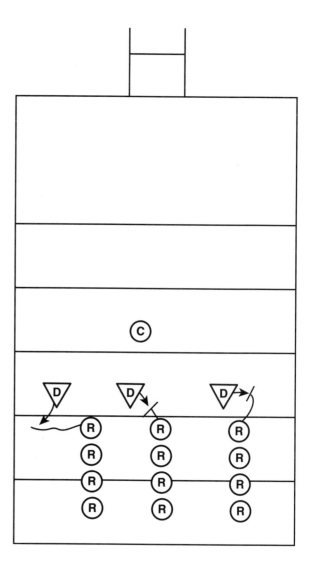

Set-up and Instructions:

Position three lines of receivers in a simulated slotback alignment. Position a defender to the inside of each receiver. On the snap count, have the defenders react by either playing soft or boxing to the outside or slanting hard to the inside. Instruct the receivers to block them accordingly. Check to make sure the block is legal. They may have to cheat to the inside if the defender is consistently slanting hard into the backfield.

148. DOWNFIELD MIRROR

Purpose:

- To emphasize foot movement and facing up to defenders when blocking downfield.

Coaching Pointers:

- Get in a good hit position before the block: Keep your arms relaxed, your knees bent, and your upper body balanced.
- Keep your feet approximately shoulder-width and move them quickly to mirror the defender's moves.
- All you want to do is **SHIELD** the defender. This is not a devastating block. Just keep your body between the defender and the ball carrier.
- Remember, keep your hips low so you can move laterally and don't overextend early.

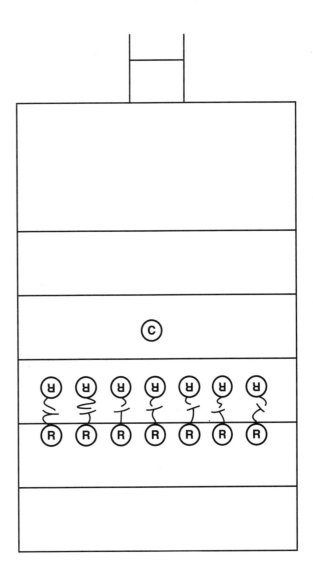

Set-up and Instructions:

Position half the receivers on a yard line, the other half facing them, approximately a yard apart. Instruct the players in one line to be blockers; the other, defenders. Instruct the defenders to move right and left randomly to try to get past the blocker. Instruct the blockers to mirror the defenders' movements and to keep their bodies in front of the defenders.

Check for a good hit position and quick feet.

Variation: A good variation on this drill is to position the receivers in two lines, a defender downfield of each line. On the cadence, have the receivers release downfield and execute a good shield block on the defender. This variation comes closer to approximating game conditions and it enables you to select certain players to model good technique.

149. SHIVER

Purpose:

- To teach the hand-shiver technique when executing a shield block.

Coaching Pointers:

- Establish a position between the defender and the ball carrier.
- Move your feet quickly to maintain that position.
- Remember during the block to always keep your hands within the frame of your body.
- Hit the defender with the heels of both hands to straighten him up and to prevent his forward progress.
- At the point of contact, lock your elbows so that your arms stay straight. If your elbows bend, the defender can break down your block.

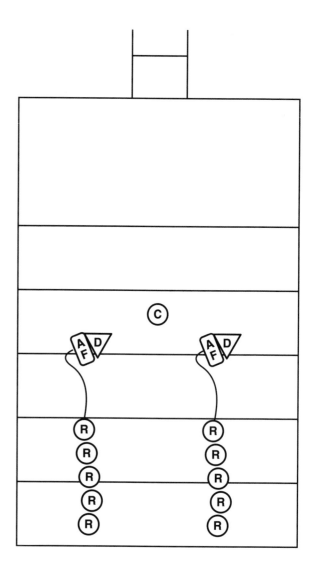

Set-up and Instructions:

Position two lines of receivers, approximately 10 yards apart on a designated line of scrimmage. Position a defender with an air flate five or six yards upfield and a couple yards outside each line. On the snap count, instruct the first receiver in each line to release and to stalk block the defender, using a hand shiver to prevent his forward progress. Use the above coaching pointers and check to make sure each receiver keeps his body between the defender and the ball, stays in a good hit position, and hits and recoils at least two or three times during the block. Give each receiver at least five or six repetitions. Use this drill when introducing and explaining the differences between play action and traditional passing attacks.

150. MOVE YOUR BODY

Purpose:

- To introduce receivers to the basics of stalk blocking.

Coaching Pointers:

- Don't let the defender move in the direction he wants to go.
- Guard him as if you're playing basketball, and you don't want him to drive to the basket.
- Stay low, keep your knees bent, your feet approximately shoulder-width.
- Be in a comfortable position, so you can move in any direction quickly.
- Nobody's expecting you to make a big hit on the defensive back, just to prevent him from getting to the ball carrier.
- Don't worry about being a tough guy; be a **nuisance!**

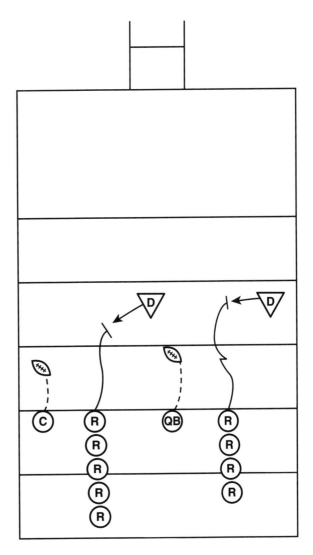

Set-up and Instructions:

Position two lines of receivers on a designated line of scrimmage. Position a defender approximately five to six yards upfield and just to the outside of the first receiver in each line. On your cadence, instruct the receivers to release upfield quickly, to break down into a good hit position when they get one or two yards from the defender and keep their bodies between the defender and a ball you will be tossing upfield. Tell the defenders to try to get to the ball to pick it up. Toss the ball to a different location on the field for each receiver and check his execution.

This is an introductory drill. Emphasize only a good hit position, quick feet, and the ability of the receiver to keep his body between the defender and the ball.

151. STALK LIVE

Purpose:

- To practice the fundamentals of stalk blocking under game conditions.

Coaching Pointers:

- Race to a position approximately a yard in front of the defender and one to two yards to his outside.

- **Get there fast** so you can get into your hit position and wait for his reaction.

- Get into a good, balanced position and be prepared to hand shiver him when he makes his move toward the running back.

- Don't try to pancake him or to block him too aggressively. He'll beat that kind of block and get to the ball carrier.

- Don't let him get to the back! Harass him, annoy him, keep your body in front of him. Don't let him get to where he wants to go!

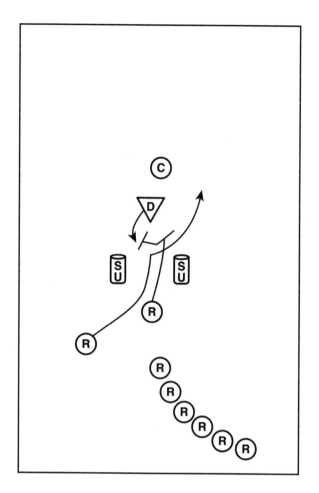

Set-up and Instructions:

Position a line of receivers on a designated line of scrimmage. Place two cones or stand-up dummies approximately five yards upfield of the first receiver, approximately three to four yards apart as illustrated. Position a defender six or seven yards upfield between the cones.

Instruct a running back or one of the receivers acting as a running back to run a sweep play, setting up and reacting off the receiver's stalk block on the defender. Tell him to run the ball any way he wants but to stay within the cones. This is a live drill. Tell the defender to tackle the ball carrier. Tell the receiver not to let him!

Alternate the defenders and the ball carriers and be sure each receiver has at least three repetitions. This drill should be used only after all the fundamental skills of stalk blocking have been mastered.

152. DOUBLE STALK

Purpose:

- To teach stalk-blocking techniques to multiple receivers.

Coaching Pointers:

- Approach the defender quickly, then break down into your hit position and wait for him to react.
- Hurry up and wait! And wait aggressively!
- When he moves, get in front of him. Keep your body between him and where he wants to go.
- Stay in your hit position so you can move laterally and have the mobility to hit and recoil.
- Don't try to knock him down! If you move at him too aggressively, you'll fall off the block.
- Harass him, hassle him, don't let him get past you to the ball carrier.

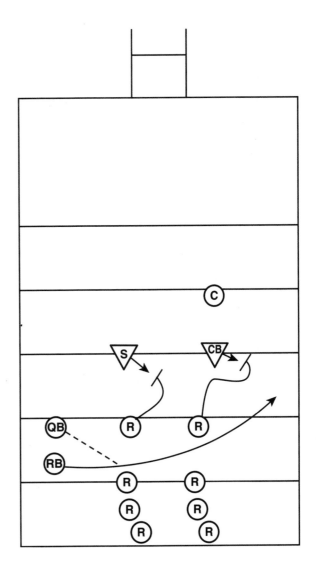

Set-up and Instructions:

Position two lines of receivers as illustrated. Position a strong safety and a cornerback in their normal alignments. Put a quarterback and a running back in the backfield. (These can also be receivers if you're working with just the receivers.) On your cadence, have the players execute a sweep play to the right or the left. Vary the direction during the drill. Instruct the inside receiver to stalk block the strong safety, the outside receiver to stalk block the cornerback. Tell the running back to try to set up the blocks for the receivers but to stay to the outside throughout the play.

Check the receivers for a quick move to their blocking assignment, a good hit position, effective lateral movement, and good shiver technique. Give each receiver at least three or four repetitions in each direction.

153. REACH BLOCK

Purpose:

- To teach tight ends how to block the outside man on the line of scrimmage when the quarterback keeps the ball on a bootleg.

Coaching Pointers:

- If the defender is on your outside and you're the tight end on the right, reach block by driving off your left leg, taking a long step with your right leg, and driving your left arm and shoulder to his outside leg.

- Stay low and position your left arm so that your hand is on the ground behind him and your left leg is spread in front of him.

- Look and act like a crab—with him caught between your arm and your leg.

- Another option: Drive into him as if to block him out of the off-tackle hole. Once you feel him fighting your pressure, pivot quickly to his outside and push him down the line. In other words, when he reacts to your pressure with pressure, use it against him.

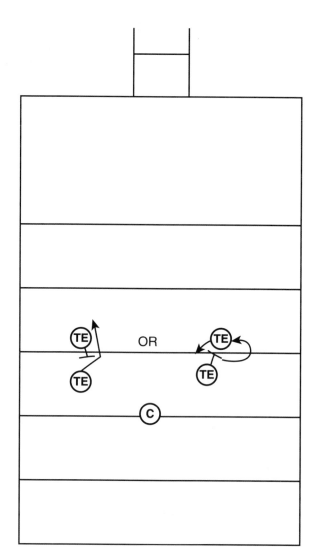

Set-up and Instructions:

Pair off the tight ends and have them alternately practice the reach block and the pressure/pivot block as described above. Be sure that each gets at least three or four repetitions. This is an excellent hook block on the outside and is particularly effective on bootleg keeps.

SECTION 6

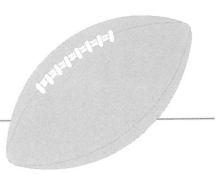

OFFENSIVE-LINEMAN DRILLS

This section focuses on the following skills:

- Stance and starts
- Pulling technique
- Base blocking
- Cross blocking
- Double-team blocking
- Sealing technique
- Pass-protection blocking
- Chip blocking
- Downfield blocking
- Screen-blocking technique

154. STANCE

Purpose:

- To emphasize the fundamentals of a good stance.

Coaching Pointers:

- Position your feet a little less than shoulder-width.

- Always point your toes straight ahead, whether you're pulling or base blocking. Never tip off the blocking scheme!

- Get a nice bend in your knees and ankles and be prepared to reach hard with your non-supporting arm. That'll give your start quickness and power.

- For more power and quickness, put about 60% of your weight on your arm.

- Keep your back parallel to the ground and bull your neck. You want to get full vision of the linemen and linebackers in your area.

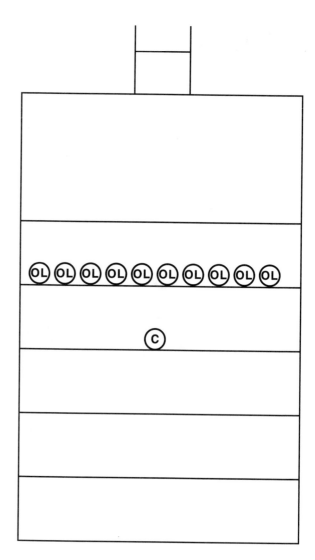

Set-up and Instructions:

Position all the offensive linemen at arm's length along the goal line or one of the yard stripes. Instruct them to stand with their feet approximately shoulder-width, the toe on the side of their supporting arm intersecting the instep of the other foot. Tell them to put their hands on their knees and to be sure their knees are almost as wide as their feet. Next, tell them to drop into their stances. Use the above coaching pointers to check the stances and to make corrections. Remind them the stance is the first and most important way to assure the power and the leverage they need to beat the defender.

155. STARTS

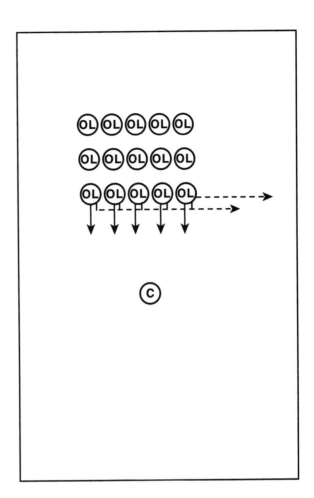

Purpose:

- To emphasize quickness and power when firing off the line of scrimmage.

Coaching Pointers:

- Always step with the foot nearer to the man you intend to block! If he's on your head, step with your up foot. If he's to either side, step with the near foot.
- Drive hard off the other foot and keep your weight low!
- Your momentum is always straight ahead, never **up!**
- Every time you stand straight up, **you get beat!**
- When you get beat, we get beat!
- Also step in the direction of your pull: right foot first when pulling right, left foot when pulling left.

Set-up and Instructions:

Position all the offensive linemen in three or four waves on one of the yard stripes. Give each wave a cadence, starting with "Down." After saying "Down," check their stances and make corrections. Then give them the snap count or say "Go!" Use the above coaching pointers as well as your own to check their starts and to make corrections. Have them start straight ahead for the first part of the drill, running only five yards. These are the critical five yards for linemen!

After a sufficient number of repetitions straight ahead, have them pull in both directions, checking for a good body lean and lead step. Put a stopwatch on them early in the season and again later to check their progress.

156. FIT

Purpose:

- To emphasize the proper stance and blocking position.

Coaching Pointers:

- Make initial contact with the front of your helmet and both arms, then slide off onto the arm you want to block with.

- **OR** Make initial contact with the front of your helmet and both hands, then drive the defender in the direction you want to take him.

- *Coach:* Teach both techniques but emphasize the head and shoulder block with junior high and secondary school football players. Base blocking with the shoulders is easier and more effective for them.

- Stay in a good hit position!

- Keep your butt down, your back straight, and your neck bulled.

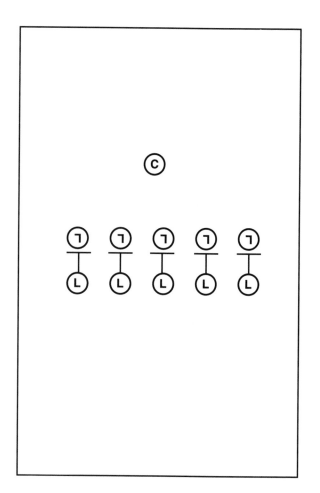

Set-up and Instructions:

Create two parallel lines of offensive linemen as illustrated. Assign one line to be the catchers; the other, the blockers. Alternate the assignments as needed. Instruct the catchers to put their arms in a catching position, the blockers to get in their stances and to fire out to make a good fit on the defender. They should not be told to explode into the defender nor to drive him, just to make a good fit. Check stances for power-producing angles and balance. Also check for head up, eyes on numbers, and either a good tight fit with the appropriate shoulder or good hand placement under the defender's breastplate.

Make corrections as needed. Take time with this drill to emphasize the proper fundamentals and to assure the right feel and fit for each lineman.

157. FIT AND PUSH

Purpose:

- To teach the fundamentals of leverage and follow-through when base blocking.

Coaching Pointers:

- Get into a good fit. Now roll your hips, arch your back, keep a good base, and drive the defender in the direction you want him to go.
- Keep a good base with your feet at least shoulder-width! Don't fall off the block or allow yourself to get pushed off!
- Drive your legs! Drive 'em! Keep your feet moving!

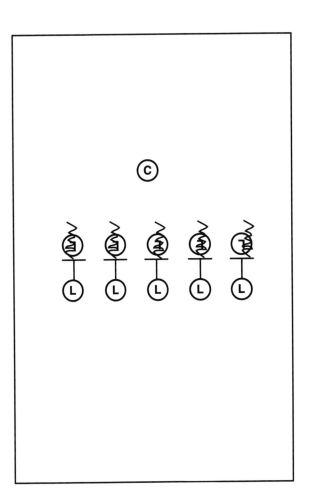

Set-up and Instructions:

Create two parallel lines of offensive linemen—one, the defenders; the other, the blockers. Alternate these responsibilities as needed. Put the blockers in a stance and have them fire out into the defenders, who will catch them. Check for a good fit: legs underneath the blockers, necks bulled, and good bases. Then tell the blockers to roll their hips, arch their backs, maintain a good base, and drive the defenders until they hear the whistle. Check for good leg drive and solid fundamentals. Use this drill in conjunction with *(156) Fit* to assure the proper sequence of fundamentals.

158. HIT, FIT, PUSH

Purpose:

- To emphasize the fundamentals of a good base block under live conditions.

Coaching Pointers:

- Get in a good stance. Assure power by getting a good bend in your knees and ankles.

- Explode into the defender. Hit him with the front of your helmet and your hands and arms.

- If you're blocking with your arms, try to lock your elbows for maximum power.

- At the point of contact, roll your hips and drive your legs. Keep your back straight and bull your neck.

- Keep a good base: feet shoulder-width, toes straight ahead, and quick, strong steps.

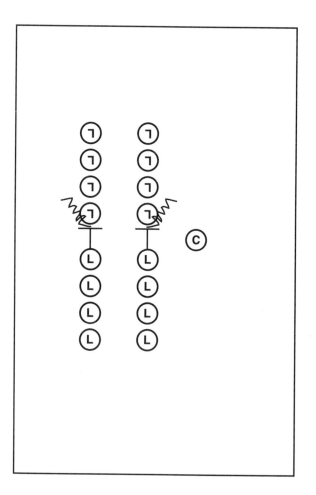

Set-up and Instructions:

Position half the offensive linemen in two lines, the other facing them as illustrated. Instruct two of the lines to be blockers, the other two to be defenders. On your cadence, have the blockers explode into the defenders, strive for a good fit, and drive the defender back. Instruct the defenders to catch the blockers but to give them as much resistance as possible. Alternate the blockers and the defenders so that each lineman gets at least four or five repetitions.

This is a semi-live drill. Future drills will focus on overcoming good defensive technique. The primary purpose of this drill is to focus on explosion, fit, and leg drive.

159. POPSICLE

Purpose:

- To emphasize a good base and strong leg drive during a base block.

Coaching Pointers:

- Go on the count—and go hard!
- Get into a good balanced stance with all the necessary power angles to help you explode out of your stance.
- Drive hard with your first step using your off arm to help drive you out of your stance.
- Keep your feet shoulder-width and use short, powerful steps to move the sled.
- Bull your neck and drive forward and **up!**
- If you can get the defender straightened up out of his hit position, you've got him beat!

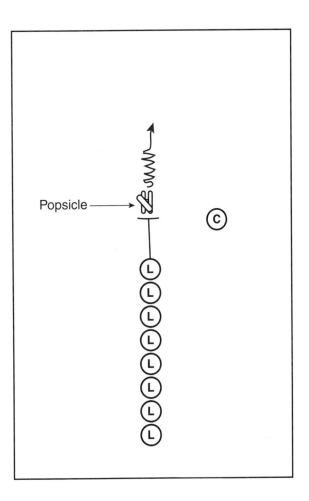

Set-up and Instructions:

Position a line of linemen in front of the one-man sled. Tell each to get into a good stance and, on the cadence, drive into and through the popsicle to make a good base block. If the block is executed well, the popsicle should lift off the ground during the first part of the block. Vary the cadence so they get used to leaving on a different snap count.

Check for a good explosion, good leg drive, and a good base. To assure a good base, tell each lineman to drive the popsicle in a straight line. On the whistle, have each fall off the sled, do a seat roll, and sprint for 10 yards. Then have each go to the back of the line. They should do everything on the run during this drill. This is a rapid-fire drill; each lineman should get at least five or six repetitions.

160. LEG DRIVE

Purpose:

- To emphasize leg drive for offensive linemen.

Coaching Pointers:

- **Explode** into the bag! Block it as if you're trying to block **through** it.
- If it weren't there, you'd end up three yards behind it!
- Rip into and up on the bag. Hit and lift! Hit and lift! Bull your neck!
- Get the defender straightened up. His strength is in his hit position. Get him **out** of it!
- After contact, drive your legs. Don't ever stop your legs.

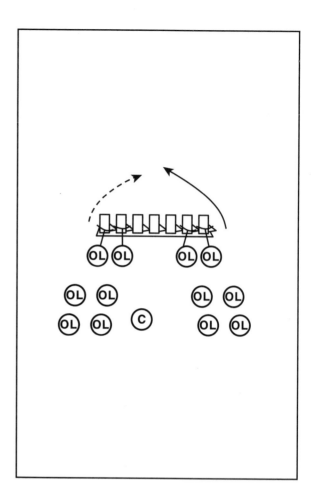

Set-up and Instructions:

Position two offensive linemen on the two outside pads on the seven-man sled. Position two more on the two pads on the other end. On the snap count, have all four linemen hit and drive the sled until they hear the whistle. The two linemen who turn the sled win that repetition. Pair off tackles against tackles, guards and centers against guards and centers, tight ends against tight ends. Find the winners within each group and have them compete with each other. Ultimately, find the best tandem and give each of them a Powerhouse® candy bar.

Run this drill often during the season. It is positively competitive and motivates each player to do his best.

161. LEVERAGE I

Purpose:

- To emphasize rolling the hips and arching the back to get leverage on a block.

Coaching Pointers:

- Hit and lift on contact! **Hit and lift!**
- Bull your neck so your head and body go forward and up, not down.
- Explode out of your stance. Always block **through** the man. If he weren't there, you'd end up two yards behind him.
- For purposes of this drill, don't drive your legs. This is the only time you'll ever do that! See how far you can move the sled with just the explosion out of your stance.

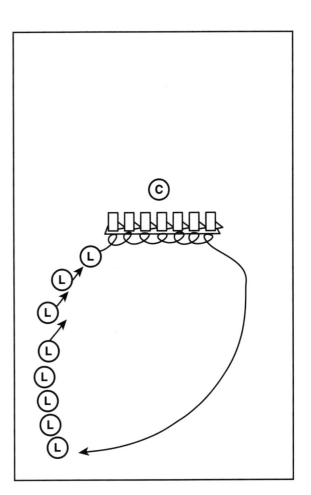

Set-up and Instructions:

Position all the linemen to the left of the seven-man sled. On the whistle, have the first man in the line get into his stance and explode into the first pad, do a seat roll and come up into his stance on the second pad. Have the second man get into his stance in front of the first pad. On the whistle, have them both explode into the pads to see how far they can move the sled. Have both do a seat roll and get into their stance in front of the next pad while the third lineman gets into his stance in front of the first pad. On the whistle, have the three linemen explode into the pads in front of them to see how far they can move the sled. Continue this process until there is a lineman in front of all seven pads.

When the first lineman rolls off the last pad, have him race to the back of the line and continue the drill. That will keep all the pads filled throughout the remainder of the drill. This is a rapid-fire drill, so be sure each lineman executes correctly. Make sure you drill **good** habits into the body memory of each player.

162. LEVERAGE II

Purpose:

- To emphasize leg drive after rolling the hips and arching the back to get good leverage.

Coaching Pointers:

- Use the same coaching pointers as in *(161) Leverage I*, but add:
- Keep your base after rolling your hips. **Don't** get pushed off the block!
- While keeping your base—feet shoulder-width!—drive your legs with three short, powerful steps, then do a seat roll off the pad and **pancake** the stand-up dummy in front of you!
- Alternate blocking technique by having them punch the pad with their hands one time, block it with their shoulders the next.

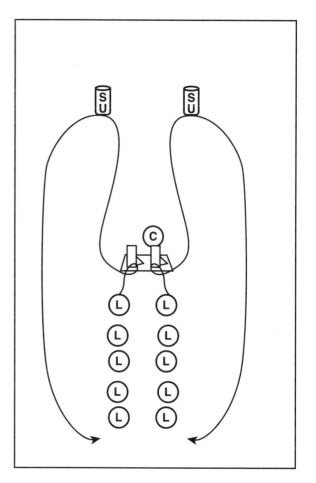

Set-up and Instructions:

Position all the linemen in two lines in front of the two-man sled. Vary the cadence so they become accustomed to a different snap count. On the snap count, have them explode up and into the pads. They should lift the two-man sled—even with you on it—if they are blocking up and into the pads. Have them alternate between blocking with their hands and with their shoulders. They should raise the sled a little higher when blocking with their hands.

Have them take three strong steps after contact, do a seat roll to the outside, get up quickly, and pancake the stand-up dummy five to 10 yards in front of them. Then have them return the dummy to its original position and hustle to the back of the line. This is a rapid-fire drill, to be used as much for conditioning as for teaching fundamentals.

163. KEEP ROLLING

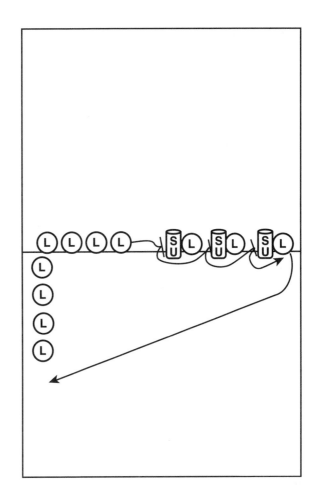

Purpose:

- To teach each lineman to feel his hips rolling under him in order to get good leverage during his block.

Coaching Pointers:

- Bull your neck and arch your back at the moment of contact. Feel your hips roll under you to give you upward power and leverage on the defender.
- If using your hands and arms, punch with the heel of each hand with a forward and upward movement and lock your elbows—if possible—to give the block added strength.
- The power of the block is in your quads. Arch your back and drive hard with your upper legs to lock on and defeat the defender.

Set-up and Instructions:

Position all the linemen so that they are straddling one of the yard stripes. Align three players holding stand-up dummies at 10-yard intervals in front of the first lineman as illustrated. Instruct each lineman to jog toward each player, being sure to straddle the yard stripe. This will assure that each maintains a good blocking base. As each lineman gets within two or three feet of a player holding a stand-up dummy, he should take a short jab step and drop to one knee. With a continuous motion, he should arch his back, feel his hips roll under him, feel the strength in his upper legs, and explode up and through the dummy.

Each lineman should do this through all three dummies. They should not hesitate when going to a knee but, instead, should roll their hips immediately and explode into the dummy. Rotate the players after each repetition and be sure that each lineman gets at least three or four repetitions. This is an excellent early-season drill for emphasizing the power produced by arching the back and rolling the hips when executing a base block.

164. PUNCH I

Purpose:

- To emphasize the essential steps when executing a good base block.

Coaching Pointers:

- When you take your first step, bring your elbows back so the upper part of each arm is parallel with your back.
- As you do this, flex your wrists so your hands are open, your thumbs pointed inward. Now you're prepared to punch the defender with the heels of both hands.
- On the second step, punch the defender with the heels of your hands. I want to hear the pop when they hit!
- On the third step, roll your hips and explode up and into the defender, driving him with your hands. Follow-through with short, powerful steps to drive him out of the hole.
- Remember to bull your neck and use the front part of your helmet to get a good fit while you punch with your hands.
- Keep a good base with your feet and stay in your hit position to maintain balance and to prevent overextension.

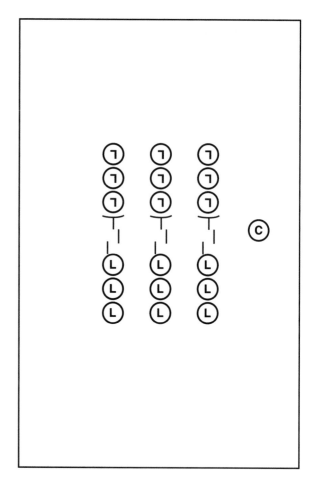

Set-up and Instructions:

Position two or three lines of linemen facing each other as illustrated. Have three of the lines be defenders; the other, blockers. Alternate the lines as needed to make sure all the linemen get at least three or four repetitions as blockers. Early in the season, especially with inexperienced players, have each blocker stop at the end of each step in order to **feel** the position and to get it into his body memory. Then have them combine the steps into one fluid motion. Make a lot of corrections. This is an important drill. It represents an early opportunity to develop good habits in your linemen.

165. STAY IN CONTACT

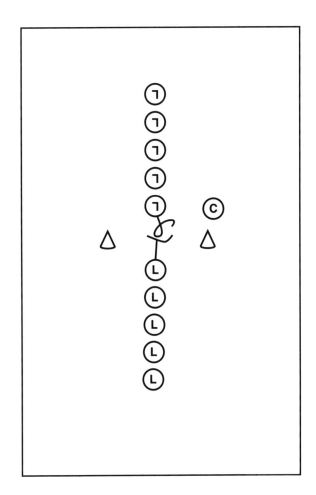

Purpose:

- To emphasize the importance of locking on—maintaining contact—during a block.

Coaching Pointers:

- Fight pressure when you feel it!
- React in the direction of the defender's spin technique. He'll try to push off you in the direction of his spin. Drive **into** the spin!
- He'll shiver you with his off hand when he tries the swim technique. Drive in the direction of the punch.
- Keep your neck bulled throughout the block and keep a good base with your feet. Never cross your feet.
- To stay locked on, you want a balanced charge and you want to see the defender.
- Solid contact, good balance, and strong leg drive will negate almost any defensive maneuver.

Set-up and Instructions:

Position two lines of offensive linemen on either side of a designated line of scrimmage as illustrated. Set two cones or stand-up dummies approximately three yards apart on the line of scrimmage. Instruct the players in one line to be defenders; the other, blockers. Tell the defenders to use one or a combination of defensive maneuvers to beat the blocker: arm under, swim, spin, bull rush, etc.

Tell the blockers the snap count and the direction you want them to drive the defender. Check each player for a good charge, a good base, and hard leg drive in order to lock on to the defender. Check also for fundamentals and levels of intensity. This is a good early season drill for teaching fundamentals and for finding players who can do the job.

166. STALEMATE

Purpose:

- To emphasize a good base and leg drive when stalemated at the line of scrimmage.

Coaching Pointers:

- Don't forget everything you've learned when a defender stalemates you on the line!
- Keep a good base and keep driving your legs!
- Keep your head up, bull your neck, and keep driving forward and up.
- **Something's** gotta give—and it won't be **you!**

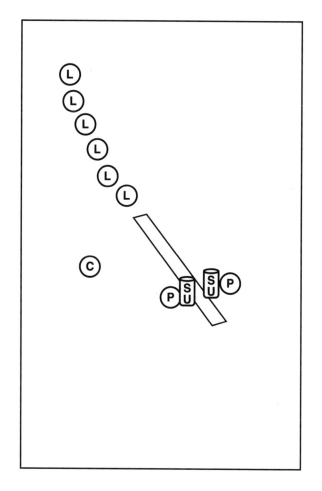

Set-up and Instructions:

Position the linemen on one end of 2" by 8" by 6' board. Position two players holding stand-up dummies approximately two feet from the other end, one on either side of the board as illustrated. Tell the blocker to get into his stance and, on the cadence, to drive into the two bags, trying to move them. Tell the two players holding the bags to stalemate the blocker. Check the blocker for a good base, a bulled neck, and continued leg drive.

Use the board to teach a good base during the block. Instruct the players with the bags to lessen their resistance when they hear the whistle and to allow the blocker to push them off the end of the board. Use this drill only after you already have emphasized blocking fundamentals. Use it especially before a game with evenly matched players.

167. DRIVE

Purpose:

- To emphasize getting to the line of scrimmage quickly and exploding into the opponent.

Coaching Pointers:

- Break out of the huddle quickly. Get to the line! Sell yourself to the defense! Let them know you mean business!
- Get there and get into your stances.
- Explode into the pad and drive the sled until you hear the whistle.
- I want to hear the pads pop, and I want to see the sled come off the ground!
- Hit and lift! Roll your hips!
- Drive hard! Keep a good base, and move your legs!

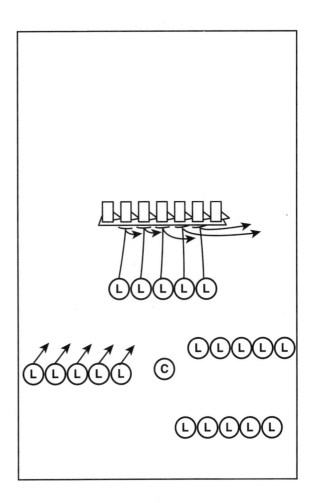

Set-up and Instructions:

Align the linemen in waves composed of the first team, the second team, and so on. Huddle the first team, give them a snap count, and break them from the huddle. They should race to a position approximately a yard from the interior five pads on the seven-man sled. Vary the cadence. On the snap count, have them drive into the sled and push it with short, powerful steps until you blow the whistle.

On the whistle, they should peel off in the same direction and the next unit should huddle up. If blocking with the right shoulder, they should peel off to the left, and vice versa. Be sure to have all teams block with both shoulders. Make corrections on the run with this drill. It should be a rapid-fire drill and is useful for conditioning linemen to race up to the line of scrimmage.

168. REACH

Purpose:

- To emphasize the fundamentals of the reach block.

Coaching Pointers:

- When the defender is shading you in the direction of the play, take a parallel step toward him, drive hard off the step, and execute a good base block.
- This is not a chip block, a seal block, or a chop block. We want a solid base block here!
- When taking your jab step, make it parallel to the line, and watch the defender closely for any quick inside penetration. If he's coming hard, come out of your step faster and make the block.
- Such a defensive move will make your job easier. If he's slanting away from you, just push him down the line of scrimmage or chip him and help out on a linebacker.

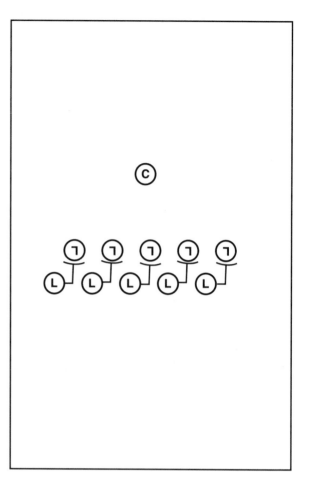

Set-up and Instructions:

Position all the linemen in two parallel lines facing each other as illustrated. Instruct one line to be defenders; the other, blockers. Alternate these assignments so that everyone gets at least four or five repetitions on offense. Tell the defenders to shade the blockers slightly, to line up on an inside or outside shoulder. Vary the cadence. On the snap count, have the blockers execute a reach block. Check for an appropriate first step, followed by good blocking fundamentals. Make a lot of corrections during this drill and have each lineman execute the block as deliberately as possible. This is the time to get the movements into their body memory.

169. SEALING

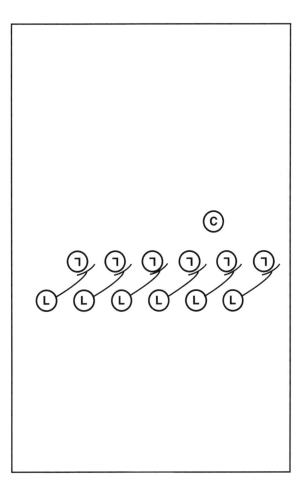

Purpose:

- To emphasize the fundamentals of the seal block.

Coaching Pointers:

- This is not a devastating block! All we want to do is eliminate penetration or prevent pursuit.

- Most of the time, you'll be blocking a defender who is head up on the blocker next to you. The blocker next to you may be pulling, so you'll have to seal the man who was head up on him.

- Remember, eliminate his pursuit or penetration! The easiest way to do it is to cut him, chop him, get your body into his legs and feet!

- Again, this is not a solid, lock-on type block. Tie him up so he can't get into his pursuit path.

- On the snap, extend your head and arms into his feet and legs—and keep driving your legs! Drive right through him, if possible.

- If you can stay on all fours and crab him, that's even better, just be sure to get into his legs!

Set-up and Instructions:

Position all the linemen in two parallel lines facing each other as illustrated. Instruct one line to be defenders; the other, blockers. Instruct the blockers to position themselves in their normal line splits. Alternate the two lines so that everyone gets at least four or five repetitions on offense. Tell the defenders to line up one man to their left or right as illustrated. Be sure they know where the block will be coming from: their right or their left. Have all the linemen execute the seal block in both directions, be sure each gets at least three or four repetitions in each direction, and make corrections as needed. This is a teaching drill, so take your time with it.

Use this drill in conjunction with *(168) Reach* so that the linemen can distinguish between the two blocks.

170. CROSS-BLOCKING

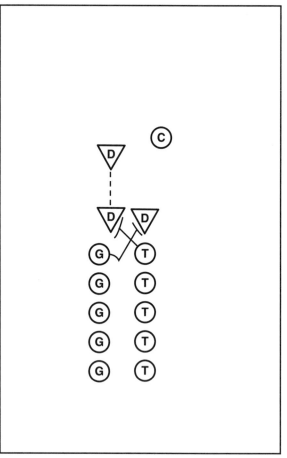

Purpose:

- To emphasize the fundamentals of the cross block.

Coaching Pointers:

- This blocking scheme may be called in the huddle when we're expecting a certain defensive alignment.
- But if you call it on the line, call it when the player next to you may have trouble with his block because of the defender's alignment.
- Remember, the player on the outside normally blocks first; the player on the inside normally blocks second.
- The first player should slant down hard, putting his head in front of the defender to prevent penetration.
- The second player should jab step in the direction of his block, look at the defender, and drive hard off his teammate's tail. Don't hesitate on the jab step! Wait just long enough for your teammate to clear in front of you.
- Use the next drill, *(171) Cross Change*, in conjunction with this drill to teach variations.

Set-up and Instructions:

Align the guards and tackles in lines as illustrated. Position defenders in front of them, varying their alignment. Sometimes have the man on the guard's head shade his inside shoulder. At other times, put a linebacker in his normal alignment, then move into the B gap to blitz. Explain why each situation requires a cross block, then have the linemen execute the blocks. Once a tandem completes its blocks, have it switch to defense. Keep alternating the players accordingly to assure that each lineman gets at least four or five repetitions.

Check for good lead steps in the direction of the blocks, quickness of execution, and blocking fundamentals. Make lots of corrections.

171. CROSS CHANGE

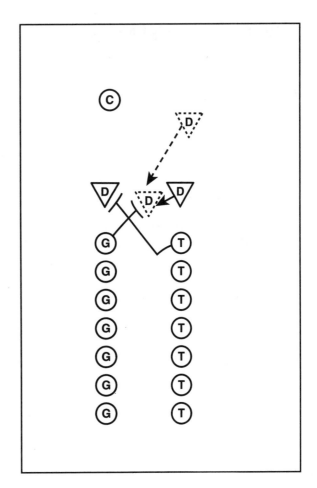

Purpose:

- To emphasize the fundamentals of the cross block with the inside man blocking first.

Coaching Pointers:

- If the cross block is called in the huddle and the defensive alignment is unexpected. . . .
- **OR** If the defense shifts when one of you calls a cross block, call "Change."
- The change call will allow the inside man to block first, the outside man to block second.
- Inside man, slant into your block immediately.
- Outside man, jab step quickly, then drive hard off the tail of the inside man.
- Remember, a good cross block is executed quickly! It allows no time for the defense to penetrate or to get into its stunts.

Set-up and Instructions:

Align the guards and tackles in lines as illustrated. Position defenders in front of them, varying their alignments. Position them head up on the guard and tackle, then shift them as illustrated before the snap. Be sure to give the offensive linemen enough time to make the "Change" call. Explain why each situation involves a change call, then alternate the players from offense to defense to assure that each gets at least four or five repetitions on offense.

Check for good lead steps in the direction of the blocks, quickness of execution, and solid blocking fundamentals.

Use this drill in conjunction with *(170) Cross-Blocking*.

172. DOUBLE-TEAMING

Purpose:

- To emphasize the fundamentals of a double-team block.

Coaching Pointers:

- The blocker **farthest** from the defender executes a DRIVE block; the blocker **closest** to the defender executes a POST block.
- A DRIVE block is a good base block. Lower the boom on the inside man and **drive** him out of the hole!
- A POST block simply prevents penetration and sets up the defender to be driven out of the hole.
- When you POST block, don't put your head to either side of the defender. Keep your head in front of him and **spread your wings** to prevent penetration!
- Try to hit the defender at the same time. That means the drive blocker is going to have to **MOVE!**

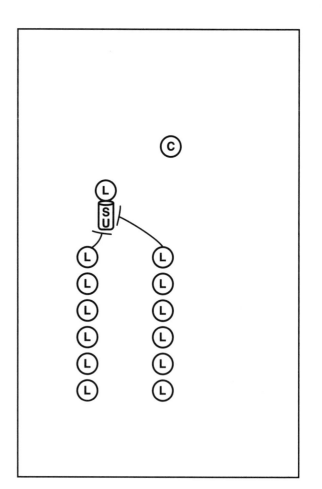

Set-up and Instructions:

Align all the offensive linemen in two lines, one player with a stand-up dummy in front of the inside line as illustrated. Use the above coaching pointers and some of your own to explain the responsibilities of the inside and the outside blockers. Alternate the dummy holder with the blockers so that all the linemen get four or five repetitions. Be sure to line up tight ends on the outside (usually drive blockers) and guards (usually post blockers) on the inside as much as possible. The tackles must learn both.

Make explanations, then check for proper execution. This is not a rapid-fire drill. Be sure to take enough time to explain, teach, and make corrections.

173. CHIP-BLOCKING

Purpose:

- To emphasize the fundamentals of chip-blocking.

Coaching Pointers:

- If the man you're supposed to block is lined up far enough away from you or if he is stunting away from you, you may not have to block him.

- You might just CHIP him; bump into him on your way to someone else to block.

- The chip block is a modified bump and shield. It will keep the defender away from the ball carrier, while you go get someone else, usually a linebacker or a safety.

- You can use your hands to chip, but keep them within the frame of your body.

- More likely, you will drop a shoulder into the defender and keep going to someone else.

- We usually can't call a chip block in the huddle, so keep your eyes open!

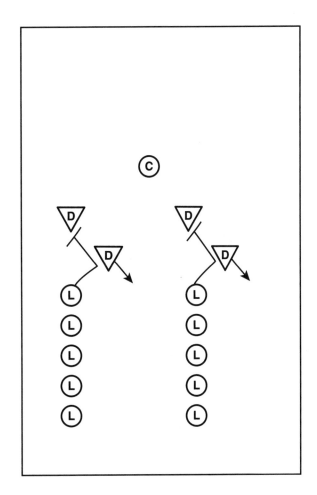

Set-up and Instructions:

Position all the linemen in two lines with four defenders in front of them as illustrated. Vary the cadence. Also vary the alignment of the defenders. Have them shade the inside of the offensive linemen or align themselves head up. If shaded, have them slant hard to the outside. If head up, have them loop hard to the outside. On the snap count, have the offensive linemen "chip" them by using their hands or by dropping a shoulder into them on their way to another defender.

Alternate the defenders and the blockers so that everyone gets five or six repetitions. This is a challenging technique for many linemen, especially young ones. Don't try this drill with very young players. They're having trouble enough mastering everything else!

174. SETTING SCREENS

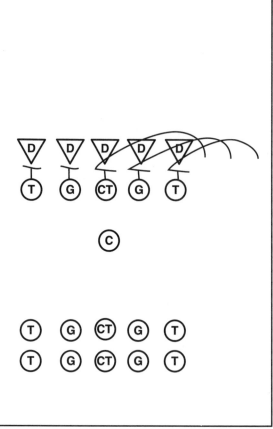

Purpose:

- To emphasize the fundamentals of screen-blocking.

Coaching Pointers:

- Block someone! For three counts! Aggressively! Don't let anyone penetrate!

- After blocking for three counts, allow your man to release past you, then move quickly to set up the screen. If you're not involved in the screen, **keep blocking!**

- Blocking to set up a screen pass does not mean that you open the floodgates!

- We want the quarterback to have enough time to sell screen—not to run for his life!

- Invite the defender to an outside release, so you can slip out behind him. If sloppily blocked, a smart defender will sense a screen and break up the play—often for a loss.

- Get to the screen quickly and concentrate on your assignment. Be prepared to block someone right away.

Set-up and Instructions:

Align the starting interior five on a line of scrimmage. Set up the remaining teams in waves behind them as illustrated. Position a defender head up on each lineman. Alternate the blockers and defenders so that all the linemen get an equal number of repetitions. Tell the defenders to rush the passer, the defensive ends to cover screen if they sense it.

Huddle the interior five and tell them to either pass protect block until the whistle or to set up a screen to the right or the left. Emphasize that the screen-blocking should be identical to the pass protection right up to the release of the defender.

Check the entire line for execution, and see how often the defensive ends sense screen. Set up screens to both sides and practice all your screens: slip, slow, swing, etc. Take time with this drill and make a lot of corrections. If enough time is spent on screens early in the year, they will become a valuable part of your offense.

175. TWO ON TWO

Purpose:

- To practice all the blocking schemes versus live stunts.

Coaching Pointers:

- Get to your blocking responsibility aggressively and quickly. The faster you get there, the more successful you'll be handling their stunts.
- Watch the defender's initial charge as you make your move to block him, then adjust your path accordingly.

Set-up and Instructions:

Position the linemen in two lines with a defender head up on each line as illustrated. Alternate the blockers and the defenders after each repetition. Huddle the blockers and give them a blocking scheme: base block, two-team, cross block, pull and seal, chip block, screen block, or pass protect. Tell them to hustle to the line and to get into their stances. Hand signal a maneuver and/or a technique to the defenders: spin, swim, slant either way, jam, twist, etc. Then call the cadence and check for proper execution.

This drill takes quite a bit of time, but it will become one of your favorite and most productive drills. It is realistic and helps linemen understand the adjustments they must make to handle defensive stunts. Use it often, at least once a week early in the season.

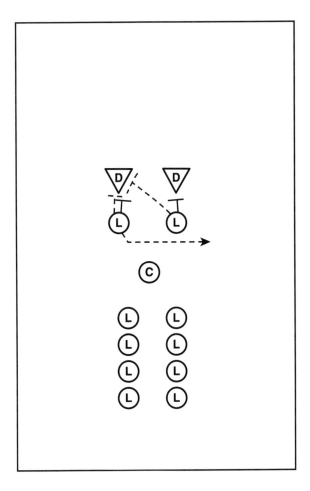

176. GET DOWNFIELD

Purpose:

- To emphasize blocking on the line of scrimmage, then getting downfield fast to make another block.

Coaching Pointers:

- The coaching pointers are identical to the other drills in this section. The primary emphasis with this drill is to encourage and motivate!
- Encourage everyone to drive hard off the line of scrimmage, then to get downfield as quickly as possible.
- Be a cheerleader and a source of a lot of positive stuff with this drill.

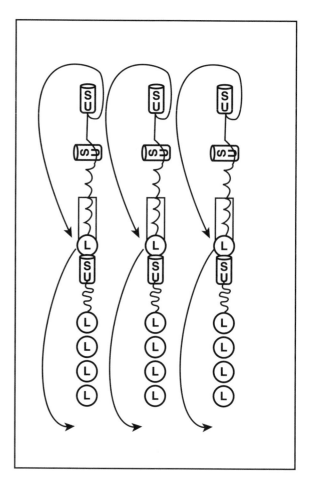

Set-up and Instructions:

Position all the linemen in three lines in front of three six- to eight-foot boards. Position a lineman holding a stand-up dummy a foot from the front of each board. Next, lay a stand-up dummy on its side five yards beyond the end of each board. Finally, position a lineman five yards farther downfield as illustrated. Be sure to alternate all the linemen so that everyone gets at least three repetitions.

Vary the cadence. On the snap count, have the first lineman in each line drive off the line of scrimmage, push the stand-up dummy the length of the board, do a seat roll, get up and hurdle the dummy, then sprint the final five yards and pancake the last dummy. Check for proper blocking fundamentals but, above all, encourage everyone to move quickly.

Vary the drill and increase its competitiveness by putting a stopwatch on everyone. Use this drill often throughout the season. It's a good conditioner and a lot of fun for everyone.

177. DO IT ALL

Purpose:

- To promote mastery of basic line-blocking techniques.

Coaching Pointers:

- Check for proper fundamentals with all the blocking techniques. Use the coaching pointers from other line blocking drills.
- This drill should be used only after the linemen have mastered the fundamentals of each block. This drill is designed to work the fundamentals into body memory.

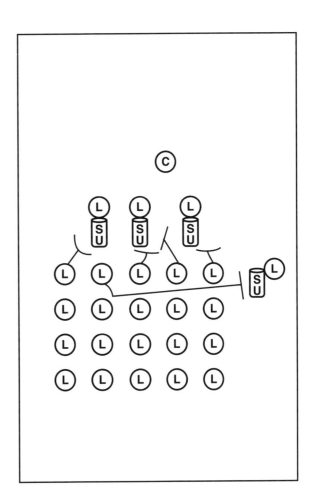

Set-up and Instructions:

Position the linemen in five waves. Position players with stand-up dummies in front of the second and third lines, between the fourth and fifth lines, and outside the fifth line as illustrated. Instruct the first lineman to seal the dummy to his inside, the second lineman to pull and trap the outside dummy, the third and fourth linemen to double team the middle dummy, and the fifth lineman to down block the dummy to his inside. See the diagram.

Alternate the linemen, irrespective of their positions, among all five places in each wave. All of them should practice each blocking technique. Take time with this drill. Give everyone at least five repetitions.

178. THE ARENA

Purpose:

- To promote challenges among linemen and to emphasize intensity during execution.

Coaching Pointers:

- This drill is not a time for coaching pointers. The coach is little more than a spectator and a cheerleader during this drill.

- If a player's performance is particularly bad, the coach may need to make a comment or two, but comments should be kept to a minimum. This drill is more motivational than instructive.

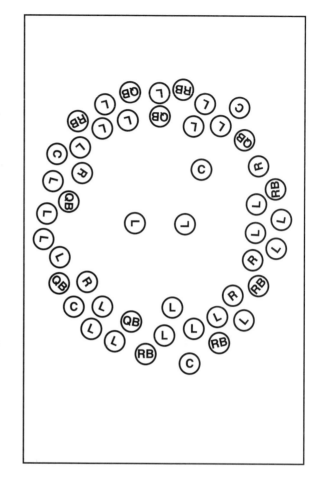

Set-up and Instructions:

A couple days before the game, tell the linemen, "OK, it's arena time! Who wants to challenge for a better position?" Tell all the linemen, maybe the entire team, coaches included, to circle the challengers to create an arena. Then, have the challenger and the man he's challenging alternate between offense and defense. Give them one or two tries each way. Prior to and during contact, allow the entire team to shout encouragement to both players—to get them pumped!

You announce the winner so that the drill doesn't become a popularity contest, but have the team applaud and shout praise for both players. Use the time to motivate young players and to congratulate veterans for their courage and effort. This is an excellent opportunity for coaches to praise players and for players to pump up for intense competition. But be careful; it can become very competitive.

Use the drill weekly. "The arena" often becomes the battle cry for extra effort during tough games.

Thanks to Paul Adams of Deerfield (Illinois) High School for this drill.

179. SET UP

Purpose:

- To emphasize the importance of pass-protection blocking by assuring the proper set up.

Coaching Pointers:

- Pinch the toe of your drive foot! Push it into the ground to give you good explosion!
- Snap up into a good hit position: legs shoulder-width, knees bent, arms up, elbows locked, and neck bulled.
- Keep your tail down and show me some chest.
- When sliding, step with your near foot, make the move quickly, and get into your hit position!

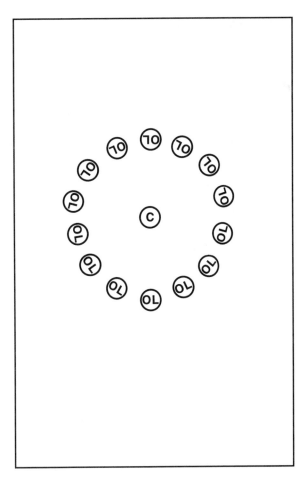

Set-up and Instructions:

Position all the offensive linemen in a circle around you. Tell them to get into their stances on the "Down" command. Check their stances for balance and power. On the snap count, have them set up either right or left to pass block or slide right or left, then set up. Each lineman should have at least four or five repetitions of setting up right, then left, and of sliding right, then left. Make a lot of corrections early in the season. Don't hurry this drill. The number of repetitions are not so important as each player's understanding and execution.

Thanks to Frank Lenti of Mt. Carmel (Chicago) High School for this drill.

180. PUNCH II

Purpose:

- To practice the fundamentals of the pass-blocking punch after executing a good set up.

Coaching Pointers:

- I don't want to see how far you can drive the defender; just keep him off the quarterback!

- Run blocking and pass blocking are different. I'm not interested in forward movement; I want to see good lateral and backward movement. Keep your body between the defender and the quarterback.

- It all starts with a good set up, followed by a solid punch move into the defender.

- Punch with the heels of both hands after you get into a good hit position. Hit the defender's numbers—on the rise. Punch out and up with your arms and hands.

- Punch only with your arms and hands. I don't want to see any other part of your body moving forward.

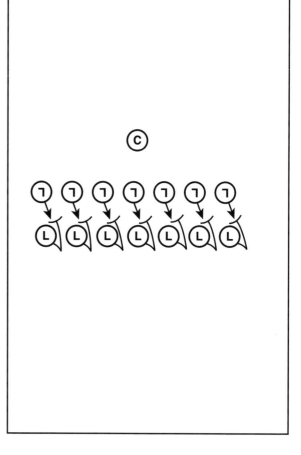

Set-up and Instructions:

Pair off all the linemen. Have them alternate between being the blocker and the rusher. On their own cadence, they should set up and punch the rusher, staying in a good hit position. The move should be very deliberate. Check for proper execution and make as many corrections as needed. This is not a rapid-fire drill. The coach should move among all the players to correct and to teach. Assure at least 10 repetitions for everyone.

181. PUNCH AND MOVE

Purpose:

- To emphasize and repeat the mechanics of punching, moving, and locking.

Coaching Pointers:

- Stay in your hit position!
- Punch hard and lock your elbows as much as possible. Keep the defender out of your body.
- Move your feet quickly from one pad to the next! Maintain good balance.
- Don't overextend. Stay balanced. Be able to move in any direction!

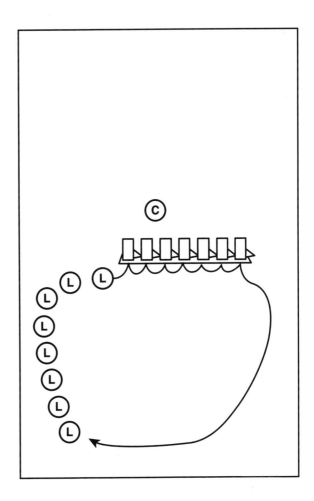

Set-up and Instructions:

Position all the linemen to the left of the seven-man sled. Have the first get into his hit position in front of the first pad. On the whistle or your command, have him punch and lock on the pad, then move quickly to the next pad. Have the remaining linemen follow in order, each punching, locking, and moving to the next pad. The more linemen hit the pads, the more the sled should rise off the ground. Some of them will want to get the sled high in the air. Discourage this. In order to raise the sled, they have to overextend their bodies. They should remain balanced and in their hit positions throughout the drill.

Check for balance, a strong hit position, a good punch and lock, and quick shuffle steps from one pad to the next.

182. HAND JAM

Purpose:

- To develop the upper body techniques and footwork needed to block effectively with the hands.

Coaching Pointers:

- Stay in your hit position at all times throughout the drill.
- Keep your arms pointed toward the defensive player, keeping your elbows locked at all times.
- Move your feet to remain in front of the defensive player. Always keep your body between him and the quarterback.
- Always keep your arms within the frame of your body.

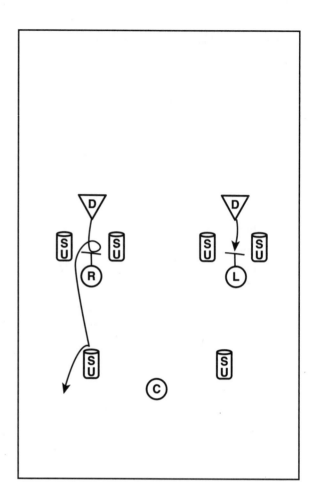

Set-up and Instructions:

Lay two sets of stand-up dummies parallel to each other, leaving approximately three yards between each set of dummies. Position a blocker on one side of each set, a defensive player on the other side facing him. Instruct the defensive player to use whatever skills are necessary to destroy the offensive player's block and to knock over the upright dummy as illustrated.

Instruct the offensive player to block the defensive player with his hands, keeping them within the frame of his body at all times. Use your cadence and allow only four or five seconds for defensive players to reach the stand-up dummy. Operate each group simultaneously or alternately and rotate the players until each has two turns on offensive and defense.

Use this drill once a week for both offensive backs and linemen to emphasize blocking fundamentals.

183. INVITE

Purpose:

- To emphasize proper positioning when pass-blocking.

Coaching Pointers:

- Move your feet quickly when adjusting to the rusher. The more your feet are on the ground, the quicker you can react!
- Invite the rusher to take a path that makes your block easier. Invite him to an outside rush, then push him that way.
- Punch the rusher and move your feet! Keep moving your feet! We want sideways and sometimes backward movement.
- Keep your back to the quarterback. Stay between him and the rusher.
- Don't overextend! If you overextend in any direction, the rusher will push you that way and get to the quarterback.
- Always stay in your hit position: legs shoulder-width, knees bent, back straight! If you get out of your hit position, **you're beat!**

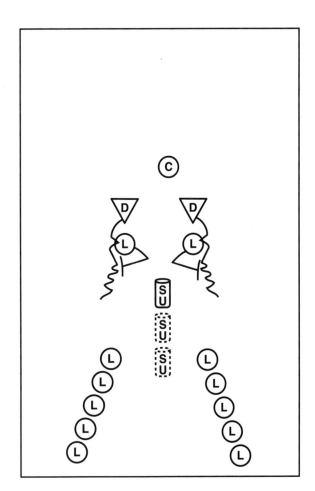

Set-up and Instructions:

Position the linemen in two lines as illustrated, each with a rusher head up. Alternate the blockers and the rushers after each repetition. Place a stand-up dummy behind the blockers to represent the quarterback's drop position. Move the dummy periodically to reflect three-step drops, seven-step drops, and sprint out moves. Vary the cadence and, on the snap, have the blockers invite the rushers to an inside or an outside path, then use proper fundamentals to keep them off the quarterback.

Check the above coaching pointers as well as your own and make lots of corrections. This is an instructive drill, so keep everyone listening. Your corrections will be as helpful for those standing in line as for those blocking.

184. MOVE YOUR FEET

Purpose:

- To emphasize quick feet and a balanced stance.

Coaching Pointers:

- Stay in your hit position. Stay balanced, and keep your feet moving. Good balance is impossible without quick feet!
- Don't crossover step! You lose a balanced position whenever you cross over.
- Move quickly to keep your body between the rusher and the quarterback.
- Always be prepared to punch and move, punch and move.

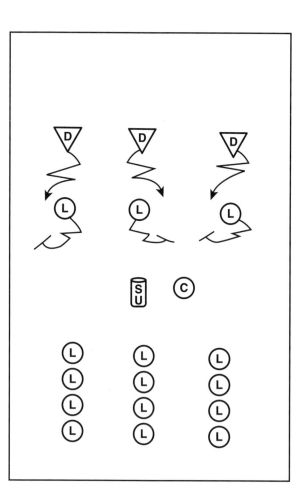

Set-up and Instructions:

Position the linemen in three lines, each with a rusher to the outside of the first man in line as illustrated. Place a stand-up dummy six to seven yards behind the middle line. Instruct the rushers to try to get to the dummy **without making contact** with the blockers. Have them feint, juke, and do whatever they can to get the blocker off balance in order to get past him.

Check the blockers for a balanced hit position and quick feet. Make sure they don't crossover step to stay with the rusher. This is a good early season drill to emphasize balance and quick feet.

185. LINE MIRROR

Purpose:

- To emphasize good lateral movement and balance when pass-blocking.

Coaching Pointers:

- Keep yourself separated from the rusher. Don't let him get into your body.
- Don't overextend; stay balanced!
- Don't crossover step! Shuffle your feet—quickly! That will give you better balance.

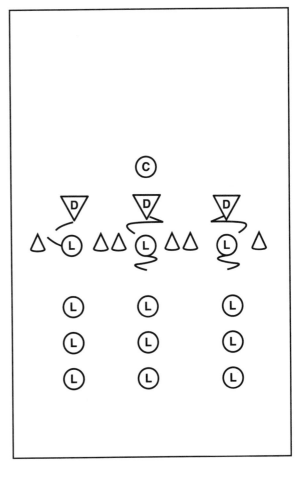

Set-up and Instructions:

Position all the linemen in three lines, a defender facing the first man in each line as illustrated. Place two cones on either side of the first man in each line, approximately five yards apart. Instruct the defender to try to get past the blocker, using whatever technique(s) he wants. Tell the blocker to mirror the moves of the defender to prevent his penetration.

Check each blocker for balance, quick feet, and a solid punch and lock. Make as many corrections as are needed. This is not a rapid-fire drill. It's a good drill for the early season and should involve a lot of instruction and correction.

186. LOCK OUT

Purpose:

- To maintain inside-out or outside-in pressure.

Coaching Pointers:

- Aim your outside leg at the rusher's crotch.
- Maintain your outside-in or inside-out pressure on the rusher.
- Whenever possible, push him away from the quarterback.
- If you let the rusher get into your body, it'll be easier for him to get the leverage he needs to beat you.
- Don't let him get his arm behind you. If his arm and shoulder get underneath and behind you, **you're beat!**

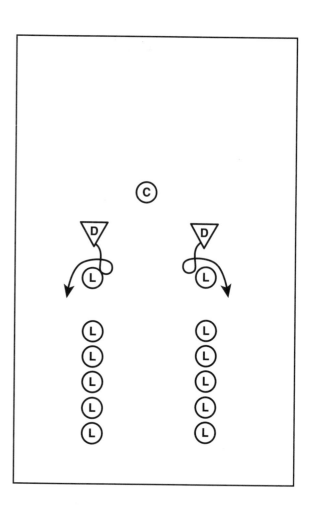

Set-up and Instructions:

Position the linemen in two lines, each with a rusher head-up on the first man in the line as illustrated. Vary the cadence. On the snap count, have each rusher work to get an arm and shoulder behind the blocker. If it doesn't work to the outside, have the rusher spin to the other side and try to get his arm and shoulder to the inside of the blocker. Have the rushers spin and swim as often as they want but to work to get either arm and shoulder behind the blocker.

Check the blockers for balanced stances, a strong punch move, good extension with the hands and arms, and quick feet.

187. TUG-O-WAR

Purpose:

- To emphasize staying in a balanced hit position throughout the pass block.

Coaching Pointers:

- Don't let the rusher push **or pull** you off balance!
- If you stay in a balanced hit position, you can move easier and **stronger!**
- Don't give the rusher any outside leverage. If he can get either arm past you or either elbow behind you, you're beat. *(The coach should demonstrate this point to make it clearer to the players.)*
- Work hard to keep the rusher locked out. He might try to push or pull you, but he should never be allowed to get into your body.

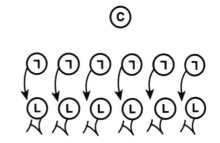

Set-up and Instructions:

Pair off the linemen and have them alternate between being blockers and rushers. Tell the blockers to get in a good hit position, to maintain it, to move their feet, and to keep the rusher locked out—at arm's length. Tell the rushers to grab the blocker's shoulders and to try to turn him by pushing and pulling him off balance.

Vary the cadence and, after the snap count, count to five or six, then blow the whistle. Check the blockers for a balanced hit position, a good lock out on the rusher, and quick lateral foot movement.

188. CHANGE DIRECTION

Purpose:

- To emphasize a balanced hit position and quick feet in order to change direction with the rusher.

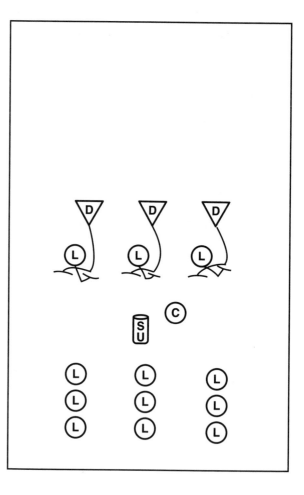

Coaching Pointers:

- Take your drop step and invite the rusher to the outside.
- Stay in a good hit position.
- Aim your outside leg at the rusher's crotch. No, we're not looking for a cheap shot, just good positioning!
- Punch for his numbers; keep your hands within the frame of your body.
- This means you have to move your feet. Don't cross over!
- Don't get out of your hit position. Stay balanced so you can change direction quickly.

Set-up and Instructions:

Position all the linemen in three lines, approximately two to three yards apart, each with a rusher to the outside of the first player in line as illustrated. Alternate the blockers and the rushers so that everyone gets at least four or five repetitions. Position a stand-up dummy six to seven yards behind the middle blocker. Vary the cadence. On the snap count, have the blockers drop step and invite the rusher to the outside. Have them get in a good hit position, punch the rusher, and aim the outside leg for the rusher's crotch.

When contact is made, have the rusher push the blocker to the outside or spin back to the inside. Tell the rushers to get to the dummy and knock it over. This drill is also a good way to find good pass rushers. Check the blockers for hit position, blocking technique, and good foot movement.

Variation: Vary the drill by allowing the rusher to move inside first and make contact, outside next. You can also put a stopwatch on each repetition. Praise linemen who hold off the rusher for a four to six count.

189. TWIST AND SHOUT

Purpose:

- To emphasize positioning for handling a stunting or a straight pass rush.

Coaching Pointers:

- Snap up into a good hit position so you can move.
- As you move out of your stance, watch the defenders for stunts.
- If the defenders twist, switch assignments, but always be in a position to move.
- Don't block too aggressively or overextend yourself. Let them come to you.

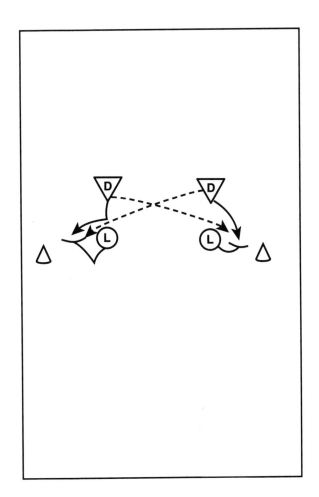

Set-up and Instructions:

Position two linemen on a designated line of scrimmage, separated by your normal line split. Align a defender head up on each lineman. Put a cone approximately two yards outside each blocker as illustrated. Hand signal the defenders to either rush head on or to execute a twist. Tell them to try to get inside the cone on their side. Whenever they do, they win. Determine an appropriate reward.

Instruct the blockers to snap into their blocking positions, to watch the defense for stunts, and to make whatever adjustments are necessary to prevent the defender from getting inside the cone. Tell the blockers that a job well done is its own reward! Check for a balanced hit position, good fundamentals, and quick feet.

190. HIT AND MOVE

Purpose:

- To drill pass-blocking fundamentals into body memory and to promote anaerobic conditioning.

Coaching Pointers:

- Keep your knees bent, your back straight, and your feet moving! **Don't stop your feet!**
- Watch the rusher! Anticipate his moves—and **be** where he wants to go!
- Move! Keep the defender away from the quarterback. When you hear the whistle, get back to your original position!
- Fast!

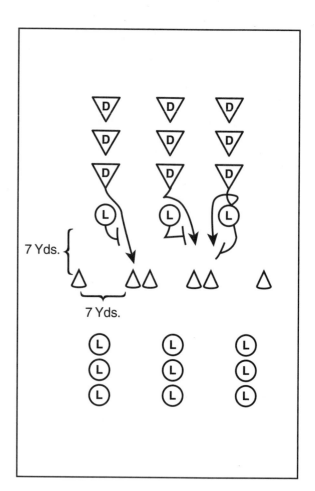

Set-up and Instructions:

Put all the linemen in three lines four yards apart. Place cones three to three and a half yards outside the first linemen in each line and seven yards behind him as illustrated. Position the remaining linemen away from the cones. Put a line of three defenders head up on each lineman and instruct them, in turn, to knock over either of the two cones to their outside. Be sure to alternate the blockers and the defenders so that everyone gets at least four repetitions on offense.

Instruct the blockers to block the first defender until they push him outside one of the two cones or until they hear the whistle. They should then run back to their original location, get into a hit position, and block the second defender. Have them do the same for the third defender. The blocker who keeps all three defenders outside the cones wins.

This is a rapid-fire drill and should be used only after blocking fundamentals have been taught and practiced. Keep all the linemen on the move and push for good blocking fundamentals throughout all three blocks.

191. ARC LINE

Purpose:

- To emphasize quick feet and a balanced hit position throughout the pass block.

Coaching Pointers:

- You can give a little ground when the rusher is bull rushing; just don't give too much!
- When the defender is bull rushing, try your best to keep him away from your body so that you can get a lower center of gravity.
- This is a dog fight, boys! Don't give up! Battle him! Keep him off the quarterback!
- Move your feet and stay in your hit position. Stay mobile!
- You have to be able to move to block a twisting lineman or a blitzing linebacker.

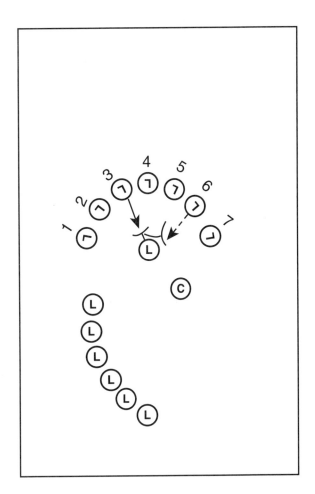

Set-up and Instructions:

Create an arc of seven linemen as illustrated. Assign each of them a number, one through seven, and instruct them to bull rush the blocker. Position a blocker in the center of the arc and tell him to be prepared to block a different rusher each time he hears a number called. Call a number every three to four seconds and watch the blocker for a balanced hit position during each block, toughness, and quick feet. Be sure to alternate the rushers and the blockers so that everyone gets at least two or three repetitions as a blocker.

This is a good, hard-hitting drill and should be used early in the season to condition toughness. Use it sparingly, however. It involves a lot of head banging!

192. HOLD THAT LINE

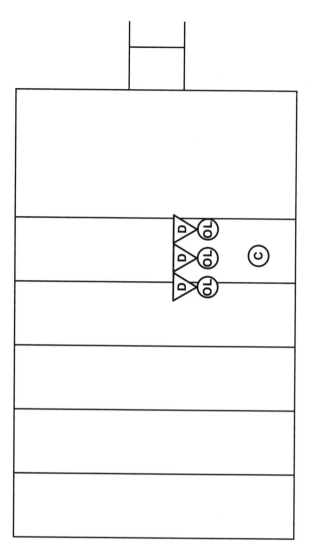

Purpose:

- To practice effective pass-blocking techniques against a hard-charging defensive rush.

Coaching Pointers:

- Stay in your hit position! Keep your knees bent and your back straight!
- Shuffle your feet! Keep your feet moving! Keep your body between the rusher and the quarterback!
- Don't overextend your body while executing the block! Stay balanced.
- Keep your arms within the frame of your body.
- Lock your elbows! Keep the defender at arm's length.
- Work until you hear the whistle! Don't assume anything!
- Set and punch! Set and punch!

Set-up and Instructions:

Position three interior linemen seven yards in from one of the sidelines within a 10-yard area, between the goal line and the 10-yard line, for example. Position a pass rusher head-up on each offensive lineman as illustrated and give him free rush to the quarterback, who will be you. Instruct the rushers to use all their pass-rushing techniques but to stay within the 10-yard area.

Give them a snap count and tell them that you will count to five. If one of the rushers touches you—gently!—within that time, the defense wins. If no one touches you, the offense wins. Don't push for a lot of repetitions with this drill. It can be very competitive. Take time to make corrections. Check for proper execution and try to match your best rushers with your best blockers.

193. OVERLOAD

Purpose:

- To practice pass-blocking techniques against an overloaded defensive front and a variety of rushing techniques.

Coaching Pointers:

- Stay with the pass protection scheme called in the huddle. Don't improvise. Effective pass protection is a team effort!

- Stay in a good hit position so you can keep your balance. Don't allow yourself to be pushed or pulled off balance!

- Refer to the coaching pointers in the individual drills. All of them apply here.

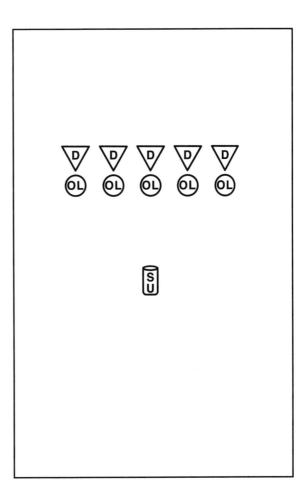

Set-up and Instructions:

Position all five interior linemen on a designated line of scrimmage. Put a rusher head-up on each offensive linemen. Script the drill. Give one script to the defense outlining their stunts on a play-by-play basis. You might even indicate the kinds of rushing techniques you want them to use. Use line slants, twists, looping techniques, and a variety of techniques.

Call pass-blocking schemes for the offensive line to check its ability to handle the scripted stunts. Place a stand-up dummy six or seven yards behind the line and tell the defense to knock it over. Give the players a five count before blowing your whistle. Be prepared to stop the drill each time players start piling up! Don't let anyone get hurt.

194. THINK BLOCKING

Purpose:

- To establish an understanding of offensive blocking assignments against likely opposing defenses.
- To promote higher order thought process about offensive assignments.
- To take away possible confusion created by the opponent's attempts to vary defensive alignments.

Coaching Pointers:

- Look at the alignment and apply your blocking rules.
- If the alignment is new to you, point to the man you intend to block. Never leave a defensive lineman unblocked!
- Learn every defensive adjustment this team makes, know your blocking assignments, and study the scouting report carefully before the game.

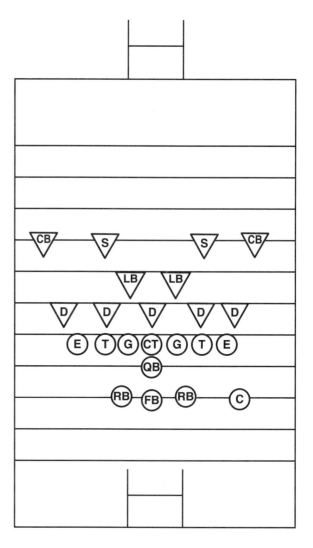

Set-up and Instructions:

Depending on the number of players on your team, alternately line up your top one, two, or three offensive teams. Place a defensive team in front of each one. Instruct the defensive team to align themselves in the upcoming opponent's favorite defense. Then call an offensive play, one you plan to run on game day, and instruct each offense: "Point to the man you will block." Periodically ask each player, "Why will you block that defensive player? How else might we block this particular defense?" Call a new play and ask the same questions.

After reviewing the defense and making corrections as needed, put the defense in a different alignment. Call a series of offensive plays. Ask the same questions: "Who will you block? Why?"

Show the offense all the defensive alignments you are likely to see on game day. Take enough time for this drill. Don't hurry it. The time spent on it—sometimes up to 45 minutes—will pay dividends on game day.

SECTION 7

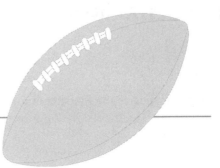

TACKLING DRILLS

Always emphasize tackling drills early in the season, usually during the first practice or two, especially before first contact. These tackling drills are designed to improve athletic performance as well as assure the safety of the players. The drills are appropriate for every position on defense. Substitute linebacker or strong safety for defensive lineman to use appropriate drills for other positions.

195. GET A GOOD FIT

Purpose:

- To emphasize the fundamentals of a good tackle, especially the fit prior to contact.

Coaching Pointers:

- Get to the ball carrier fast and break down into your hit position.
- Bend your knees, get your feet shoulder-width, bull your neck, and wrap your arms.
- Don't drop your head; **never drop your head!** You have all kinds of mask in front of you to protect your face.
- Face up to the ball carrier, drive your shoulder into his midsection, and wrap your arms.
- Hold that position. I want to see what you look like.

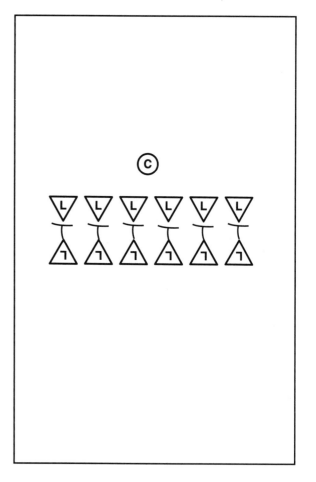

Set-up and Instructions:

Pair off the defensive linemen and tell one to be the ball carrier; the other, the tackler. Instruct all of them on the proper fundamentals, then have them alternate making a good fit at half speed. Have the ball carrier simply stand in his position. Tell the tackler to approach him at half speed, break down into a good hit position, then form up by pushing his shoulder into the ball carrier's midsection and wrapping his arms.

Check for all the above coaching pointers as well as some of your own and make a lot of corrections, emphasizing a bulled neck and every other safety precaution you think of. This is an important early season drill. A lot of time should be devoted to teaching the proper fundamentals. Nothing in football causes more injuries than a poorly executed tackle.

Think about scheduling your practice to sequence right into the next drill, *(196) Go for Form*.

196. GO FOR FORM

Purpose:

- To emphasize good tackling fundamentals.

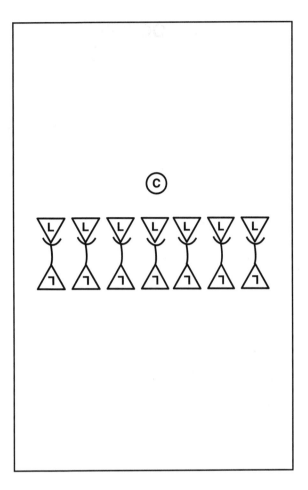

Coaching Pointers:

- **ALWAYS** bull your neck during contact! Use the muscle pad in the back of your neck to absorb the blow.
- Never align the spine! Never be looking at the ground when you try to make a tackle!
- If possible, get into a good hit position prior to contact. Roll your hips and use your legs to drive him back.
- Always tackle **through** the ball carrier; otherwise, you'll absorb most of the blow.
- Wrap your arms around the ball carrier's legs or buttocks. In order to wrap them well, you have to get deep into the ball carrier's body.

Set-up and Instructions:

Pair up the defensive linemen and have them face each other approximately a yard apart. Have one be the ball carrier; the other, the tackler. Conduct this drill at half speed. Tell the ball carriers to approach the tackler with a moderate forward lean and to drape themselves over the tackler's shoulders at contact. Tell the tacklers to get into good hit positions, to bull their necks, to face up to the ball carrier, to drive their shoulders into the ball carrier's midsection, and to wrap their arms and lift.

If executed properly by both players, the tackler should be able to lift the ball carrier and walk a few steps with him. Obviously, pair off the players according to size and strength and keep the drill at half speed. Be sure each lineman gets at least five repetitions. This is an excellent introductory drill because it teaches the fundamentals and enables you to emphasize safety.

197. POP THE POPSICLE

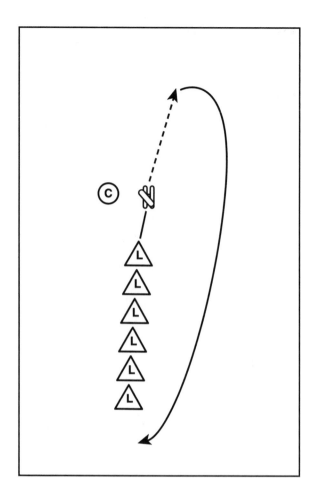

Purpose:

- To practice tackling fundamentals and leg drive.

Coaching Pointers:

- Be under control as you approach the popsicle.
- Never run full speed at a ball carrier—unless you have him right where you want him!
- Club the pad with your arms and wrap them immediately.
- Roll your hips on contact and lift the sled as you drive it.
- Drive with a good base! Keep your feet approximately shoulder-width and drive with short, powerful steps.

Set-up and Instructions:

Position all the defensive linemen in front of the popsicle and have each execute a good fundamental form tackle on the sled. Check for the above coaching pointers. If the hit is solid and the leg drive is good, the sled should move straight ahead. Whenever it moves off to either side, the hit isn't straight on or the base and leg drive are wrong.

This is a rapid-fire drill. Have each lineman go to the back of the line as soon as he executes his tackle. Be sure that each lineman gets at least four or five repetitions with each shoulder.

198. FACE UP

Purpose:

- To emphasize good mobility and sound tackling fundamentals.

Coaching Pointers:

- Stay in your hit position and keep your feet moving!
- Get your head on a swivel and find the ball carrier.
- Get to him quickly and face up. Don't crossover step to get to him. Shuffle step!
- If you can't face up, tackle him across the bow.
- Whether across the bow or face up, hit and lift! Climb his body!

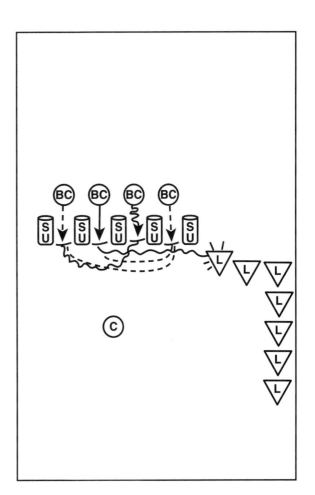

Set-up and Instructions:

Position five stand-up dummies on their sides, approximately two to three yards apart. Position a line of tacklers as illustrated. Put a ball carrier in each gap between the dummies approximately two to three yards from the gap. Use linemen as ball carriers but be sure to alternate them so that everyone gets at least three or four repetitions. Hand signal the ball carriers when you want them to move into the gap as if running the football. Have them hit the gaps in random order and only at half speed.

Instruct the first tackler to face the dummies and to get into his hit position. Instruct him to shuffle quickly to each gap when a ball carrier enters it. When he gets to the ball carrier, have him face up, hit, lift and release, then drop back behind the dummies and look for the next ball carrier entering a gap. He should continue moving from gap to gap—facing up, hitting, and lifting—until all the ball carriers have moved.

Check for good shuffle movement and hit position. This is not a live drill, but it is excellent for emphasizing defensive movement.

199. OFF THE GROUND

Purpose:

- To emphasize agility and good fundamentals when getting off the ground to make a tackle.

Coaching Pointers:

- If you get tripped, blocked, or fall down, get off the ground quickly and get into your hit position.
- Keep your feet moving, locate the ball carrier, and make the tackle.
- Don't cross over with your feet; you'll be out of position.
- I want to see good tackling fundamentals!

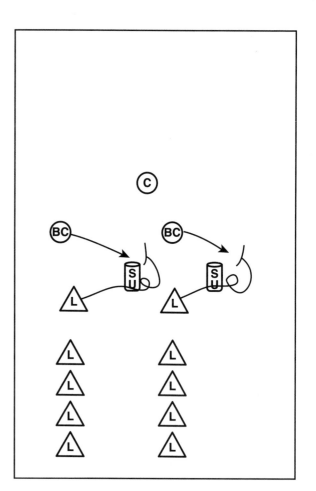

Set-up and Instructions:

Position the linemen in two lines, a stand-up dummy eight to nine yards to the right of each line. Position a ball carrier (he can be a lineman) five yards in front of each line as illustrated. Tell him to run to a position approximately two to three yards in front of the stand-up dummy and to allow himself to be tackled. Instruct the lineman to race to the dummy, cross body it, and get up as quickly as possible. Once up, he should get into his hit position, move his feet, and form up the ball carrier.

This drill doesn't have to be live. The important thing is that the linemen move well and get into position to make a fundamentally sound tackle. Be sure to run the drill in both directions and to assure at least four or five repetitions for each player.

200. INSIDE-OUT

Purpose:

- To emphasize the correct pursuit path and good tackling fundamentals.

Coaching Pointers:

- Maintain an inside-out pursuit path on the ball carrier. Don't let him get to the outside.
- Stay under control! If you approach him too aggressively, he'll be able to make a move, and you'll miss the tackle.
- Stay in your hit position and shuffle your feet.
- Make him commit, then go get him!

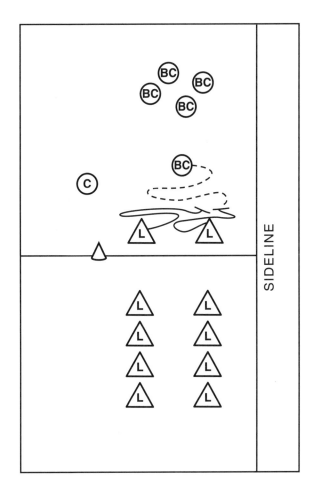

Set-up and Instructions:

Position the defensive linemen in two lines just inside one of the sidelines and a yard in front of a yard stripe. Place a cone or a stand-up dummy 10 yards inside the sideline on the yard stripe. Position five or six ball carriers five to six yards in front of the linemen, facing them as illustrated. Instruct the ball carrier to spin, juke, do anything he can to beat the linemen. Every time he gets over the yard stripe, he runs one less sprint after practice.

Instruct the linemen to maintain an inside-out path on the ball carrier; in essence, to squeeze him inside the 10-yard area so he has nowhere to go. Once the ball carrier makes a forward move, both linemen should be in a position to tackle him—from an inside-out angle. The drill can involve live tackling or simply facing up and forming the ball carrier. It is most effective if it is run live.

Use this drill only after the linemen have had a chance to master tackling fundamentals.

201. USE YOUR HEAD

Purpose:

- To develop the ability to attack and defeat the ball carrier from different angles.

Coaching Pointers:

- **Above everything else,** keep your head up and your neck bulled throughout the tackle. Never drop your head!

- Put your head in front of the ball carrier whenever you angle tackle. Drive and lift the same way you do when tackling head on.

- Don't grab with your arms! Get your head across the bow and drive a shoulder into his body.

- Always stay in your hit position and chug your feet prior to contact.

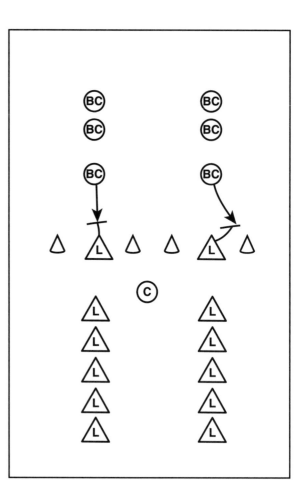

Set-up and Instructions:

Position the defensive linemen in two lines, with a ball carrier about three yards in front of the first man in each line as illustrated. Place two cones approximately two or three yards outside the first lineman in each line. Hand signal the ball carrier to run straight ahead or to angle to either side of the lineman and to try to beat him and pass the cones. Tell the lineman to stay in a good hit position and to use good tackling fundamentals when stopping the ball carrier.

Check for good foot movement, a good hit and lift on contact, safe and effective head position, and aggressive arm movement.

202. GOAL LINE

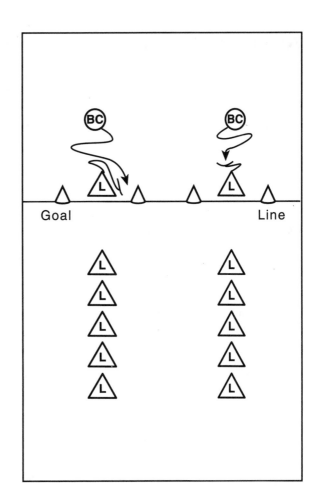

Purpose:

- To emphasize proper tackling fundamentals.

Coaching Pointers:

- Stay in your hit position and keep your feet moving!
- Force the ball carrier to commit but keep him away from the goal line.
- Remember, he doesn't have to run straight ahead! So don't overcommit!
- Hit him and lift to prevent forward momentum.
- Get your shoulder into his body and grab cloth and anything else you can!

Set-up and Instructions:

Position the defensive linemen in two lines, the first man in each line in the end zone a yard in front of a designated goal line. Position a ball carrier head up on each lineman approximately three yards in front of him. Place two cones on the goal line approximately five yards apart on either side of each lineman. Instruct the ball carrier to get into the end zone any way he can. Tell the linemen to tackle him before he can get in.

Check for a good hit position, chugging feet, a driving tackle, and a controlled move toward each ball carrier. Motivate the players even further by developing a reward system for the ball carriers who score and the linemen who consistently keep them out of the end zone.

203. IN HOT PURSUIT

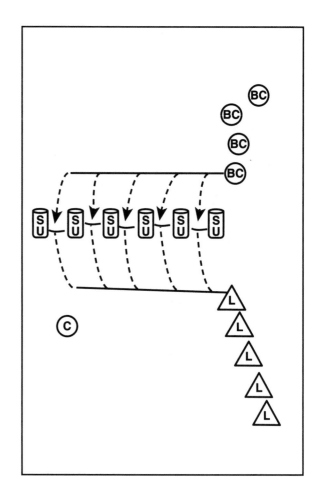

Purpose:

- To emphasize tackling fundamentals and the proper pursuit path.

Coaching Pointers:

- Don't overrun the ball carrier. Keep him in front of you!
- Don't allow him to cut back on you.
- Tackle across the bow. Keep your head in front of the ball carrier and get a shoulder into him as you lift.
- Keep your head up at all times! You'll do a better job tackling and you won't get hurt!

Set-up and Instructions:

Place six stand-up dummies on their sides, each about two yards apart. Position ball carriers (they can be linemen) on one side of the bags, the tacklers on the other side. Hand signal the ball carriers which hole you want them to run through. Tell them to start whenever they want. Instruct the linemen to run with them, always maintaining inside-out leverage on the ball carrier. Tell them to close on the ball carrier when he hits a particular hole and to tackle across the bow.

Be sure to run the drill in both directions. Check for the above coaching pointers as well as your own and make corrections. Be especially critical of players who arm tackle or drop their heads.

204. FIND THE BALL

Purpose:

- To practice good tackling fundamentals and learning to find the ball.

Coaching Pointers:

- Get into a good hit position and keep your feet moving while you search for the ball.
- Wait aggressively!
- Move to the ball carrier as soon as you see him and execute a fundamentally sound tackle.
- Get your head across the bow and get a shoulder into his body.
- Climb him to get leverage and to take away his forward momentum.

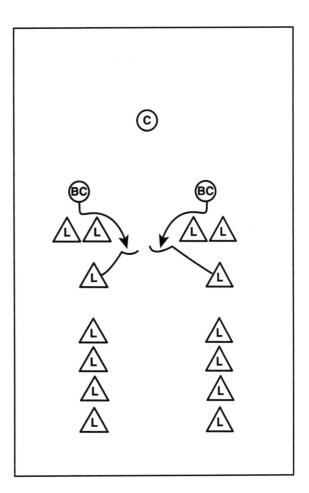

Set-up and Instructions:

Position all the linemen in two lines. Align two linemen, shoulder to shoulder, in front of the first player in each line so they can hide the ball carrier behind them. Position a ball carrier behind the two linemen and hand signal the direction you want him to run.

Instruct the tackler to get into a good hit position, to keep his feet moving, and to tackle the ball carrier across the bow as soon as he sees him. Alternate the ball carriers and the stationery linemen so that everyone gets at least three or four repetitions. This is a good drill after tackling fundamentals have been mastered. Players like this drill. Just be sure no one arm tackles or drops his head.

205. RICOCHET

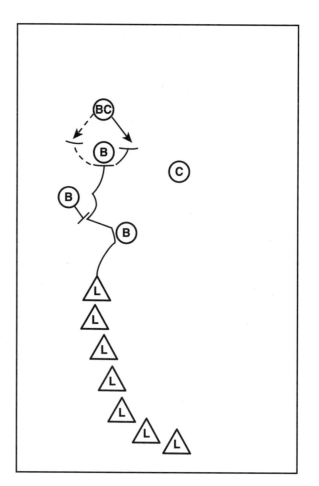

Purpose:

- To practice defeating blockers and tackling the ball carrier.

Coaching Pointers:

- Rip through angle blocks and use your frontal techniques on head-on blocks.
- Don't waste a lot of time on the blockers. Hit them and shed them! We're not punishing blockers; we're tackling the ball carrier!
- Emphasize a good base and a good hit position throughout this drill. Keep your feet shoulder-width and be sure to shuffle step; otherwise, you're going to get knocked off balance.
- Tackle the trunk of the ball carrier's body and lift! Push him back with good leg drive.

Set-up and Instructions:

Position the linemen in one line as illustrated. Position three blockers in front of them, staggered at three-yard intervals as illustrated. Position a ball carrier three yards behind the blockers. Instruct each lineman to meet and defeat each of the blockers. He'll probably use a right arm rip technique on the first, a left arm rip technique on the second, and a good punch move and separation on the last. Tell him to find the ball carrier as he defeats the final blocker and to tackle him across the bow. The ball carrier may go right or left depending on your hand signal.

Check for good hit positions, punch and separation, rip technique, and tackling fundamentals. This is an excellent drill—one of my favorites. It emphasizes fundamentals under quasi-game conditions and can become very competitive. For this reason, give each lineman only one or two repetitions.

206. SIDELINE

Purpose:

- To emphasize using the sideline to tackle a ball carrier or to force him out of bounds.

Coaching Pointers:

- Stay on his back hip. Don't let him cut back or outrun you. Pin him against the sideline.
- This means you have to run under control, in a good hit position.
- If he needs a first down, he's going to unload on you. You attack him!
- Keep your neck bulled throughout the hit. The sideline is a dangerous place where lots of players get injured.
- If you pin him well, he may just go out of bounds, but don't **expect** that— and **don't relax** because that's when he'll cut back on you!

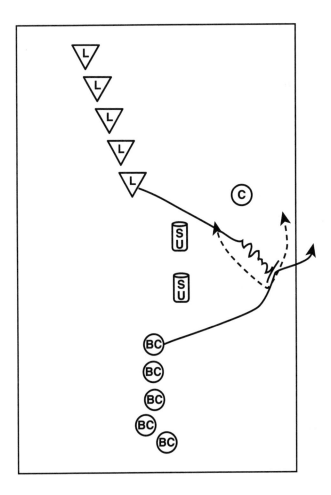

Set-up and Instructions:

Place two stand-up dummies seven or eight yards from the sideline. Position the ball carriers (they can be linemen) 10 to 12 yards from the sideline. Position the tacklers opposite them, 15 yards upfield as illustrated. Instruct the ball carriers to put the ball in their outside arm and to race toward the sideline, always staying inside the dummies. Tell them to outrun the tackler or to cut back on him if they can.

Tell the tacklers to leverage the ball carrier against the sideline and to maintain a good hit position and a controlled approach. This drill can involve some violent contact, so rarely should it be live. The purpose of the drill is to teach sideline leverage. Simply have the tacklers face up to the ball carrier and execute good tackling fundamentals without unloading on him.

207. CREATING TURNOVERS

Purpose:

- To practice forcing fumbles while executing good tackling fundamentals.

Coaching Pointers:

- Sometimes late in the game, we need the ball. But remember, we never just tackle the ball. If you're the only tackler, put your face on the ball but execute good tackling fundamentals.
- Your first job is to stop the runner!
- If several tacklers are assisting you, you can work on grabbing the ball but only if you are sure the ball carrier is going to be tackled!

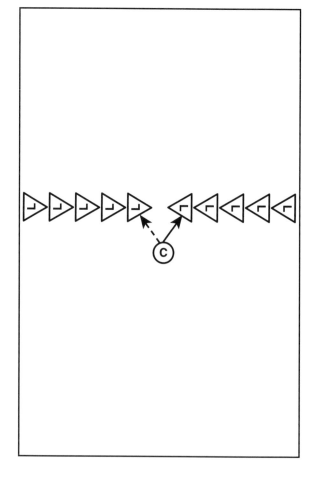

Set-up and Instructions:

Position the linemen in two lines facing each other as illustrated. They should be only two yards apart. Stand between them with a football. Toss the ball to one of them. He will be the ball carrier; the other, the tackler. Instruct the ball carriers to run at three-quarter speed, to allow themselves to be tackled, and to drop the ball when the tackler puts his face on it.

Instruct the tacklers to use good tackling fundamentals but to aim at the football with the front part of their helmets. Remind them never to drop their heads, even when trying to dislodge the football. Tell them to emphasize form when making the tackle. This is only a semi-live drill.

Vary it early in the season by making it live. It's also a good drill for simply practicing tackling fundamentals. When you liven it up, keep the ball carrier and the tackler relatively close to each other. The purpose of the drill is not to promote collisions, just good tackling.

208. THE STRIPPER

Purpose:

- To emphasize stripping the football when making a tackle.

Coaching Pointers:

- Remember, your first job is to make the tackle!
- During the tackle, if you can come down hard on the ball-carrying arm of the runner or punch the ball from underneath, do it! But be sure you stop the runner.
- This drill is not live, but I want to see good fundamentals!
- In a game or scrimmage situation, you will drive with your shoulder, strip with one arm, wrap up with the other, and spin the runner to the ground.

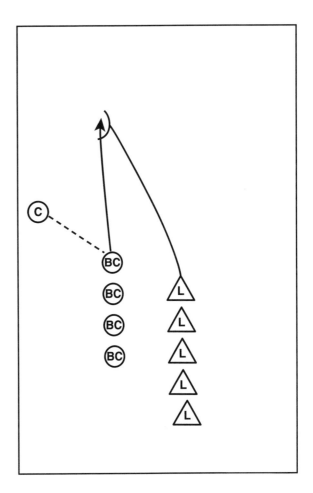

Set-up and Instructions:

Place the defenders in two lines facing upfield. Designate one line as ball carriers; the other, as tacklers. Stagger the ball carriers in front of the tacklers as illustrated. Instruct the ball carriers to run at half to three-quarter speed and to expect a hit from behind. Tell the tacklers to chase down the ball carrier and to strip the ball. Make sure they also get their near shoulder into the runner and wrap him up with their other arm.

Neither player should go to the ground. Focus only on wrapping up and stripping the football.

209. WHO WANTS IT?

Purpose:

- To promote competition between the offense and defense.
- To emphasize blocking as well as tackling fundamentals.

Coaching Pointer:

- Use all the coaching pointers mentioned so far in the tackling and blocking drills. This is an instructional drill, but it is primarily a time for the coach to promote some healthy competition and to allow both offense and defense to get fired up!

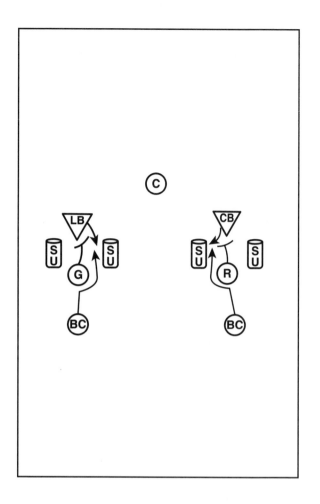

Set-up and Instructions:

Lay two or three sets of stand-up dummies on their sides, each set approximately three yards apart. Pair off blockers and tacklers according to their respective positions on offense or defense. For example, have nose guards go against centers, linebackers against guards, tackler against defensive ends, and so on. Position a ball carrier three to four yards behind each set as illustrated and tell them to try to run between the bags on the coach's cadence.

This is a highly competitive drill and teaches desire and toughness as well as fundamentals. It is a good early season drill for promoting competitive attitude as well as blocking and tackling fundamentals.

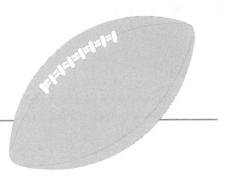

SECTION 8

DEFENSIVE-LINEMAN DRILLS

This section focuses on the following skills:

- Stance and starts
- Forearm shiver
- Hand shiver
- Pass rushing techniques vs. linemen: swim, arm under, bull rush, etc.
- Beating the back's block
- Meeting the trap block
- Breaking the double-team block
- Submarine technique
- Attacking the gaps
- Technique during linebacker stunts
- Executing the "twist" technique
- Head-on tackling
- Tackling across the bow

210. STANCE

Purpose:

- To emphasize line stances and variations based on defensive assignment.

Coaching Pointers:

- Your primary responsibility as a defensive lineman is to beat the opponent's block, to get rid of him, and to get to the ball.
- The right stance will make these jobs easier.
- If our defensive call requires you to read or to move, I want you in a balanced stance: feet shoulder-width, weight evenly distributed between feet and hand, bulled neck, and tail elevated.
- If we're in an attack front, I want a three-, maybe a four-point stance: feet shoulder-width, 65% of your weight forward, bulled neck, and tail elevated.

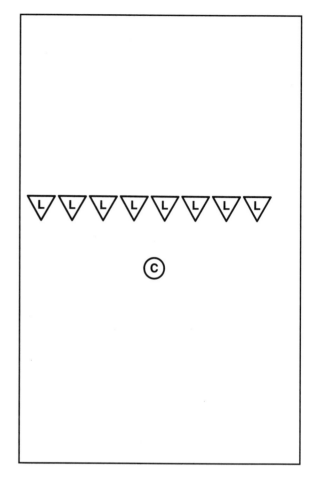

Set-up and Instructions:

Position all the defensive linemen in a straight line facing you. Tell them to get into the appropriate stance based on your command. Alternate your commands among: "Three-point read!" "Four-point read!" "Three-point attack!" and "Four-point attack!" Once they get into the designated stance, check them for proper weight distribution, comfortable positioning, bulled neck, elevated tail, and power angles in the knees and ankles.

Make lots of corrections and take a lot of time with this drill. The linemen won't get excited about it, but it pays off in the long run.

211. EXPLOSION OFF MAN

Purpose:

- To emphasize the defensive take-off based on the opponent's movement.

Coaching Pointers:

- Go when your opponent moves! Don't listen to the quarterback!
- Focus on the man in front of you. See and listen to nothing else!
- His movement should shock you into an explosive take-off.

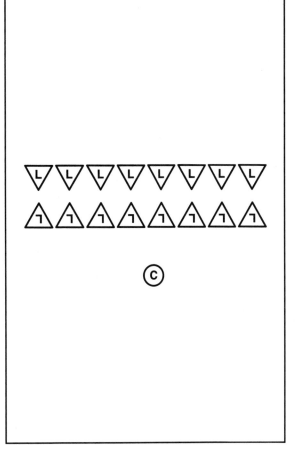

Set-up and Instructions:

Pair off the defensive linemen, one a blocker; and the other, a defender. Have them alternate these responsibilities so everyone gets at least five or six repetitions as a defender. On your command, have them get into their stances. Instruct each defensive lineman to move only when the man on him moves. Emphasize this point vigorously before and during the drill! It pays to pound it into their heads!

Stand behind the defensive linemen so only the blockers can see you. Hand signal the snap count to them. Then give a cadence designed to draw the defenders off side. Occasionally, have the blockers fire out immediately after the "Down" call, even before the cadence starts. Check the defenders for focus, stance, and explosiveness. Again, make a lot of corrections. This responsibility has to become second nature to them.

212. EXPLOSION OFF BALL

Purpose:

- To emphasize the defensive take-off based on the movement of the ball.

Coaching Pointers:

- Go only when the ball moves! Don't listen to the quarterback! His job is to confuse you.

- Focus only on the ball! For that brief moment before the play starts, nothing else exists.

- Let the ball's movement shock you into an explosive take-off.

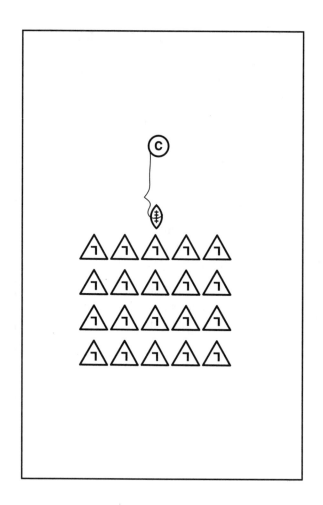

Set-up and Instructions:

Put all the defensive linemen in waves of five players each. Place an old football with a rope attached in front of the middle man. Remind each wave to take-off only when the ball moves. Start the cadence and move the ball unpredictably. Watch each lineman for stance, focus, and explosiveness. As with the previous drill, make a lot of corrections. This reaction must become second nature to all the defensive linemen.

213. HIP HOP

Purpose:

- To emphasize upper body explosion and a good hip roll when reacting to a blocker.

Coaching Pointers:

- For purposes of this drill, stay on your knees and focus only on exploding with your shoulders and arms and getting your hips under you for power.
- Push your pelvis forward and roll your hips under you for power.
- Leverage your back this way as you explode your arms and hands up and into the blocker.

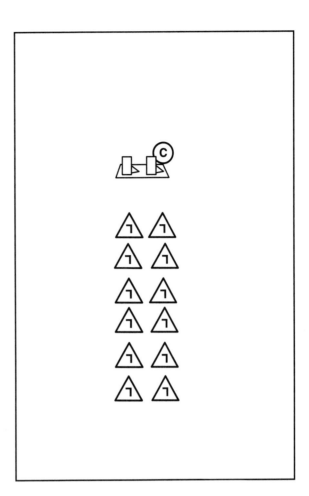

Set-up and Instructions:

Position all the defensive linemen in front of the two-man sled. Have the first two players get on their knees while you stand next to the sled. Tell them that when the sled moves to explode upward with their arms and hands and to roll their hips under them so that the sled rises at contact. Push the sled slightly to get each pair started and watch for good upper body explosion, leverage, and take-off. Be sure that each lineman gets at least seven or eight repetitions. This should be a rapid-fire drill. Linemen who don't execute correctly should be told to repeat the movement immediately.

214. HIP EXPLOSION

Purpose:

- To emphasize hip roll, upward lift, and upper body explosion when destroying a block.

Coaching Pointers:

- Go on the ball! As soon as that ball moves, **you** move!
- And move **fast!** Explode into the blocker. Get your hips underneath you and drive up hard with your legs.
- Exaggerate your bulled neck and keep your shoulders back. That's the position you want for good upward lift.
- Aim your hands at his chest, punch hard and lock your elbows, and roll your hips and drive your legs.
- Feel those hips come underneath you. That's where your power is.

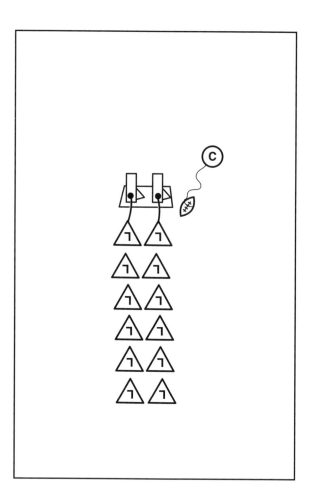

Set-up and Instructions:

Position all the defensive linemen in front of the two-man sled. You stand to the side with an old football attached to a rope. Drop the football within the vision of both players and instruct them to explode into the sled as soon as the football moves. If you haven't attached an old football to a piece of rope yet, do it right away. This is an essential piece of equipment for drilling defensive linemen. Too many coaches drill fundamentals without conditioning linemen to move on the ball. That is a serious mistake. In fact, many of them use a verbal cue to start the drill, which further conditions the linemen to be influenced by the opposing quarterback's cadence.

Check for the above coaching pointers and some of your own. They should be exploding the hands and arms into the blocker/sled while rolling their hips under them for power and leverage. Make lots of corrections.

215. KEEP YOUR BASE

Purpose:

- To emphasize a solid base when neutralizing an offensive block.

Coaching Pointers:

- Explode into the blocker and destroy his block by driving up and into him. Maintain a balanced charge by keeping your feet at least shoulder-width when you drive.

- You have to have a good base to prevent the blocker from pushing you in either direction.

- Keep the base by driving with short, choppy, powerful steps. Don't try to take long strides. Long strides eliminate your base.

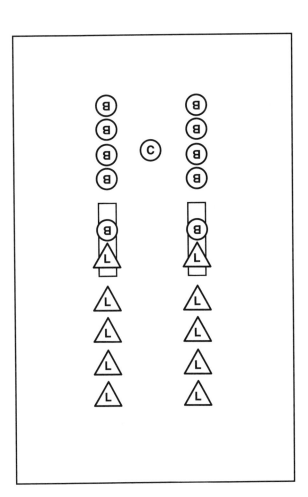

Set-up and Instructions:

Position the defensive linemen at both ends of two 2" × 8" boards as illustrated. Have the two lines facing you be blockers; the other two, defenders. Get the players into their stances and tell them to go on the blocker's movement. Tell the defensive linemen to explode into the blocker, make a good hip roll, punch and separate, and maintain a good base while driving their legs.

This is a good drill for both offensive and defensive linemen. The lineman who fails to maintain his base hits the board with his foot and loses the battle. Both players win stalemates. This is an excellent drill for teaching base and leg drive. Use it early in the season to establish good habits.

216. SHADE HIP

Purpose:

- To emphasize hip roll and upward explosion when in a shade position.

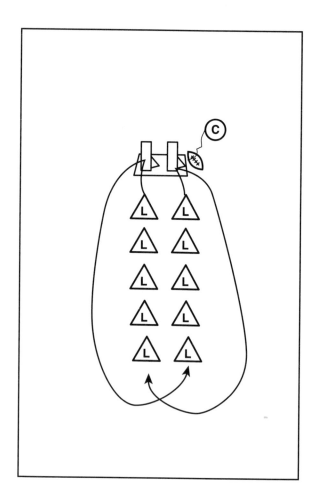

Coaching Pointers:

- When shading an offensive lineman, explode your upper body and roll your hips the same way you would if you were head up.

- The difference is punch and lift with your arm nearer the blocker and jam him from the outside with your off arm to control the gap.

- Always step with your inside foot, the foot nearer the blocker. Your outside leg is your drive leg.

Set-up and Instructions:

Position all the defensive linemen in front of the two-man sled. Offset each player outside their respective pads to simulate a shade alignment. Toss the football on a rope within the vision of both players. Instruct them to explode into the pad as soon as the ball moves. Emphasize the above coaching pointers as well as your own. Be sure all the linemen get an equal number of repetitions on both pads.

Check for good movement off the ball, a good hip roll, and a strong jam with the outside hand. Make a lot of corrections.

217. SHADE RIP

Purpose:

- To emphasize a rip move with the inside arm and shoulder when shaded.

Coaching Pointers:

- Go on the ball and go hard!
- Jam hard with your outside arm and hand. Simultaneously rip your arm nearer the blocker into and through him to gain inside leverage.
- If you can get your arm and shoulder past him, you've got him beat!
- Drive your legs hard throughout this maneuver and maintain thrust **into** the blocker so he can't push you out of the hole.

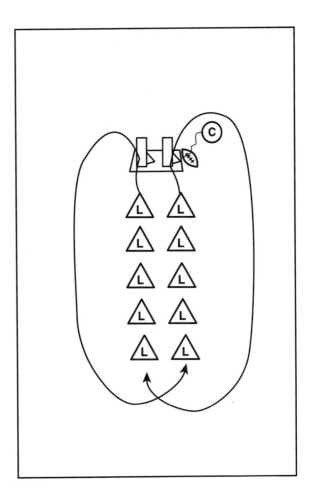

Set-up and Instructions:

Position all the defensive linemen in front of the two-man sled. Stand off to the side and toss the football on a rope within vision of the two front players. Instruct them to go on the ball movement and to rip through the outside of each pad. Each lineman should jam the pad with his outside hand and arm and rip to the outside of the sled with his inside arm and shoulder. Be sure the players go on the ball movement and that they explode into and through each pad. A rip maneuver is wasted without quickness off the ball.

Check for a good bulled neck, shoulders back, and a strong hip roll as well as a strong jam and rip move. Make a lot of corrections.

218. RIP AND MOVE

Purpose:

- To emphasize a strong hip roll, rip move, and quickness to the ball carrier.

Coaching Pointers:

- Step with your inside foot and drive hard with your outside leg to maintain pressure on the blocker.
- Jam with your outside hand and arm and rip with your inside arm and shoulder to beat the blocker through the gap.
- Try to maintain a balanced hit position in order to be able to react to the ball carrier.
- Go to the ball—hard!

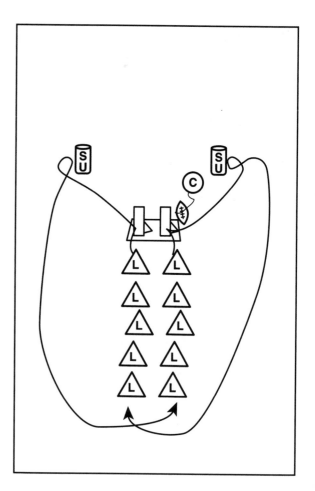

Set-up and Instructions:

Position all the defensive linemen in front of the two-man sled. Place a stand-up dummy five yards off to the side as illustrated. Stand to the side and toss a football on a rope within the vision of the first player in each line. Instruct them to go on the ball, to rip through the outside of the pad, and to tackle the stand-up dummy across the bow so that after wrapping it up they roll with it.

Use this drill when you feel confident that your linemen are comfortable with the fundamentals of the hip roll, punch, and rip move. It is a rapid-fire drill and can be used as much for anaerobic conditioning as for instruction.

219. POP AND MOVE

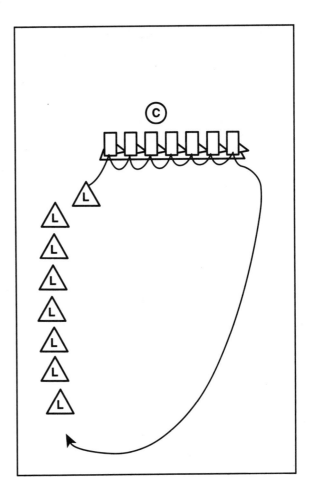

Purpose:

- To emphasize a good punch, leverage, separation, and movement.

Coaching Pointers:

- Don't overextend on the sled. We're not trying to knock it over; we're working on punch and separation.
- Lock your elbows after the punch; get some separation from the blocker.
- Keep a good base; stay in your hit position. After the punch and separation, you'll have to move to the ball carrier.
- Shuffle your feet; don't cross over!

Set-up and Instructions:

Position all the defensive linemen to the left of the seven-man sled. Instruct them, one at a time, to move from pad to pad, punching, separating, and staying in a hit position. When they release off the last pad, have them return to the back of the line and continue working on the sled until they hear the whistle.

Be sure they move from right to left as well as from left to right on the sled. Check for a good hit position, quick feet, a strong punch move with locked elbows, and good separation from each pad. This is a good early practice drill and, with some teams, becomes a part of their daily routine.

220. HIT AND SHED

Purpose:

- To emphasize a strong punch-and-move technique.

Coaching Pointers:

- Read the blocker's head! Don't let him put it where he wants to put it!
- If he comes straight at you, punch with both hands and lift and lock.
- If he drives to either side of you, shuffle in that direction, stay in your hit position, and punch into his numbers, then lift and lock.
- Once you've gotten good separation, lock him out, find the ball, and get rid of him.
- Move your feet! Move your feet! Stay face up!

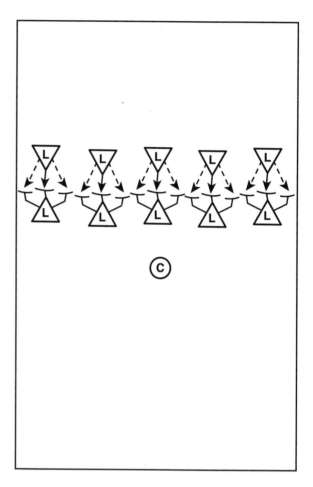

Set-up and Instructions:

Pair off the defensive linemen so they are facing each other along a designated line of scrimmage. Have them alternate between being blockers and defenders. Stand behind the defenders and hand signal the blockers to block straight ahead or to try to get their heads on either side of the defender. Have both defenders and blockers get into their stances, bull their necks, and go on your hand movement.

Check the defenders for a good hip roll, quick feet, a good punch move, good lockout and separation, and the ability to go on the blocker's first move. Be sure each lineman gets at least two or three repetitions reacting to the blocker's three different head movements.

221. SHIVER TECHNIQUE

Purpose:

- To practice the forearm and hand-shiver techniques.

Coaching Pointers:

- A powerful forearm doesn't come from your arm or shoulder! It comes from your legs!
- Rip up with the forearm and shoulder, but come out of a good hit position so you're exploding up and into the defender.
- Hit, rip, and lift!
- Also be in a good hit position when you deliver a strong hand shiver. Hit the defender's breastplate with the heel of each hand and lock your elbows.
- Keep good separation between you and the defender.

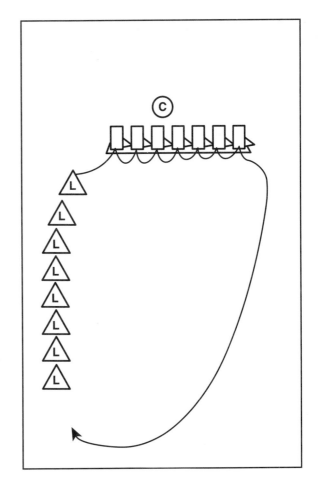

Set-up and Instructions:

Position all the linemen to the left of the seven-man sled. Instruct them, in order, to hit each pad with a strong forearm, then return to the back of the line. They should shuffle step between each pad and get into a good hit position before delivering each blow. When all the linemen have had two repetitions, instruct the first man to deliver a hand shiver on each pad.

After two repetitions, have them go to the right of the seven-man sled and deliver two forearm shivers and two hand shivers in the opposite direction. Each lineman should have at least two repetitions with each technique in both directions. Because this drill is rapid-fire, each can probably have more than two repetitions.

Keep them moving, but keep them executing correctly. This is an excellent drill for getting proper execution into body memory.

222. PLAY THE ANGLES

Purpose:

- To promote reaction time and the fundamental skills needed to destroy blocks coming from different angles.

Coaching Pointers:

- Anticipate blocks from every angle!
- Once you identify the blocker, **attack him** and destroy the block.
- Don't get your weight too far forward when you're reading line blocks. Keep your weight over your knees to prevent a premature forward movement and to help your explosion.
- When attacking an outside blocker, punch with your near shoulder and forearm, step with your near foot, and pivot into a hip roll for leverage.
- Destroy the head-on block with all the frontal techniques we've worked on so far.

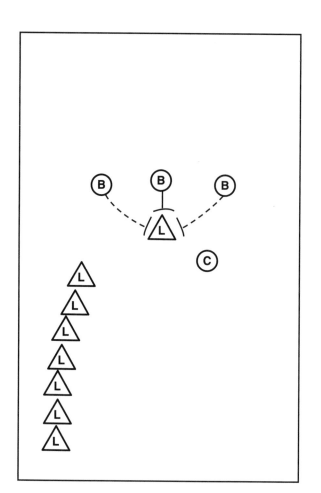

Set-up and Instructions:

Position all the defensive linemen in one line, the first man in the line with his back to you. Position three blockers in a triangle in front of the first defender. Place the first blocker a yard off the defender; the other, two approximately two and a half yards to the outside as illustrated. Point to the blocker you want to attack the defender. Be sure the other two remain in their stances. Check each defender for the correct technique to destroy a head-on or an angle block.

Alternate all the blockers and defenders to be sure each gets at least four or five repetitions. As the defensive linemen master their techniques, make the drill more difficult by having all three blockers move but only one hit the defender. Hand signal the assignments to all three blockers.

223. PUNCH AND REACT

Purpose:

- To emphasize explosion, hip roll, a strong punch move, and reaction to the ball.

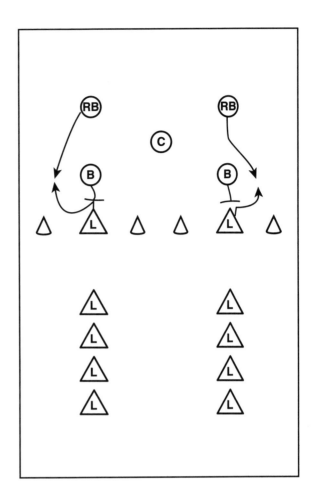

Coaching Pointers:

- Explode into the blocker, punch hard, get good separation, and find the ball.
- Strive to lock your elbows in order to **get and keep** good separation!
- You be in control! You can give ground a little when finding the ball, but keep your hips under you for leverage and always be able to shed the blocker in order to get to the ball.
- When you find the ball and move to it, don't just try to **escape** the blocker! Get rid of him! Push him away from you.

Set-up and Instructions:

Position the defensive linemen in two lines, each with a blocker in front of the first man. Position a cone up to a yard and a half on either side of each line as illustrated. Position a ball carrier three to four yards behind each blocker. Instruct the defensive lineman to go on the blocker's movement, to punch and control the blocker, and to shed him to get to the ball. Tell the ball carrier to delay one count, then to run to either side of the blocker but to stay within the cones. Remind him that he's not a tackling dummy, that he should run hard in order to beat the defensive lineman.

Although this drill is included in the defensive linemen section, it's good for offensive linemen and backs as well. Chew out the running back who goes down like a sacrificial lamb and the blocker who gets manhandled! Without a maximum effort from everyone, no one learns anything!

224. RIP THROUGH

Purpose:

- To emphasize the use of the hands and the rip technique when a blocker approaches from an angle.

Coaching Pointers:

- **NEVER** take the path of least resistance when avoiding a blocker to get to the ball carrier.
- Always rip across the blocker's face on an inside-out path.
- He'll invite you to go behind him. **Don't accept** the invitation! You'll immediately be out of position. Give a little ground if you have to. Just be sure to maintain your proper pursuit path.
- Jam him with your outside hand and square up your shoulders. Then defeat the block with a throw or a rip move to the outside.
- Rip hard enough to get leverage, then go to the ball carrier—on an inside-out path.
- Don't overpursue; always leave room to let the ball carrier come back to you.

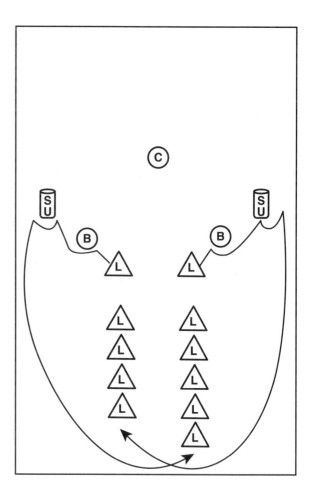

Set-up and Instructions:

Position the defensive linemen in two rows, each with a blocker to the outside and a stand-up dummy five yards behind the blocker as illustrated. On the blocker's movement, have the defensive lineman explode into him, seeking to gain outside leverage. He should use his hands to punch and get separation, then rip his inside arm to the outside of the blocker to destroy the block.

Vary the blocker's movement with a hand signal. Have him angle right at the defender or box the defender to prevent pursuit. Check for good fundamentals: shuffling with the feet, punching and separating, and ripping hard to the outside.

225. BEATING THE CUT BLOCK

Purpose:

- To enable defensive linemen to react to and defeat the cut block.

Coaching Pointers:

- A good back is going to try to set you up before he blocks you.
- He's going to make you think he plans to block you high, then he's going to cut you!
- So stay low! Keep your knees bent and stay in a good hit position.
- Be sure to shuffle step in order to maintain your balance.
- Get your hands on the blocker immediately to control him.
- If he **does** get into your legs, don't be afraid to drop step and give a little ground.
- Sometimes you have to give ground to protect the outside.

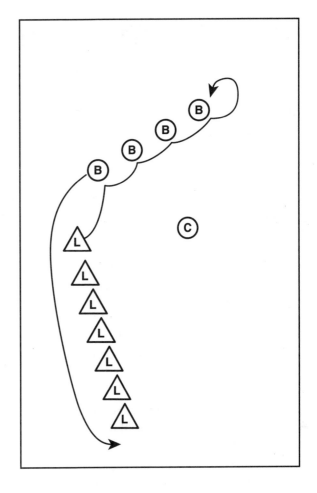

Set-up and Instructions:

Stagger three or four blockers in the backfield, two to three yards apart and angled away from the defender as illustrated. Position a defensive lineman three to five yards downfield of the first blocker and tell him to move laterally from blocker to blocker, defeating each one until he gets to the end of the line. Tell him to then become one of the blockers and have one of the blockers go to the end of the line of defenders.

Be sure that all the defensive linemen get at least two or three repetitions **in each line**. This is an important drill for all defensive linemen but especially for defensive ends. Check for a good shuffle step, use of hands, and the ability to stay to the outside.

226. BEATING THE DOUBLE-TEAM

Purpose:

- To practice defeating a double-team block.

Coaching Pointers:

- Always keep in mind that tight line splits, especially on the outside, suggest a possible double-team.
- Explode into the first man, usually the post block, and use the proper leverage to defeat his block.
- Once you see or sense outside pressure, get low and drive into it with your outside leg.
- If you're getting moved, get on your inside knee and try to split the double-team or make a pile.
- If you're not getting moved, stay low to either split the block or to spin off the outside man.

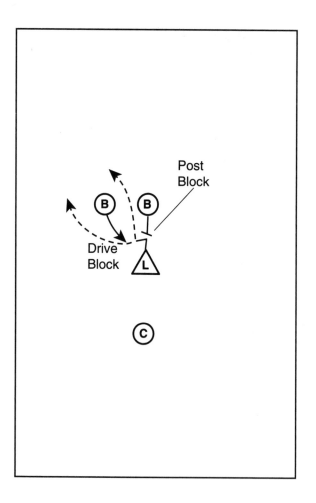

Set-up and Instructions:

Divide the defensive linemen in groups of three. Have them take turns being the defender. Position the defenders on a line of scrimmage in a gap between the two blockers. On your signal, have the blockers try to double-team the defender to one side or the other. Be sure to alternate all the players so that each one gets at least two or three repetitions in both positions. This drill can take a lot of time. The potential for injury is small and the need to know how to beat a double-team block is great!

Check for good defensive technique, especially staying low and showing the quickness to split the block or spin to the outside.

227. READ THE BLOCK

Purpose:

- To emphasize the ability to react to and defeat different blocking techniques.

Coaching Pointers:

- Use the hit and shed techniques we've worked on to beat the blocker who comes right at you or tries to get his head to either side.
- If the man on your head pulls in either direction, look quickly to either side or into the backfield for a blocker.
- If the man on your head drops into pass protection, use your pass-rushing techniques.

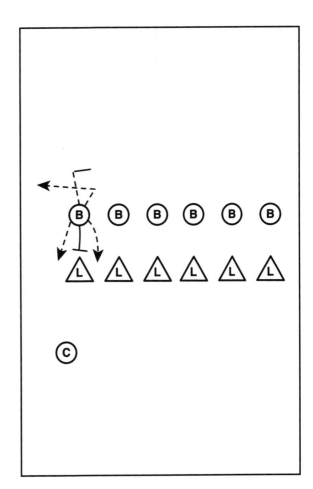

Set-up and Instructions:

Pair off the defensive linemen: one as a blocker; the other, as a defender. Stand behind the defenders and hand signal the blockers which of five techniques to use: straight ahead, head to the right, head to the left, pull in either direction, or drop to pass protection. Have the defenders and the blockers get into their stances and go on your hand movement.

Check the defenders initially for their ability to react to the blocker's first movement. Simultaneously, look for good defensive technique: hip roll and base, punch, lockout and separation, quick feet, and good pass-rushing technique.

228. READ THE BLOCKS

Purpose:

- To emphasize the ability to react to and defeat different blocking combinations.

Coaching Pointers:

- Focus on **movement!** Don't look directly at the man in front of you, but see him and the two blockers to either side peripherally.

- Go on movement, and understand that the block may come from the man on your head, the man to either side of you, or both of them!

- React to pressure and use different techniques.

- Rip across the face of a down block; spin out of or split a double team; rush a pass block; use the right technique against certain blocking schemes.

- **Ask questions** when you get beat or are confused!

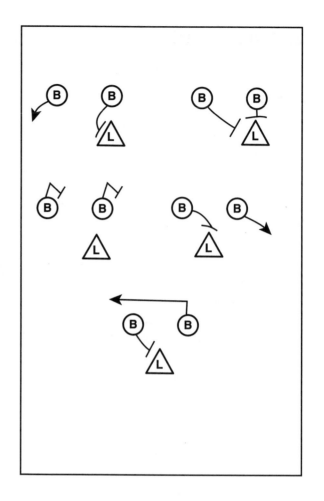

Set-up and Instructions:

Separate the defensive linemen into groups of three and have them alternate so that each player gets to be the defender at least two times. Position all the groups on a line of scrimmage with you behind the defenders. Hand signal each blocking scheme to the two blockers and use a designated gesture to start them. The diagram illustrates five different blocking possibilities. Designate them one at a time to each group. Vary the defender's alignment by positioning him head up on either blocker or in the gap.

Test each defender's reaction to body movement periodically by having one of the blockers flinch or false start. Run the groups simultaneously and check for good defensive technique. Review the coaching pointers in several of the earlier drills. This is an excellent drill for the linemen after they have mastered the basics because of its game-like situations.

229. CONTAINING

Purpose:

- To emphasize the proper pursuit path to maintain outside containment responsibilities.

Coaching Pointers:

- If the man on your head tries to seal, cutoff, or reach block, use the appropriate defensive technique to beat him and maintain your outside leverage.
- Go to the next level and do the same to the back who may try to cut or chop you.
- If you have outside containment responsibility, don't let **anyone** get outside you! You have a lot of help to the inside; very little, if any, to the outside!

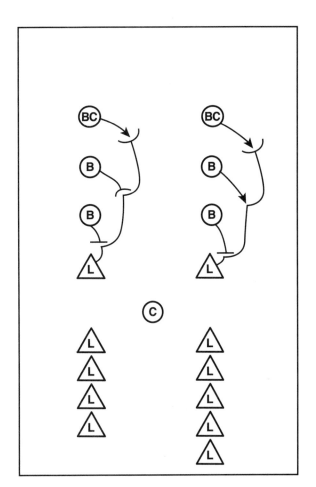

Set-up and Instructions:

Position all the defensive linemen in two or three parallel lines facing upfield, approximately five or six yards apart as illustrated. Position a blocker head up on the first man in each line, a blocking back three yards behind him, and a ball carrier three or four yards behind both.

On your hand gesture, have the blocker head up on the first man in each line and try to cut him off from outside pursuit. Once the defender defeats that block, have him continue on his outside contain and defeat the back's attempt to cut or chop him. Once he defeats that block, have him face up to contain the ball carrier or to angle tackle him. Have the backfield blocker wait a count or two before he tries to block the defender and have the ball carrier wait a count or two before he runs the ball.

Check for good shuffle movement, use of hands, and other defensive techniques. This is a good drill for all defensive linemen but especially for defensive ends.

230. BEATING THE TRAP

Purpose:

- To enable defensive linemen to sense and defeat a trap block.

Coaching Pointers:

- Attack the man on your head or just to your inside first with a good punch and hip roll.
- If he wants to downblock on someone to the inside, slide with him and push him hard so that he is unable to execute his block.
- As you slide with him, look to the inside for a trapper coming your way. Attack his inside shoulder!
- Don't wait for him to hit you; you hit him and force the play outside!
- Stay low! Shock him!

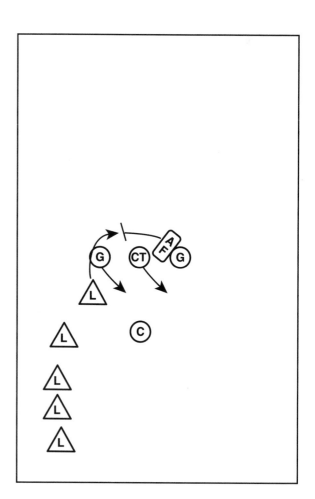

Set-up and Instructions:

Align two offensive guards and a center in their normal positions. Position a defensive lineman head up or shaded to the outside of one of the guards. Be sure to put the lineman on both sides of the center so he gets practice meeting the trap with both shoulders. Also be sure to alternate all the blockers and linemen so that everyone gets at least two or three repetitions both ways.

Give the trapping guard an air flate and tell him to try to trap inside the defensive lineman so that he gets outside leverage. Tell the defender to slide with and push the downblocking guard and to attack the trapping guard with his outside shoulder—so even if he only achieves a stalemate, he is filling the hole.

Tell them to go only half speed at first. In fact, they can walk through it initially so that the defenders get a feel for the correct path. Tell the guard to toss the shield (air flate) for the final set of repetitions and liven it up in order to simulate game conditions.

231. FOUR ON TWO

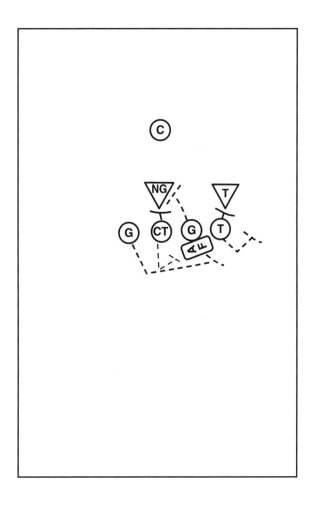

Purpose:

- To master basic defensive adjustments to offensive blocking schemes and techniques.
- Specifically, to react to and destroy trap blocks.

Coaching Pointers:

To the tackle:

- Any time you are unblocked, look to the inside for a trap block or to the backfield for a kickout block.

To the noseguard:

- Fight pressure from the center and, if double-teamed, make a pile in the gap.

To the tackle when stunting:

- Take a hard lead step across the offensive tackle's face, using a good rip technique with your right forearm and shoulder, then control the B gap.

- When you sense a trap block, attack the trapper! Don't wait for him to attempt the block. Attack him and jam the hole as he comes down the line of scrimmage!

Set-up and Instructions:

Put a center, two guards, and one tackle on the line of scrimmage. Give the right guard an air flate to use when executing a trap block. Position a noseguard on the center's head (sometimes offset, depending on your defensive alignment) and a defensive tackle, either head up or on the offensive tackle's outside shoulder. Stand behind the two defensive players to signal blocking schemes to the offensive linemen. Possible variations include: base blocks on the noseguard and tackle; base block tackle and two-team noseguard; pass-protection block; seal block on nose and tackle/both guards pull; and two-team noseguard and trap tackle. When the guard traps the defensive tackle, have him use an air flate in order to protect the two players. Be sure the tackle attacks the guard. This is one of the primary purposes of this drill.

232. SUBMARINE

Purpose:

- To emphasize good submarining technique.

Coaching Pointers:

- Get into your normal stance. Drive **hard** out of it! Focus, focus, focus on the offensive lineman's first move!
- Keep your neck bulled and your head up so you don't go into the ground.
- As you move under the offensive lineman's block, get your knees and arms underneath you as quickly as possible.
- Push off your arms and knees to elevate and immobilize the blocker.
- Don't use this technique until we tell you to.

Set-up and Instructions:

Pair off the defensive linemen, each pair with a stand-up dummy. Instruct them to alternate between offense and defense. Using the above coaching pointers, tell the defensive linemen to hit the base of the stand-up dummy, to drive at least two to three feet beyond it, and to raise up immediately on their hands and knees. Tell the defender to stand to the side of the dummy and to hold the top so that the dummy doesn't fall when the offensive lineman hits it. He should secure the top so the dummy becomes a pendulum.

Have them alternate responsibilities so each lineman gets at least four repetitions. This technique is more important for some linemen than for others and should not be used at will or repeatedly during a game. It should be used when your best player for that position is getting beat or on a goal-line defense.

233. BLOWING THE GAP

Purpose:

- To emphasize the proper technique for attacking the gap, especially on a goal-line stand.

Coaching Pointers:

- Get your tail up in the air and your nose sniffing grass!
- We don't care if we are telegraphing our technique. I want you in the gap **right now!**
- I want you to end up at least a yard in the backfield, on all fours if possible, flat on your stomach if necessary.
- Tie up the linemen and let the linebackers be heroes! They can clean up.

Set-up and Instructions:

Position the defensive linemen in two lines with two blockers to the outside of the first man in each line as illustrated. You stand behind the defenders and, on your hand movement, have the blockers fire into the defender. Instruct the defenders to explode through the gap so that their heads are between the blockers and well into the backfield. Tell them to try to get to all fours, but if they can't, at least to get good penetration into the backfield.

Alternate the blockers and the defenders so that everyone gets at least four or five repetitions. Check for a good stance and quick penetration into the gap.

234. BEATING BACKS

Purpose:

- To practice defeating backfield blockers.

Coaching Pointers:

- Remember, a back **really** doesn't want to block you! He prefers trying to run away from you!
- Once you identify the blocker, attack **him!**
- So if he comes at you high, he's only trying to set up for a cut block or a chop block. He wants to hit you as low as possible!
- So stay low. Stay in your hit position and use your hands on the blocker.
- Depending on his attack, punch and lift or drive a forearm into him and lift—OR—if he tries to cut you, push him into the ground.
- Remember also that if you're taking on a fullback in order to maintain outside containment, you don't have to beat him to death. Just don't let him take you off your feet. A stalemate works as well as anything else. Keep your outside arm free.

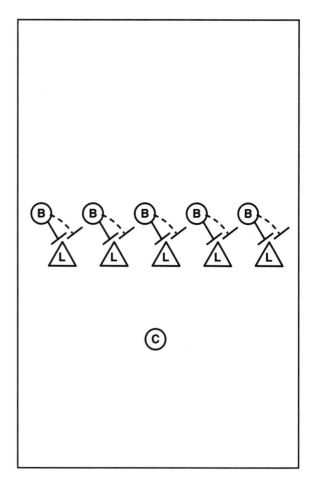

Set-up and Instructions:

Position half the defensive linemen on a line of scrimmage. Position the other half in a fullback alignment to their inside as illustrated. On your cadence (vary it to try to get a defender to jump), have the fullbacks try to kick the defenders out or chop them. Hand signal the kind of block you want for each repetition. Be sure the defender attacks the blocker but always under control so he doesn't get chopped.

Alternate the blockers and the defenders so each lineman gets at least three or four repetitions. This should not be a long drill. Chop blocks can cause injury, so emphasize staying in a **low** hit position. **The lower they get, the more upward leverage they can use when the fullback tries to kick them out and the better they can hand play a chop block.**

235. TAKING THE RIGHT PATH

Purpose:

- To emphasize the correct pursuit path for all defensive linemen.

Coaching Pointers:

- Get off the ground and take the right pursuit angle to the runner!
- Don't ever think you're out of the play! Stay on your pursuit path; you may make the game-saving tackle!
- Don't flatten out your pursuit path! You should be on a collision path with where the ball **will be!**

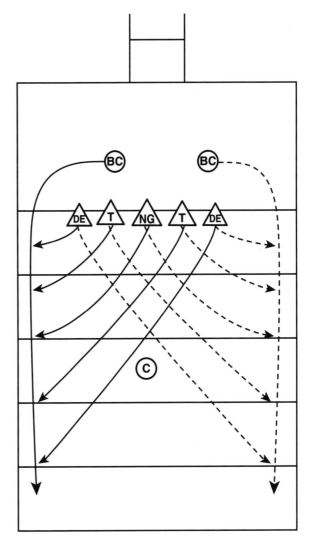

Set-up and Instructions:

Position all the defensive linemen in their normal alignments. Alternate your faster linemen in the backfield as ball carriers. Position them as illustrated. On your command, have all the linemen hit the ground. Simultaneously, have the ball carrier run up the sidelines as fast as he can. Tell the defenders to stay on their pursuit paths and touch him at 10-yard intervals as diagrammed. Notice the dotted lines that illustrate the pursuit paths for the opposite side of the field.

Be sure all the linemen execute their pursuit paths to both sides of the field, at least two to three times. This is an excellent drill at the end of the week to remind linemen of the importance of pursuing correctly. It's also a good end-of-practice conditioner, especially if the entire defensive team is involved.

236. TAKING OFF I

Purpose:

- To emphasize a good take-off when rushing the passer.

Coaching Pointers:

- OK, let's assume an obvious passing situation! I'm taking off your leash! Go get the quarterback!
- But stay in your rushing lanes! We want to rush the quarterback and either sack him or hurry his throw. We also want to **contain** him!
- Take a good, long first step! Get a lot of forward lean. You want to close the distance between you and the blocker as quickly as possible.

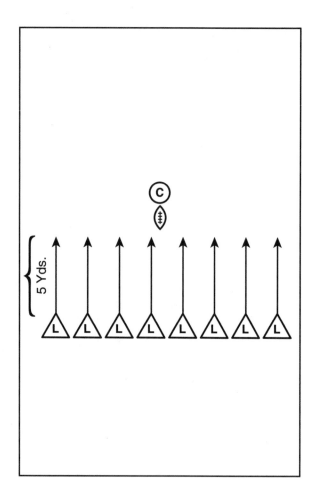

5 Yds.

Set-up and Instructions:

Position all the defensive linemen on one line of scrimmage. Position yourself five yards upfield facing the linemen. Hold a football on the ground as if to snap it. Tell the linemen to get off the ball quickly, elongating their first step and sprinting the five yards as fast as they can. Check for stances and a good forward lean, lift the ball, and watch for a long first step and quick feet. Call out the names of the winners.

Establish some competition. Help the smaller, faster players realize that quickness and speed compensate for size. Size alone doesn't make for a good pass rusher. Quickness and good fundamentals will help them play a lot of football.

237. TAKING OFF II

Purpose:

- To emphasize a fast take-off when rushing the passer.

Coaching Pointers:

- Remember your good, long first step!
- Don't stand up! Keep a good forward lean.
- Drive your arms and legs! Get here!
- Don't move until my arm moves, but then move as fast as you can!

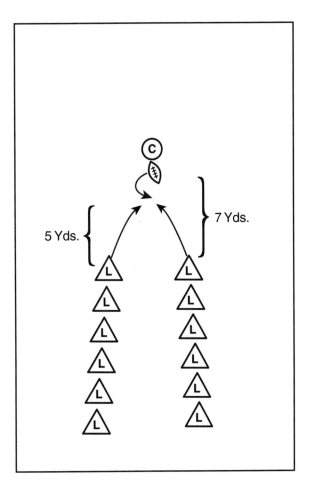

Set-up and Instructions:

Position all the linemen in two parallel lines facing you. Position yourself seven or eight yards in front of them. Hold a football, point up, prepared to toss a spiral in the air. Hold the football approximately waist high and instruct the linemen to get in good stances and to take-off when the ball first moves. Toss the ball up in the air and slightly forward so that it comes down approximately five yards in front of the linemen.

The linemen should take-off as soon as your hand moves and compete to catch the football. The lineman who catches it is the winner. Continue to pair off the linemen until one emerges as the fastest. This kind of competition is healthy. Players like this drill. It's not only fun but very effective in emphasizing a good take-off.

238. GOING IN CIRCLES

Purpose:

- To emphasize running fishhooks around pass blockers.

Coaching Pointers:

- Get around the cones as fast as you can!
- Lean as far to the inside as you can. The sharper your lean, the smaller your blocking surface! The blocker will have a tougher time getting his hands on you.
- If you slip, get up immediately and keep running!
- Remember, you'll be leaning into a blocker. His body will prevent you from falling.

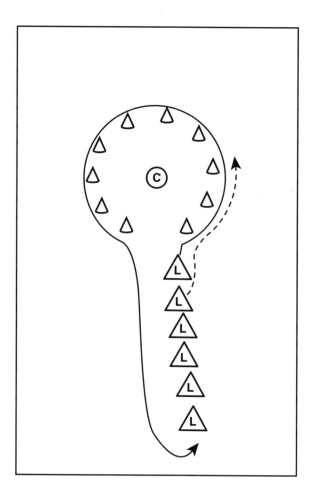

Set-up and Instructions:

Place nine or 10 cones in a circle, approximately six to seven yards in diameter. Put the rushers in a line facing the circle as illustrated. On your cadence, have each lineman run the circle as fast as possible, leaning as far as possible to the inside. The lineman who tips over a cone occasionally is doing a good job. Early in the drill, have them all run the circle so that five or six linemen may be running the circle at once.

After everyone gets warmed up, have them run the circle individually. Put a stopwatch on each of them to promote a little friendly competition. Encourage them to cheer each other on. Be sure each lineman gets at least two or three repetitions **in each direction.**

239. BULL OR PULL

Purpose:

- To emphasize the proper "feel" for vulnerability in the pass blocker's body position.

Coaching Pointers:

- Punch the heels of your hands into the blocker's pads and grab the breastplate.
- Lock your elbows to maintain separation.
- When you push him, how hard does he push back?
- If he pushes hard, pull him and throw him by you.
- If he continues to give ground, roll your hips and bull rush him.

Set-up and Instructions:

Pair off all the defensive linemen and have them alternate being the blockers and the rushers. Have the rushers get a fit on the blockers, their hands in position on the blocker's pads. Then have them close their eyes and **feel** the blocker's body tension. Tell the blockers to exaggerate one of two reactions: forward pressure or backward movement. If the rusher feels strong forward pressure, he should pull the blocker forward and throw him away. If he feels backward movement, he should roll his hips and execute a strong bull rush.

This is a relatively short drill. Give each lineman two or three repetitions being the rusher. This is a good preliminary drill to others in this section. Its purpose is to remind rushers of the need to use the blocker's movements against him.

240. BASIC TECHNIQUES

Purpose:

- To emphasize the basic techniques to be used when rushing the passer.

Coaching Pointers:

- The technique you use will be determined by the strengths and weaknesses of your opponent.
- They also will be determined by his size and his blocking tendencies.
- No matter what technique you use, your goal is to get outside leverage, to get an arm next to and behind the blocker. Once you get either arm behind him, you've got him beat!

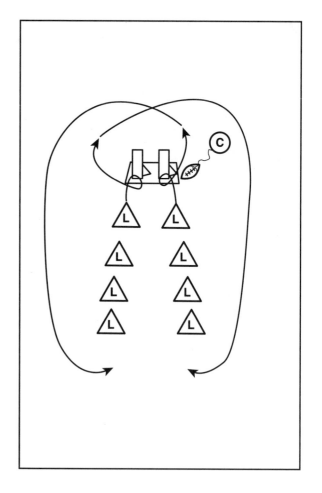

Set-up and Instructions:

Position all the linemen in two lines facing the two-man sled. You stand alongside the sled with your football on a rope. When you move the football, have the linemen explode off the line and execute the move you designate prior to the snap. Have them practice three techniques: the swim, the arm under, and the spin. With the swim and the arm under, have them jam the pad of the sled with their outside hand and either lift the inside arm and swim over the blocker or drop the inside shoulder and push under and past the blocker.

When they execute the spin, have them hit the pad head on and immediately pivot the upper body while they drive off the leg opposite the spin. Most important, have them whip the arm opposite the spin to gain momentum and to separate themselves from the blocker.

Tell them the arm under is effective against a tall blocker or one who stays high during the block. The swim is effective against a short blocker or one who stays low during the block.

The spin is effective at any time but particularly against a less mobile blocker or the blocker who leans hard into them.

241. SPIN THE SQUARE

Purpose:

- To develop the ability to spin away from pass blockers.

Coaching Pointers:

- Get your body on the blocker and get him to lean hard into you. Once he does, spin in the direction of your containment responsibility.

- If you have outside contain, don't spin to the inside—unless you've been pushed behind the quarterback and you're spinning back to him.

- Whip your outside arm hard when you start the spin. It will give you momentum during spin and will separate the blocker from you after the spin.

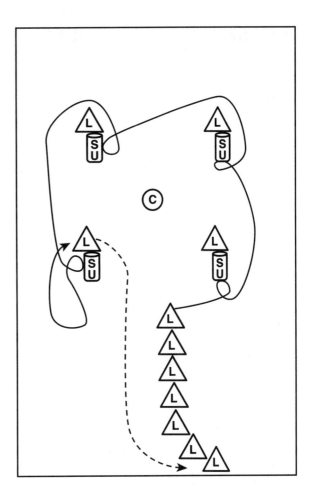

Set-up and Instructions:

Create a square by placing four stand-up dummies five yards apart, each with a lineman holding it. Position the remaining linemen at the base of the square and instruct them to hit each dummy and spin hard to the outside. Be sure to replace the bag holders so that everyone gets at least four or five repetitions. Also be sure to have the linemen run the square in both directions.

Run this drill early in the season and run it often. Spinning off blockers is one of the hardest techniques for pass rushers to learn.

242. REFINED TECHNIQUES

Purpose:

- To refine the basic pass-rushing techniques by executing them against live blocking.

Coaching Pointers:

- Know the blocker! What are his strengths? Weaknesses?
- When you make contact, feel by his body movements what he wants to do and let those movements work against him.
- If he's leaning hard into you, pull him by you or spin on him.
- If he's blocking tall with forward lean or can be pulled off balance, get your arm under and drive past him.
- If he's blocking short, can be pulled off balance, or has a poor blocking base, use your swim technique.
- Much of what he does will be determined by what **you** do!

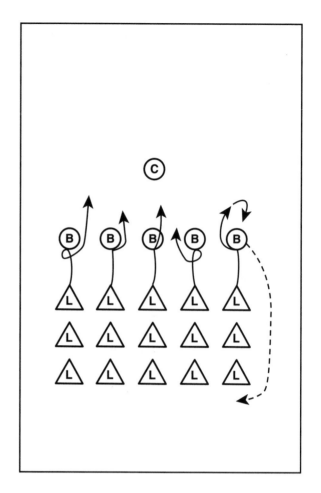

Set-up and Instructions:

Position all the linemen in waves of four or five players. Tell the first wave to take a step forward and turn to face the second wave. Instruct that wave to be blockers, the second wave to be pass rushers. Tell the pass rushers to see if they can **juke** the blocker off balance; otherwise, tell them to punch and grab the blocker and to use his movements against him. If he leans too hard, pull him by or spin. If he's off balance or has a poor blocking base, use an arm under or swim technique. If he's leaning backward or is off balance, bull rush him. **Feel** his pressure or lack of it, his balance, his reactions to you!

Tell the linemen when they are blockers to exaggerate their movements to help the rushers. When the linemen become proficient with these techniques, have the blockers do their best to block them. Continue the drill so that each wave of rushers becomes the next line of blockers. Be sure that everyone gets at least two or three repetitions. This drill uses waves so everyone gets a chance to see or be seen. Both are motivating and instructive.

243. VARY THE SQUARE

Purpose:

- To employ a variety of pass-rush techniques.

Coaching Pointers:

- Refer to the coaching pointers and instructions in the drills *(240) Basic Techniques* and *(242) Refined Techniques* for instructional elements.

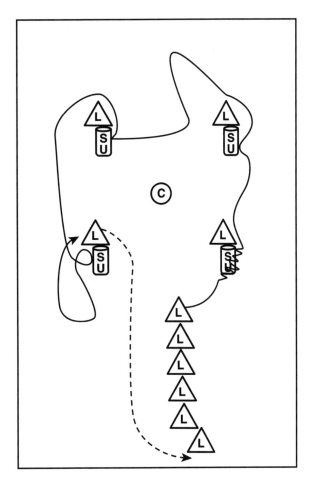

Set-up and Instructions:

Create a square of four stand-up dummies five yards apart, each being held by a lineman. Position the remaining linemen at the base of the square and instruct them to hit each bag, using a different pass-rush technique on each. Have them bull rush the first bag, put an arm under the second bag, swim the third bag, and spin off the last bag.

Be sure to alternate the bag holders so that every lineman gets at least two or three repetitions **in each direction.** Use this drill before defensive scrimmages to remind defensive linemen of their pass-rushing options. Be sure to tell them you want to see every technique used at least once around the square.

244. SMART RUSH

Purpose:

- To practice rushing techniques for beating backfield pass blocking.

Coaching Pointers:

- Use your technique—whatever it is— early. Backs, especially small ones, will often try to chop you.
- So stay low! You can move faster, use your hands better, even spin more quickly.
- Initially, attack the inside of the back, then make a move to his outside. Backs don't want to give you an inside path to the quarterback. Some tend to overprotect the inside.
- A big back may try to take you on high. If he remains fairly stationary, bull rush him.
- At least **start** a bull rush! If he reacts aggressively into you, spin on him.
- Don't be **too** aggressive! A smart back will chop you. Always use a controlled rush on a back.

© 2001 by Michael D. Koehler

Set-up and Instructions:

Position the defensive linemen in three or four waves of five players each as illustrated. Position five linemen approximately five yards downfield from the first wave and off to the side. Tell them they are backfield blockers. Use your ball on a rope to start each repetition. Tell the rushers to use good pass-rushing technique to defeat the block. Alternate the blockers and the rushers after each repetition and be sure that each lineman gets at least four or five repetitions.

Variation: Invite the backs to join you. Have one of the linemen challenge them to a contest. This kind of competition makes for a very spirited drill—sometimes too spirited! Be careful that no one gets hurt. When overly aggressive linemen get chopped by a smart back, they not only learn a lot—they can be seriously injured.

245. GET UP AND GO

Purpose:

- To practice getting off the ground after being chopped, defeating a second blocker, and tackling the ball carrier.

Coaching Pointers:

- Get off the ground as fast as possible! You're still in the play!
- Attack the inside half of the blocking back's body, then bull rush him or make a move based on his reaction.
- Control your rush! Don't charge blindly. You'll get chopped again!
- For purposes of this drill, maintain outside leverage. Don't let the quarterback get outside you.

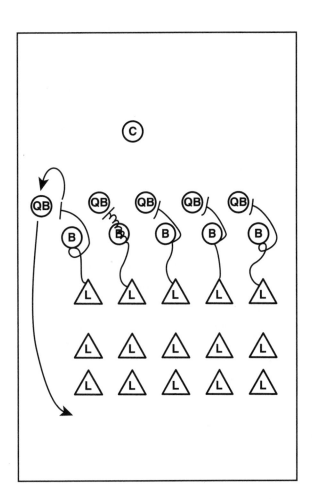

Set-up and Instructions:

Position the linemen in waves of five players. Instruct the first wave to lie down on their backs, their heads facing upfield. Position a blocking back five yards deep and to the outside of the first wave as illustrated. Position a quarterback three yards behind the blocking back and a yard or two to his outside. Both the blocking backs and the quarterbacks can be linemen. Just be sure to alternate them so everyone gets at least two or three repetitions. *Vary the drill* by inviting the backs to join in, but be careful. The competition between them can get intense, sometimes too much so!

Have the linemen get off the ground as quickly as possible, encounter and defeat the blocking back, and wrap up the quarterback. The linemen don't have to tackle the quarterback, just face up to him and wrap him up. Tell the quarterback once in a while to try to scramble outside the pass rusher. Climb all over the rusher if the quarterback is successful. Emphasize his outside contain responsibility.

246. DISCIPLINE

Purpose:

- To emphasize rushing fundamentals and practice the discipline to stay in pass-rush lanes.

Coaching Pointers:

- Prior to your **explosive** take-off, know the rushing technique you plan to use.
- Use secondary techniques based on the blocker's reactions.
- If pushed out of your lane, use a countermove to get back into it.
- Stay in your lane! You don't have free rush unless we tell you it's OK.
- If you can't get to the quarterback, read his passing motion and get your hands in the air!

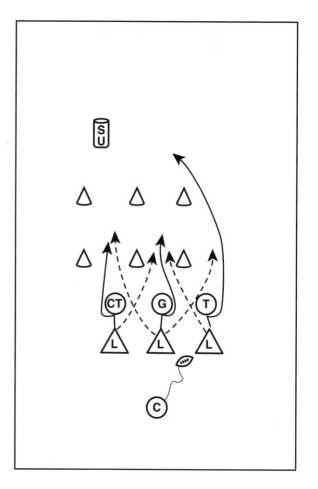

Set-up and Instructions:

Position an offensive center, guard, and tackle in their normal alignments. Position a defensive lineman on the head of each. Early in the season, align the defenders randomly. Later (numbers permitting), as players settle into a position, align a noseguard on the center, a defensive tackle on the guard, and a defensive end on the tackle. Place a stand-up dummy seven yards deep in the backfield to simulate the quarterback. Position six cones as illustrated and identify the spaces in between as pass-rush lanes. Instruct the pass rushers to stay in the lanes and to use whatever technique they can to get to the quarterback. Use your football on a rope to start each repetition. Be sure each defender gets at least two repetitions in each direction.

Variation: Have the defenders use inside or outside twist moves. Huddle the defense between each repetition to call the stunt and hand signal the snap count to the offense. Encourage the defenders to execute their stunts quickly but to stay in their pass-rush lanes.

247. CORRAL THE QUARTERBACK

Purpose:

- To practice staying in a disciplined relationship with the quarterback when he scrambles out of the pocket.

Coaching Pointers:

- Put pressure on the quarterback! Get to him! But stay in your lanes!
- If you have outside containment, **keep** outside containment!
- If you have inside responsibility, don't chase to the outside.
- Shuffle your feet and stay in a good hit position!
- Be mobile! Be able to move.

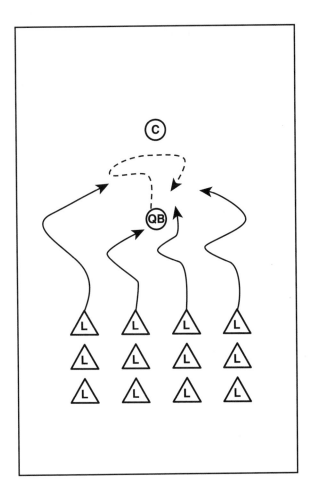

Set-up and Instructions:

Position the linemen in waves of four. Tell the defensive tackles to take the two inside positions; the defensive ends, the outside. Early in the season, don't worry about these assignments. You may still be searching and most players should learn both responsibilities anyway.

Position a quarterback (he can be a lineman—a quick one!) seven yards deep in the backfield. Use your ball on a rope or a designated movement to start each repetition. Tell the rushers to attack the quarterback and to stay in positive relationship with each other to prevent a successful scramble.

Tell the quarterback to drop back farther, run in either direction, drop back and run; in essence, do anything he can to get inside or outside the rushers.

Once the rushers become proficient with pass-rush techniques, **vary the drill** by positioning blockers in front of each lineman. Check for their pass-rush techniques as well as their disciplined relationships with each other.

248. HELP THE BLITZ

Purpose:

- To emphasize the lineman's responsibility when linebackers or safeties are blitzing.

Coaching Pointers:

- Your primary job is to make two men block you so you open a lane for the blitzer!

- Put your outside shoulder on the inside shoulder of the man on your head. Work to get into the gap in order to make contact with the next man to the inside.

- Force the man on your head to block you as **you** move to block the next man to the inside!

- Tie up both men so that no one is in the lane to block the blitzer.

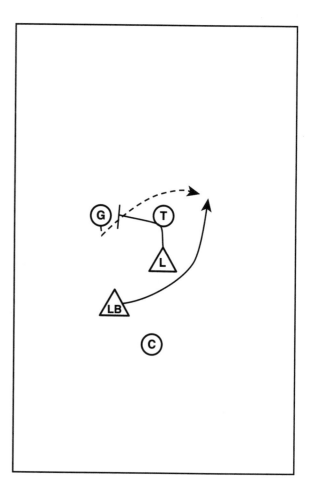

Set-up and Instructions:

Divide the linemen into groups of four. Tell one to be an offensive guard, one an offensive tackle, one a linebacker, one the defender. Have them line up as illustrated and have them alternate responsibilities after each repetition. Hand signal a cadence to the two men on offense. On the snap, have the defender drive through the inside shoulder of the man on his head and make contact with the next man in. In this case, have him drive into and past the tackle in order to make contact with the guard.

Tell the guard to hesitate a split second, then try to area block the linebacker. Tell the linebacker to drive off the defender's tail and get into the backfield. Tell the defender, **if he has to,** to move head up on the tackle or shade his inside eye to get to the gap faster. This will depend on his quickness and desire.

This is an excellent drill, but it need be run only three or four times all season.

249. BAT THE BALL

Purpose:

- To develop the skill to read the quarterback's throwing intentions in order to obscure his vision or to knock down the ball.

Coaching Pointers:

- Read **these keys**: the quarterback's non-throwing hand, his non-throwing arm, and the football.
- When he releases his hand, he's preparing to throw the ball. If you're close enough for a sack, try harder!
- If you're **not** close enough, get under control and raise your arms into his field of vision.
- Once the ball moves away from the front of his body and his throwing elbow is raised, jump to knock down the ball.
- Don't jump unless he's starting his passing motion, and **never pass rush with your arms up!** Your primary job is to get to the quarterback! Raise your arms only if you can't get to him!

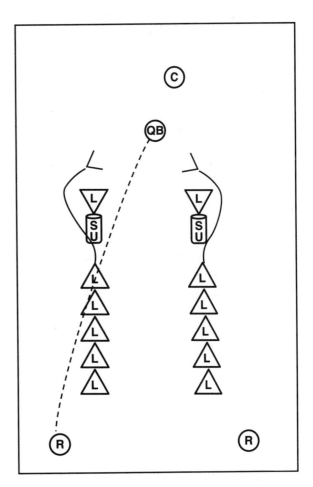

Set-up and Instructions:

Position the defensive linemen in two lines, one on either side of a quarterback who is five to six yards away facing them. Position two linemen 12 to 15 yards downfield as receivers. Have two additional linemen hold stand-up dummies facing each line. Instruct the dummy holders to give ground but to use just enough resistance to prevent the rushers from getting to the quarterback. Tell the rushers to bull rush the dummies at three-quarter speed and to watch the quarterback's passing indicators. Be sure to alternate the receivers and bag holders so that everyone gets at least two or three repetitions.

Check to see that they raise their hands and/or jump at the right time to obscure the quarterback's vision or to knock down the ball.

250. COUNTERMOVE

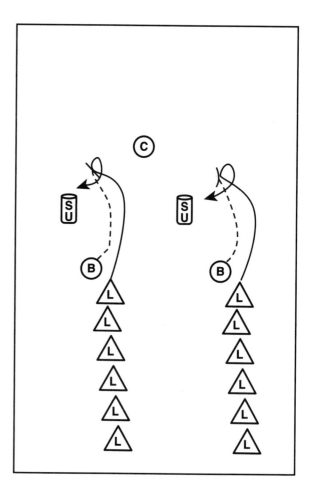

Purpose:

- To develop the skill to counterback to the quarterback when pushed beyond him by a blocker.

Coaching Pointers:

- First of all, focus on beating the blocker but know where you are in relation to the quarterback.

- When you see you're about to be pushed past the quarterback, exert as much outward pressure as you can to keep the blocker pushing you in the same direction.

- Then spin back against his pressure to the inside.

- **Don't ever** spin to the inside if you have contain responsibility—**unless** you've been pushed past the quarterback. At that point, a spin to the inside still gives you the outside leverage you need to pressure the quarterback.

Set-up and Instructions:

Position the linemen in two lines facing upfield, an offensive blocker just to the side of the first man as illustrated. Place a stand-up dummy six yards into the backfield to simulate the quarterback in his dropback position. Instruct the rushers to move hard to the outside of the blocker in an attempt to fishhook around the blocker.

Tell the blockers to feel free to drive the rushers hard to the outside past the stand-up dummy. Tell the rushers to counterback quickly to the inside once they see they have been pushed beyond the stand-up dummy. They should execute an inside spin move. Alternate the rushers and the blockers so everyone gets at least two repetitions **in both directions.**

251. RUSH THE GAP

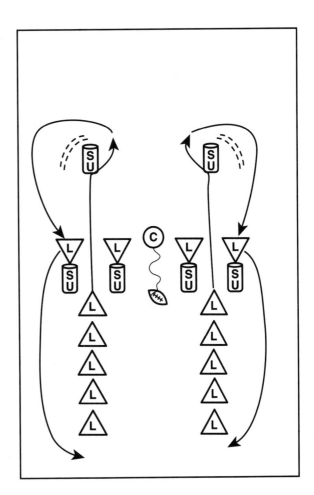

Purpose:

- To emphasize proper techniques for splitting two blockers on obvious passing situations.

Coaching Pointers:

- Get through the gap! Be especially poised to go on the ball. You still don't have **free** rush, but we're turning you loose. We'll take the blame if you miss run action.
- Go get the quarterback!
- Get your tail up and your head down. This is a time to blow off the line!
- Your first step—a long one—should get you over the line of scrimmage.
- Create a small blocking surface by turning your torso so you literally **squeeze sideways** through the gap.
- And keep driving your legs! You need speed to blow the gap!

Set-up and Instructions:

Position the linemen in two lines facing upfield. Position two linemen, each holding a stand-up dummy on either side of the first player in each line. Stand between the two lines with your football on a rope to start each repetition. Tell the rushers to get off the ball as fast as they can. Place a stand-up dummy six or seven yards into the backfield to simulate the quarterback. Shout your challenge: Who's gonna get to the quarterback first?

Check for a good stance, a long first step, and a pivoted torso to squeeze through the dummies. Check also for good leg drive and an evident desire to get to the quarterback. As the season progresses, motivate the players further by putting a stopwatch on them.

SECTION 9

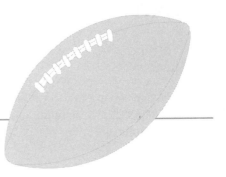

LINEBACKER DRILLS

This section focuses on the following skills:

- Stance/hit position
- Delivering a forearm blow
- Executing the rip technique
- Middle linebackers: reading the triangle
- 52 and 44 backers: reading backs through the line
- Executing stunts
- Camouflaging/faking stunts
- Maintaining pursuit paths
- Staying in a good hit position
- Dropping to pass coverage
- Jamming a tight end
- Breaking on the ball
- Maintaining an inside-out pursuit path
- Maintaining an outside-in responsibility

252. WAVE

Purpose:

- To practice staying in a good hit position and shuffle stepping along the line of scrimmage.

Coaching Pointers:

- **Never** get out of your hit position! It gives you mobility, strength, and good upward lift. Stay in it right to the point of making the tackle.
- When pursuing along the line of scrimmage, shuffle step. Don't cross-over step. If you do, you're blockable and immediately out of position. Keep your shoulders **squared** to the line of scrimmage!
- Be mobile! Be able to move in any direction. The only way to do that is to have a good bend in your knees and a good base with your feet.

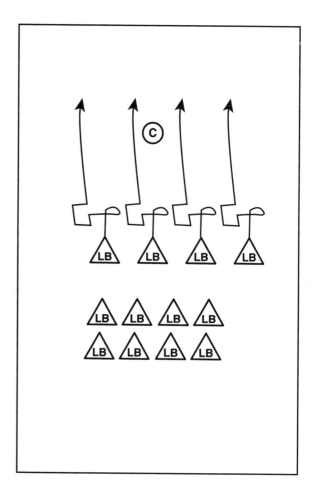

Set-up and Instructions:

Position all the linebackers in waves of four or five. Have each wave shuffle right, left, back, forward by pointing in the direction. They should move as soon as you point with no wasted steps. Their movements will be awkard if they get out of a good hit position, so remind them often to stay low, to shuffle their feet, and to use their arms.

Use this drill early in the season to teach proper linebacker movement, then often during the season as a conditioner prior to the use of the other drills in this section.

253. SHUFFLE AND GO

Purpose:

- To emphasize the importance of shuffle stepping when pursuing the ball.

Coaching Pointers:

- Don't crossover step! Shuffle! When going to the right, right foot sideways, followed by left foot. The left foot should never cross over the right.
- Stay in your hit position! Keep your arms in front of you to ward off blockers, and keep a good bend in your knees for mobility and power.
- In this drill, whether moving sideways, forward, or backward, **NEVER** get out of your hit position!

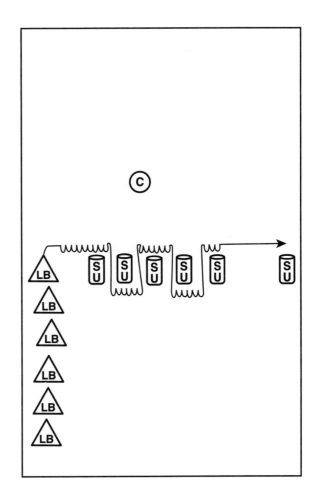

Set-up and Instructions:

Position the linebackers to the left of a series of stand-up dummies facing you as illustrated. On your command, the first linebacker should set up in front of you in a good hit position. On your next command, he should shuffle to the right in front of the dummies. He should shuffle, back pedal between one and two, shuffle, race forward between two and three, shuffle, back pedal between three and four, shuffle, race between four and five, then turn and sprint past the sixth stand-up dummy. Be sure to have the linebackers shuffle in both directions.

Check for a good hit position throughout the drill, quick feet, squared shoulders, and a bulled neck.

254. FOLLOW ME

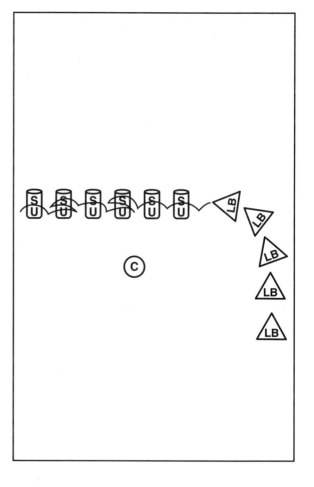

Purpose:

- To emphasize a good hit position and mobility while pursuing the ball carrier.

Coaching Pointers:

- Stay in your hit position to maintain your mobility!
- Keep your eyes on me and shuffle step over the dummies.
- Don't waste any steps! Move, move!

Set-up and Instructions:

Lay five or six stand-up dummies on their sides, approximately one yard separating each dummy. Position all the linebackers on either side of the dummies and instruct the first man in the line to shuffle step over the dummies, staying facing you. You can move right or left in front of him—if you need the exercise!—or you can point in the direction you want him to move. Have him change direction each time you point right or left.

This is a rapid-fire drill. It's as much a conditioner as a learning experience for the linebackers. Be sure each linebacker has at least three repetitions over the bags.

Make the drill more challenging—and fun—by having one of the players play catch with each linebacker as he goes over the bags.

255. SHUFFLE DOWNHILL

Purpose:

- To emphasize moving downhill to attack the line of scrimmage.

Coaching Pointers:

- Shuffle over the dummies. Do not crossover step.
- Think **ATTACK** when shuffling along the line of scrimmage. Blockers are objects to be **ATTACKED.** They don't control you. You control them!
- Keep your shoulders square, your head up and neck bulled, and your knees bent and weight forward. Never get out of your hit position.
- If you get out of your hit position, you lose mobility and power when delivering a blow.

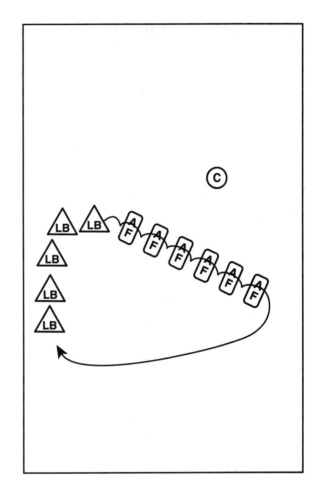

Set-up and Instructions:

Lay six air flates on their side approximately two to three feet apart. Position the linebackers to either side facing you. On your command, have them get into a good hit position. On your next command, have them shuffle over the bags, staying low and moving their feet quickly.

Remind them the dummies are going downhill to emphasize the importance of attacking the line of scrimmage while they are pursuing the ball. Remind them also they are shuffle stepping to prevent cutbacks. They must be able to move in all directions in order to react to ball carriers.

256. SHUFFLE AND READ

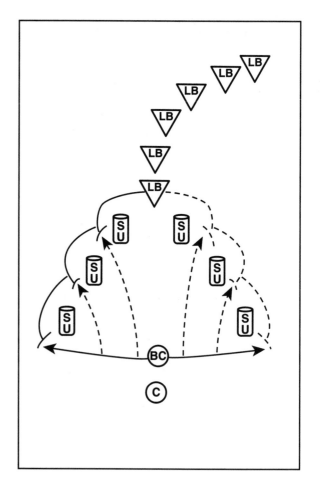

Purpose:

- To emphasize the importance of attacking the line of scrimmage, reading the ball carrier, and facing up.

Coaching Pointers:

- Read the ball carrier's direction and shuffle step downhill.
- Read his cut and face up with him.
- For purposes of this drill, don't worry about tackling him; just face up.
- **DO NOT** let him cut back on you.
- You should never have to move back uphill.
- Every time you have to go back uphill, you have overpursued the ball.

Set-up and Instructions:

Set up six stand-up dummies as illustrated, three downhill to the right, three to the left. Position a linebacker in the middle facing another linebacker acting as a ball carrier. On your command, have the ball carrier move either right or left and cut into hole one or two or keep running hard to the outside.

Be sure the linebacker stays in a hit position and shuffles downhill. When the ball carrier cuts into a hole, the linebacker should be in a position to face up to him. He should **not** overpursue. If he does, **GET HIS ATTENTION!** Overpursuit is the linebacker's cardinal sin.

257. TWO-POINT CONTACT

Purpose:

- To emphasize the fundamentals of the forearm blow.

Coaching Pointers:

- Stay in your hit position! A powerful forearm comes from your legs!
- The strength of the blow comes when you drive **up** and into the blocker.
- **Bull your neck!** When you explode up, keep your neck bulled so you can protect yourself with the front part of your helmet and the muscle pad in the back of your neck.
- As you make contact with your helmet, make simultaneous contact with your arm and shoulder, pushing up and out with your arm after initial contact.
- Contact should be made as you explode up and out of your hit position.
- Remember, you attack blockers! Defeat them.

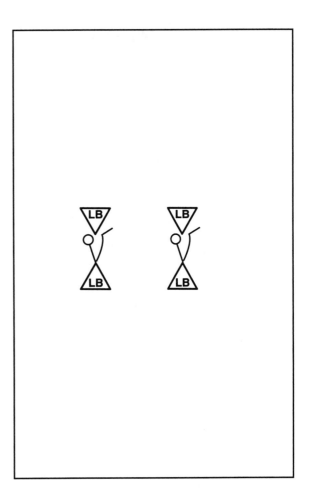

Set-up and Instructions:

Pair off all the linebackers. Have them alternate being blockers and linebackers. Early in the season, conduct this drill at half speed. Have the blockers get into three-point stances and fire out on the linebackers. Position the linebackers two to three yards in front of the blockers. On your signal, have the blockers move toward the linebackers. Have the linebackers stay in their hit positions, get low, maintain a good base, and rip up through the blocker with the two-point contact as described above. Remember, this drill is only half speed. The primary emphasis is proper form.

Check for all the above pointers and all of your own.

258. THREE-POINT CONTACT

Purpose:

- To practice the fundamentals of the hand shiver.

Coaching Pointers:

- Emphasize many of the same fundamentals outlined in the coaching pointers for *(257) Two-Point Contact.*

- Keep your neck bulled and use your helmet to protect your head. Don't drop your head at contact. If contact is made with the blocker, it should be made with the front part of your helmet.

- Watch the blocker for the technique he plans to use.

- If he comes right at you, to initiate contact, punch out and up with the heels of your hands, then explode up with your legs, rolling your hips under you for leverage.

- Attack the blocker, gain control of him, then get rid of him.

Set-up and Instructions:

Pair off the linebackers. Have them alternate between being a blocker and a linebacker. Tell the blocker to get into a three-point stance and, at half-speed, to base block the linebacker. Tell the linebacker to stay in a good hit position, to make contact—again, at half speed—with the front part of the helmet and the heels of both hands, and to explode up with the legs and roll the hips. Form is more important than anything else during this drill.

Early in the season, aggressiveness and toughness are secondary to the proper fundamentals. You know who the tough guys are, or you'll soon find out. The toughest guy, without the proper fundamentals, gets beat. Watch for the proper form and make lots of corrections.

259. POP THE SLED

Purpose:

- To practice the fundamentals of two- and three-point contact on either the popsicle or the two-man sled.

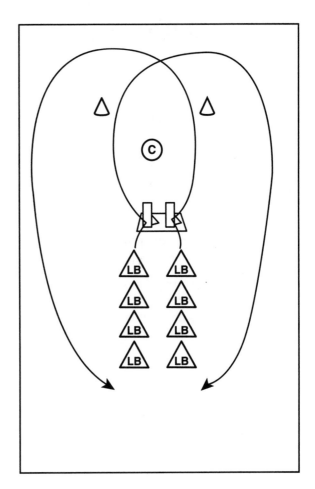

Coaching Pointers:

- Get in a solid hit position: good base, good bend in the knees, arms hanging comfortably in front of you, bulled neck.
- On the whistle, explode into the pad with good two- or three-point contact, drive in and up with your legs, roll your hips underneath you, and get separation from the sled.
- On the whistle, push off the sled to the outside and sprint to the cone.

Set-up and Instructions:

Position the linebackers in two lines in front of the two-man sled. (This drill can be used with a popsicle, too.) Have them get into a good hit position and, on your signal, explode into the pad, using two- or three-point contact. Be sure each linebacker gets at least three repetitions with both kinds of contact. Also be sure each linebacker works both sides of the sled during the drill. When using two-point contact, the linebacker should hit the pad with his inside arm, keeping the outside hand free to jam the pad in order to maintain outside leverage. Have them release to the outside on your next signal and sprint to a cone 10 yards upfield.

This is a rapid-fire drill, to be used after the linebackers have mastered the fundamentals of two- and three-point contact.

260. POP AND GO

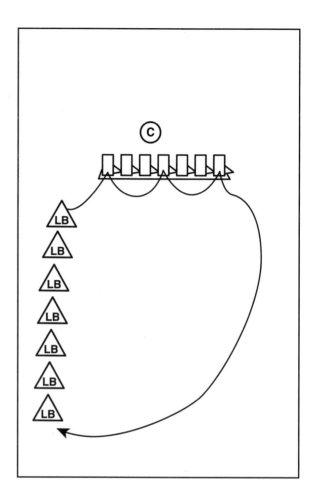

Purpose:

- To master the fundamentals of three-point contact.

Coaching Pointers:

- Maintain a good hit position and shuffle from the first pad, to the middle pad, to the last pad on the sled.
- On each pad, execute good three-point contact—hit, punch, lift, separate!
- Explode up with your legs and roll your hips under you!
- We're not trying to push the sled over! I just want to see it pop up with each hit.

Set-up and Instructions:

Position all the linebackers to the left of the seven-man sled. On your signal, have them execute good three-point contact on the first pad, the middle pad, and the last pad on the sled. After they hit the three pads, the linebackers should go to the back of the line and continue with the drill until they all get at least three repetitions. After the three repetitions, have them line up to the right of the sled and get three repetitions in the opposite direction.

This is a rapid-fire drill. The linebackers should have mastered the basic fundamentals of three-point contact prior to this drill. You should have to make few corrections, just keep them moving to be sure the techniques get into body memory.

261. CONTROL THE BOARD

Purpose:

- To practice the fundamentals of two- and three-point contact in a live but controlled situation.

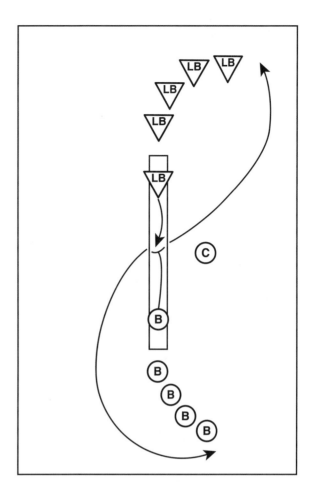

Coaching Pointers:

- When the blocker fires out at you, **attack him!**
- Stay in a solid hit position and try to get underneath his block.
- If you can get underneath his block, use three-point contact to hit, lift, and separate.
- If he is too low, use two-point contact to try to get your arm underneath him to gain control.
- Maintain a good base with your feet, or you'll slip on the board.
- Drive the blocker back off the board or throw him to either side.
- If he drives you off, he wins!
- Who's going to control the board?

Set-up and Instructions:

Position the linebackers in equal lines on either side of a six-foot 2" × 6" board. Tell one side to be blockers; the other side, linebackers. Tell the blockers to straddle the board about a yard from the end, get into a three-point stance and, on your signal, block the linebacker. They should try to push the linebacker off the board.

Tell the linebackers to straddle the board about a yard from the end of the board, get into a good hit position, and defeat the block with either two- or three-point contact.

This is a very competitive drill. Use it only to see if the linebackers are using proper fundamentals under live conditions. Two repetitions for each linebacker is usually enough.

262. QUICK RIP

Purpose:

- To emphasize the basics of the rip technique.

Coaching Pointers:

- When a blocker tries to cut you off by getting between you and your path to the ball, rip your inside arm past his head and drive off your inside leg to get your arm and body to his outside.

- Drive your arm as soon as you see he is taking a cutoff path.

- The faster you get your inside arm to his outside, the quicker you get the leverage you need to defeat his block and to stay on your pursuit path.

- This is an aggressive move. Don't try to sneak your arm past him; drive it past him!

- Do it legally! We're not telling you to punch the opponent or to purposely hurt him. Just get your arm to his outside!

Set-up and Instructions:

Pair off the linebackers and have them face each other: one is a blocker; the other, a linebacker. Be sure they alternate these responsibilities so each linebacker gets at least four or five repetitions as a linebacker. This is a non-contact drill. Instruct the blockers to take one step either straight ahead, right, or left. Tell the linebackers to react to the blockers' movements by either stepping into three-point contact or by making a right or left rip movement.

If the blocker takes one step forward, the linebacker should take one step forward, staying in a good hit position and popping up with both hands and the front part of his helmet. If the blocker steps either right or left, the linebacker should drive hard in that direction with his inside foot and rip his inside arm to a position that would be outside the blocker. Each takes just one step. Watch for good hit positions and strong initial movement. This is a good introductory drill.

274

263. RIP CONTACT

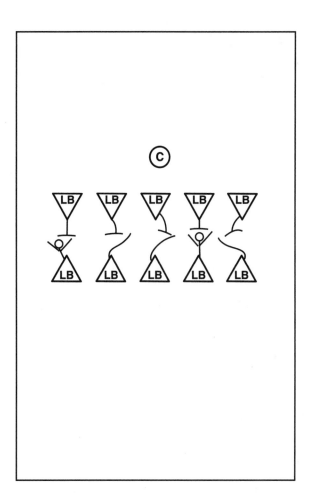

Purpose:

- To practice the fundamentals of the rip technique to secure outside leverage.

Coaching Pointers:

- When the blocker tries to seal or reach block or cut you off to one side or the other, he's doing it for a reason. Always be prepared to beat his block to get to the outside.
- **NEVER** take the path of least resistance when avoiding a blocker to get to the ball carrier, so never go **behind** him!
- Always rip across the blocker's face on an inside-out path.
- Give a little ground if you have to. Just be sure to maintain your proper pursuit path.
- Rip with your inside arm, that is, drive your inside arm forcefully past the blocker's head to his outside.
- Rip hard enough to get leverage, then go to the ball carrier—on an inside-out path.
- Don't overpursue; always leave room to let the ball carrier come back to you. You have lots of help to the outside.

Set-up and Instructions:

Pair off the linebackers. Have them alternate between being blockers and linebackers. Tell the blockers to get into three-point stances and—at half speed—to block the linebacker straight on or to try to angle to either side of him. Tell the linebackers to use two- or three-point contact for the straight shoulder block and a good rip technique for the angle block.

Check to make sure they stay in good hit positions and execute the proper fundamentals. Each linebacker should have at least four or five repetitions, especially early in the season. Use this drill often during the preseason. It does a good job getting the fundamentals into body memory.

264. BLAST RIP

Purpose:

- To teach linebackers the fundamentals of blasting with the shoulder, punching with a two-hand shiver, and ripping to the outside of blockers.

Coaching Pointers:

- Remember, a good shoulder blast starts with your legs!
- So get in a good hit position with a good knee bend so you're able to explode up and into the blocker!
- Stay in your hit position—always!—before and during the blast, the rip, and the tackle!
- Bent knees give you the power to explode up, into, and through blockers and ball carriers.
- Also remember, a shoulder blast and a rip are aggressive moves! They're not dirty—just hostile. So mean business when you deliver them!

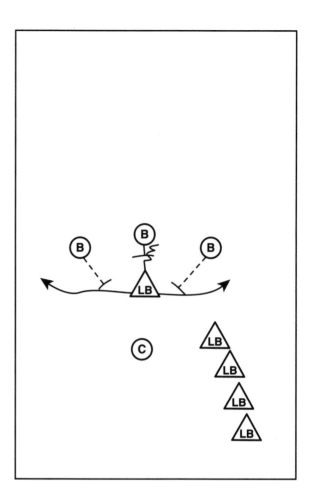

Set-up and Instructions:

Position three linebackers in an arc as blockers. Number them one, two, and three. Position a linebacker in front of them in a good hit position. When the middle blocker approaches him, he should attack him with a shoulder blast and a two-hand shiver. When one or three approaches him, he should rip through the block to the blocker's outside.

Check for a good hit position, good leg explosion up and into the blockers, a forceful rip move to either side, and a return to a balanced hit position after each move. Alternate the linebackers through the arc so everyone gets at least two or three repetitions of defeating the blockers.

265. TEMPO PURSUIT

Purpose:

- To emphasize the proper inside-out pursuit path.

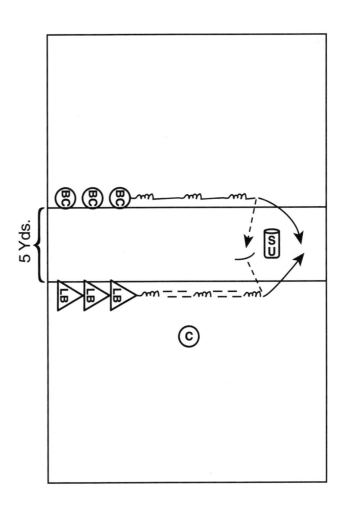

Coaching Pointers:

- Don't overrun the ball carrier!
- If he cuts back on you, he's got a straight shot to the end zone.
- This means that you have to adjust your path and your speed to maintain your inside-out pursuit path. Always stay inside the ball carrier, maybe a yard behind him.
- While you're making such adjustments, stay in your hit position and move downhill along the line of scrimmage, staying squared up to potential blockers.
- Shuffle step until the ball carrier runs full speed. Then you can crossover step.

Set-up and Instructions:

Position the linebackers along one of the yard lines. Position two or three ball carriers five yards upfield of them as illustrated. The ball carriers can be linebackers. Be sure to alternate them so that everyone gets at least two or three repetitions.

Tell the ball carrier to alternately jog and sprint across the field until he reaches the stand-up dummy near the far sideline. Just before he reaches the dummy, he should either cut back on the linebacker or sprint hard to run outside the dummy. Tell him he can fake a cutback and go wide or fake going wide, then cut back.

Instruct the linebacker to stay a yard behind the ball carrier, to shuffle step when the ball carrier jogs, to cross over when the ball carrier sprints, and to execute the proper tackle when the ball carrier either cuts back or runs to the outside. The drill can involve live tackling or form tackling. I usually make it live early in the season; dummy, later on.

266. NO CUTBACK

Purpose:

- To emphasize the proper pursuit path to prevent cutbacks.

Coaching Pointers:

- You're not doing this all alone! You have lots of help to the outside.
- The defenders on the outside are forcing the ball carrier back to the inside—to you.
- Your job is to squeeze him to the outside, so he has nowhere to go.
- The outside defenders will contain outside-in. You contain inside-out so that, if he cuts back, you make the tackle.
- **<u>DO NOT OVERPURSUE!</u>**

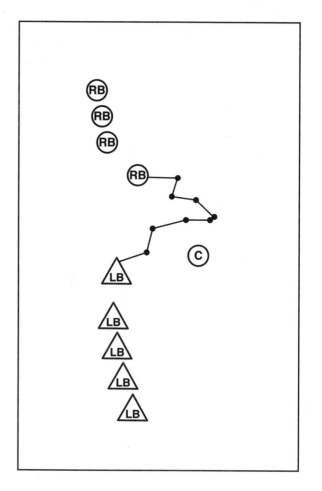

Set-up and Instructions:

Divide the linebackers into two groups: one to be running backs; the other, inside linebackers. Position both lines as illustrated. Tell the running backs to try to beat the linebacker to the outside or to cut back on him to the inside. They should try to get the linebacker to overpursue, then cut back against him.

Tell the linebackers to maintain an inside-out pursuit path on the running backs. The running back should always be a step or two ahead of the linebacker. This drill is not live. Tell the linebackers to simply wrap up the running back.

Be sure all the linebackers alternate running back and linebacker responsibilities so everyone gets at least three repetitions executing an inside-out pursuit path.

267. MOVE AND HIT

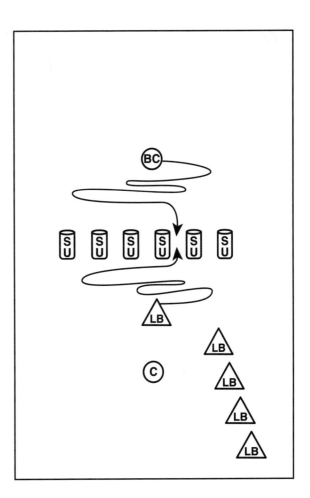

Purpose:

- To emphasize good lateral movement before executing a tackle.

Coaching Pointers:

- Stay in your hit position and shuffle step along the line of scrimmage.
- Keep your knees bent and a good base with your feet to maintain your mobility.
- While you're mirroring the ball carrier's movements, be sure to stay a yard behind him to maintain inside-out leverage.
- You should always tackle him across the bow or straight up, never outside-in.

Set-up and Instructions:

Lay five or six stand-up dummies on their sides each approximately two yards apart. Position a ball carrier (he can be a linebacker) on one side of the middle bag, a linebacker on the other. You stand behind the linebacker and hand signal the ball carrier to run right or left. After three or four changes of direction, point to a gap between any of the bags. The ball carrier should run into that gap and the linebacker should tackle him across the bow or straight up.

Try to move the ball carrier so the linebacker gets out of position. Be sure each linebacker gets at least two repetitions. They don't need many more than that. This can be a very competitive drill. It's also a good early season drill for identifying kids with the mobility, strength, and aggressiveness to play linebacker.

268. ONE, TWO, THREE

Purpose:

- To emphasize good open-field tackling fundamentals.

Coaching Pointers:

- Never run full speed at the ball carrier in the open field. You'll lose lateral mobility if he makes a cut.
- Stay at 80% to 90% of your full speed and take a good collision path with him, always trying to keep him pinned to one direction.
- Normally, you'll tackle him high, above the waist or at the numbers. We don't want you to give yourself up at his feet.
- If he has nowhere to go when hitting a hole, giving yourself up may be OK, but not in the open field.

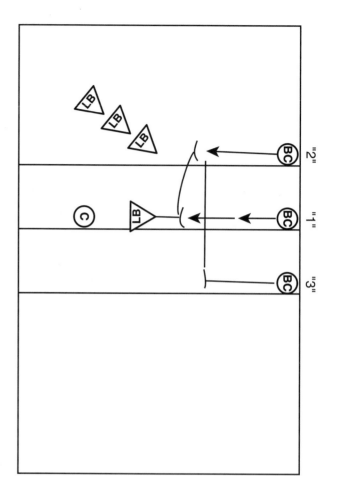

Set-up and Instructions:

Position three ball carriers (they can be linebackers) on a sideline approximately five yards apart. Assign each a number. Alternate the numbers after each repetition. Position a linebacker at midfield in front of the middle runner. Call a number and have the first runner run toward the linebacker. Give all the runners the option of cutting back on the linebacker.

Have the linebacker take the proper collision path with the ball carrier. Have him face up to the ball carrier and form tackle him. Then call another number and have the linebacker take a collision path with the second ball carrier. Do the same with the third ball carrier.

Check to be sure the linebackers maintain the proper speed and take a collision path with the ball carriers, preventing cutbacks. This is a good drill at any time during the season to remind linebackers of proper pursuit fundamentals.

269. BOARD OF EDUCATION

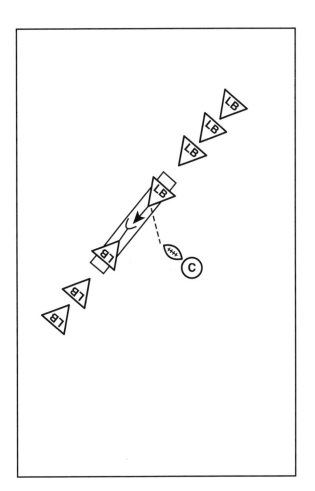

Purpose:

- To emphasize good tackling fundamentals on the line of scrimmage and in the open field.

Coaching Pointers:

- Tackle high in the open field. I don't care if you don't drive him back. I want the runner on the ground.

- Always keep a good base when tackling: foot at least shoulder-width and a good bend in the knees. If you don't keep a good base, you're going to slip on the board.

- **ALWAYS** bull your neck when tackling, even in the open field or when hitting a ball carrier low. The muscle pad in the back of your neck will protect your head.

- When you catch a ball carrier in the hole with nowhere to go, I want a solid hit with good leg drive. Push him back where he came from!

Set-up and Instructions:

Position the linebackers in two lines facing each other on either end of a six foot 2" × 6". Have the first two linebackers in each line straddle the board one foot from each end. Be sure there are no size or weight mismatches. Tell them to get into good hit positions. You stand to the side of the middle of the board with a football. Toss the ball unpredictably to one of the linebackers. He will be the runner; the other, the tackler.

Just before you toss the ball, say "In the hole" or "Open field." The tackler should either drive the ball carrier back or tackle him high. This can be a very competitive drill, so keep the repetitions at a minimum. It should be used early in the season to evaluate the players' live execution of fundamentals. It is generally unnecessary later in the season.

270. INSIDE-OUT

Purpose:

- To defeat two blockers, using the forearm and rip techniques, to maintain an inside-out pursuit path, and to execute a form tackle, preferably across the bow.

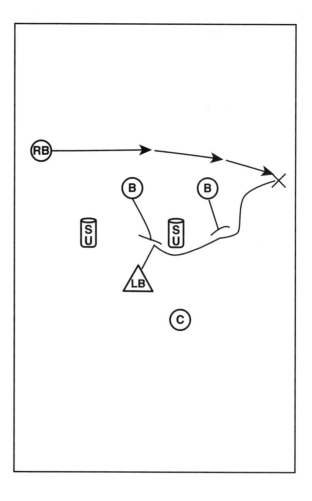

Coaching Pointers:

- Maintain a good stance/hit position.
- Use effective leverage when defeating the first block, using the helmet, shoulders, and forearm.
- Defeat the second block with a strong rip-through technique.
- Maintain an inside-out pursuit path, never allowing the running back a cut-back possibility.
- A good pursuit path should result in a tackle across the bow.

Set-up and Instructions:

Lay two stand-up dummies parallel to each other, approximately three yards apart. Position a blocker between the dummies, one yard back. Position another blocker alongside him, one to two yards outside the second dummy. Position the running back three yards deep and two yards outside the first dummy. Finally, position a linebacker between the two dummies on the defensive side of the ball, head up on the first blocker.

Instruct the running back to run a sweep, allowing him to cut back if he can. Tell the blockers to block the linebacker, allowing the second blocker to cut block, base block, or shield block. Instruct the linebacker to defeat each block, maintaining an inside-out pursuit path and to stop the running back, no more than five yards downfield. Emphasize the inside-out pursuit path, even to the point of missing the tackle. Remind the linebacker he will have sufficient help to the outside but must not allow a cutback move.

271. OUTSIDE CONTAIN

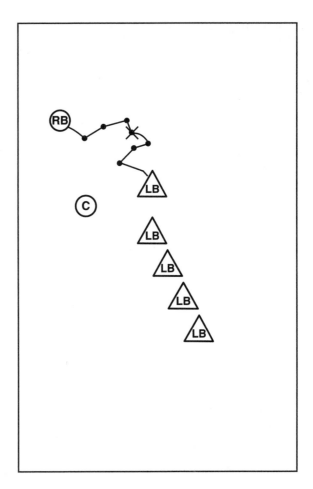

Purpose:

- To emphasize the basics of the containment responsibility for outside linebackers.

Coaching Pointers:

- You have a lot of help to the inside! Your job is to prevent the ball carrier from getting outside you.

- Remember, **nothing** gets outside you!

- Get used to it. The people on the inside will get more tackles than you will. Your job is to force everything back to the inside.

- The more aggressive you become, the more mistakes you will make. Be patient.

- Every time you penetrate into the backfield, angle penetrate! Angle into the backfield. Don't move straight ahead. You'll leave a hole between you and the defensive tackle.

Set-up and Instructions:

Position the outside linebackers in their normal defensive alignment. Position a running back to the inside (he can be a linebacker). On the running back's movement, tell the linebacker to take the appropriate angle to maintain outside-in containment. If the running back comes straight at him, as with a power play, the linebacker should angle into the backfield to pressure him to the inside. If the ball carrier takes a parallel path or gets depth in the backfield, as with a sweep, option or quick pitch, the linebacker should shuffle along the line of scrimmage to string out the play, always staying just outside the ball carrier and waiting for him to commit.

Emphasize PATIENCE! The more anxious an outside linebacker is to make a tackle, the more likely he is to make mistakes.

272. READ THE BACK

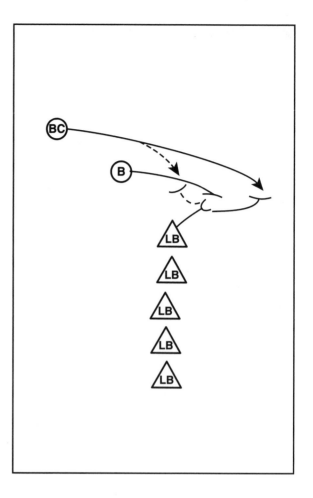

Purpose:

- To teach linebackers to control and shed blockers while reading the ball carrier's motion.

Coaching Pointers:

- Use two-point or three-point contact on the blocker and get good separation while reading the ball carrier.
- Shed the blocker when the ball carrier commits to a certain direction.
- Don't be afraid to give a little ground while reading the ball carrier. The tackle is the important thing.
- Don't let the ball carrier cut back on you. Don't commit until he commits.
- If he tries to cut back, you'll be faced up to him. But if he runs to the outside, tackle him across the bow.

Set-up and Instructions:

Position all the linebackers in one line facing upfield. Position a blocker five yards farther upfield and five yards to the inside. Place a ball carrier five more yards upfield and six or seven yards to the inside of the blocker as illustrated. The blocker and the ball carrier can be linebackers but be sure to alternate them so everyone gets at least two or three repetitions.

Tell the blocker to cutoff block the linebacker, then try to shield him away from the ball. Tell the ball carrier to help set up the block, then to run either to the outside or try to cut back on the linebacker. Check for the above coaching pointers. Check especially for good three-point contact, good separation, and quickness to the ball.

You can have the linebackers either tackle the ball carrier or just form him. The focus of the drill is to beat the block and to get to the ball carrier without allowing him to cut back.

273. BEATING THE CHOP

Purpose:

- To practice the fundamentals of defeating a chop block.

Coaching Pointers:

- Learn to watch the ball carrier peripherally! **Feel** where he's at! The guy who wants to get you is the blocker! Keep your eyes on him/them.
- Too many defenders focus only on the ball carrier, and they end up getting alley-ooped!
- Watch the blocker. When he starts to chop you, he'll telegraph it by dropping his head and shoulders.
- Get the heels of both hands onto the top of his helmet and his shoulder pads and push yourself off him.
- To do this, you have to be in a good hit position and squared up to the blocker(s).

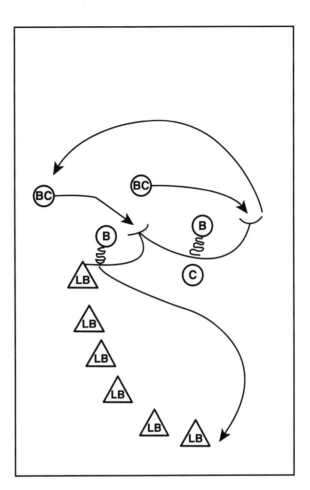

Set-up and Instructions:

Position a line of linebackers three yards off a designated line of scrimmage. Position one blocker a yard to a yard and a half to his inside, another blocker three yards inside him and one to two yards upfield as illustrated. Position a ball carrier two to three yards to the side of each blocker as illustrated.

On your signal, have the ball carrier run half speed to the outside and have the first blocker execute a chop block on the linebacker as he moves downhill on his pursuit path. The linebacker can either tackle or face up to the runner, grabbing him with both arms. As soon as he tackles the ball carrier, preferably across the bow, have him get into his hit position just to the inside of the next blocker and repeat the process.

Extra linebackers can be blockers and ball carriers, but be sure to alternate everyone so each linebacker gets at least three repetitions. Check for the above coaching pointers, but especially for focus on the blockers and a good feel for the ball carriers.

274. BREAK THE SHIELD I

Purpose:

- To emphasize the fundamentals for beating a shield block.

Coaching Pointers:

- No matter what, be sure to maintain your pursuit path. Don't get out of position when trying to beat a shield block.
- Don't let the blocker turn his hips so that the runner gets a possible cut-back lane on you.
- If the runner has committed to a certain direction, and the blocker is between you and the runner, use a swim or a rip technique to get to the runner.

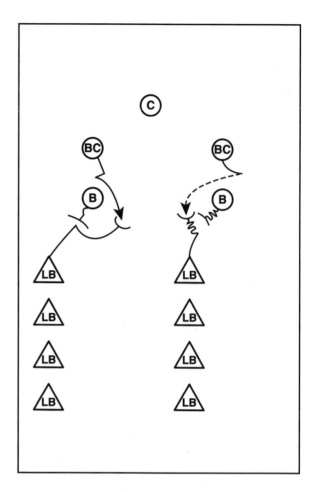

Set-up and Instructions:

Position the linebackers in two lines as illustrated. Position a blocker five yards upfield of the first man in each line and five yards to his inside or outside as illustrated. Position ball carriers five yards upfield of the blockers. Use linebackers for the blockers and the ball carriers, but be sure to alternate them so everyone gets three or four repetitions during the drill.

Instruct the linebackers to attack the blocker and the ball carrier on an inside-out path, to destroy the block, and to make the tackle—but not to allow the ball carrier to cut back. Use the above coaching pointers to make corrections.

Tell the blocker to shield block the linebacker; in essence, to keep his body between the linebacker and the ball carrier. Tell the ball carrier to run straight ahead behind the shield blocker **OR** to cut back on the linebacker as indicated by the dotted line on the illustration.

This is a good drill for learning to beat downfield blocks and to stay on the right pursuit path.

275. BEAT THREE BLOCKS

Purpose:

- To practice beating different kinds of blocks on a single play.

Coaching Pointers:

- Review the coaching pointers for the techniques for defeating different kinds of blocks. Reemphasize them during this drill.

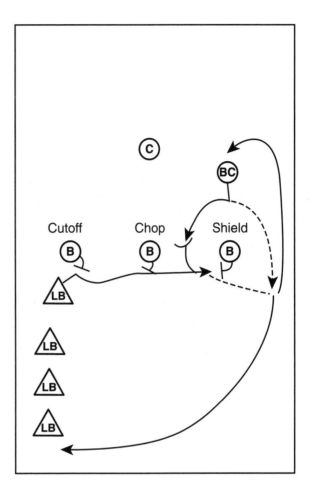

Set-up and Instructions:

Position three blockers in a straight line across the field, approximately five yards apart as illustrated. Position a linebacker shaded to the outside of the first blocker. Finally, position a ball carrier four or five yards behind the third blocker. The blockers and ball carrier can be extra linebackers. Just be sure to rotate them so everyone gets at least two repetitions of beating the blocks.

Instruct the first blocker to cutoff block the linebacker, the second blocker to chop him, and the third to shield block him. Tell the ball carrier to run as soon as the linebacker reaches the third blocker. He can run outside the shield blocker, but he should try to cut back behind the linebacker.

Instruct the linebacker to move downhill and to defeat each block, being sure the ball carrier does not cut back on him. He must tackle the ball carrier inside-out or across the bow. Even if the ball carrier uses the shield block effectively and beats him to the outside, his performance is still OK. His performance during the drill is **perfect** if he beats the shield block and tackles the ball carrier across the bow.

Watch for a good shuffle step, good use of hands, a strong rip technique, and a good hit position throughout the drill.

276. CONTAIN TWO

Purpose:

- To practice the outside-in pursuit path for outside linebackers and the inside-out pursuit path for inside linebackers.

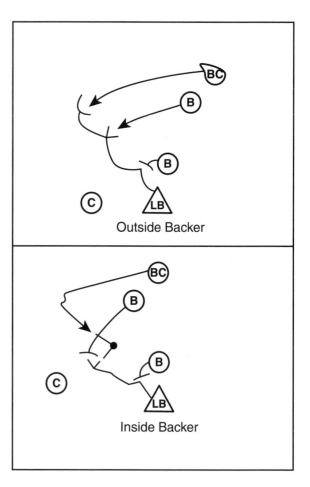

Outside Backer

Inside Backer

Coaching Pointers:

For Outside Linebackers:

- Take on the blockers with your hands or your inside arm. Keep your outside arm free to react to the ball carrier and to get to the outside quickly. **Do not lose** your contain responsibility.

- You must always tackle the ball from an outside-in direction.

For Inside Linebackers:

- Always pursue and tackle the ball carrier from an inside-out direction. You should always make your tackle across the bow or faced up to the ball carrier.

- Use two- or three-point contact or your hands to defeat the blockers. Focus on them and watch the ball carrier only peripherally.

Set-up and Instructions:

Position one blocker on the line and one in the backfield. Position a ball carrier to the inside of the blocker in the backfield. Tell the outside linebackers to align themselves just to the outside of the blocker on the line and have that blocker be a tight end. Tell the inside linebackers to align themselves in a 50 defensive set and have the blocker on the line be an offensive guard.

Tell the tight ends to hook or reach block the outside linebackers, the backfield blocker to chop him, and the ball carrier to try to get to the outside. Tell the guards to cutoff block the inside linebackers, the blocker in the backfield to chop him, and the ball carrier to try to cut back on him.

Check the linebackers for proper execution: good hit position, foot movement, use of hands, shoulder and hand shiver technique, and tackling fundamentals. This is an excellent drill for linebackers who have mastered the basic techniques for defeating blockers.

277. FILL THE LANE

Purpose:

- To read the ball carrier, to fill the lane, to get in a good hit position, and to make a good angle tackle.

Coaching Pointers:

- Stay in your good hit position and keep your feet chugging until the running back commits to a lane.
- Then get to the lane as **fast** as you can!
- You want to be there waiting in your hit position when the ball carrier comes through the lane.
- No one expects you to get there that fast all the time, but strive for that! Get there and **wait aggressively!**
- Remember your inside-out pursuit path. Make a good angle tackle—across the bow!

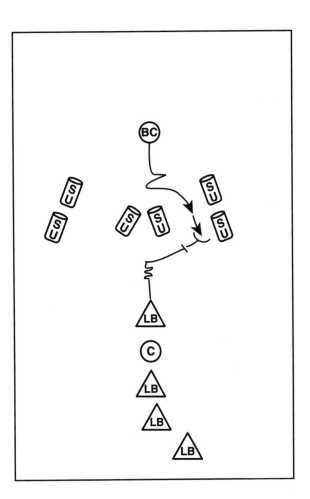

Set-up and Instructions:

Lay two stand-up dummies on their sides to form a V. Lay down two more dummies just to the outside of each of these two as illustrated. Position a ball carrier five yards from the closed end of the V and a linebacker facing him about five yards from the open end of the V.

Tell the ball carrier to run through one of the two lanes. He can fake as often as he wants before running the lane. Instruct the linebacker to race to the bottom of the V and to wait aggressively for the ball carrier to commit. Then have him execute a good angle tackle or **form** the ball carrier at the correct angle. You might want to have the linebackers form the ball carrier to avoid injuries. The most important part of the drill anyway is the linebacker's read and his quickness to the lane.

278. DOOR

Purpose:

- To promote reaction time, aggressive waiting, and angle tackling.

Coaching Pointers:

- Shuffle to the right and stay in your hit position. Chug your feet and wait aggressively until you see the back.
- When you see the back, drive toward him, closing the distance between him and you.
- Maintain a good hit position with a good base and forward lean.
- Gather as you close the distance and tackle through the back, driving your legs and wrapping your arms.
- Bull your neck throughout the drill. **Never drop your head!** Use the muscle pad on the back of your neck to protect your head.

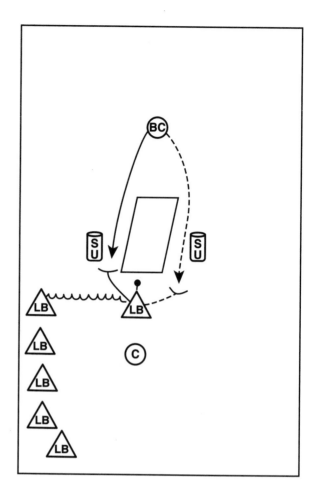

Set-up and Instructions:

Position all the linebackers in a line two or three yards to the left of a door or a 4' × 6' piece of well-sanded plywood. Place a stand-up dummy two yards from each side of the door. Position a ball carrier behind the door. This drill is so good, it's worth taking the time to find a door or a piece of plywood. Have a team manager or one of the linebackers hold the door upright from behind. Be sure to rotate the linebacker.

On your signal, have the first linebacker in the line shuffle to his right so he is poised in front of the door in a good hit position. Tell him to wait aggressively, to chug his feet, and to be poised to move. Tell the ball carrier to wait a count or two after the linebacker gets into position, then to run to either side of the door—between the door and the stand-up dummy. He can run to either side and he should run as fast as he can to see if he can beat the linebacker.

The linebacker should watch for him, react, and make a good angle tackle. This is an excellent drill for emphasizing reaction time. Players **like** it, too.

Thanks to George Kelly at the University of Notre Dame for this drill.

279. TRIANGLE

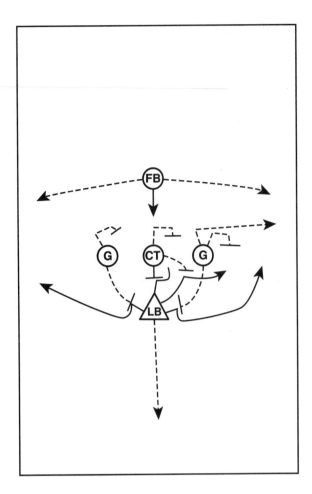

Purpose:

- To know where the point of attack is, based on the combined movements of the "triangle": the two guards, the center, and the fullback.

Coaching Pointers:

- Watch the triangle's **pattern** of movements. Don't watch just the fullback.

- When the center seal blocks, the block will usually be in the direction of the offense's play.

- The guards will **usually** pull in the direction of the offense's play.

- If the offensive right guard pulls but the center seals to his right, watch for a play in the direction **opposite** the guard's pull. Some offensive teams will "influence pull" their guards to misdirect the defense.

- Rip through the center's onside seal or the guard's down block. **Never** take the path of least resistance **behind** either of them!

- Drop to your hook zone when the linemen pass-protect block, looking for an immediate receiver to either side and always watching for a draw play up the middle.

Set-up and Instructions:

Position a center, two guards, and a fullback in their normal alignment. Position the middle linebacker over the center. Stand behind the middle linebacker to signal the blocking scheme(s) to the offensive players. Possible blocking schemes include: center base block on linebacker/guards base block; either guard down block linebacker; center seal block in direction of both guards' pull; guard base block, center seal, other guard pull *(illustration);* linemen pass protect block; or other.

This drill is especially effective for middle linebackers, but it is important for all linebackers, some of whom might find themselves in this position as the season wears on. Appropriate adjustments can also be made to accommodate linebacker reads in other alignments.

280. 52 READ

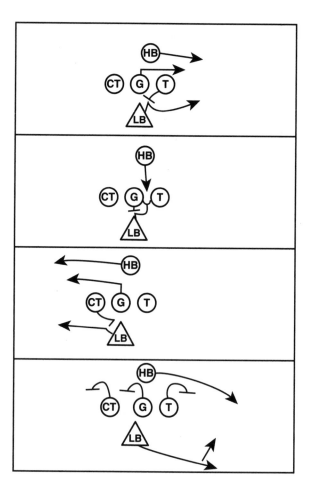

Purpose:

- To teach inside linebackers to read through the line to their backfield keys.

Coaching Pointers:

- The plays run by the offensive backfield are designed to fool you, but the line—almost always—will tell you where the ball is going.

- So look at the backfield through the line. The pattern of blocks you see will tell you where the ball is going.

- Try to read three linemen, the one in front of you and the one on either side of you.

- Read the **pattern** of their movements.

- Then pick up the back behind them. Watch the halfback in his home position. If there's no halfback, read the fullback.

Set-up and Instructions:

Position a center, guard, and tackle in their normal alignments. Position a halfback in his home alignment. Position the linebacker in his base alignment, head up on the guard, about three yards off the line of scrimmage. Huddle with the offense and give them a variety of blocking schemes. The guard can base block or pull either way. The center can seal block; the tackle can down block; the center and guard can two-team an imaginary noseguard, and the halfback can block the linebacker. Or they all can pass block. Several alternatives are diagrammed.

Tell the linebacker to read the pattern of blocks and to react accordingly. When he reads pass block, have him drop to his hook zone and look immediately to the imaginary tight end on his side—and have him drop fast. When he reads seal or down blocks, have him use his rip technique. When he reads base block, be sure he uses a good two- or three-point technique. This is a good drill and should be used often to condition linebackers to read through the line.

281. QUICK BLITZ

Purpose:

- To emphasize the basics of the blitz move.

Coaching Pointers:

- Stagger your feet a little, your drive foot back a little more than usual.
- Get in a good hit position, your weight forward.
- Anticipate the snap count and drive hard out of your stance into the gap.
- Take a long first step and drive your arms hard to get good forward movement.
- When you hit the gap, turn sideways to reduce your body surface and to be able to squeeze through the line.

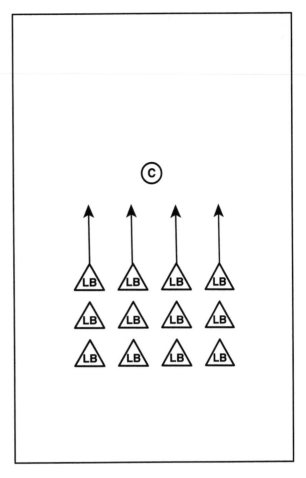

Set-up and Instructions:

Position all the linebackers in waves of four or five. Instruct the first wave to get into their hit positions, stagger their feet a little for a quick forward start, and drive out of their hit positions as if blitzing. This is a race. Remind them not to telegraph a blitz with too much forward lean but to get enough to get into the backfield quickly.

Vary your cadence to try to draw them offside and watch for the above coaching pointers. This is a good introductory drill and should be used before the other blitz drills. This drill is especially good for young football players.

282. BLITZ TECHNIQUE

Purpose:

- To practice the fundamentals of blitzing.

Coaching Pointers:

- Appear to blitz when you're **not** and appear not to blitz when you **are!**
- Show blitz, then go back to base alignment—then blitz!
- Anticipate the blitz with a forward lean and stagger your stance a little more than usual, so you can drive off your back leg for a quicker start.
- Get through the gap! Turn your shoulders to get through a tighter space and to provide a smaller surface for the blockers.
- Get a feel for the quarterback's cadence to get a jump on him. But always have enough body control to prevent yourself from going offside.

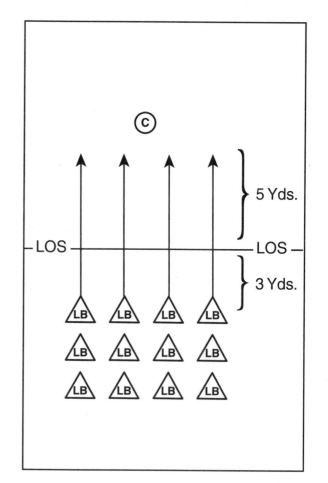

© 2001 by Michael D. Koehler

Set-up and Instructions:

Position the linebackers in waves of four or five, the first wave three yards off a designated line of scrimmage. Stand eight yards in front of them and instruct them to get in their hit positions. On your cadence, have them blitz straight ahead to see who gets the best jump and who covers the eight yards the fastest. Tell them this is a race. That will motivate them to get a good jump, sometimes a jump that's too good, another important lesson they need to learn.

283. SCRAPE TECHNIQUE

Purpose:

- To practice the inside and the outside scrape maneuvers.

Coaching Pointers:

- This is another blitz maneuver. So show it sometimes and don't do it.
- Show it, go back to base, then do it.
- Remember, when scraping off an inside or an outside lineman, scrape as tight on his tail as possible.
- Go where he **is**, not where he **was!**
- If you scrape off his original alignment, you'll take too wide an arc and get into the backfield too late.
- When scraping to the inside, drive off your outside leg; when scraping outside, drive off your inside leg.
- Anticipate the quarterback's cadence. It's easier to stop yourself from going offside when you're scraping.

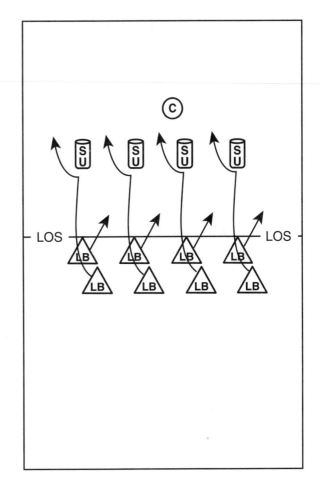

Set-up and Instructions:

Pair off the linebackers and have them alternate between being the scraping linebacker and the down lineman. Have all the pairs face you on a single line of scrimmage. Place a stand-up dummy 10 yards in front of each pair. Tell them they're racing to see who knocks over the stand-up dummy first. On your cadence, have them scrape either inside or outside. Vary the cadence to try to draw them offside and be sure that each linebacker gets at least three repetitions scraping both inside and outside.

284. STACK TECHNIQUE

Purpose:

- To practice the blitz from a stack position.

Coaching Pointer:

- Refer to the coaching pointers in *(282) Blitz Technique* and *(283) Scrape Technique.*

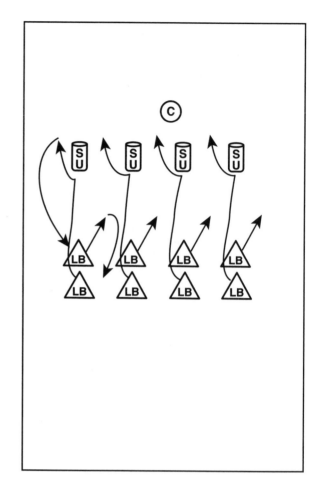

Set-up and Instructions:

Pair off the linebackers and have them alternate between being the blitzing linebacker and a down lineman. Align them on a designated line of scrimmage and have them race to knock over the stand-up dummy that is positioned 10 yards in front of them as illustrated. Try to draw them offside with your cadence. Be sure to have them blitz both ways. This drill is a good complement to the other blitzing drills. Run two or three of the drills in combination so the linebackers understand and practice the similarities in each.

285. SHOW BLITZ

Purpose:

- To practice showing the blitz to the offense without running it.

Coaching Pointers:

- Show blitz often on defense but not so often that it loses its effect.
- Show blitz especially on an obvious passing situation, on second and medium, or when the quarterback audibilizes most of his calls.
- Show blitz but be sure to get back in your base alignment quickly enough to be in a good ready position.
- Don't show blitz and then be off balance or out of position.

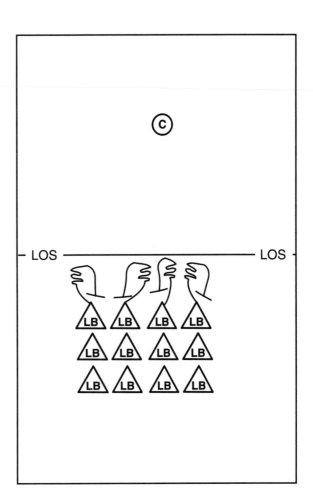

Set-up and Instructions:

Position the linebackers in waves of four or five on a designated line of scrimmage. Stand in front of them and tell each to show blitz, then to get back into a good ready position prior to the snap. Vary your cadence to get them out of position or off balance and make a lot of corrections. This is a good early season drill to condition linebackers to show a lot of movement on defense but to be careful about being in position prior to the snap of the ball.

Also be sure to expect good movement during defensive scrimmages and games. Make sure they translate this drill into performance by expecting it of them as often as possible. This drill can be quite short; run it in conjunction with other blitzing drills to emphasize the relationship between blitzing and showing blitz.

286. DROP, BREAK, AND CATCH

Purpose:

- To emphasize a quick drop to the hook zone, a good break on the ball, and good pass-receiving skills.

Coaching Pointers:

- As soon as I bring the ball up to pass it, drop quickly to your hook zone.
- Get there fast, looking to the outside for the tight end or slotback.
- Keep your eyes on me but turn and go! Crossover step! Get there fast!
- As soon as you get there, get into your hit position immediately and be prepared to break on the ball.
- Read my eyes and my passing motion to determine where I am likely to throw the ball.
- Break on the ball just before it leaves my hands.
- Catch it at its highest point with both hands, then shout "Bingo!"

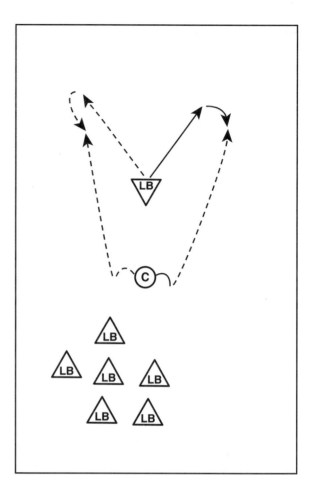

Set-up and Instructions:

Position the linebackers behind you and have them, one at a time, race to a position three yards in front of you. Tell them to get into a good hit position immediately and, as soon as you raise the ball, to drop to their hook zone. Have them drop to their left if you raise the ball to your right, to their right if you raise the ball to your left. Use the above coaching pointers to assure proper execution. Check especially for a fast drop, a quick look to the tight end, a good read on your passing motion, a fast break on the ball, and good pass-receiving techniques.

This is a rapid-fire drill. Have the linebackers move quickly so everyone gets four or five repetitions. This is a good preliminary drill for many of the other pass-coverage drills in this book. It's also a good pregame warm-up drill.

287. DROP READ

Purpose:

- To emphasize the correct reads for the linebacker as he drops to the hook zone.

Coaching Pointers:

- As soon as the ball is snapped, read the near back **through the line** to determine where the ball is going!
- If the linemen in front of you snap up into pass blocks, start the drop to your hook zone.
- Get back there **fast!** Keep your head pivoted to see the quarterback but **get** to the hook zone!
- Look to the nearer receiver immediately, a tight end or a slot back for the closer pass-receiving threat.
- Do this as you drop. If there's no immediate threat, get your head on a swivel as soon as you get into your hook zone and find any receiver(s) coming into your area.
- Stay with the receiver peripherally and read the quarterback's eyes and passing motion to determine if he's ready to throw the ball.
- Move in the direction of his eyes and motion!

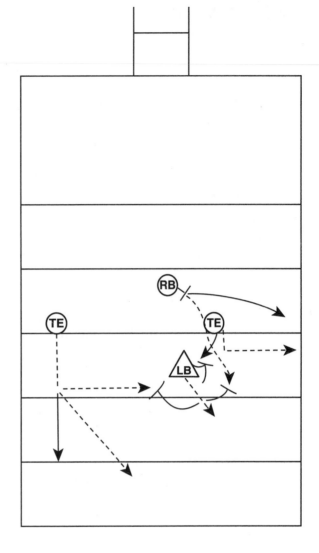

Set-up and Instructions:

Position the inside linebackers in their normal alignment. If he's a middle linebacker, position him appropriately and have him drop to his designated hook zone. If he's a 52 backer, have him drop to hook zone on. Use the linebackers as tight ends and running backs as well, but be sure they alternate so everyone gets at least three repetitions in his normal alignment.

On your cadence, have the receivers run designated patterns. Alternate the patterns as illustrated. Have the near tight end slant in for a quickie pass one time; square out to the flat, another. Have the backside tight end square into the hook zone one time; run straight upfield, another. Have the running back block and swing sharp one time; just block, another.

Vary the patterns but be sure one of the receivers enters the linebacker's hook zone on each repetition. Check for the above coaching pointers and all of your own.

288. SWIVEL

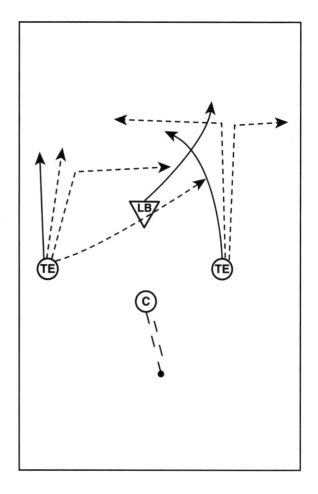

Purpose:

- To emphasize a quick look to the tight end and swivel technique to find immediate receivers.

Coaching Pointers:

- As soon as that lineman snaps up in front of you, drop to your hook zone—quickly!
- When you take your first step back, look immediately to the tight end or slotback on your side of the center.
- Adjust your drop path depending on what he's doing.
- If he's slanting in, find the quarterback and look for an interception or a quick hit on the tight end.
- If he's leaving your area, keep dropping to your hook zone and get your head on a swivel to find receivers from the off side coming into your area.
- If you find any, look to the quarterback for his intended receiver and look for a possible interception or a pancake tackle.
- Remember, look to the tight end first, a back out of the backfield, an offside receiver, then a back delaying out of the backfield.

Set-up and Instructions:

Stand in the middle of the field or have a quarterback stand in the middle of the field. Align a tight end in his normal position to the right, another receiver aligned as a tight end or a wingback to the left. Position a 52 linebacker or a middle linebacker in his normal alignment. The illustration shows a 52 linebacker. As you or the quarterback drop (three- or five-step), have the linebacker drop to his hook zone, immediately looking to the tight end on his side, then to the offside receiver. Have the receivers run different but complementary routes each time. Examples are included in the illustration. Watch the linebackers for good drops, good reads, and good mobility.

289. JAM TIGHT

Purpose:

- To practice the proper techniques for jamming the tight end.

Coaching Pointers:

- Position yourself head up or just to the inside of the tight end.
- Do not allow him to take an inside release!
- When he starts his outside release, go with him, jamming him all the way.
- Stay in a good hit position to maintain your mobility.
- Don't unload on him; just hassle him.
- As you jam him, maintain your inside leverage so that you are pushing him to the outside, watching the quarterback as you go.
- Release him when you reach the flat, then resume your pass coverage.

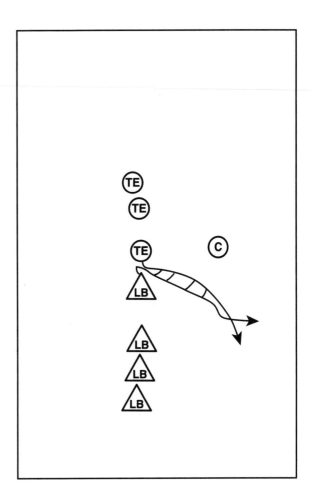

Set-up and Instructions:

Divide the linebackers into outside linebackers and tight ends. Be sure to alternate all of them so each linebacker gets at least three repetitions of jamming the tight end. Align each linebacker head up on the tight end and remind him not to allow an inside release. Stand behind the linebackers to hand signal the start of each repetition to the tight end.

When the tight end releases, check each linebacker for a good hit position, good jamming technique, and steady movement to the flat.

290. BREAK ON BALL

Purpose:

- To practice reading the quarterback's passing motion in order to get a good break on the ball when it is thrown.

Coaching Pointers:

- Drop to your hook zone—quickly!
- As you go, look to the outside for the most immediate receiver, in most cases, the tight end or a slotback.
- If you see no immediate receiver, get your head on a swivel and look for the backside tight end, for any receiver coming from the backside, or for a receiver coming out of the backfield.
- When you pick up a possible receiver, look to the quarterback for his intentions.
- Your keys are his non-throwing hand, his non-throwing arm, the football, and his eyes.
- If he lets go of the ball with his non-throwing hand and initiates his passing motion, move to the area he's looking at.
- Be prepared to either intercept the ball or to make a tackle.

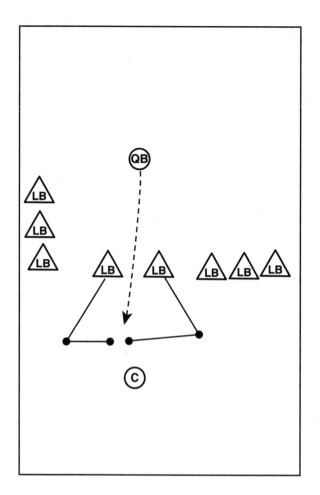

Set-up and Instructions:

Position the linebackers in their normal alignments. Position a quarterback seven yards behind the line of scrimmage. Tell him to simulate reading the secondary and picking out a receiver. Then have him throw the ball to an imaginary receiver in the general vicinity of the inside linebackers. Tell him to throw it in such a way as to allow the linebackers to intercept it—if they break correctly.

Tell the linebackers to drop to their respective hook zones, to simulate looking for receivers in their area, then to read the quarterback's eyes and passing motion in order to get a good break on the ball. Have them shout "Bingo" each time they intercept the ball.

291. MAN-TO-MAN

Purpose:

- To teach the techniques for man-to-man coverage on backs and tight ends.

Coaching Pointers:

- Read an offensive lineman, next to the tight end or in front of the back, to make sure it's a pass.
- When you know it's a pass, get to your man as fast as possible.
- Move to him on a straight line, laterally if necessary, to get inside leverage.
- Force him to take an outside path and stay on his shoulder, especially in the end zone. There is **no such thing** as a cushion in the end zone!

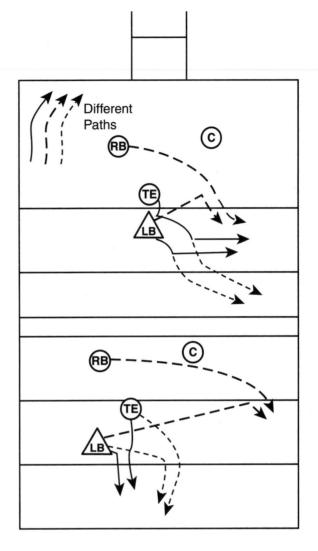

Set-up and Instructions:

Position a linebacker in his normal relationship with a tight end or a running back as illustrated. Use extra linebackers as offensive personnel but be sure to alternate them so all the linebackers get three or four repetitions of man-to-man coverage. On your cadence, have the receiver run a predetermined route. Have the receivers try to run "in" routes: swing sharps, slants, square ins, posts. Make sure the linebackers secure inside leverage. Or have the receivers run "out" routes: swing wides, slant outs, square outs, flags. Make sure the linebackers get to the receiver quickly and stay on the outside or upfield shoulder, focusing on the receiver until he reaches for the ball.

DEFENSIVE-BACK DRILLS

This section focuses on the following skills:

- Stance and starts
- Reading backfield keys through the line
- Taking a drop step during initial read
- Executing the backpedal
- Drop-stepping during the backpedal
- Maintaining the cushion based on opponent speed
- Man-to-man coverage versus zone
- Coverage in or close to the end zone
- Jamming wide receivers
- Breaking on the ball
- Interception technique
- Executing the head-on tackle
- Tackling across the bow
- Stripping technique

292. STANCE

Purpose:

- To emphasize the fundamentals of a good stance.

Coaching Pointers:

- Keep your feet shoulder-width or less.
- Stagger your feet, your dominant foot intersecting the instep of your other foot.
- Get a good bend in your knees. I want you moving as soon as the ball is snapped.
- Improve your mobility by stooping your shoulders and your upper body forward, so all your weight is over your legs.
- Keep your head up and read your key **through the line.** The line will tell you quickly whether it's pass or run.
- Relax your arms to keep your body balanced.
- This is your ready position. Be ready to **move!**

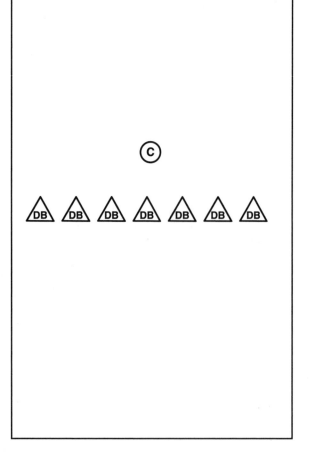

Set-up and Instructions:

Position all the defensive backs at arm's length on a line of scrimmage. On the command "Set," have them get into their stances. Make corrections—lots of them. Be sure to check for the above coaching pointers and all of your own. Without the correct stance, defensive backs can lose mobility and compromise their ability to cover pass or run.

293. STARTS

Purpose:

- To emphasize the fundamentals of a good start from the ready position.

Coaching Pointers:

- Your first step is **always** backward!
- Call it a **read step.** It's the split second you read your keys to determine if the play is pass or run and where the ball is going.
- Your first step is always backward because your primary responsibility is to protect against a pass. You have at least seven good defenders in front of you to stop the run. Look behind you! How many do you see there?
- This is not the time to come out of your ready position. Keep your shoulders stooped and your weight over your legs. Keep your legs bent to maintain your mobility.
- You have to be able to move easily **in any direction.** You can't do that if you're standing straight up.

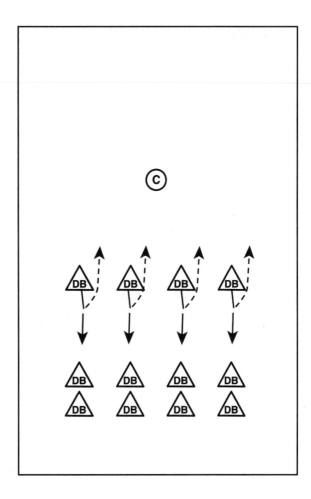

Set-up and Instructions:

Put the defensive backs in waves of four or five. On the "Set" command, have them get into their stances. Make corrections. On the "Go (split-second delay) Pass" command, have them continue dropping back. Check to make sure their weight is evenly distributed and they keep a good bend in their knees. On the "Go (split-second delay) Run" command, have them react off their back step to a forward motion. Three or four forward steps is enough to check to make sure they maintain a ready position.

Do the same thing with each successive wave and make sure every back gets at least four or five repetitions. This is an important drill.

294. BACKPEDALING

Purpose:

- To emphasize the fundamentals of backpedaling.

Coaching Pointers:

- Stay in your ready position, your knees bent and your weight over your hips.

- Move your arms forcefully to give yourself momentum backward.

- Reach back with your feet and **pull** yourself backward.

- Do not straighten up—at any time! Once you straighten your body and lose the bend in your knees and waist, you lose your ability to move backward or to cut in any direction.

- Your weight should be evenly distributed—over your knees—so you can move your feet quickly.

- Take a comfortable stride, not too long, not too short—long enough to move quickly.

- When you cut to the ball, plant your back foot and drive hard to get your momentum moving forward.

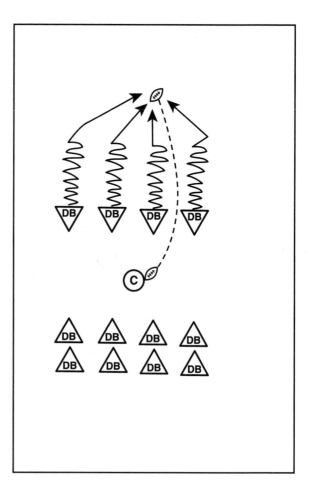

Set-up and Instructions:

Position the defensive backs in waves of four or five. Instruct the first wave to jog five yards downfield, turn, and face you. Have them start backpedaling as soon as you raise the football to a passing position. Hold the ball stationary to keep them in their backpedal. Throw the ball to one of them, high enough to enable the other defensive backs to react to the ball, too. Tell them all to jump and reach to catch the ball. No one should catch the ball in the basket. Everyone must catch the ball with his hands, reaching for it with arms fully extended.

Check on a good backpedal and a good drop step to make the cut to get to the ball. Be sure they all get at least five or six repetitions to force the proper motion into their body memory.

295. OPEN HIPS

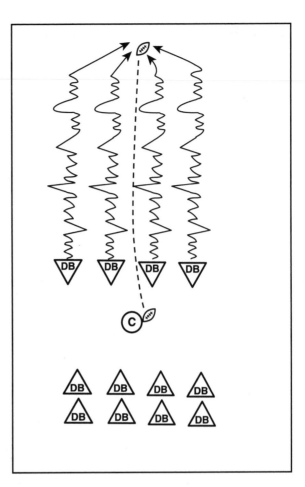

Purpose:

- To practice opening the hips while backpedaling.

Coaching Pointers:

- Stay in your ready position and keep your weight over your hips and the balls of your feet.
- Backpedal quickly and, when I point in a direction, open your hips in that direction, then resume your backpedal.
- Open your hips by pushing off one foot and drop stepping with the other so that your body pivots in the direction that you drop step.
- Then resume your backpedal until the next change of direction.

Set-up and Instructions:

Position all the defensive backs in waves of four or five. Have the first wave move five yards upfield and face you. Start them in a backpedal by raising the football to a throwing position. Have them open their hips in the direction that you point the football. After they open four or five times, throw the ball up for grabs. Be sure they go for the ball aggressively by jumping for it and fully extending their arms.

Have the first wave return while the second wave gets into position. This is a rapid-fire drill—if all the defensive backs are executing properly. It's essential that these fundamental moves get into body memory as soon as possible in the season, so give everyone at least five or six repetitions of this drill.

296. DROP STEP

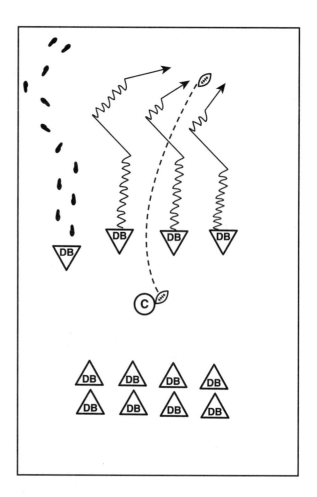

Purpose:

- To emphasize the drop step for changing directions when covering receivers who cut.

Coaching Pointers:

- Get in a good stance and backpedal hard on my signal.

- Keep your weight balanced and drive your arms to gain momentum.

- Change direction every time I move the ball.

- When the receiver makes a cut, plant your forward foot, drop step with your back foot, and crossover step to change directions with him.

- If you're running diagonally to the left (demonstrate these steps), to change direction plant your right foot, drive off it, drop your left foot behind you, pivot, and cross over hard with your right foot. (Now demonstrate a change of direction if running to the right.)

- Never turn your back on the receiver. You'll lose him. Always plant, drop step, and cross over to remain faced up to the receiver.

Set-up and Instructions:

Position the defensive backs in waves of four or five. Tell the first group to move five yards upfield and face you. Start the drill by snapping the football into passing position. Have the defensive backs cut—using the plant, drop step, and crossover technique—each time you point the football in a different direction. After they cut three or four times, throw the ball in the air and have them go up for it as if grabbing a rebound. Be sure they get off the ground and extend their arms.

Check for a good stance, start, drop step, and aggressiveness toward the ball.

297. TURN AND RUN

Purpose:

- To practice the fundamentals of turning and running with a receiver when he's committed to a deep route.

Coaching Pointers:

- When you're convinced the receiver is committed to a deep route, get out of your shuffle and turn and run with him.
- Stay faced up with him and always be prepared to react to the ball or to break if he should make a late cut.
- Stay as close to him as possible without interfering.
- To get out of your shuffle, drive hard off the opposite foot and drop step as deep as possible with the other foot.
- Drive the near elbow to help pivot your body and accelerate into a forward sprint.

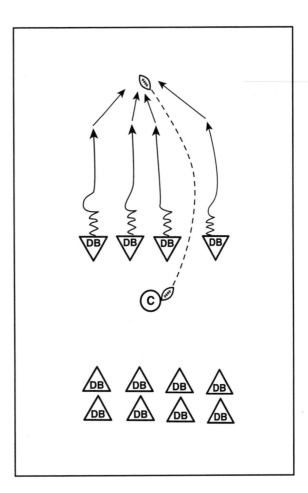

Set-up and Instructions:

Position the defensive backs in waves of four or five, the first wave facing you as illustrated. Tell them to get into good stances, then start the drill by snapping a football into passing position. Tell them to turn and run when you raise the football above your head. After they are in a full sprint, throw the ball up for grabs and have them all react to it aggressively. They should all jump for it and fully extend their arms.

298. HAND AWAY

Purpose:

- To emphasize the fundamentals of pushing the receiver's outside hand away from making a reception.

Coaching Pointers:

- Backpedal and full pivot to run with the receiver when he runs a deep route.
- Turn your back to the quarterback and watch the receiver.
- When his eyes and hand movement indicate that he's about to catch the ball, close the distance between you and him.
- When he extends his arms to reach for the ball, slap his upfield hand with your downfield hand. In other words, if he's the right end and you're the left cornerback, slap his right hand with **your** right hand.
- If, for some reason, you miss his hand and he catches the ball, you'll still have your upfield arm free to tackle him.

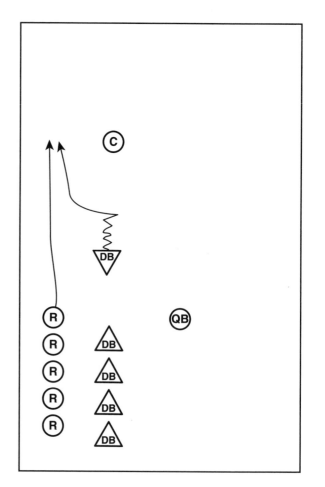

Set-up and Instructions:

Position half the defensive backs in a line facing upfield; the other, half in a parallel line acting as wide receivers. Position a quarterback in his normal alignment. Instruct the receivers to run streaks or fade routes and to catch the ball. Tell the defensive backs to backpedal, then to turn and run with the receivers. Tell them to focus on the receiver's arms and to slap his hand with their hand to prevent him from catching the ball. Use the above coaching pointers. Use this drill in conjunction with *(297) Turn and Run* to combine the fundamentals of covering a deep route.

299. HANGING TIGHT

Purpose:

- To emphasize the need to run with a deep receiver and to play the ball.

Coaching Pointers:

- Once the receiver breaks your cushion, turn and run with him.
- Stay in your shuffle as long as you can and keep your cushion.
- When the pass is deep, however, turn and run with the receiver—**and stay with him!**
- Try also to maintain position so that if the ball is long, he has to run into **you** to get at it.

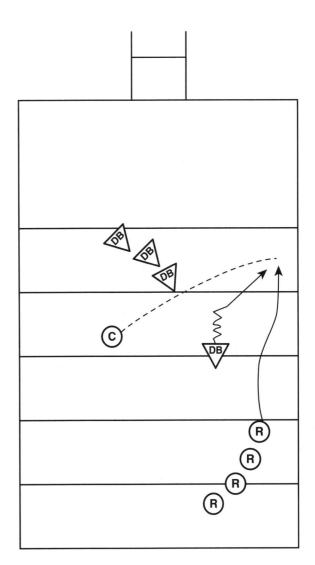

Set-up and Instructions:

Position half the defensive backs in a cornerback alignment seven or eight yards in from the sideline. Position the other half as receivers on a designated line of scrimmage. Position yourself as the thrower approximately parallel to the defensive back who will be covering the receiver as illustrated.

On your cadence, have the receiver execute a fade or streak pattern and tell the defensive back to stay with him. Tell him to backpedal, then turn and run with the receiver, watching his eyes and hands to know when to play the ball.

You throw the ball sometime after they pass you. Try to lead the receiver and check to see the defensive back gets and maintains good position and uses his hands effectively to break up the pass.

300. BREAK TO THE BALL

Purpose:

- To emphasize the fundamentals of breaking back to the ball.

Coaching Pointers:

- A receiver's sudden cut or any of several running plays may cause you to break out of your backward movement.

- This is why you must remain in your ready position with your weight evenly distributed—so you can make such a move.

- To break back to the ball, plant your back foot hard, step in the direction you want to go with your other foot, and crossover step if necessary. Come back at a 45-degree angle.

- You can't do this if your backward lean is too pronounced, so **keep your weight evenly distributed over your hips and the balls of your feet!**

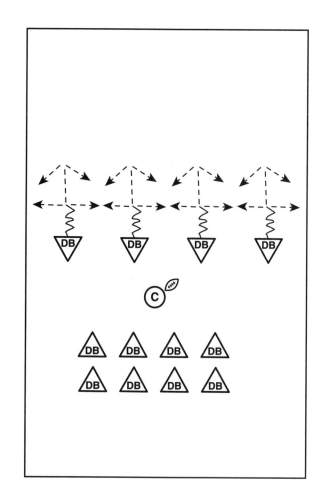

Set-up and Instructions:

Position the defensive backs in waves of four or five, the first wave facing you as illustrated. Tell them to get into good stances and have them go into a backpedal by snapping the football into passing position. They should continue the backpedal as long as you don't move the football. Use these variations:

1. Point the ball in either direction to have them drop step and open in that direction.
2. Raise the ball above your head to have them turn and run with an imaginary receiver.
3. After they turn and run, point the ball in either direction to have them break back to the ball.

Vary these as the drill is conducted so they are unable to anticipate what you want them to do. Be sure they break back at a 45-degree angle. The variations are illustrated with dotted lines.

301. W BREAK

Purpose:

- To practice the fundamentals of breaking back to the ball.

Coaching Pointer:

- Refer to the Coaching Pointers in *(300) Break to the Ball.*

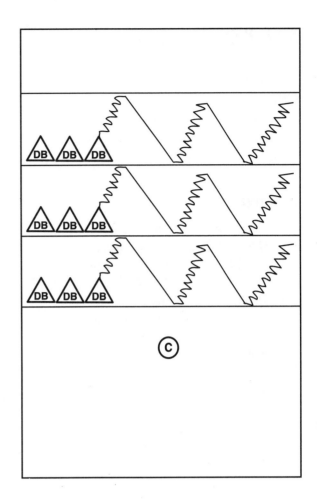

Set-up and Instructions:

Position groups of four or five defensive backs at five-yard intervals across the field as illustrated. On your command, have the first back in each group begin backpedaling at a 45-degree angle. When they have gone five yards, have them break back at a 45-degree angle, then continue to backpedal and break back until they have crossed the field.

Check for proper fundamentals, the most important of which is proper body positioning throughout the drill. This is a rapid-fire drill. Try for as many repetitions as possible.

302. DOUBLE CUT

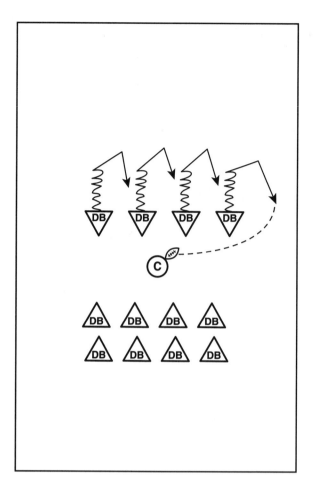

Purpose:

- To practice making two cuts: out of the backpedal and back to the ball.

Coaching Pointers:

- Review the Coaching Pointers in *(295) Open Hips, (296) Drop Step,* and *(300) Break to the Ball.* Use them while conducting this drill.

- If you're going to pick off an outside pass or close on a delayed running play, you have to break to the ball quickly.

- Do it by planting your upfield foot and driving hard back to the line of scrimmage. Step in the direction of the line of scrimmage with your other foot and cross over hard to sprint back to the line.

- Maintain a low center of gravity to make all your cuts. The straighter you stand, the less mobility you have.

Set-up and Instructions:

Position all the defensive backs in waves of four or five, the first wave facing you as illustrated. Have each wave backpedal by snapping the football up into passing position. Point the ball to have them open up and run at a 45-degree angle in a certain direction. Point the ball again to have them break back to the line of scrimmage. Throw the ball to one of the backs.

Check for proper stance, backpedaling, open hips, and low center of gravity. Be sure that each back gets at least two or three repetitions cutting both ways. This is a good drill for practicing and correcting several pass-coverage techniques at one time.

303. BREAK WITH PARTNER

Purpose:

- To emphasize the fundamentals of backpedaling and breaking on the ball.

Coaching Pointers:

- Review the Coaching Pointers in *(296) Drop Step, (297) Turn and Run,* and *(300) Break to the Ball.*
- Be sure to make as many corrections as possible, especially early in the season.

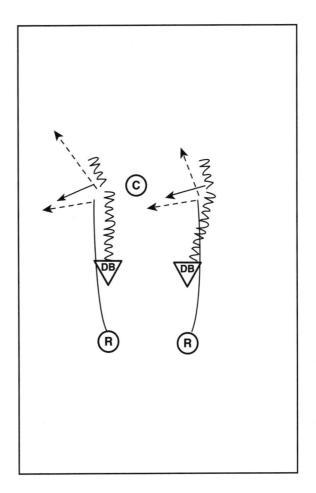

Set-up and Instructions:

Position two defensive backs in front of two receivers as illustrated. Hand signal the pass routes to the receivers and, on your cadence, have them execute the routes at three-quarter speed. Watch the defensive backs for proper stance, backpedal, change of direction, and break to the ball after it's thrown.

Throw the ball to one of the receivers but instruct both backs to break when it is thrown. This is a rapid-fire drill. Try for as many repetitions as possible.

304. WATCH IT IN

Purpose:

- To emphasize receiving and pass-interception fundamentals.

Coaching Pointers:

- Always catch the ball with your hands—and always look it in!
- Watch the ball during flight and watch it hit your hands.
- I want to see your heads turned so your eyes are looking at the ball in your hands after you have caught it.
- Ease it in; don't fight it.
- Don't run with it until you catch it!

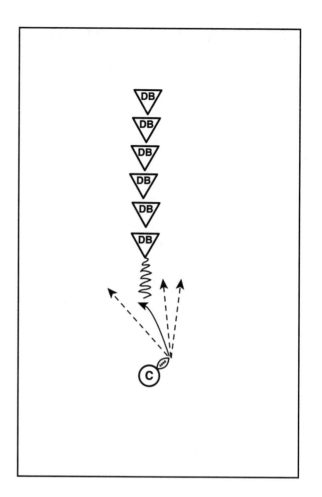

Set-up and Instructions:

Position a line of defensive backs in front of you. One at a time, have them run toward you at half speed. Throw a football to each: high, low, or off to either side. Tell them to focus on the ball and to catch it with their hands. Emphasize the above coaching pointers, especially having their eyes focusing on the ball in their hands after they have caught it. Early drills have to exaggerate important fundamentals if they are to get into body memory.

305. READ THE KEYS

Purpose:

- To emphasize techniques for intercepting the ball.

Coaching Pointers:

- While you're in your backpedal, watch the quarterback peripherally for keys to where he intends to throw the ball.
- If you have no immediate receiver to cover, watch the quarterback completely.
- Especially watch his body positioning! After he drops and sets up, he'll survey the field. Once he pivots his body in a certain direction, **if you're not covering anyone,** move in that direction.
- The longer he takes before he pivots, the more likely he is to throw in that direction.

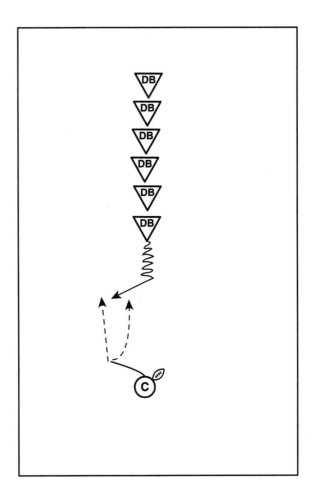

Set-up and Instructions:

Position the defensive backs in one line facing you as illustrated. If you have a lot of backs, make a second line and use a back-up quarterback or another coach to throw the ball. Tell each back to jog toward you. After he takes three or four steps, pivot your body in a certain direction. Tell him to break on your pivot, then throw the ball in that direction and tell him to catch it with his hands, looking it in all the way.

Throw the ball high or low and emphasize good pass-receiving fundamentals.

306. COVER THE TREE

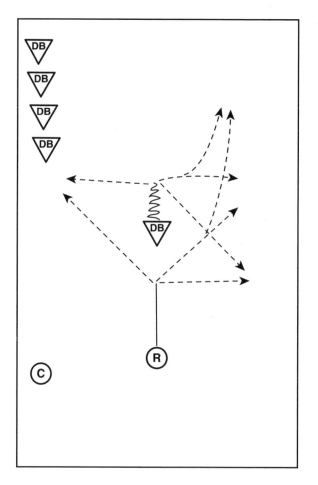

Purpose:

- To practice all the moves required to cover a variety of pass routes.

Coaching Pointers:

- Review the coaching pointers in *(294) Backpedaling, (295) Open Hips, (296) Drop Step, (297) Turn and Run* and *(300) Break to the Ball* for key elements during this drill.

- Remember, if you make a good break and cut in front of the receiver to intercept the ball—*you'd better intercept it!*

- If you miss it, the receiver has an open road to the end zone!

- Better yet, maintain good position. Be in a position to knock the ball down with your inside arm and to tackle the receiver with your outside arm if he catches the ball.

Set-up and Instructions:

Position a line of defensive backs six or seven yards upfield and facing a receiver (can be a defensive back) as illustrated. If your arm can stand it, you be the quarterback. Otherwise, have a quarterback throw the ball to the receivers. Tell each receiver what pattern to run and check the defensive back for stance, backpedal, maneuverability, and ability to break on the ball.

Remind each defensive back to maintain proper leverage on the receivers. This drill doesn't focus on interceptions but on incomplete passes. We'll take an interception, but—more important—we don't want the opposing team to gain yardage.

Check for the above coaching pointers and for aggressiveness to the ball. This drill is to be used after the fundamentals of pass coverage have been mastered. It does a great job requiring defensive backs to use all their skills. Use more lines of defensive backs and receivers, depending on your numbers.

307. DEFLECT THE BALL

Purpose:

- To emphasize quick reactions and concentration on the football in flight.

Coaching Pointers:

- Watch the football! Nothing exists but that football.
- If it's deflected, adjust accordingly.
- Be relaxed while watching the football and making an interception. The more relaxed you are, the quicker your reflexes.
- Catch the ball **with your hands!**

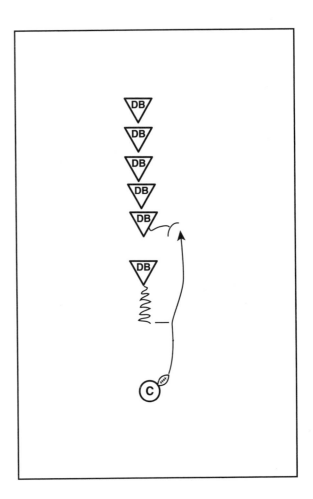

Set-up and Instructions:

Position all the defensive backs in a line facing you. Have the first back in the line jog toward you. Throw the football just over his head so he has to reach up for it. Tell him to **deflect** the ball, just barely touching it to change its flight. You don't want him to tip it. When some defensive backs tip the ball, they look like they're trying to set a volleyball! You just want the ball deflected. That's what's likely to happen in a game and it's a better drill for quickening reflexes. Then have the second back in the line catch the ball. Once he does, have him tuck it in and yell "Bingo" or "Oskie."

308. DUCK

Purpose:

- To emphasize quick reflexes and concentration on the ball in flight.

Coaching Pointers:

- Watch the ball and relax your body.
- Focus hard enough so you see nothing but the ball.
- Keep your hands in a ready position to catch the ball, not in front of your face but halfway up your body, elbows pointed out.

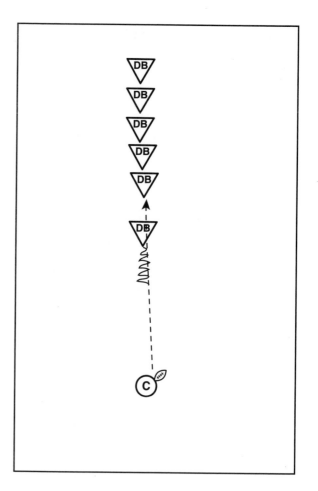

Set-up and Instructions:

Position all the defensive backs in a line facing you. Tell the first back to jog toward you. Throw the ball at his head and tell him to duck at the last second. Have the back behind him catch the ball. Check for concentration and ball-receiving fundamentals.

This is a quick drill and should be combined with others. The backs need only two or three repetitions.

309. DEFLECT OR DUCK

Purpose:

- To emphasize quick reactions and concentration on the ball.

Coaching Pointer:

- Review the coaching pointers in *(307)* *Deflect the Ball* and *(308) Duck.*

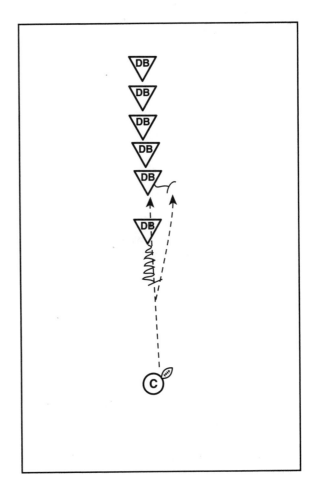

Set-up and Instructions:

Position all the defensive backs in one line facing you. Have the first player in the line jog toward you. After he takes three or four steps throw the ball at or slightly above his head. Instruct him to either duck or deflect the ball. Tell the second player in line to catch the ball.

Be sure the second player in line is at least three or four yards behind the first player so he has time to react to the ball. If he's too close, the drill is useless and he could jam a finger or two.

Use this drill after you've covered the coaching pointers in *(307) Deflect the Ball* and *(308) Duck.* It provides a more enjoyable test of their reaction time.

310. GO DEEP

Purpose:

- To practice the fundamentals of covering a deep pass.

Coaching Pointers:

- For purposes of this drill, backpedal with the receiver and watch for when I (or the quarterback) pivot my shoulders.

- When I pivot my shoulders, you open out of your backpedal, pivot, and sprint down the sideline with the receiver.

- Battle him for the ball! Get off the ground as high as you can, extend your arms, and catch the ball with your hands.

- If you can't catch it, **knock it down. Don't** let him catch it!

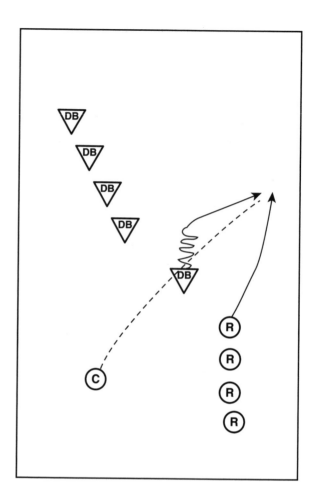

Set-up and Instructions:

Position half the defensive backs in one line facing you, five yards upfield and seven yards in from the sideline. Position the other half in a wideout position, five yards in from the sideline as illustrated. Instruct the wide receivers to run a fade pattern, three-quarter speed at first, then full speed.

Tell the defensive backs to backpedal and to maintain a cushion. When they see you (or the quarterback) open your shoulders, they should make a full pivot and sprint down the sideline with the receiver. Pivot your shoulders as soon as the receiver has run five or six yards. That way, the pass will be short enough to save your shoulder and to emphasize the purpose of the drill.

Check each defensive back's stance, backpedal, full pivot, and aggressiveness to the ball.

311. WATCH THE HANDS

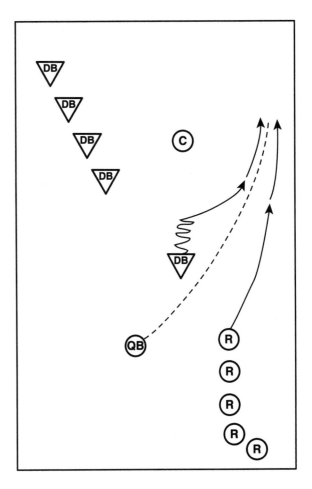

Purpose:

- To emphasize the technique of watching the receiver's hands to know when he plans to catch a long pass.

Coaching Pointers:

- Backpedal, then turn and go with the receiver when you see he's committed to running deep.
- Focus on **him!** Watch his hands. When his hands move to catch the ball, push your inside hand up toward the ball.
- If you've closed the distance between yourself and the receiver, look for the ball, too.
- If he catches the ball, strip it with your inside hand. Keep your outside arm free to make the tackle.

Set-up and Instructions:

Position half the defensive backs as wide receivers 10 yards in from the sideline. Position the other half of the defensive backs six yards upfield and five yards inside the receivers as illustrated. On your cadence (or a quarterback), have the receivers run streak or fade patterns. Instruct the defensive backs to backpedal, then to full pivot and run with the receivers, facing them and watching their hands for an indication of when the ball will arrive.

Use the above coaching pointers as well as your own to check for good stances, backpedal, open hips, and coverage on the wide receiver. Also watch for the defensive back's focus on the receiver's hands.

Make sure to alternate all the defensive backs so everyone gets at least two repetitions from both sides of the field.

312. PICK OR HELP

Purpose:

- To emphasize breaking on the quarterback's passing motion and intercepting the ball or helping to tackle the receiver.

Coaching Pointers:

- Get in your backpedal and watch the receivers and the quarterback peripherally. If you maintain the right cushion, you should be able to see all of them.
- When the quarterback pivots his shoulders to go into his passing motion, break in the direction of his intended pass.
- If you break fast enough on a fly or a post pattern, you should be able to pick off the ball.
- **Intercept it at its highest point.**
- If you can't get there to pick off the ball, get there fast enough to make or help out on the tackle.

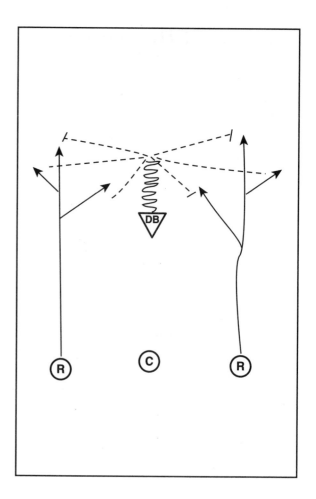

Set-up and Instructions:

Position a defensive back in the middle of the field as a free safety, 12 yards upfield from you or a quarterback. Assign two other defensive backs to be wide receivers and position each of them 15 yards outside on opposite sides of the field. Have all the defensive backs take turns being receivers but be sure everyone gets at least two or three repetitions as the free safety.

Huddle the receivers and give them specific patterns before each repetition. One can run a fly pattern; the other, a post or a flag. Have the receivers go on your cadence and instruct the free safety to break on your passing motion. Throw the ball to either of the receivers. Check each free safety for a good stance, backpedal, and break on the ball. Also be sure each gets up in the air with extended arms to intercept the ball.

313. BREAK AND PICK

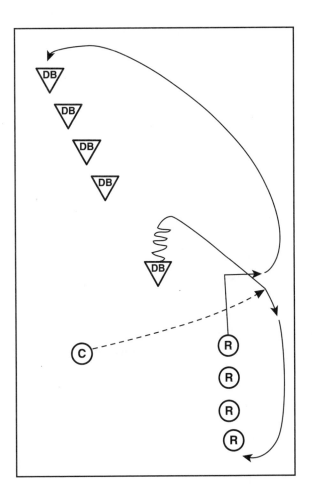

Purpose:

- To emphasize the importance of breaking quickly on the ball to make an interception.

Coaching Pointers:

- Maintain a good center of gravity during your backpedal to have the mobility to make a good break on the ball.
- Watch the quarterback's motion peripherally while focusing on the receiver.
- Don't round off the break. Plant and come back hard.
- Extend your arms and use your hands to intercept the ball.

Set-up and Instructions:

Position half the defensive backs in a line facing you, the first man aligned as a cornerback in man coverage, shading the inside of the receiver. Position the other half of the defensive backs as wide receivers. Be sure to alternate all the players so everyone gets at least two repetitions on both sides of the field.

Instruct the wide receivers to run six- to seven-yard square outs. Tell the defensive backs to break as soon as you open your shoulders toward the receiver. Have them break hard at a 45-degree angle to pick off the ball. Check for the above coaching pointers, especially the arm extension and the use of the hands to intercept the ball.

314. BREAK ON COMEBACK

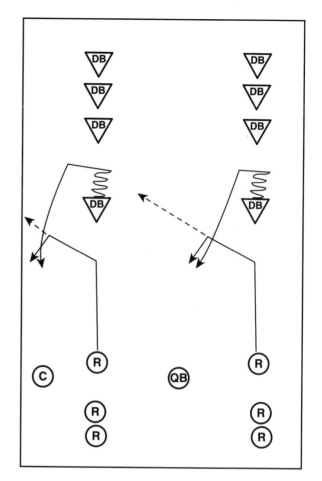

Purpose:

- To practice the fundamentals of breaking on an interception line with a receiver running a comeback route.

Coaching Pointers:

- Get in a good stance and maintain your cushion while backpedaling with the receiver.
- When he cuts to his flag pattern, open your hips and go with him, maintaining a cushion of two to three yards. Stay with him if he continues running the flag.
- If he then runs a comeback route, plant hard with your upfield foot and drive back on an interception line with the ball.
- Keep a slight upfield cushion on the receiver so that you can knock the ball down with your hand closer to the quarterback or tackle the receiver with your other arm.

Set-up and Instructions:

Position half the defensive backs in two lines facing the offense as illustrated. Position the rest of the defensive backs in two lines as receivers. Instruct the receivers to run corner comebacks. They should run a flag pattern and, after four or five steps, execute a comeback route.

The defensive backs should backpedal, open their hips in the direction of the flag, then break hard off their upfield foot when the receiver executes a comeback route. To keep them honest, keep the receiver on a flag pattern every fifth or sixth repetition.

Check for good fundamentals, a strong break back to the ball, and good positioning on the receiver.

315. END ZONE COVERAGE

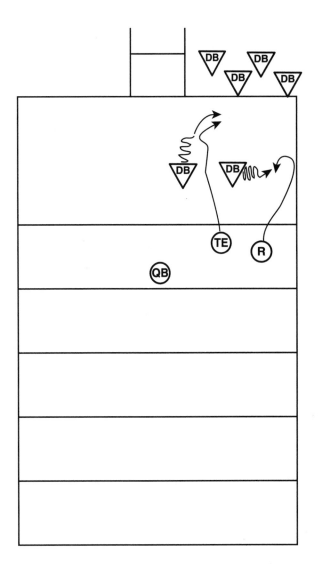

Purpose:

- To emphasize the fundamentals of covering receivers in or near the end zone.

Coaching Pointers:

- Imagine yourself covering someone in a basketball game. That's end zone coverage.
- In or near the end zone, don't worry so much about maintaining a cushion.
- In fact, you want to stay on the receiver's shoulder—one, to make a quicker move to the ball; two, to maintain position to prevent him from releasing inside or outside of you.
- Remember, a good cushion in the end zone is exactly what you don't want!
- In the end zone, you don't have to worry about him running with the ball after he catches it. **You don't want him to catch it!**

Set-up and Instructions:

Position a quarterback, a tight end, and a wingback in their normal alignments (they can be defensive backs). Put some defensive backs behind the end zone and two defensive backs in the end zone as illustrated. Give the receivers patterns and throw the ball to one of them. Instruct the defensive backs to use man-to-man coverage to prevent a reception. Check for the above coaching pointers and any of your own.

Remind the defensive backs to shorten or eliminate their cushions, to stay in their ready positions to maintain their mobility, and to focus on the receiver but to pick up the quarterback peripherally if they can.

This is a good drill, especially late in the week before a game to remind the defensive backs of their end zone responsibilities.

316. BREAK THE SHIELD II

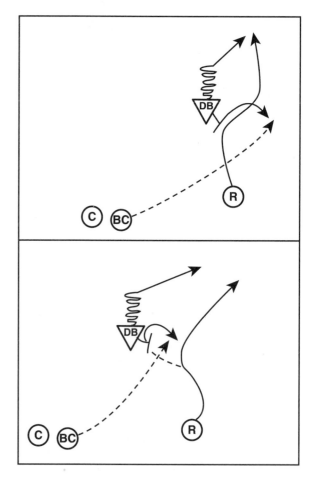

Purpose:

- To emphasize reaction to the blocker and ball carrier when the play becomes a run.

Coaching Pointers:

- Once you determine an apparent pass play has become a run, you have to contend with blockers.
- The man you're covering is often the primary blocker.
- He may try to cut or stalk block you.
- Whatever he does, your eyes should be directly on him, and you should make contact with him, find the ball, get good separation, and shed him to get to the ball carrier.
- Never avoid or run around the blocker. You'll be out of position. Remember, you have an area to cover and a proper pursuit path to take.
- Punch the blocker with the heels of your hands—high if he's stalk blocking, low if he tries to chop you.
- Find the ball carrier and whip the blocker or use a rip or swim technique to get past him to make the tackle.

Set-up and Instructions:

Position a defensive back six to seven yards upfield as a cornerback. Position a receiver on a line of scrimmage. Position a defensive back next to you as a potential ball carrier. Tell the receiver and the defensive back next to you whether the play is going to be run or pass. Start the play on your cadence and have the receiver run a pattern—and either complete it or stalk block the defensive back. If it's a stalk block, have the defensive back standing next to you run. Tell him to try to get outside the cornerback.

Remind the defensive back that cornerbacks have outside-in responsibility and **<u>nothing</u>** can get outside them! Check his positioning and technique accordingly. Have the defensive back chest butt and wrap up the runner. This drill doesn't have to be live.

Variation: Have the defensive backs play safety, too. Remind them that the safety's responsibility is usually inside-out, but he's freer to get to the ball. Take your time with this drill and be sure that the corners and the safeties get enough repetitions playing their respective positions.

317. SQUEEZE PLAY

Purpose:

- To practice the contain and inside-out responsibilities of the secondary.

Coaching Pointers:

- Whatever your responsibility, once you determine it's a run, focus on blocker.
- What kind of block does he intend? How am I going to beat it?
- Get your hands into him, get separation, find the ball, and get rid of him to make the tackle.

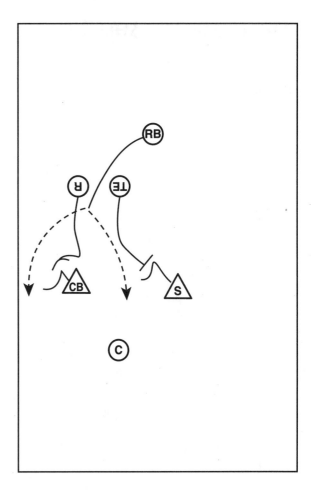

Set-up and Instructions:

Position a cornerback and a safety in their normal alignments. Use extra defensive backs to be a wide receiver, a running back, and a tight end. Give the running back a ball and have him run a sweep. Be sure to align everyone so the ball is run to both the right side and the left side of the center. Tell the wide receiver to try to block the cornerback to the inside, in essence to take away his outside containment. Have the tight end simply shield block the safety, keeping himself between the safety and the ball.

Tell the cornerback to maintain outside-in pressure and the safety to squeeze the play inside-out. Tell them to destroy the blocks (see *(316) Break the Shield*) and make the tackle. This drill can be live or, more likely, dummy. Just have the defensive backs face up with the ball carrier, chest bump, and wrap up.

Make sure they stay in good, ready positions and execute good fundamentals in destroying the blocks.

318. HEAD-ON TACKLING

Purpose:

- To practice the fundamentals of head-on tackling.

Coaching Pointers:

- Review the coaching pointers in *(319) Waiting Aggressively.*
- Get in front of the ball carrier as fast as possible and wait aggressively.
- Get as low as possible for a head-on tackle, especially if the ball carrier is big.
- Backs don't like to be hit low. They'd rather drop a shoulder into you and punish you.
- Get a good bend in your knees and hit him as low as possible.
- **Bull your neck!** Protect your head! Be smart!

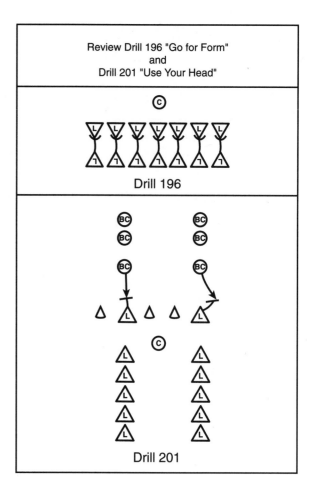

Set-up and Instructions:

Review *(196) Go for Form* and *(201) Use Your Head* for set-up and instructions. Use the coaching pointers contained in each and incorporate the above pointers when coaching defensive backs.

319. WAITING AGGRESSIVELY

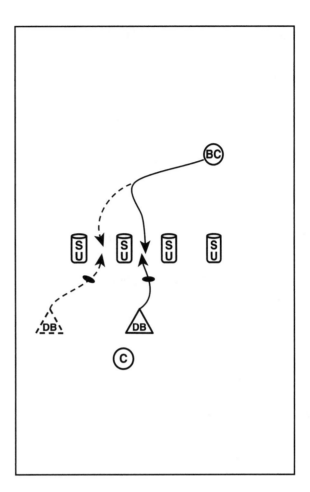

Purpose:

- To emphasize good tackling fundamentals.

Coaching Pointers:

- Get in your ready position and read your backfield key **through the line.**
- When the line tips you off where the ball is going and you see the ball carrier approaching the line, race to a position a yard and a half in front of him and get into your hit position.
- **Don't** try to time your movement toward him so you'll get to a contact spot about the same time he will.
- **Get there first!** And get a good bend in your knees, your feet a little wider than usual, so that when you hang your arms in front of you, your hands will touch the top of the grass.
- Stay this low, especially if the ball carrier is big. The hit position will give you good mobility so that you can cut in either direction.
- Watch where the ball carrier wants to go, get there first—and **wait aggressively!**

Set-up and Instructions:

Position four stand-up dummies on their sides approximately a yard and a half apart. Position a ball carrier (he can be a defensive back) four yards behind the the first dummy. Position a defensive back in either his safety or cornerback position and tell him to get into a good ready position. Stand behind the defensive back and point to the hole you want the ball carrier to hit. On your cadence, have him run the hole.

Tell the defensive back to race to a position approximately a yard to a yard and a half in front of him and wait aggressively to make the tackle. He should get into a good, low hit position and be prepared for a straight-on tackle or a tackle across the bow. If he's a safety, he should approach inside-out; if he's a cornerback, he should approach outside-in. This drill can be live early in the season, but it should be dummy most of the time. Simply have the defensive back race to his position, then face up on the ball carrier and form him.

320. BALANCE

Purpose:

- To teach defenders to race to a position in front of a ball carrier, face up to him, and react for the tackle.

Coaching Pointers:

- Race to a position approximately four to five yards in front of the ball carrier and quickly get into your hit position.
- Be balanced: feet shoulder-width, knees bent, back straight, neck bulled, and arms relaxed in front of you.
- Let's call this—waiting aggressively!
- Watch the ball carrier's midsection. He can fake you out with his head, even his feet, but not his midsection.
- If he cuts, tackle him across the bow, that is, keep your head in front of him and swing him to the ground!

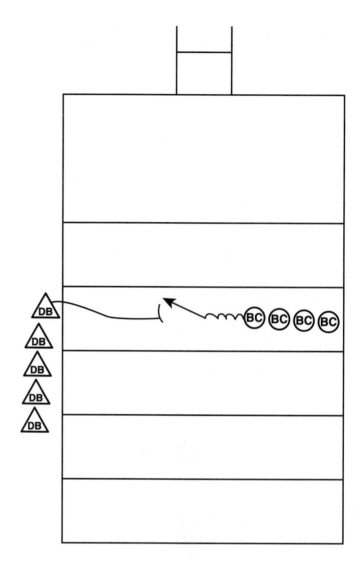

Set-up and Instructions:

Position the defensive backs (or linebackers) on a sideline between two 10-yard stripes as illustrated. Position ball carriers midfield between the same two stripes. Instruct the first ball carrier at midfield to advance the ball toward the sideline and avoid the tackler. Tell him, however, that he can make only one cut.

Tell the defender to race to a position four to five yards from the ball carrier and set up in his hit position. Check for the above pointers and use some of your own. Make sure the tackler doesn't race to and through the ball carrier so quickly and so aggressively that he misses the tackle. This is a good drill early in the season to teach balance and to identify kids who like contact.

Thanks to Greg Royer, coach, at Deerfield (Illinois) High School for this drill.

321. PLAY RUN OR PASS

Purpose:

- To read the proper line key, to react to run or pass, and—when run—to defeat the wide receiver's stalk block.

Coaching Pointers:

- Read through the line to backfield action. Read the tackle!
- If he snaps up into pass protection, keep backpedaling.
- If he releases downfield, forget pass and look for a stalk block from the wide receiver.
- You're a cornerback, so maintain outside-in pressure on the running back. Do not allow the stalk blocker to shield you from the sideline.
- Use the proper technique to defeat the stalk block and make the tackle.

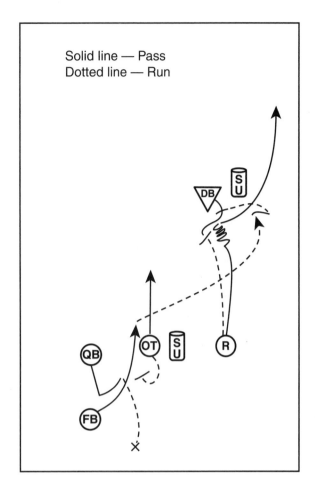

Solid line — Pass
Dotted line — Run

Set-up and Instructions:

Position a quarterback, a fullback, an offensive tackle, and a wide receiver in their normal alignments (they all can be defensive backs) as illustrated. Position a cornerback in his normal alignment. Place a stand-up dummy in the tight end's alignment, just outside the tackle. Place one more dummy 10 yards upfield and five yards in from the sideline.

You be the quarterback or find one for this drill. Instruct the quarterback to belly ride the fullback off tackle and either give him the ball or pull it out and drop back to pass. If it's a pass play, have the wide receiver run a fade or a streak down the sideline after his stalk block. Tell the tackle to release straight ahead on a running play or set up to pass block on a passing play. Tell the wide receiver to stalk the cornerback and either release for a pass or shield block him for a run.

If the running back keeps the ball, have him try to run down the sideline and knock over the stand-up dummy. If he does, he and the wide receiver win. If the cornerback beats the shield block and faces up to and grabs the running back, he wins. This is a great drill for reading keys, covering pass, and reacting to the run.

322. PICK 'N GO

Purpose:

- To practice intercepting the ball and shield blocking.

Coaching Pointers:

- As soon as you see the quarterback's shoulders open, move in that direction.
- Pick off the ball, then use your blockers effectively to get all the yardage you can.
- Yell "Oskie" or "Bingo" after you intercept the ball to get help from your teammates.
- Blockers, get to the ball carrier as fast as you can and either cut the tacklers or shield block them. **Keep them away from the ball carrier!**

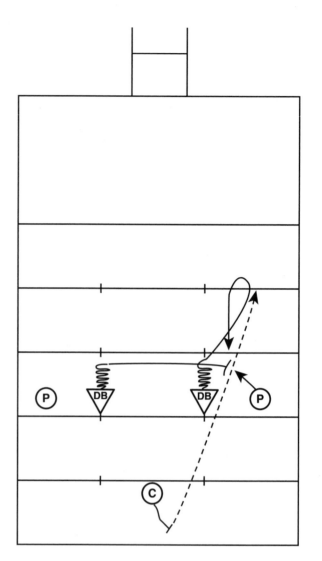

Set-up and Instructions:

Position two defensive backs on the hashmarks approximately 10 yards in front of you. Position two more defensive backs as tacklers parallel with them and five yards in from the sidelines as illustrated. You or a quarterback drop three steps and open your shoulders to throw the ball deep in either direction. When you initiate your drop, the defensive backs should start to backpedal. When they read your shoulders open, they should cut in that direction and intercept the ball.

As soon as the ball is caught, the defensive back who catches it should pivot and start to return it. At the moment the defensive back catches the ball, the tackler on that sideline should try to tackle him. The defensive back on the other hash should race to the far sideline fast enough to shield block the tackler. Tell the players that the shield block is live but that tackling is dummy. If the tackler breaks the defensive back's shield block, tell him to simply touch the ball carrier.

This is an excellent drill for emphasizing movement to the ball when it's in the air and for reading the quarterback's motion. Once the quarterback's shoulders open, both backs should be racing to the sideline. The drill is also good for practicing the shield block.

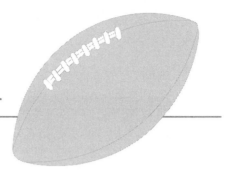

DRILLS FOR THE ENTIRE TEAM

This section focuses on a variety of general drills for the entire team.

323. PURSUIT PATHS

Purpose:

- To emphasize the appropriate pursuit paths on defense.

Coaching Pointers:

To inside linebackers and safeties:

- Pursue inside-out! Never overrun the ball!
- Defensive containment will force the ball **back** to you! When the ball is forced back to you, you better be there to make a tackle!

To the defensive ends, outside linebackers, and cornerbacks:

- Pursue outside-in! Never let the ball get outside you!
- Contain the runner; force him back to the inside. That's where all your help is!

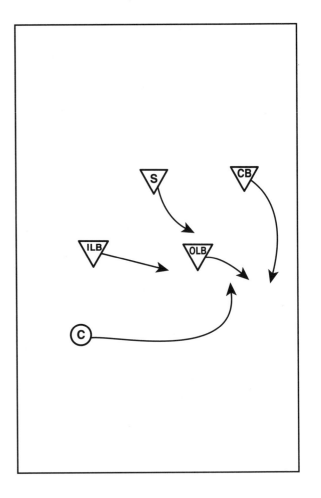

Set-up and Instructions:

Position one linebacker, one safety, one defensive end or outside linebacker, and one cornerback as illustrated. You be the ball carrier. Start walking to the right and instruct the defenders to walk their pursuit paths based on your movement. Repeat this several times. Do it both to the right and to the left, so all defensive personnel get a chance to practice their pursuit paths.

Check for an inside-out path from the inside linebacker and the safety, an outside-in path from the outside linebackers and the corners. Remind them that they are **squeezing** the ball carrier into defensive coverage, giving him nowhere to run. Remind them also that defensive players who get too anxious to make tackles often make mistakes. Defense involves a team effort.

Finally, run the ball to either side, checking for correct pursuit paths, appropriate shuffle movements from the linebackers, and quick reactions from the defensive backs. Be sure also that all defenders are in good hit positions when you start moving the ball upfield. This is an excellent preseason drill for teaching defensive reactions.

324. CONTAIN, FILL, PURSUE

Purpose:

- To emphasize the importance of contain, fill, and pursuit responsibilities on defense.

Coaching Pointers:

To the linebackers:

- Read your key and take an inside-out path at the ball.
- Never overpursue! Never allow the ball carrier to cut back on you!

To the safeties:

- Read your keys and take an inside-out pursuit path to the ball.
- Always think **pass** first; never get beat deep.
- Always read one or more offensive linemen with your key. The line will tell you if it's pass or run.

To the corners:

- Think pass first!
- Read an offensive lineman to determine if it's pass or run!
- If run, always pursue outside-in!
- You are a secondary contain man!

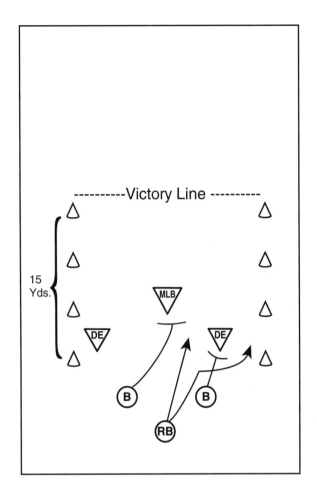

Set-up and Instructions:

Develop a 15-yard square with cones. Use a goal line or a sideline as the "victory line." Position two offensive blockers and a ball carrier as illustrated. Then, position a middle linebacker and two defensive ends as illustrated. When the run is to the right, the right blocker is instructed to kick out the defensive end; the left blocker is told to block the middle linebacker. The offside defensive end is instructed to take a proper pursuit path to prevent a score. The ball carrier reads the blocks and runs to daylight. The offensive team gets two tries to cross the victory line.

If the offense scores, they win five points. If the defense stops them, the defense gets five points. Run at least 10 repetitions to determine a winning team. Alternate other teams of players as well and keep their scores. Winners get fewer sprints or milk shakes, whichever you can afford!

This is a highly competitive drill; blow the whistle early. It's excellent for identifying players early in the season who like to hit. It's also very instructional.

Thanks to Don Drakulich, head coach, at Aviano (Italy) High School for this drill.

325. STATIONS

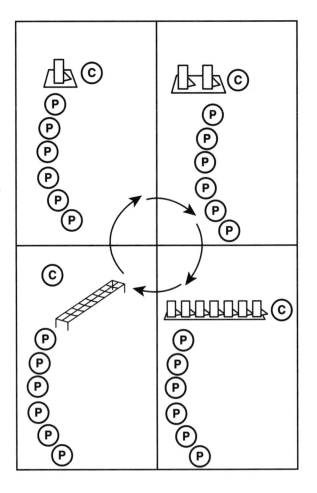

Purpose:

- To emphasize techniques and fundamentals and to improve physical conditioning.

Coaching Pointers:

- Work smart! Work hard! Work fast!
- Also be sure to tell the coaches at each work station to coach on the run. These are rapid-fire drills.

Set-up and Instructions:

Set up four work stations: the one-man sled, the two-man sled, the seven-man sled, and a quickness station. After calisthenics, the entire team divides into four groups. The first group tackles the one-man sled; the second group tackles the two-man sled; the third group forearm and hand shivers the seven-man sled; and the quickness group works on foot speed and proper running form. (See Section 2 for agility drills.) Each station is assigned a coach, who is enthusiastic and demanding of the players.

The "station" concept is good for all teams because it improves fundamentals and improves conditioning. It also reduces practice-related injuries, an important element for teams with small numbers or a great many injuries.

Thanks to Jeff Johnson, head coach, at Marquette (Ottawa, IL) High School for this drill.

326. FULL TEAM PURSUIT

Purpose:

- To check defensive alignment and execution.
- To check proper pursuit angles.
- To improve physical conditioning.

Coaching Pointers:

- Break the huddle and hustle to the line.
- Check your alignment.
- Be on your proper pursuit path and get there fast!
- Get back in the huddle quickly.

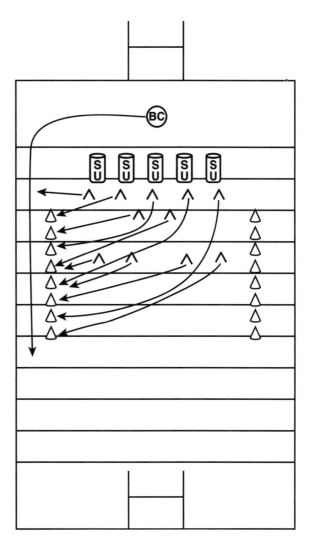

Set-up and Instructions:

Huddle the defensive team in front of five stand-up dummies and a ball carrier as illustrated. Call an alignment with or without stunts in the huddle. Have the defensive team break the huddle and hustle to the line. On your cadence, have them fire out of their stances and execute their assignments, penetrating across the line only one yard.

On the command "Hit it," have them fall to their stomachs and get up as quickly as they can. Simultaneously, have the ball carrier start running between the sideline and the cones that have been set up at five-yard intervals. Tell the defensive team to pursue the ball carrier with the proper collision angles. As soon as they come to their assigned spot near the cones, have them run in place until they hear the whistle, at which point they sprint back to the defensive huddle.

If the repetition isn't executed to all the coaches' satisfaction, the team is to repeat the repetition. After five perfect repetitions, put in a new defensive team. Each team should have five repetitions to both sides of the field.

327. HALF LINE

Purpose:

- To master blocking assignments and techniques and to improve offensive timing.

Coaching Pointers:

- If you have any questions about your assignments, ask.
- Prove you know your assignment by executing it at top speed.

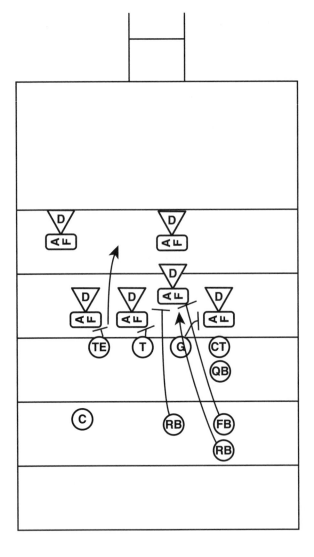

Set-up and Instructions:

Position a full backfield behind a half line. Position defensive personnel in varying alignments, each with an air flate. Tell the defenders to react to the play by executing their proper pursuit paths. At the end of each play, have them hustle back to the line for the next play. You call it on the line of scrimmage.

Run as many offensive plays as possible within a 10- to 15-minute time period. Be sure to execute to both sides of the line. This is a good time to practice the offense you plan for an upcoming opponent. Plays requiring pulling guards or misdirection should be run later in the practice. Make corrections and answer questions on the run.

This is a good drill for all teams but especially for teams with a limited number of players.

328. PERFECT PLAYS

Purpose:

- To work on offensive execution, timing, and promoting conditioning.

Coaching Pointers:

- Break the huddle like you mean it!
- Hustle up to the line of scrimmage!
- Make sure you have the right line splits.
- **DO NOT** fumble the ball!
- We'll add five more plays each time **anyone** goes offside!
- Get back to the huddle as fast as you can.

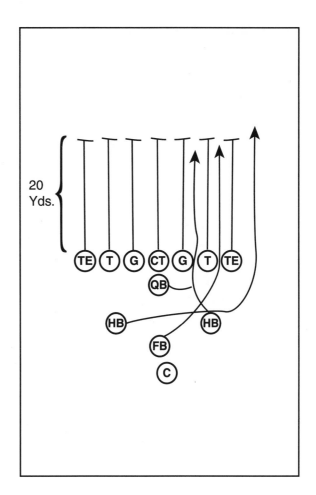

Set-up and Instructions:

At the end of practice, align the first team, second team, etc., in the end zone. Tell them they have 15 minutes to run 20 **perfect** offensive plays. Have the plays scripted; focus on plays you plan to use in an upcoming game. Huddle the teams one at a time and call a play. The team must break the huddle, sprint to the line of scrimmage, execute the play to perfection, and sprint 20 yards downfield, where they huddle again. Younger players might sprint only 10 yards. Coaches should use their discretion. If anyone fails to put forth enough effort or makes a mistake, the play doesn't count.

The teams that complete 20 plays in 15 minutes are praised by the coaches and dismissed. The teams that don't complete the plays run sprints, the number depending on their ages and levels of physical conditioning.

Extra players should stand alongside one of the teams and sprint the 20 yards.

Thanks to Jeff Johnson, head coach, at Marquette (Ottawa, IL) High School for this drill.

329. TWO-MINUTE

Purpose:

- To simulate the hurry-up conditions late in a close game.

Coaching Pointers:

- Call the play on the line of scrimmage unless we call a time out or, for whatever reason, the clock is stopped.
- **Get out of bounds** unless you have a clear shot at the end zone!
- Hustle, hustle, hustle! Time is the enemy!

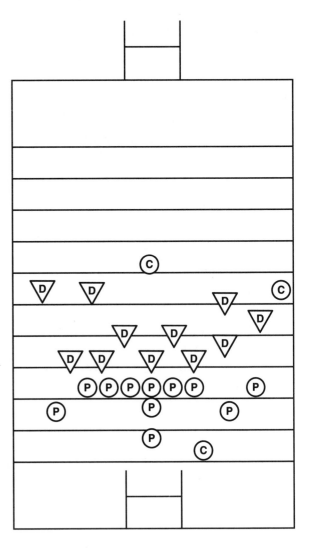

Set-up and Instructions:

Put the first team on its own 20-yard line, a defensive team in the upcoming opponent's favorite alignment, which probably will include some kind of a prevent defense. Simulate game conditions by sending in plays from the sidelines or by having the quarterback call pass plays at the line of scrimmage. Use a stopwatch to shout time remaining and have another coach shout out down and distance.

Have someone running alongside the team to hurry them up, to create as much pressure as possible. Early in the season, stop the drill to make corrections. As the season progresses, try not to stop the drill for any reason. It should be as pressure-packed as you can make it.

330. HURRY-UP OFFENSE

Purpose:

- To execute offensive plays against the opponent's likely defenses.

Coaching Pointers:

- Check fundamental skills and techniques but watch especially for a knowledge of assignments and execution.

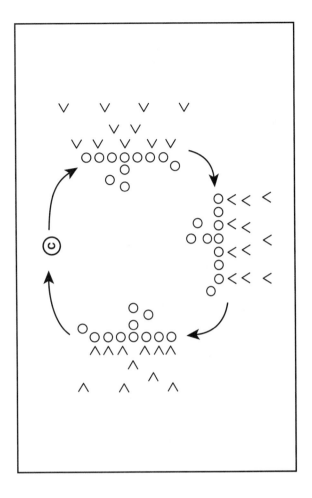

Set-up and Instructions:

Depending on the number of players on the team, position the first, second, and third teams facing north, east, and south. Align one of the upcoming opponent's defenses against each team. You stand in the west position and call the plays you plan to use in the game. Have each team execute the plays against each defense, one play for each cycle. After each team runs the play against each of the three defenses, change the play.

You should be able to run every play you plan to use in the upcoming game against every defense you expect from the opponent. Keep the teams moving but make corrections. This may be one of the last times during the week that you get to check assignments and execution.

331. SAFE SCRIMMAGE

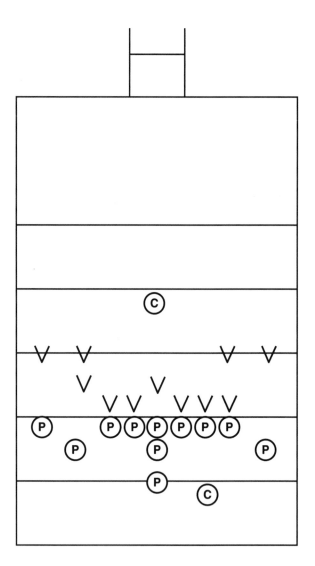

Purpose:

- To practice offense and defense under semi-live conditions.

Coaching Pointers:

- Check fundamentals, execution and knowledge of assignments and be sure each player abides by the following rules.
- Don't blindside anyone, especially the quarterback.
- Pass plays are live to the ball but no tackling.
- Running plays are live to the ball but form tackle only.
- **<u>No tackling below the waist!</u>**

Set-up and Instructions:

Conduct a routine scrimmage but emphasize the above points, especially if your team is experiencing more injuries than normal. *Safe Scrimmage* is also a good idea for young players, who are unusually prone to injury. In fact, I used *Safe Scrimmage* throughout most of the season, once the staff felt confident the players knew their fundamentals and were enjoying contact. We were unwilling to risk injury with a group of players who really didn't need contact during most of the week.

332. WALK THROUGH

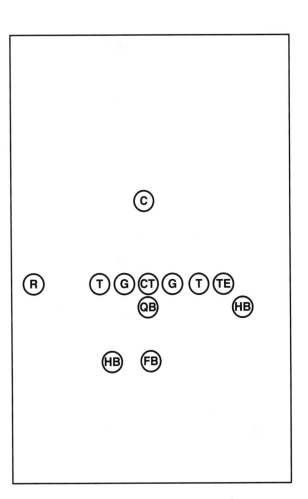

Purpose:

- To promote the learning of new plays by affecting all the modalities.

Coaching Pointers:

- When introducing new plays, promote learning by emphasizing the following process:
- Explain and describe the plays. (Auditory modality.)
- Model key elements of the play for them. (Visual modality.)
- Have them walk through the plays. (Kinesthetic modality.)

Set-up and Instructions:

Position the offensive teams so that each faces you from a different angle as illustrated. Introduce the new plays by using the above process. Encourage questions—as many as possible. After having them walk through the plays, have them run through them at half speed two or three times. Finally, have them execute the plays at full speed.

There should be no criticism during this drill, just corrections. This is a time for learning. Criticism is more appropriate after they have had sufficient time to master the plays.

333. PASSING BACK-TO-BACK

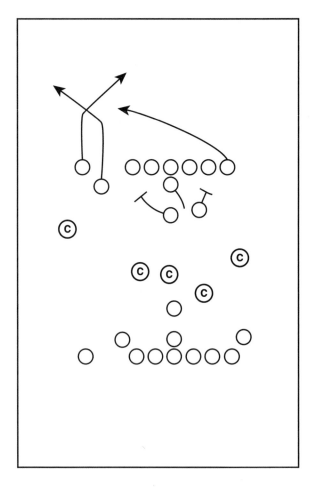

Purpose:

- To practice the passing attack.

Coaching Pointers:

- Review the receiver drills for specific coaching pointers. This drill emphasizes execution and a knowledge of assignments.

Set-up and Instructions:

Position the first and second offensive units back-to-back in the middle of the field. Position the coaching staff in between them so they can watch both teams alternately execute their pass plays. Instruct both teams to watch each other. This is an especially good way for the second team to learn the execution of their assignments.

This drill can be run with or without defensive teams. To run the drill live, have the offensive teams execute against a live pass rush and defensive backs go live to the ball. At other times, have no defense or only a skeleton defense with the secondary going live to the ball. This drill should never involve tackling. Tackling in a passing drill accomplishes nothing and invites injury.

334. SMART

Purpose:

- To establish an understanding of offensive blocking assignments against likely opposing defenses.

Coaching Pointers:

- Look at the alignment and apply your blocking rules.
- Learn every defensive adjustment this team makes, know your blocking assignments, and study the scouting report carefully before the game.

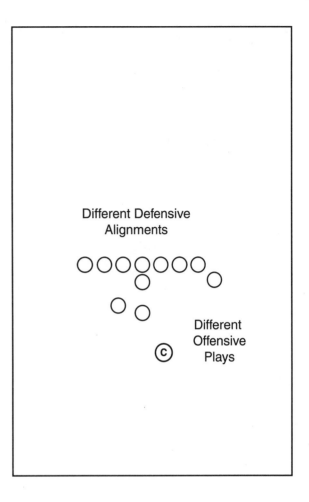

Set-up and Instructions:

Line up your first offensive team. Place a defensive team in front of them. Position the defensive team in the upcoming opponent's favorite defense. Then call an offensive play, one you plan to run on game day, and instruct the offense to point to the man you will block. Then ask, "Why will you block that defensive player? How else might we block this particular defense?" Call a new play and ask the same questions.

After reviewing the defense and making corrections as needed, put the defense in a different alignment. Call a series of offensive plays. Ask the same questions: "Who will you block? Why?"

Show the offense all the defensive alignments you are likely to see on game day. Then do the same with the second and third offensive teams. Answer all questions and take time for explanations. This is a good drill early in the week to prepare the team for an upcoming opponent.

335. QUICK RECOGNITION

Purpose:

- To learn or review offensive assignments.

Coaching Pointers:

- Use this drill late in the week to review offensive assignments. It is a complement to *(334) Smart*. Use *Smart* early in the week.

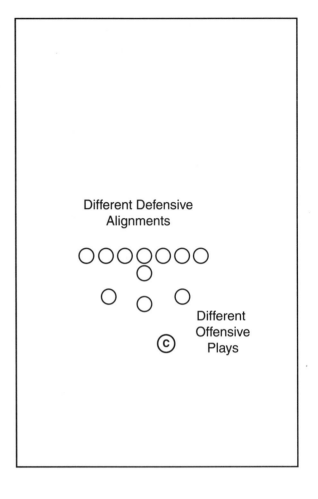

Different Defensive Alignments

Different Offensive Plays

Set-up and Instructions:

Align your first offensive team against a defense. Tell the offensive team to turn around and to face you, their backs to the defense. Then tell the defense to align themselves in one of your upcoming opponent's favorite defenses by using a predetermined hand signal: one, two, three, etc. With the offensive team still facing you, call a play and give them a snap signal, then tell them to turn around. Two or three seconds after they turn around, say "Down." They need not get into their stances. Then give them the cadence. On the snap count, have them point to the man they will block.

Using the command "Down" and a snap count approximates game conditions and doesn't allow any of the linemen to watch another blocker for a clue as to his own blocking assignment. They get a quick look at the defensive alignment, must make an individual decision prior to the snap count, and then point to the man they will block. This is an excellent pregame drill. I used it every week just before game day.

336. FUN TIME

Purpose:

- To practice special plays.

Coaching Pointers:

- Review the appropriate drills on fundamentals to assure proper execution.
- Create one or two special plays that capitalize on player skills, are strategically effective, and, most of all, are fun to practice.
- Have fun introducing them but be sure the players learn them.

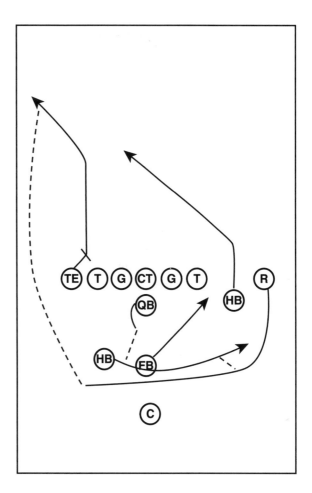

Set-up and Instructions:

Develop one or more special plays: end around pass, halfback pass, quarterback or tight end screen, tackle eligible. Be sure to capitalize on the talents of your athletes: the tackle with good hands, the halfback who can throw the ball, etc. Also be sure the plays are strategically effective against an upcoming opponent's defensive alignments and tendencies. Introduce the plays and be sure the players have fun executing them. A little out of the ordinary can do a lot to overcome tension or tedium.

Practicing such plays is not only a break in the routine; it can also provide elements of strategy that can be surprisingly helpful on game day.

337. OUT OF THE POCKET

Purpose:

- To practice adjustments in the passing attack when the quarterback is forced from the pocket.

Coaching Pointers:

- Tell receivers of their expected adjustments whenever the quarterback is forced from the pocket and has to improvise.
- If you're to the side of the quarterback, maintain your current depth but work to the outside with him. If you come to the sideline, turn upfield.
- If you're on the side away from the quarterback, change directions to his side of the field and find an open area. Don't run to an area already occupied by an onside receiver. If you're deep, stay deep and wave your arms.

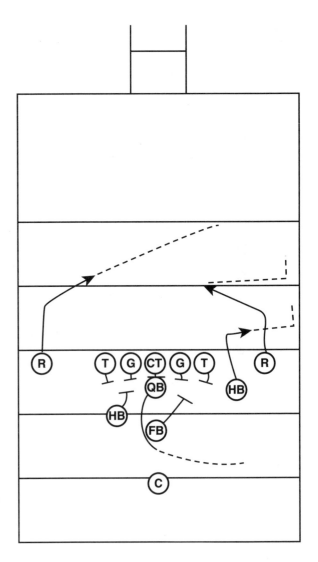

Set-up and Instructions:

Early in the season, call a passing play but have the quarterback race out of the pocket in either direction. Tell the receivers what adjustments to make. Practice the adjustments until the receivers understand them and can execute them consistently.

Throughout the remainder of the season, when practicing the passing attack, periodically tell only the quarterback to allow himself to be forced from the pocket and to start scrambling. Expect the receivers to make their adjustments. After a few surprises and reminders early in the season, the teams will run their adjustments routinely.

338. READ BLITZ

Purpose:

- To teach players how to read and react to stunts.

Coaching Pointers:

- Always follow your blocking rules.
- When you approach the line, watch for keys from defensive players that they may be stunting.
- When linemen twist, they'll get their weight back on their haunches.
- When linebackers red dog, they'll get a forward lean and adjust their stances.
- When safeties blitz, they'll line up a little closer than usual to the line of scrimmage.
- Remember, you're usually blocking an area when you pass block—no matter who comes into it.
- Don't be afraid to talk to each other before the ball is snapped. Let the guy next to you know what you're seeing. **Point** to the man you may be blocking if you have to.

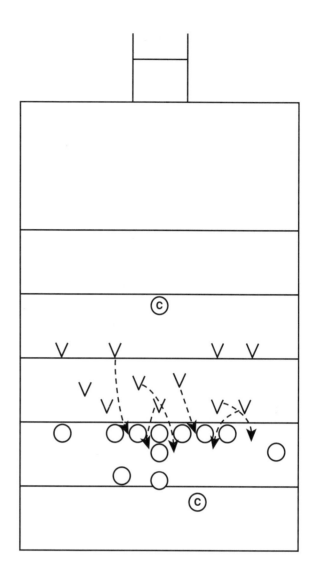

Set-up and Instructions:

Position an offensive team and a defensive team on the field. Have the defensive coach call stunts (red dogs, blitzes, and twists) and have the offensive team execute a pass play. Check for proper execution of the pass play, including fundamentals, and make sure the linemen and backs are picking up the stunts. This is a good drill late in the week to keep the linemen alert and to practice anticipated stunts from the upcoming opponent.

339. GET TO THE BALL

Purpose:

- To emphasize pass-rush techniques and pursuit to the ball after it's thrown.

Coaching Pointer:

- Review pass-rush techniques and responsibilities. Also review defensive back responsibilities and techniques. Use them as coaching pointers throughout the drill. Be sure to emphasize hustle when pursuing to the ball.

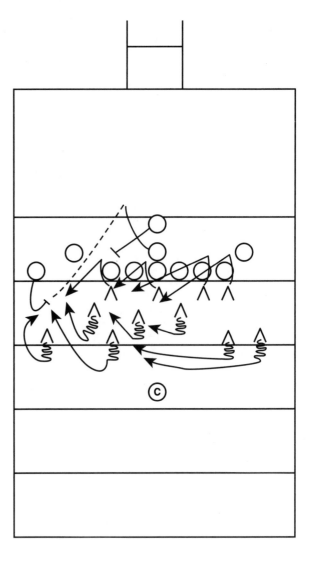

© 2001 by Michael D. Koehler

Set-up and Instructions:

Position an offensive and a defensive team in the middle of the field. Have the quarterback execute a three- or a five-step drop and throw the ball to a predetermined receiver. Have the defense use proper pass-rush and coverage techniques. Once the ball is thrown, have the entire defensive team run to the receiver. Tell him to remain stationary and instruct all 11 defenders to touch him.

354

340. HIT A DUMMY

Purpose:

- To promote team conditioning and unity.

Coaching Pointers:

- Emphasize enthusiasm and effort throughout the drill. This drill should be fun and provoke a lot of healthy competition.

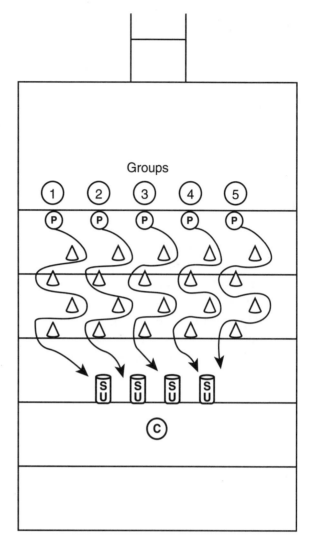

Set-up and Instructions:

Divide the team into five groups. Each group should cheer for its members during competition. Position cones in front of each group as illustrated. Be sure they're far enough apart to challenge the runners. Position four stand-up dummies 10 yards from the last cone, and approximately three yards apart.

Instruct one player from each group to run to the outside of each cone and sprint to one of the dummies and knock it down. One of the runners from one of the groups will be too late to knock down a dummy. Have him and his group do 20 push-ups and 10 up-downs.

Then have the next set of runners negotiate the cones. Continue the drill until every player has had a turn to run the cones. Have everyone run a lap and go in.

341. WHAT'S THE PLAY

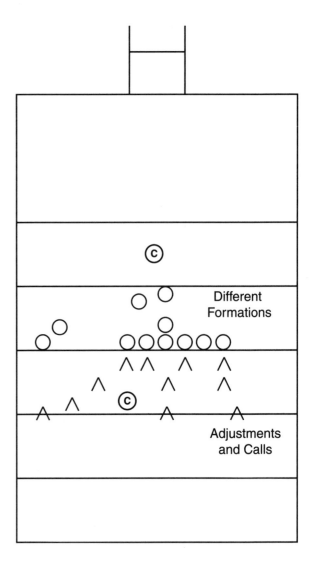

Purpose:

- To determine if the defensive team has read its scouting report and understands the proper adjustments by offensive formation.

Coaching Pointers:

- Expect every linebacker and defensive back to call out the likely play each time they see a different offensive formation.
- Expect the linemen and the linebackers to make whatever adjustments have been planned for that week.

Set-up and Instructions:

Align the defensive team in its base defense. Put an offensive scout team in front of them. Have a scout team coach call all the opponent's offensive formations you expect to see. Each time a new formation is called, expect the linebackers and defensive backs to shout out the tendencies by pointing to the holes where they are likely to see a play. Also have them name the play.

Expect also to see the defensive team make whatever alignment adjustments have been made for that week. Run all your defenses and be sure that each defensive team gets a repetition.

This is an excellent drill for late in the week to make sure the defense is prepared for the opponent. It also is a very intimidating experience for the opponent on game day Nothing disturbs an offense more than having the defense predict where the ball is going!

342. FIVE YARDS IN

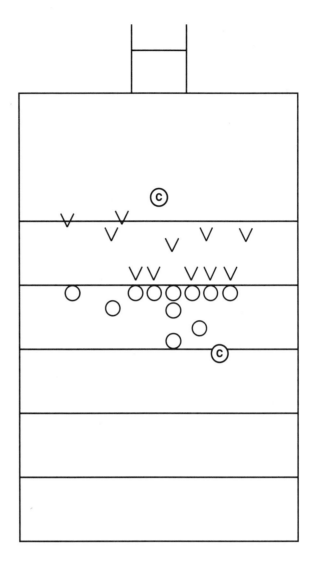

Purpose:

- To practice goal-line defense.

Coaching Pointers:

- Position a scout team on the five-yard line. Position the first-team defense against them and tell them to play their goal-line defense.
- Check fundamentals as well as defensive assignments.

Set-up and Instructions:

Position a scout team or the second-team offense on the five-yard line going in. Tell the first-team defense to play its goal-line defense. Call a mixture of running and passing plays to evaluate line play and secondary coverage. Challenge the scout team to score. Promise everyone on the team a soda if they score twice on the defense. This is a good drill for late in the week to check assignments and to get the defensive team fired up.

343. TACKLING STATIONS

Purpose:

- To emphasize tackling fundamentals and to promote safety.

Coaching Pointers:

- Review the entire tackling section of this book for coaching pointers and emphasize them, especially those involving safety, to the entire team as groups of players move from station to station.

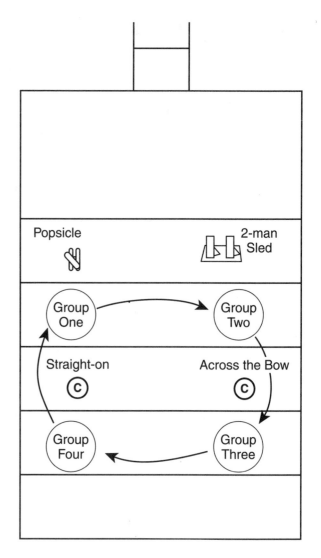

Set-up and Instructions:

Divide the team into four groups. Establish four tackling stations at different corners of the field. Put the popsicle in one corner, the two-man sled in another. Position coaches in the other two corners, one to cover tackling across the bow; the other, straight-on tackling. Neither of these last two stations should involve live tackling. Both stations should emphasize effective and safe form and should match up players according to size and strength.

Assign a group to each station. Rotate the groups every 10 to 12 minutes. Be sure to emphasize proper fundamentals at each station, not simply to have the players go through the motions. Proper execution is safe execution. When coaching tackling, player safety is the most important consideration. This drill is especially effective in that regard because it provides a daily opportunity for coaches to work closely with players.

344. QUICK PURSUIT

Purpose:

- To teach proper pursuit paths.

Coaching Pointer:

- Review the other materials in this book regarding defensive pursuit by position and emphasize them during this drill.

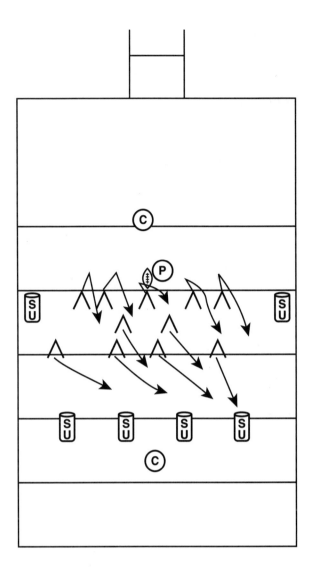

Set-up and Instructions:

Align the first-team defense on a designated line of scrimmage. Have an extra player or the team manager kneel in the center's position holding a football on the ground. Have a coach stand four yards deep in the backfield. Place six stand-up dummies as illustrated at different locations on the field.

To start the drill, the coach/quarterback calls a defensive alignment. When the player or manager holding the football raises it off the ground, the defensive team should surge forward and look at the coach. When the coach points to one of the six dummies on the field, the team should pivot and sprint to the dummy, staying in their proper pursuit paths and being careful not to follow in the same path as another teammate.

The first player to the dummy should knock it over, the others should touch it. When the last player touches it, they should sprint back to their defensive alignment and wait for the next snap, at which point they should race to a different dummy. Each defensive team should race to all six dummies and coaches should watch them carefully for proper pursuit paths.

This is a great drill, especially late in the week as a reminder to pursue quickly to the ball.

345. OSKIE

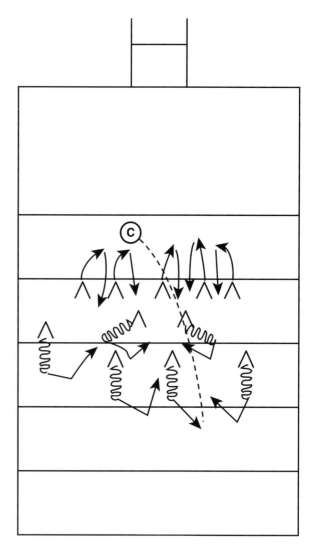

Purpose:

- To emphasize breaking on the pass after the ball's been thrown.
- To emphasize blocking after the ball is intercepted.

Coaching Pointers:

- Review pursuit angles by position in other sections of this book.
- Also review and emphasize proper pass-receiving skills for defensive backs.
- Make sure the defensive back shouts "Oskie" or "Bingo" after he intercepts the ball.

Set-up and Instructions:

Position the defensive team in its normal alignment. You stand where the quarterback would be after a five-step drop. Shout "Down" to get the defense in their stances and hit positions. Instruct them to fire off the ball when you take one backward step. Get the attention of anyone who goes offside.

Tell the line to stay on their rush paths and the linebackers and secondary to drop or backpedal to coverage. Throw the ball to one of the defensive backs. Make him run for it or jump for it. Be sure the other defenders also break to the ball. Once he catches it, he should shout "Oskie!" At this point, the other defenders should form a wave of blockers for him. When the ball is returned 15 yards, have the team sprint back to its original alignment for another repetition.

Make corrections and expect a lot of hustle during this drill. This drill is a conditioner as well as a teaching tool and is very useful during the early season.

SECTION 12

SPECIAL-TEAM DRILLS

This section focuses on the following skills:

Kickoff
- Kicking skills and technique: deep, onside, squib, etc.
- Receiver and return technique: deep and onside
- Making the most of wall protection
- Coverage: staying in lanes
- Receiving: wall return and blocking technique

Punt
- Punting skills and technique: fundamentals, and deep, short, and sideline kicks
- Snapping skills and technique
- Receiver and return technique
- Practicing the fair catch
- Punt coverage: staying in lanes and maintaining outside-in pressure

Extra Point
- Kicking skills and technique
- Holder skills and technique
- Snapper skills and technique
- Blocking techniques
- Reacting to a poor snap (punt and extra point)

346. PLACE KICKING

Purpose:

- To emphasize the fundamentals of place kicking.

Coaching Pointers:

- Most important, keep your head down and get a good plant with your non-kicking leg.
- The good plant will give you power, so keep your weight back, then roll hard over the plant leg while kicking the ball.
- Your knee should be locked at the point of contact, and your kicking leg should follow-through in the same locked position.
- Keep your head down. If your head comes up, your weight will tend to go forward, and you'll lose some of the pivot that gives the kick power.

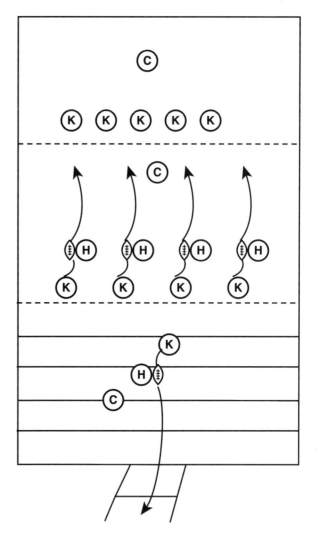

Set-up and Instructions:

Position the place kickers on a designated line of scrimmage in front of you. Instruct them to stand with their feet together, their bodies leaning slightly forward, their non-kicking foot slightly ahead of their kicking foot. On your signal, have them execute their kicking motion at half-speed. They should exaggerate everything: the plant, the head down, and the follow-through.

Next, have a holder position a football for each. Instruct the kickers, on your signal, to kick the football at half-speed. The kicking motion—and their feel for it—is still most important at this point. In fact, don't have them aim at the upright. Have them just kick the football into open field. The distance of the kick is unimportant. Important are the kicking motion, contact with the ball, and the ball's trajectory.

Finally, place them in front of a crossbar and let them kick away. Check for the proper fundamentals. This is a time for teaching and correcting.

347. BAD SNAP

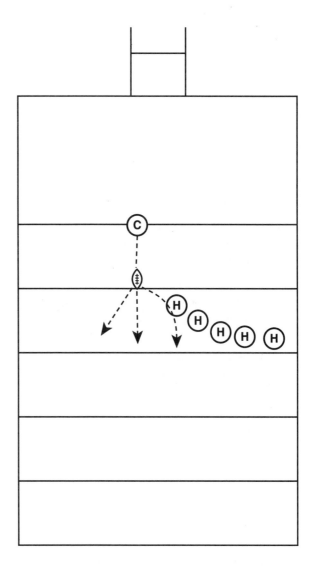

Purpose:

- To teach proper positioning to holders.
- To enable holders to handle bad snaps.

Coaching Pointers:

- Kneel on the knee closer to the center. This may vary depending on individual preference.
- Keep the opposite foot underneath you to maintain a balanced stance and to be able to stand as quickly as possible in the event the snap is high.
- Position yourself as low to the ground as possible, keeping your head erect and your stance as open as possible to keep your knee out of the way during reception and positioning of the ball.
- Your arms should be relatively parallel to the ground, your hands wide open.
- Be as relaxed as possible in order to move quickly.
- Keep your eyes on the ball until it is kicked.

Set-up and Instructions:

Position one holder facing you, approximately six to seven yards away. Check his stance for coaching pointers. Underhand spiral pass the ball to him, snapping the ball either perfectly, too high, or too low. Be sure he positions the ball with the hand closer to the kicker (this, too, may vary, depending on right- or left-handedness), using only enough pressure to keep the ball erect. Also be sure he focuses only on the ball and looks at it and holds it until the ball is kicked. Be sure he is close enough to the ground to field low or bouncing snaps. Emphasize FOCUS, FOCUS, FOCUS.

Alternate holders until every holder has had two or three repetitions.

348. KICKING OFF

Purpose:

- To emphasize different techniques for kicking off.

Coaching Pointers:

- Remember, the power of the kick comes from your plant foot. If you plant hard and don't slide, you'll hit the ball with more force.
- Keep your head down so you get the full pivot of your body over your plant leg.
- **Feel** the motion of your body during the kick. Watch the ball and **feel** your entire body as you kick the ball.
- Kick the ball on the bottom band when kicking deep, the middle of the ball when squib kicking, and the top band when kicking onside.
- When kicking onside, get high on the toes of your plant foot so that you can pound **down** on the top of the ball.
- If you kick down on it, the ball will take a big bounce almost immediately.

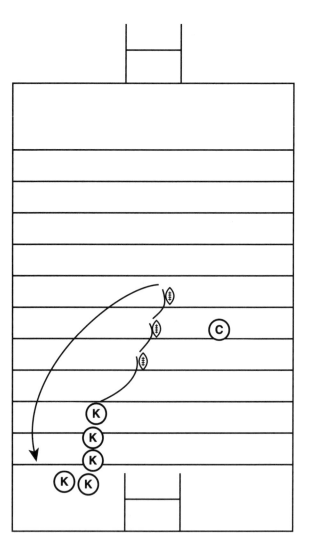

Set-up and Instructions:

Position footballs on kicking tees at 10-yard intervals: one on the 30, the second on the 40, the third at end field. Position the kickers on the 15 or the 20 and instruct them to kick the footballs consecutively: kick, keep head down, kick second ball, keep head down, kick third ball. Tell them not to watch the balls in flight but to keep their heads down and to prepare to kick the next ball.

Their focus should be on a feel for the kicking motion: approach, plant, kick (knee locked at impact), follow-through. This is a good early season drill for finding kickers and for working the kicking motion into body memory.

349. ONSIDE KICKING

Purpose:

- To practice the fundamentals of onside kicking.

Coaching Pointers:

- Approach the ball much the same way you would if you were kicking it deep, except for the angle you take.
- On your last step, elevate your body, get up on the toes of your non-kicking foot, raise the foot of your kicking leg, and come down hard on the top band of the ball.
- **Pound** the ball into the ground! If you do it well, the ball will take a giant hop!

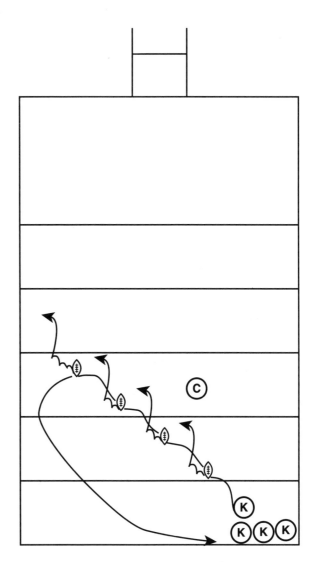

Set-up and Instructions:

Stagger four footballs on kicking tees seven or eight yards apart, each five yards farther upfield than the last, as illustrated. Instruct the kickers to kick each ball consecutively, emphasizing the above coaching pointers for each kick. Have them approach, kick, gather, approach, kick, gather, etc., until all four balls are kicked. Remind them on each kick to **feel** the motion: elevate, raise foot, pound down on the ball. During the drill, some kickers will do better than others. Identify those who are doing it well and have the others watch them, then do it themselves.

Most coaches spend too little time on onside kicking and other special teams drills. Devote some time to this drill early in the season. It **will** pay dividends in the future.

350. STAYING IN LANES

Purpose:

- To emphasize the importance of staying in lanes when covering kickoffs.

Coaching Pointers:

- Stay in your lanes! Don't avoid blockers! Hit, hold, and react to the ball.

- This doesn't mean slow down! Run downfield as fast as you can!

- Race past a blocker if you can get to the ball carrier; otherwise, hold your position and stay in your lane.

- When you close to the ball, maintain your lanes. Keep your relative relationships with each other.

- Close to the ball as soon as you locate it. If you're in the middle of the coverage, go directly to the ball.

- If you have contain responsibility, maintain an outside-in approach to the ball.

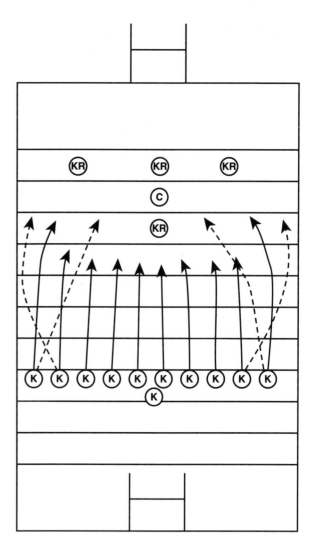

Set-up and Instructions:

Position the first, second, and third kickoff teams in waves on the 40-yard line. Position three deep returners inside the receiving team's 10-yard line, a short returner on the 25. Instruct each team in turn to get downfield fast. With your back to the kicking team, point to one of the four returners. Have the kicking team go on the whistle. As they approach the receiving team's 40-yard line, have the designated returner raise his hand. Check to see that the kicking team stays in their lanes while closing on the ball.

Use this drill early in the season and sometimes prior to actual special teams practice to remind players of the need to stay in their lanes. Make lots of corrections to emphasize the importance of staying in their lanes. Getting out of a lane happens more often than most coaches care to remember and it can be very costly in big games.

351. KICK RECEIVING

Purpose:

- To emphasize the fundamentals of catching kickoffs.

Coaching Pointers:

- Get under the ball fast! Race to get there! Camp out under it.
- As the ball comes down to you, reach up for it with your hands. Your hands should be under the ball, thumbs out.
- As the ball approaches your hands, ease it down into the basket: your forearms parallel, your elbows six to eight inches apart, your upper arms touching your chest.
- Bend at the knees while receiving the ball to cushion the catch.
- Soft! Everything is soft! Baby it in! Get tough after you catch it!

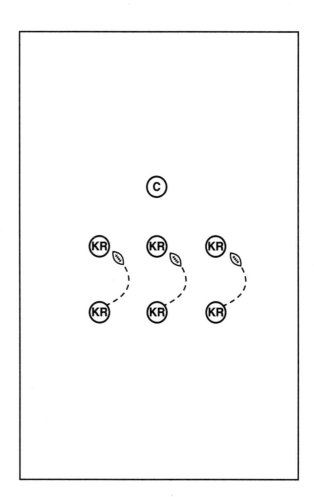

Set-up and Instructions:

Pair off the kick returners. Give each pair a football and tell them to loft the ball to each other, throwing it higher and higher after each repetition. Each returner should catch the ball as indicated above. Check for a soft catch in the basket and a good bend in the knees to cushion the catch.

When the returners become proficient at catching the ball, they can practice catching it on the run to give themselves some momentum. Delay such a technique, however, until they have mastered the basics.

352. WALL BLOCKING

Purpose:

- To emphasize the fundamentals of wall blocking during the return of a kickoff or a punt.

Coaching Pointers:

- Get to the wall right now! We'll give you a specific place to be and a job to do. Get there fast to do it!

- When a tackler approaches your area, wait for him to commit himself, then move toward him aggressively but under control.

- Don't try to pancake him unless you have a clear shot! If you move at him too aggressively, he'll sidestep you, and you'll miss the block.

- Shield block him! Pass block him, aggressively but not so aggressive that you fall off the block.

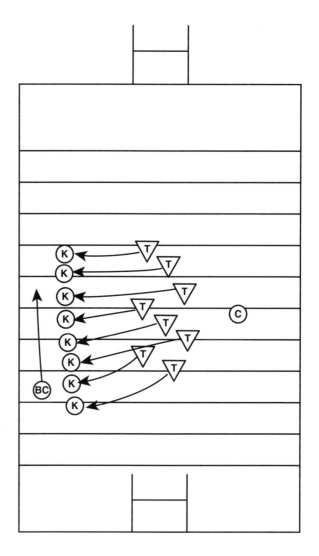

Set-up and Instructions:

Initiate the drill by positioning the blockers in a wall five yards apart and approximately seven yards in from the sideline. At first, have an equal number of tacklers approach them and tell the blockers to face up to and grab a tackler. Check for a good hit position, foot movement, and fit with the tackler.

As the blockers master these fundamentals, vary the drill by having them actually block the tacklers for at least two or three counts. Tell the tacklers to avoid the blocks and to try to touch the ball carrier running behind the wall.

Finally, run several actual kickoffs. Check the blockers for quickness to the wall and execution of proper fundamentals when blocking. Run a couple live kickoffs just to simulate game conditions, but don't run too many. Kickoff and punt coverage can cause injuries.

353. PUNTING

Purpose:

- To emphasize the fundamentals of punting the football.

Coaching Pointers:

- Place your hands on both sides of the football, one near the front, the other near the back.
- Don't put either hand underneath the football. The placement of the ball on your kicking foot will be too inconsistent.
- To receive the snap, show your hands to the center and stand with your kicking foot forward so that your non-kicking foot intersects it at the instep.
- As you catch the ball, take a short step with your kicking foot, then a long step with your non-kicking foot and kick the ball.
- Stand upright during the initial motion. Guide the actual drop of the ball with the hand on the same side as your kicking foot.
- The hand should be on the side of the ball.
- To drive the ball deep, your foot should make contact with the ball when the ball is knee-high.
- To kick the ball high but short, kick the ball when it is higher off the ground.

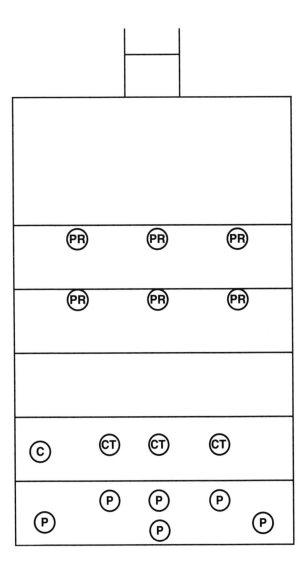

Set-up and Instructions:

Position three or four deep snappers five to 10 yards apart along a designated line of scrimmage. Alternate the punters behind them. Early in the season, look at a lot of punters. Many times you'll find a sleeper with an unusually live leg.

Check to be sure the punters are moving while the snap is in the air. They should be moving toward the ball, in essence, starting their punting motion. Check also for the above fundamentals, especially the placement of the hands on the ball. Poor hand placement will cause poor drops and some surprisingly bad kicks—at times when you least want them.

354. DROPPING THE BALL

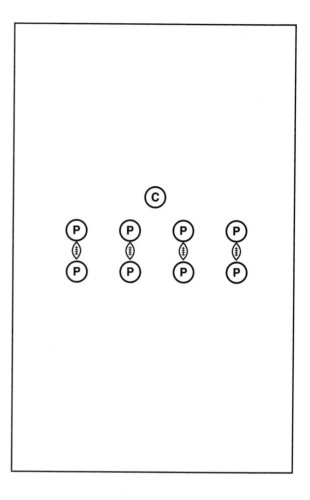

Purpose:

- To emphasize a good ball drop when punting the football.

Coaching Pointers:

- The drop is critical to a good punt! A poor drop leaves the ball at an angle, which results in a lousy kick!

- Depending on how well you can point your toes, you want to drop the ball at an angle that assures a good fit with your foot.

- Place the ball on your foot; don't just drop it!

- Practice the drop by holding the ball in front of you as if to kick it. Bend your body forward a little and drop the ball. If dropped correctly, the ball should hit the ground and make one full revolution backward.

Set-up and Instructions:

Pair off all the punters. Give each pair a football and tell them alternately to drop the ball as indicated in the coaching pointers. When the ball hits the ground, it should make one full revolution backward. The punters are paired off for this drill to assure that someone is watching them. So do some creative pairing. Put the kid with a live leg but a poor drop with the veteran who drops the ball well.

Check all the punters for a good grip on the ball and a good drop. Even the liveliest leg on the team will never be a good punter unless he learns how to drop the ball.

355. DELIBERATE PUNT

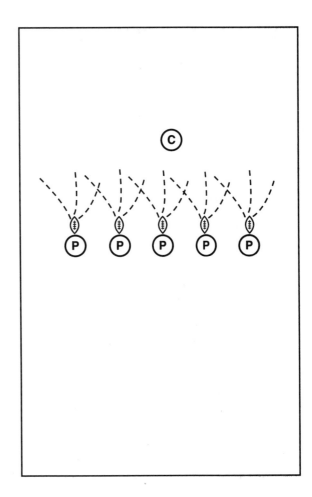

Purpose:

- To emphasize the fundamentals of the punting motion.

Coaching Pointers:

- I want your punting motion to be only half speed, less than half speed!
- The ball should go a maximum of 10 to 15 yards.
- Slowly take the proper steps; get the ball out in front of you; drop it deliberately on your foot; keep your head down; and get a good follow-through with your leg.
- To direct the ball to either sideline, catch the ball first, then step in that direction.
- Don't change anything about your kicking motion, just angle yourself in the direction of where you want the ball to go.
- When aiming the football, kick very deliberately, focusing on your motion.

Set-up and Instructions:

Position all your punters on a designated line of scrimmage facing you. Give each a football. Tell them to put their kicking foot forward, then, on your signal, to stride into the kick, moving at half speed. Their heads should be down, and the kicking motion should be very deliberate.

Check for proper footwork, a good drop, and proper follow-through. After they punt the ball straight ahead four or five times, have them angle kick to both sides, still at half speed. Conclude the drill by having the punters kick the ball at full speed, straight ahead and angled to both sides of the field.

356. DEEP SNAPPING

Purpose:

- To practice the fundamentals of the deep snap.

Coaching Pointers:

- Put the hand of your dominant arm on the front of the ball and slightly under it.
- Spread the fingers of your other hand and put it on top of the front of the ball.
- Get in your stance, your legs spread wider than usual, your head down, the ball in front of you.
- Don't put a lot of weight on the ball. If you do, it will tend to sail over the punter's head.
- Extend your arms well in front of you while holding the ball. That will give you a good range of motion.
- Spin the ball with your hands as you snap it through your legs.
- Follow-through with your arms! Reach through your legs for the punter!

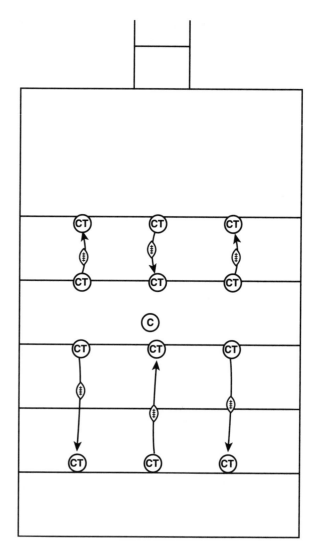

Set-up and Instructions:

Pair off the deep snappers and give each pair a football. Have them play catch by placing both hands on the ball as described above with the ball above their heads. Instruct them to snap it to each other, exaggerating their follow-through and putting a nice spin on the ball.

Have them do this for three or four minutes, then have them get into their stances and snap the ball to each other. Tell them to start only five or six yards apart to get a feel for the motion. After three or four more minutes, tell them to get 13 yards apart and snap the ball as if to a punter.

Check for all the above coaching pointers and, especially early in the season, make lots of corrections.

357. PUNT COVERAGE

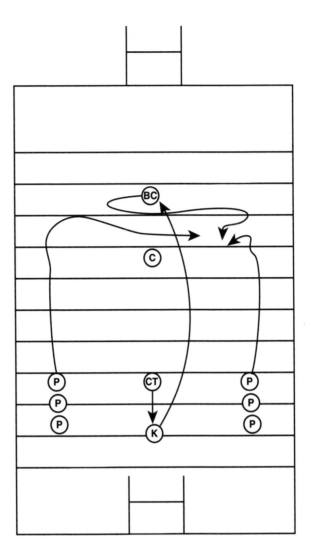

Purpose:

- To emphasize the fundamentals of outside containment during punt coverage.

Coaching Pointers:

- More punts are run back for touchdowns because of breakdowns on the outside than anywhere else on the field!
- If you have outside containment on the punt receiver, get downfield as fast as possible and close to the ball on an angle.
- Find the ball as you're running downfield, so you can close correctly.
- Whenever you're parallel to the ball carrier, that is, on the same yard line he is, you'd better be tackling him!
- Get outside right away, then stay there, even as you close on the ball carrier.
- Always close on an angle!

Set-up and Instructions:

Position outside-contain people, even those who **might** be able to do it, in lines on opposite sides of the field as illustrated. Have the first man in each line cover the punt, emphasizing his outside-in containment responsibility. Remind each to find the ball and to close on the ball carrier with the right angle, so he squeezes the ball carrier to the inside—where he has a lot of help.

Use this drill independently of other drills early in the season in order to have the time to teach containment responsibility. As the season progresses, when you are doing team drills, use this drill periodically during the team drills to reemphasize good outside-in containment.

358. PUNT RECEIVING

Purpose:

- To emphasize the fundamentals of catching punts.

Coaching Pointers:

- First of all, this is not like catching kickoffs. Kickoffs usually fall predictably; punts don't!

- So watch the trajectory of the ball after it's punted. If the ball turns over, that is, if the **front** point comes down, the ball usually will come at you—with some movement from right to left.

- If the ball **doesn't** turn over, that is, if the front point **stays up,** the ball will fall **away** from you. Be prepared to move forward to catch it.

- This means that you have to get under the ball **right now!** Camp out under it in order to be able to move to make the right catch.

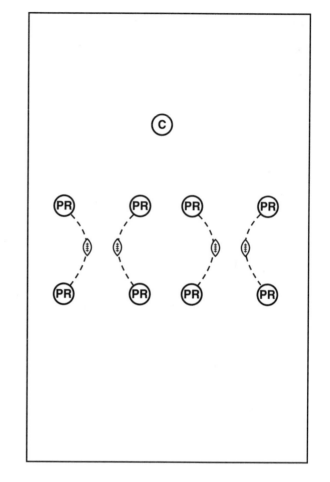

- As with catching a kickoff, reach up with your hands but cushion the ball into the basket. (See *(351) Kick Receiving* for reminders of this technique.)

- Use your legs! Bend your body at the knees and the waist to cushion the ball as you bring it into your body.

- When fair catching the ball, get your hand high in the air and wave it as if washing a windshield—vigorously!

Set-up and Instructions:

Pair off the punt returners and have them toss a football higher and higher in the air to each other. Check to be sure they are reaching up with their hands and cushioning the ball into the basket and bending at the knees and waist to soften the catch. Have them also practice a fair catch signal on every third or fourth repetition. After 10 or 12 repetitions of throwing the ball to each other, have them catch punts. Again, make lots of corrections. Good habits start early.

359. SNAPPING FOR PLACE KICKS

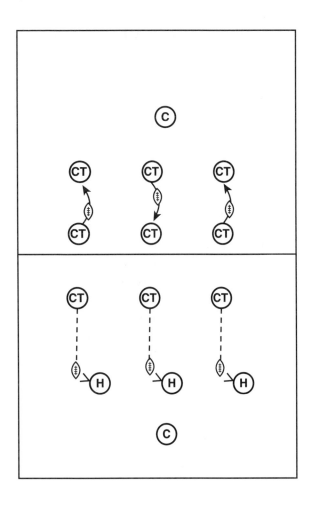

Purpose:

- To practice the fundamentals of snapping the ball for extra points and field goals.

Coaching Pointers:

- Review the fundamentals for gripping the ball and getting into the proper stance by reading the coaching pointers in *(356) Deep Snapping.*

- This is a shorter snap than a deep snap, so you don't need the same zip on the ball.

- Feel this snap! Feel the motion, and don't change it, no matter what the defense says or does!

- As you complete the snap, reach back to the holder's hands—as if you want to touch them.

- Remember, stance, grip, snap, follow-through.

- After you complete the snap, pop up and brace yourself for the defensive charge.

- **Don't** think about the charge before or during the actual snap! **Get the ball to the holder!**

Set-up and Instructions:

Have the snappers for extra points and field goals pair off and play catch with a football, gripping the ball with both hands and snapping it over their heads. After six or seven repetitions, have them alternate snapping and being a holder. For the first few repetitions, have them look between their legs while snapping the ball to each other. For the next three repetitions, have them keep their heads down but close their eyes, then snap the ball. Have them open their eyes a second later. Have them alternate between opened and closed eyes until the snaps are all accurate.

Emphasize the need to **feel** the motion, especially with closed eyes. This will get the snapping motion into their body memory.

360. PLACE-KICK BLOCKING

Purpose:

- To practice the fundamentals of blocking for extra points and field goals.

Coaching Pointers:

- If you're an interior lineman or a tight end, get in your stance and be foot to foot with the man next to you.

- As soon as the ball moves, pivot a quarter turn to the inside and brace yourself on the man to your inside.

- Allow **no penetration** between him and you!

- If you're a blocking back, line up sideways facing the outside, your inside leg intersecting the legs of the tight end.

- Don't line up any wider! Remember, the tight end is going to close down; you don't want to help create an opening between the tight end and you.

- **Don't be suckered to the outside**—to block someone who goes wide—then permit someone to race hard to the inside. Protect the inside first, then bump to the outside.

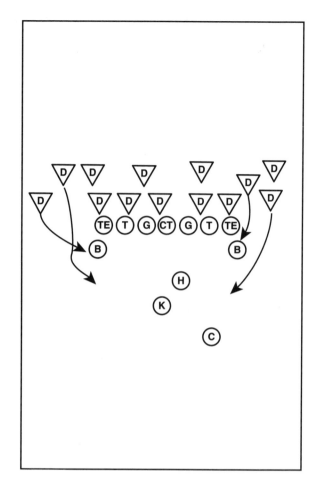

Set-up and Instructions:

Position the extra point teams in waves and have them take turns blocking. Put 11—**or more**—defensive players on the field and tell them to block the kick. Be sure to give the outside rushers a variety of stunts to use to try to entice the outside blockers out of position. Remind the kicking team that, if they execute correctly, they can hold out 15 or 16 rushers—maybe more!

Check for the above coaching pointers and all of your own. This drill can be a lot of fun, and it can identify weaknesses in the line or reinforce the skills and determination of everyone on the team. Once in a while, give a milk shake to anyone who blocks a kick. That will make the drill more game-like.

361. FIRE!

Purpose:

- To practice the team's reaction to a snap that nullifies the possibility of a kick.

Coaching Pointers:

- Sometimes a snap is so wide or so high that the holder can't get it down for the kicker.
- When that happens, the first man to see the bad snap shouts **FIRE!**
- Then, everyone shouts **FIRE!**
- When you hear "fire," execute your assignment.
- You might have to release for a pass or execute a run. We'll let you know exactly what your responsibility is. Whatever it is, do it immediately when you hear **FIRE!**

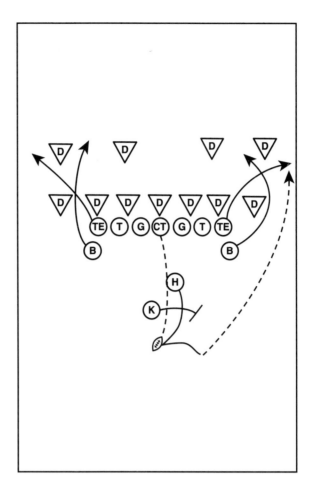

Set-up and Instructions:

Position the extra-point teams in waves and have them block for extra points as in the drill *(360) Place-Kick Blocking.* Whenever you plan to use this drill, set up the defense in its normal alignment for extra points. For every four or five extra-point attempts, plan one bad snap so the team has to shout "fire" and execute their assignments. Be sure the bad snaps are random so the blocking team can't anticipate them. In fact, sometimes don't have even one bad snap. Call the bad snap when the kicking team seems complacent or needs a reminder about their assignments.

NOTES

NOTES

NOTES

NOTES